Contemporary Research in E-Marketing

Volume 2

Sandeep Krishnamurthy
University of Washington, USA

IDEA GROUP PUBLISHING
Hershey • London • Melbourne • Singapore

Acquisitions Editor:	Renée Davies
Development Editor:	Kristin Roth
Senior Managing Editor:	Amanda Appicello
Managing Editor:	Jennifer Neidig
Copy Editor:	Joyce Li
Typesetter:	Cindy Consonery
Cover Design:	Lisa Tosheff
Printed at:	Yurchak Printing Inc.

Published in the United States of America by
Idea Group Publishing (an imprint of Idea Group Inc.)
701 E. Chocolate Avenue, Suite 200
Hershey PA 17033
Tel: 717-533-8845
Fax: 717-533-8661
E-mail: cust@idea-group.com
Web site: http://www.idea-group.com

and in the United Kingdom by
Idea Group Publishing (an imprint of Idea Group Inc.)
3 Henrietta Street
Covent Garden
London WC2E 8LU
Tel: 44 20 7240 0856
Fax: 44 20 7379 3313
Web site: http://www.eurospan.co.uk

Library of Congress Cataloging-in-Publication Data

Contemporary research in e-marketing / Sandeep Krishnamurthy, editor.
v. <2 > cm.
Includes bibliographical references and index.
ISBN 1-59140-824-5 (h/c) — ISBN 1-59140-825-3 (s/c) — ISBN 1-59140-826-1 (eisbn)
1. Internet marketing. I. Krishnamurthy, Sandeep, 1967-
HF5415.1265.C67 2006
658.8'72—dc22

2004016288

British Cataloguing in Publication Data
A Cataloguing in Publication record for this book is available from the British Library.

Contemporary Research in E-Marketing
Volume 2

Table of Contents

Preface

It is a pleasure to announce the second volume in the Contemporary Research in E-Marketing series. Volume 1 in this series was released in 2004 and has been very well received. This volume builds on the intellectual capital of Volume 1 by a compilation of interdisciplinary papers on the topic of e-marketing.

The Internet and the Web continue to evolve at a rapid pace. Examples of innovative applications of these technologies in the domain of marketing abound. E-marketing has become standard practice all over the world. This volume offers an exciting set of papers that use different perspectives, theories, and research methodologies to enrich the burgeoning e-marketing literature.

The first paper by Sanjeev Swami and Ram Krishna, "Evaluation of Web Sites on Information and Entertainment Properties: The Role of Involvement," provides an excellent empirical examination of consumer involvement on how Web sites are evaluated. Web sites receive a continuum of visitors in terms of motivation. Some care deeply about the topic of the site and others are not so engaged. Swami and Krishna provide us with empirical data on the impact of involvement on online consumer behavior. Their results show that the consumer's information and entertainment profiles significantly affect utilitarian and hedonic evaluations of involvement. They also find positive and significant relationships between the evaluations of involvement and affect toward the Web site.

Most people think that products sold on eBay tend to be low-value, low-price products that one would encounter in a yard sale. It would perhaps be very surprising to many readers to learn that eBay Motors is the largest part of the company with an annual sales of $7.5 billion. The second paper by Mark Sena and Gerald Braun, "An Examination of Consumer Behavior on eBay Motors," studies transactions in this product category. The findings of their study suggest that within selected data ranges, such factors as seller feedback ratings, number of pictures in item description, and seller type (dealer vs. individual) may affect the percentage of retail value that sellers are able to earn in eBay Motors auctions.

Too often, discussions of e-marketing are limited to examples from America or Europe. If we are to acknowledge the truly global nature of e-marketing, it is imperative that we learn about the best practices in other areas of the world. The third chapter by Sanjeev Swami is titled, "Job Search at Naukri.com: Case Study of a Successful Dot-Com Venture in India." This chapter is an in-depth analysis of an Indian company that has successfully competed with Monster India to establish an online portal for job hunters.

Everyone agrees that providing customers with value is vital to the success of an online enterprise. Yet we know little about how one must design a Web site to maximize the consumer experience and to provide the greatest value. Thomas Porter fills this gap with his chapter, "User-Centered Design and Marketing: Online Customer Value." Blending insights from marketing, consumer behavior, and human–computer interaction (HCI), Porter provides an incisive analysis of how Web design needs to be focused on the user. The model proposed in the paper based on means-end theory provides a theoretical explanation for linking Web site features and functions to perceptions of value by consumers.

Communication is central to every marketing effort. In today's multifaceted technology environment, consumers are inundated with marketing communications from all sorts of advertisers on all sorts of devices. The chapter by Merrill Warkentin, Robert Moore, and Melissa Moore, "A Synthesis and Analysis of Behavioral and Policy Issues in Electronic Marketing Communications," provides an interdisciplinary synthesis of recent research concerning emerging electronic marketing communications. The chapter explores how different levels of marketing information acquisition and integration could impact consumer perceptions and behaviors.

The next chapter by Shailey Minocha, Liisa Dawson, Ann Blandford, and Nicola Millard, "Providing Value to Customer in E-Commerce Environments: The Customer's Perspective," comes to us from the United Kingdom. Borrowing from the HCI literature and using intensive research, these authors provide us with a new way to understand online service quality and maximize the total consumer experience (TCE). Their framework of online service quality (E-SEQUAL) promises to have a major impact on the practice of e-marketing. This article also represents a truly remarkable collaboration with members of academia and industry.

Online brands help us make sense of the abundance of information online. Encountering a familiar brand online is akin to meeting a friend in an alien environment. Yet managing brands online provide unique challenges. In the chapter by Subir Bandyopadhyay and Rosemary Serjak, "Key Success Requirements for

Online Brand Management," we learn about what the brand manager can do to manage brands online and integrate them with physical brands for a successful consumer experience.

Daniela Andreini's chapter, "The Evolution of the Theory and Practice of Marketing in Light of Information Technology," is a theoretical examination of the place of e-marketing in the marketing theory literature. This Italian author provides an exhaustive analysis of the different theoretical perspectives of e-marketing and then integrates it with the known theoretical frameworks in marketing.

The next chapter comes to us from Spain. The work of José Manuel Ortega Egea and Manuel Recio Menéndez, "The Internet and Global Markets," is a theoretical overview of how the Internet is affecting global markets.

Online marketing research may well be the killer application that e-marketers have been waiting for. Online focus groups provide us with unique advantages. The biggest stated disadvantage may be that we lose body language and hence, an understanding of how things are said and not just what is said. The next chapter by Peyton Mason, Boyd Davis, and Deborah Bosley, "Stance Analysis: Social Cues and Attitudes in Online Interaction," introduces us to the notion of stance and describes how we could measure this construct using multivariate techniques, using an ongoing example taken from an online financial focus group. They review differences in stance between online real-time focus groups and online chat, as well as between online and face-to-face focus groups; and finally, they proffer examples of stance analysis in two very different online focus groups: older adults discussing financial services and teenagers discussing clothes. Their work could very well be the missing piece in our understanding of online research and is a must-read for everyone interested in using the Internet as a research tool.

The next chapter comes to us from an Austrian author—Maria Madlberger—who provides us with a fascinating comparative analysis in her paper, "Application of Internet-Based Marketing Instruments by Multichannel Retailers: A Web Site Analysis in the United States and the United Kingdom." Her findings are provocative. She found that the observed multichannel retailers still prefer "traditional" retail marketing instruments on their online shops and often do without innovative Internet-based marketing instruments such as personalization or content and information offering. Additionally, they did not find fewer-than-expected differences between the observed U.S. and U.K. retailers.

The next chapter comes to us from S. Ramesh Kumar, and his work, "The E-Mode of Brand Positioning: The Need for an Online Positioning Interface," takes on the issue of the positioning of online brands. Drawing from global as well as Indian examples, Kumar provides us with potential positioning frameworks.

The chapter by Manlio Del Giudice and Michel Polski is titled, "Locked In By Services: Willingness to Pay More and Switching Behavior in a Digital Environment." They discuss a dynamic model of cognitive and behavioral e-loyalty. Using results from an empirical study, their chapter focuses on the determinants of the switching behavior online and on the opportunity to change Web site usability using a powerful lock-in strategy.

The last chapter is by Peter O'Connor which comes to us from France. His paper titled, "A Comparative Analysis of International Approaches to the Protection of Online Privacy," compares the self-regulation approach epitomized by the United States with the comprehensive omnibus legislative approach mandated by the European Union.

This collection of articles is expected to add to an already-considerable literature and to enhance our understanding of this intrinsically interdisciplinary and global phenomenon.

Sandeep Krishnamurthy
University of Washington, Bothell, USA

Chapter I

Evaluation of Web Sites on Information and Entertainment Properties: The Role of Involvement

Sanjeev Swami, Indian Institute of Technology, Kanpur, India

Ram Krishna, Tata Consultancy Services, India

Abstract

This paper addresses the role of consumer involvement in Web site evaluation. We investigate the factors that lead the consumer to be involved with one site more than another. Based on previous research, we use the psychological constructs, information-seeking tendency, and focused attention (Baumgartner & Steenkamp, 1996; Novak, Hoffman, & Yung, 2000) to define the "information profile" of a consumer; and sensation-seeking tendency and mood variability to define the "entertainment profile" of the consumer (Eliashberg & Sawhney, 1994). The information and entertainment factors are hypothesized to affect consumers' utilitarian (need, value) and hedonic (interest, appeal) evaluations of involvement, respectively, and ultimately, the affect toward the Web site (Holbrook & Hirschman, 1982; Mano & Oliver, 1993; Zaichkowsky, 1985, 1994). We examine these evaluations for various Web sites, whose respective information and entertainment profiles are defined using elements such as informativeness, organization, and entertainment properties (Chen & Wells, 1999). The Web site properties are hypothesized to moderate the relationships between individuals' profiles and their evaluations of involvement and affect. We conducted our study using three surveys: (1) collection of data for classifying Web sites on information and entertainment properties, (2) collection of data for measurement of involvement, and (3) collection of data for time-based measurement of involvement. Our results show that the consumer's information and entertainment profiles significantly affect utilitarian and hedonic evaluations of involvement. We also find positive and significant relationships between the evaluations of involvement and affect toward the Web site. Further, we find that the Web site's information-specific properties moderate the relationship between information profile of the consumer and his/her utilitarian evaluation of involvement. A set of results from representative time-based evaluations of involvement shows that the respective elements of evaluation of involvement show increase/ decrease over time if there is a match/mismatch between the user and site properties.

Introduction

The Internet has evolved as a dynamic new medium of information, entertainment, and commerce. Penetration levels have increased dramatically and new business opportunities have been created online (Hanson, 2000). Analysts have remained upbeat about the potential of e-commerce and predicted that traditional U.S. companies using digital marketing will spend $63 billion on it annually by 2005; and that online retailing in Europe will grow to 152 billion Euros in 2006 (Forrester Research, 2001; Forrester Research BV, 2001). However, amidst all the excitement about the Internet, the importance of the most significant entity behind all this attention—the consumer—must be recognized. This is important since the consequences of the lack of in-depth understanding of the consumer could be devastating as manifested in many dot-com failures (Mahajan, Srinivasan, & Wind, 2002; Varianini & Vaturi, 2000).

In general, online consumers are younger, more educated, and more affluent than the general population (Hanson, 2000). Consumers visit the Web for entertainment (e.g., multiuser games, online discussions or chat rooms, music, videos), buying goods or services (e.g., online banking, online shopping, financial services, electronic catalogs, reverse auction), searching for information (e.g., reading news, searching online databases), communication (e.g., e-mail, chat), and education and training (e.g., interactive education, online training) (Hanson, 2000; Kolakata & Whinston, 2000; Korgaonkar & Wolin, 1999; Krishnamurthy, 2002; Nielsen, 1999a). However, a concern appears to be the fact that 80% of individuals do not revisit Web sites (Nvision, 1999).

This suggests that winning the online consumer requires a deeper analysis and understanding of his/her behavior and developing an appropriate marketing strategy. The first step in this direction should be converting casual first-time visitors into loyal users who are inclined to revisit the site. This recommends development of "sticky," or involving Web sites, which encourage repeat-visit behavior by the consumer.

Previous researchers and practitioners agree that the need to develop a comprehensive understanding of consumer behavior and creating a compelling online environment are essential for future growth of the Internet and e-commerce (Bezos, 1999; Cognitiative, 1999; Dholakia & Bagozzi, 2001; Haubl & Trifts, 2000; Hoffman & Novak, 1996b; Novak et al., 2000; Weber, 1999). However, relatively little is known from the consumer behavior perspective about the factors underlying an involving Web site and the outcomes of the experience of visiting such a Web site.[3]

The objective of this paper is to provide a simple, managerially useful, and conceptually interesting framework of online consumer behavior during a visit to a Web site. We develop and test a Web site evaluation model, which is based on the central concept of consumer involvement. The model helps us investigate factors that lead the consumer to be involved with one site more than another. Based on the psychological constructs from previous research, we use the factors information-seeking tendency (Baumgartner & Steenkamp, 1996; Novak et al., 2000) and focused attention (Novak et al., 2000: Webster, Trevino, & Ryan, 1993) to define "information profile" of a consumer. Similarly, the factors sensation-seeking tendency and mood variability (Eliashberg & Sawhney, 1994; Zuckerman, 1979) define "entertainment profile" of the consumer. The information and entertainment factors affect consumers' utilitarian and hedonic evaluations of involvement, respectively, and ultimately, the affect toward the Web site (Hirschman & Holbrook, 1982; Holbrook & Hirschman, 1982; Mano & Oliver, 1993; Zaichkowsky, 1985, 1994). We examine these evaluations for various Web sites, whose respective information and entertainment profiles are defined using elements such as informativeness, organization, and entertainment properties (Chen & Wells, 1999). In this paper, our analysis is focused on content sites and not on retailing Web sites. However, the implications of our results can readily be extended and interpreted in the context of retailing Web sites.

Some previous studies (e.g., Chen & Wells, 1999; Novak et al., 2000) have investigated the impact of similar factors as discussed above. However, the proposed study differs from these works in an important way. We investigate the role of involvement on the visitor evaluation of a *Web site*, not as a general customer experience in online environments, as treated in the previous works. The critics of flow research also appear to favor managerial usefulness of measuring consumer involvement while he/she is at a site over a general conceptualization of flow in online environment. For example, Dholakia and Bagozzi (2001) have "acknowledged the complexity and multidimensionality of the flow construct (e.g., Novak et al., 2000). This complexity potentially undermines the managerial usefulness of the construct. For example, given that a consumer experiences flow during a particular session, it is not clear how this knowledge could be used by individual marketers, since the experience may be created as part of the overall session, rather than a particular Web site. A company may take all the trouble to create a compelling Web site for an online consumer, only to have him/her visit a badly designed, slow Web site next, and not experience any of the postulated positive flow consequences. Rather than inducing flow, marketers may find it more productive to optimize the consumer's experience while he/she is at their Web site" (p. 168). Accordingly, in this paper, our analysis begins after the Web user has decided to visit the site. The user may access the site as a result of a predefined search, based on a list of favorite sites, or finds it accidentally. We want to investigate which factors lead the consumer to be involved with one Web site than another.[4]

The investigation of involvement is important because the insights generated would help the development, design, and evaluation of involving Web sites, a major objective of Web marketers. Moreover, the involvement-based model could aid in further understanding of the general flow (Novak et al., 2000) in digital environments (DEs).[5] Flow can be seen as cumulative of sequence of actions during a Web visit, and not necessarily to a specific site.

The rest of this paper is organized as follows. In the next section, we provide background research, the proposed model, hypotheses, and underlying constructs. In the following sections, we present the research design and explain the data collection procedure. We then present the analysis and interpretation of empirical results. We conclude with discussion of managerial implications, limitations of the present study, and directions for future research.

Background and Hypotheses

The Internet is regarded as an "infotainment" media, since Web sites usually have both information and entertainment elements (Eighmey, 1997). We operationalize a site's information properties by informativeness and organization of information elements, and the site's entertainment properties by entertainment properties and organization of entertainment elements (Chen & Wells, 1999). Similarly, a Web user is conceptualized as a mix of information and entertainment profiles.[6] The individual information type is operationalized by information-seeking tendency and focused attention (Novak et al., 2000) and individual entertainment type is operationalized by sensation-seeking tendency and mood variability (Eliashberg & Sawhney, 1994). Consistent with the information-entertainment classifications, we propose the evaluation of a site to consist of utilitarian and hedonic components. We propose that the utilitarian evaluation of involvement is a function of an individual's information profile, and hedonic evaluation is a function of an individual's entertainment profile. Both utilitarian and hedonic components of the evaluation are expected to lead to more positive affect of the consumer toward the Web site (Mano & Oliver, 1993). We present the key constructs of our study in Figure 1.

We classify the relevant previous studies into the following three broad components of our conceptual framework.

Figure 1. Conceptual framework for involvement-based evaluation of Web sites

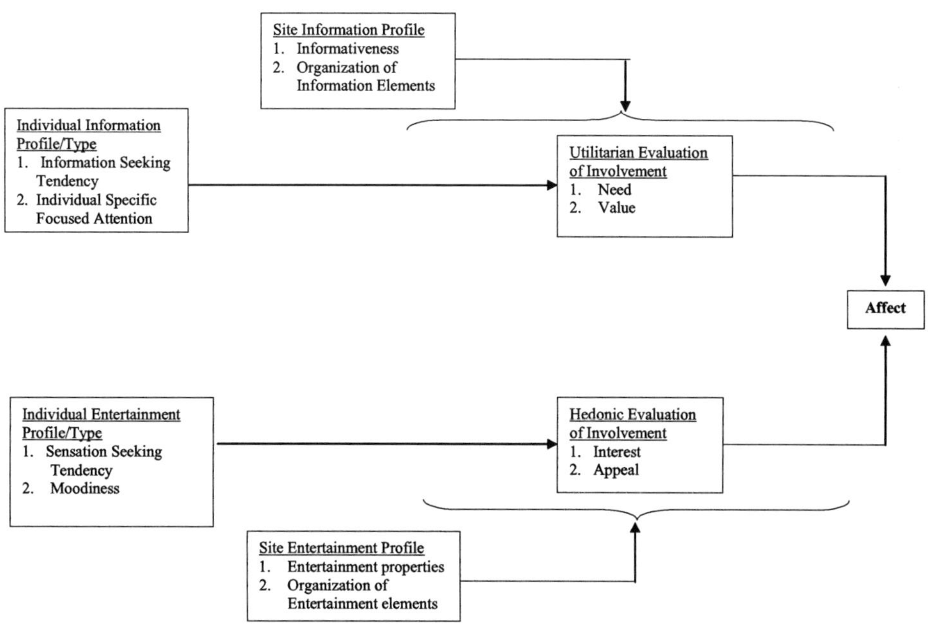

Web-Based Consumer Behavior

Previous researchers have investigated the impact of some relevant factors on the user experience in the Web environment. Hoffman and Novak (1996a) propose the concept of "flow" in Web-based environments, which has been found useful in describing a user's interaction with computers (Csikszentmilyahi, 1977, 1990). Flow is described as a sense of playfulness due to which Web users are able to perceive a sense of control, focus attention, and cognitively enjoy interacting in the Web environment. Novak, Hoffman, and Yung (2000) describe the flow on the Web as a cognitive state experienced during online navigation that is determined by (1) high levels of skill and control, (2) high levels of challenge and arousal, and (3) focused attention. Flow induces complete involvement of the actor with his activity (Mannell, Zuzanek, & Larson, 1988).

Because of the association between the notion of flow and involvement, some underlying constructs of the present study, such as focused attention or information-seeking tendency, are similar to those used in flow-based conceptualizations by Hoffman and Novak (1996a) and Novak et al. (2000). The first factor that is considered important from the involvement perspective is the "information profile" of a user. The relevance of a user's information profile has been supported extensively in extant literature (Baumgartner & Steenkamp, 1996; D'Ambra & Rice, 2001; Eighmey, 1997; Korgaonkar & Wolin, 1999). Consumers use the Web for self-education and information needs. Users have been found to agree strongly with their usage of the Web for acquiring useful information quickly, easily, and in an inexpensive manner (Korgaonkar & Wolin, 1999). The factors used in defining the information profile of a Web user are as follows:

Information Seeking Tendency[7]*:* A consumer's information-seeking tendency controls his/her behavior toward search for the latest information. If a person is of high information-seeking tendency, he/she tries to update his/her knowledge from various sources. A person with high information-seeking tendency would be eager to immediately check a new piece of information (Baumgartner & Steenkamp, 1996; Novak et al., 2000).

Focused Attention: Focused attention refers to a "centering of attention on a limited stimulus field" (Csikszentmihalyi, 1977, p. 40). Webster, Trevino, and Ryan (1993) note that the computer functions as a limited stimulus field. A person with high focused attention concentrates more during a visit to a Web site, is able to extract more information, and is deeply engrossed.

In addition to the information-seeking perspective, users also engage in the Web for the sake of fun, leisure, and enjoyment (D'Ambra & Rice, 2001). Consumers use the Web to track and watch movies online and participate in their production (Childers, Carr, Peck, & Carson, 2001). Web sites such as Ifilm.com or Intertainer.com offer features such as playing original films, movies-on-demand, or delayed broadcast of network shows. Web marketers have made use of the Web-based entertainment opportunity to promote the movie, *Tom Cats* (Mathews, 2001). Even apparently less entertainment-oriented sites such as Amazon.com recognize the importance of the entertainment aspect by "thinking of ways to make online shopping experience more fun" ("Stakes Are High," 1999, p. D8). For example, several Web sites are enabled with flash capabilities to aid their entertainment aspects.

Holbrook and Hirschman (1982) and Hirschman and Holbrook (1982) earlier proposed this experiential or hedonic perspective of consumer behavior contrasting it with the cognitive problem-solving perspective. They describe consumers as seeking fun, fantasy, sensory stimulation, and enjoyment. Novak et al. (2000) also allude to the experiential aspect of the Web in their constructs of "challenge" and "arousal." Dayal, Landesberg, and Zeisser (2000) urge Web marketers to provide the "promise of fun and adventure" while building strong digital brands. In the movies, Eliashberg and Sawhney (1994) build upon the experiential view of consumer behavior and present an innovative modeling approach to studying the dynamics of the hedonic consumption experiences. They propose the enjoyment of the experience as an outcome of stable individual difference factors (e.g., sensation-seeking tendency, moodiness), temporary moods, and the emotional content of the experience. Based on the above discussion, we describe the following constructs as defining the "entertainment profile" of a Web user.

Sensation Seeking Tendency: This is referred to as an individual's need for varied, novel, and complex sensation and experiences, and his/her willingness to actively seek out such experiences (Zuckerman, 1979). Individuals who desire a greater degree of emotional stimulation are in general expected to enjoy more stimulating activities, engage in more variety seeking, and are more willing to try and adopt new products (Raju, 1980).

Mood Variability or Moodiness Parameter: Individuals vary in the frequency with which they tend to undergo mood changes. An individual's mood may change during the experience. The duration of a mood may be small or large (Zuckerman, 1979) depending on the *moodiness* of the individual as determined by his/her susceptibility to undergo mood transitions.[8]

Involvement-Based Evaluation of Web Sites: Utilitarian and Hedonic Dimensions

Beginning with the seminal paper by Zaichkowsky (1985), several researchers have discussed research issues related to the involvement construct (Bearden & Netemeyer, 1992; Costley, 1988; Day, Stafford, & Camacho, 1995). Zaichkowsky (1985) defines involvement as "a person's perceived relevance of the object based on inherent needs, values, and interests" (p. 342). The Personal Involvement Inventory (PII) developed in the 1985 paper was mainly validated with respect to various product categories. However, in a later work, Zaichkowsky (1994) extended the validation of the involvement construct to advertisements. This work also suggests that the involvement construct may be broken into two subscales representing a cognitive and affective grouping.

Other researchers have also focused on two major dimensions of product relevance. The first dimension is the traditional notion of utilitarian performance, whereby the product is seen as performing a useful function, while the second is that of hedonic or aesthetic performance, whereby the product is valued for its intrinsically pleasing properties (Hirschman & Holbrook, 1982; Mano & Oliver, 1993).

Several researchers have investigated the hedonic versus utilitarian dichotomy in the context of the Web (Childers et al., 2001; Dholakia & Bagozzi, 2001; Hammond, McWilliam, & Diaz, 1998; Novak et al., 2000; Wolfinbarger & Gilly, 2001). The results from the above studies suggest that the major outcomes for the utilitarian consumers are freedom, control, and goal attainment, and those for the experiential consumer are fun or experience itself. Childers, Carr, Peck, and Carson (2001) propose the usefulness dimension of the product as a stronger predictor of attitudes in a more utilitarian environment and the enjoyment dimension as a stronger predictor of attitudes in a more experiential environment.

Zaichkowsky (1985) defines involvement in terms of the factors such as need, value, interest, and appeal. Similar measures of involvement have also been used in the Web-related studies of involvement (e.g., Childers et al., 2001; D'Ambra & Rice, 2001; Eighmey, 1997; Novak et al., 2000). Following Mano and Oliver (1993), we classify need and value factors of Zaichkowsky's (1985) definition of involvement as related to the utilitarian evaluation of involvement, and interest and appeal factors as related to the hedonic evaluation of involvement.

The above discussion implies that the information profile of a consumer would affect his/her utilitarian evaluation of a Web site (e.g., Hammond et al., 1998; Wolfinbarger & Gilly, 2001). We propose that a person with higher information-seeking tendency would find a Web site more needed and valuable than a person with low information-seeking tendency. Accordingly, the person with higher information-seeking tendency would be more involved with the site. A consequence of the greater involvement would be that the user would report positive affect toward the site. The outcome of this positive affect would be that such a person would revisit the site more frequently and/or would spend more time on the site during a session. Similarly, a person with higher focused attention would concentrate more during a visit to a Web site, and would be able to extract more information than a person with low focused attention, and therefore, would find the Web site more needed and valuable. This discussion is summarized in the hypotheses below:

Hypothesis 1(A). The higher the information-seeking tendency of a Web site user, the higher will be his/her utilitarian evaluation of involvement (i.e., need and value of information sought) toward the Web site.

Hypothesis 1(B). The higher the focused attention of a Web site user, the higher will be his/her utilitarian evaluation of involvement (i.e., need and value of information sought) toward the Web site.

Similarly, since every Web site might offer some level of emotional stimulation, it is expected that a person with high sensation-seeking tendency would find a Web site more interesting and appealing than a person with low sensation-seeking tendency (e.g., Hammond et al., 1998). Similarly, individuals with higher moodiness would be more likely to switch to good mood if they find the Web site interesting and appealing. Moods have been defined as mild, pervasive, and generalized affective states rather than intense emotions (Isen, 1984). Subjects in positive moods have been shown to perceive and evaluate stimuli more favorably than in other moods. This is usually attributed to three processes: (1) peripheral effects, (2) decreased elaboration, and (3) biased evaluation (Batra & Stayman, 1990). For the impact of positive moods to be effective, the individual difference variable of moodiness becomes important. This refers to the susceptibility to undergo mood transitions during a hedonic consumption experience. Underwood and Froming (1980) conceptualized this variable on the dimensions of (1) the average level of an individual's mood on the happy–sad continuum, (2) the intensity with which a person reacts to any mood experience, and (3) the frequency of mood transitions.

The moodiness variable is also related to theories of human temperament (Buss & Plomin, 1975). Temperament has been defined as "the individual differences in reactivity and self-regulation, where reactivity refers to the excitability, responsibility, responsivity, or arousability of the individual" (Rothbart & Derryberry, 1981, p. 40). In the above sense, the moodiness (or reactivity) variable in the individual entertainment profile mirrors the role of the focused attention variable in the individual information profile. Based on the above discussion, we expect that the site would interest and appeal more to a person with high mood variability than a person with low mood variability. This discussion is summarized in the hypotheses below:

Hypothesis 2(A). The higher the sensation-seeking tendency of a Web site user, the higher will be his/her hedonic evaluation of involvement (i.e., interest and appeal of entertainment sought) toward the Web site.

Hypothesis 2(B). The higher the mood variability of a Web site user, the higher will be his/her hedonic evaluation of involvement (i.e., interest and appeal of entertainment sought) toward the Web site.

Utilitarian performance of a product is seen as the product performing a useful function. Utility generates a more general form of affect (e.g., liking or disliking). Affect refers to the way a consumer feels about an attitude object. Mano and Oliver (1993) link the two types of evaluations explained above with the affect generated by the user. Thus,

Hypothesis 3(A). The higher the utilitarian evaluation of involvement of a user toward a Web site, the more positive will be his/her affect for the site.

Hypothesis 3(B). The higher the hedonic evaluation of involvement of a user toward a Web site, the more positive will be his/her affect for the site.

Web Site Properties and Evaluation: Moderator Effects

Previous studies concerned with factors underlying creation and maintenance of effective Web sites (or site design) have used similar elements, such as organized information, clarity, interface design, ease of access, simplicity, speed, style, interactive aids, and overall neatness (Eighmey, 1997; Harvard Management Communication Letter, 2000; Haubl & Trifts, 2000; Hoque & Lohse, 1999; Nielsen, 1996, 1999b; Reddy & Iyer, 2002). Similarly, Zeithaml, Parasuraman, and Malhotra (2000, 2002) introduced the concept of e-service quality (eSQ) in the context of shopping on the Internet and define it as the extent to which a Web site facilitates efficient and effective shopping, purchasing, and delivery of service. They propose some criteria, such as information availability and content, ease of use, privacy/security, graphic style, and fulfillment/reliability, that consumers might use in evaluating eSQ. In a related work, Loiacono, Watson, and Goodhue (2002) established a scale called WEBQUAL with underlying dimensions such as information quality, interaction, trust, response time, intuitiveness, visual and emotional appeals, innovation, flow, integrated communication, business processes, and customer service.

A related stream of research is concerned with consumers' rating of Web sites. For example, sites such as BizRate.com or SurveySite.com provide customer ratings of many online stores in diverse product categories. BizRate.com's online research panel of over 400,000 online buyers, who rate Web sites on 10 quality dimensions, such as Web site performance (e.g., layout, links, pictures, images, speed) or product information (e.g., quantity, quality, relevance) (Reibstein, 2001).

Based on the above literature streams, we propose that a Web site comprises of elements that can be classified into two broad classes: information and entertainment. Using a range of values on the information and entertainment spectrums, we could generate "profile" of a Web site. For example, a Web site with "high-low" profile would provide much information, but not too much entertainment (e.g., Web sites related to computer languages or stock market). Similarly, a web site with "low–high" profile would provide much entertainment, but not too much information (e.g., Web sites dedicated to movies or pop singers).

Site information profile consists of informativeness and organization of information elements, and entertainment profile consists of entertainment properties and organization of entertainment elements. The informativeness of a Web site is defined in terms such as informative, intelligent content, knowledgeable, resourceful, and up-to-date. The entertainment properties of a Web site are defined by adjectives such as fun, exciting, cool, imaginative, and flashy. Organization of entertainment elements refers to how well the entertainment elements are organized in an engaging manner.

We propose a moderating effect of a Web site's profiles on users' evaluation of involvement with a Web site. A moderator effect implies that the moderator variable (site-specific profile) modifies the form of the relationship between the predictor variable (individual profile) and the criterion variable (utilitarian and hedonic evaluation of involvement). For example, if a person is seeking some information and obtains the required information from a Web site, then his/her utilitarian evaluation of the site would be more than in the case of a site that does not provide the required information (Novak et al., 2000). Thus,

Hypothesis 4(A). The better the informativeness and organization of a Web site, the greater the positive impact of the information-seeking tendency of a Web site user on his/her utilitarian evaluation of involvement of the Web site.

Hypothesis 4(B). The better the informativeness and organization of a Web site, the greater the positive impact of the focused attention of a Web site user on his/her utilitarian evaluation of involvement of the Web site.

Similarly, an individual's enjoyment of hedonic consumption experiences is affected by the degree of match between the emotional stimulation provided by the experience, and the stimulation sought by the individual. The enjoyment level is higher when the emotional content of the Web site matches the individual's sensation-seeking tendency and is lower when there is discrepancy between the emotional content of the Web site and the individual's desire to seek (or avoid) emotional stimulation (Eliashberg & Sawhney, 1994). Therefore, a person with higher sensation-seeking tendency would find a Web site with high entertainment properties more interesting and appealing than a Web site with low entertainment properties (Underwood & Froming, 1980). Thus,

Hypothesis 5(A). The better the entertainment properties, and their organization, of a Web site, the greater the positive impact of the sensation-seeking tendency of a Web site user on his/her hedonic evaluation of involvement of the Web site.

Hypothesis 5(B). The better the entertainment properties and their organization of a Web site, the greater the positive impact of the mood variability of a Web site user on his/her hedonic evaluation of involvement of the Web site.

If a person visits a Web site with high information/entertainment properties, it is expected that the utilitarian/hedonic component of involvement will lead to more positive affective experiences than if he/she visits a Web site with low information/entertainment properties (Mano & Oliver, 1993).

Hypothesis 6(A). The better the informativeness and organization of a Web site, the greater the positive impact of the utilitarian evaluation of a user on his/her affect toward the Web site.

Hypothesis 6(B). The better the entertainment properties and their organization of a Web site, the greater the positive impact of the hedonic evaluation of a user on his/her affect toward the Web site.

Research Design

We conducted our study in three stages. In Stage 1, we collected data for classifying Web sites on information and entertainment properties. In Stage 2, we collected data for the measurement of involvement. In Stage 3, we collected data for time-based measurement of involvement.

The Sample

The surveys were conducted with a sample consisting of 44 engineering undergraduate/postgraduate students in the 18–25 age group. The sample composition mainly comprised male respondents (42 out of 44). Some respondents participated in more than one survey, while others participated in only one survey. The exact details of the contact scheme are discussed later in the methodology section. The respondents have easy access to high-speed Internet connections. They are quite active users of the Internet for various purposes. The first two surveys were conducted over a period of 4 weeks. The third survey took an additional four weeks to complete.

Scales

We used existing scales for measuring the constructs of sensation-seeking tendency, mood variability, individual specific focused attention, informativeness, entertainment properties, utilitarian and hedonic evaluation of involvement, and affect. In some cases, we modified the existing scales to make them compatible with the local conditions and the constructs of model to be tested. Exact scales used in the surveys are found in Appendix 1.

A six-item scale measured *information-seeking tendency*. We modified the *exploratory behavior* scale of Novak et al. (2000) to generalize it to measure the individual willingness to seek information (e.g., "I try to update my knowledge from various media"). *Individual specific focused attention* is also similar to Novak et al.'s (2000) scale. The scale comprised of four items (e.g., "When visiting a Web site my attention is focused"). *Sensation-seeking tendency* was measured by a six-item scale. We adapted this scale from Zuckerman (1979). The five-item *mood variability* scale closely follows Underwood and Froming's (1980) reactivity construct.

The five-item *informativeness* scale is similar to Chen and Wells's (1999). The informativeness of a Web site is defined by elements such as informativeness, intelligent contents, knowledge, resourcefulness, and currency. This factor builds upon the informative/relevant scales that have emerged in previous studies of print advertisements and television commercials. The seven-item *organization of information element* scale was adapted from two sources. Three items (e.g., "Interacting with the Web site is slow and tedious") are taken from Novak et al. (2000) and four items (e.g., "I find this Web site not messy to use") from Chen and Wells (1999) depending on their suitability to the Web environment. The five-item *entertainment* scale was constructed using five items from Chen and Wells (1999). The entertainment properties of a Web site are defined by adjectives such as fun, exciting, cool, and imaginative. These terms are similar to raters' evaluations of television commercials, such as "merry," "amusing" (Wells, Leavitt, & McConville, 1971), "lots of fun to watch," "clever and quite entertaining" (Schilinger, 1979), and "fast, held attention, and interesting" (Moldovan, 1984). *Organization of entertainment element* scale (Reibstein, 2001) consists of three items (e.g., "This Web site has animation elements").

Utilitarian evaluation of involvement construct (Mano & Oliver, 1993) comprises of two separate scales. The first scale *need* is composed of six items (e.g., "vital," "needed," "essential," "fundamental," "beneficial," and "useful"). The second scale *value* is composed of seven items (e.g., "important," "means a lot to me," "relevance," "valuable," "matters to me," "of concern to me," and "significant"). Similarly, *hedonic evaluation of involvement* construct (Mano & Oliver, 1993) also comprises of two separate scales. The first scale *interest* is composed of three items (e.g., "exciting," "interesting," and "fascinating"). The second scale a*ppeal* is composed of two items (e.g., "appealing," and "desirable"). The *affect (positive/negative)* scale is similar to Novak et al.'s (2000). The scale has four items (e.g., "After visiting the Web site I feel pleased").

Items in the sensation-seeking tendency scale are scored as either true or false. A seven-point semantic differential scale is used for the items of utilitarian and hedonic evaluation scales. For the rest of the scales, each item is scored on a five-point scale, ranging from "strongly disagree" to "strongly agree."

Tests for Main Effects

We use multiple regression technique for hypotheses testing. Hypotheses 1(A) to 3(B) are related to main effects. We examine these effects at both overall (i.e., pooling the observations of all the respondents of all the Web sites) and site-specific levels.

Hypotheses 1(A) and 1(B) are related to the relationship between individual information profile (independent variable) and utilitarian evaluation of involvement (dependent variable). Therefore, we perform regression analysis by specifying the following model,

$$Y_1 = \alpha_1 {*} X_1 + \alpha_2 {*} X_2 + e_1$$

where Y_1 is utilitarian evaluation of Web site involvement, and X_1 and X_2 are individual specific information-seeking tendency and focused attention, respectively. Similarly, Hypotheses 2(A) and 2(B) are related to the relationship between individual entertainment profile (independent variable) and hedonic evaluation of involvement (dependent variable). The regression model is as follows,

$$Y_2 = \beta_1 {*} X_3 + \beta_2 {*} X_4 + e_2$$

where Y_2 is hedonic evaluation of Web site involvement, and X_3 and X_4 are individual sensation-seeking tendency and mood variability, respectively. Hypotheses 3(A) and 3(B) are related to the effect of utilitarian evaluation and hedonic evaluation of involvement (independent variables, Y_1 and Y_2) on affect (dependent Z_1). The regression model is as given below:

$$Z_1 = \gamma_1 {*} Y_1 + \gamma_2 {*} Y_2 + e_3$$

Tests for Moderator Effects

Hypotheses 4(A) to 6(B) are related to moderator relationships. Since we define the moderator variables of site profiles as dichotomous (high–low), the moderator analysis falls into Case 2 of Baron and Kenny's (1986) classification of testing moderation (pp. 1175–1176). The method suggests use of similar regression equations as used for main effects, but in the case of moderator effects, the regression is performed separately for respective Web sites in high or low classification of information or entertainment properties. The type of each Web site signifies the level of moderator variable. For example, the sites rediff, mapsofindia, and indiainfoline represent the high information case. The difference in regression coefficients of combined pool of respondents of these sites could be compared with a combined pool of respondents of low information sites such as allindia, indiafm, and nazara. If the statistical significance of difference between regression coefficients is established by Chow (1960) test, then the hypothesized moderating effect of information profile (Hypotheses 4 and 6A) could be supported in the above example.

Data Collection

In the first survey, we collect data for classifying Web sites, and in the second survey, we collect data for measurement of involvement. In the third survey, we collect data for measure of involvement after some fixed duration of time. Initially, before the first survey, we follow judges-based procedure to select the Web sites for conducting the three surveys.

Selection of Web Sites

We classified Web sites in a 2×2 (Information properties × Entertainment properties) matrix on the basis of the level (high or low) of their information and entertainment properties. To initiate the selection of the Web sites, we use www.bestindiansites.com's "Top 50 Web Sites" appraisal, which uses parameters such as traffic ratings by various traffic ranking tools, cross-links with search engines/other sites, ratings on various quality parameters (e.g., load time, browser compatibility), HTML validity, content, site design, and listings in major search engines. The following steps were taken for primary selection of Web sites:

Step 1: We used "Top 50 Web Sites" data by www.bestindiansites.com for six months prior to the study. We give one point if the Web site appears in the Top 50 list in a week, and zero otherwise. We then sum to get the total number of times a Web site appeared in the list during the six months.[9]

Step 2: Using a cutoff value of 70%, we discarded the Web sites that appeared in the list less than 70% of time.[10] A reduced pool of 46 Web sites was obtained after this step.

Step 3: The above short-listed Web sites were classified on the basis of information and entertainment properties of Web sites. The classification was done by three *independent judges*, who were postgraduate students and used the Web (for surfing, literature search, paper downloads, etc.) for the previous two years on average of over 30 hours per week. The judges were asked to check the general criteria that the Web sites are easy to understand by the 18 to 25-year-old student respondents, and the Web sites are of general interest (i.e., without any cultural or regional biases). In each quadrant of the 2×2 matrix, we retained only those Web sites for which there were no differences among judges. This resulted in a set of 20 Web

Table 1. Web sites classified by the judges on the basis of information and entertainment properties

		Entertainment Properties	
		High	Low
Information Properties	High	www.rediff.com	www.mapsofindia.com
		www.123india.com	www.timesofindia.com
		www.indiainfo.com	www.naukri.com
		www.indiatimes.com	www.indiainfoline.com
		www.indya.com	
		www.webindia.com	
	Low	www.khel.com	www.allindia.com
		www.smashits.com	www.dgreetings.com
		www.indiafm.com	www.theholidays.com
		www.nazara.com	www.indiaserver.com
		www.paheli.com	www.ciol.com

sites as shown in Table 1. To validate the classification by the judges, we then contacted a larger group of respondents as discussed below.

Survey 1: Classification of Web Sites

Survey 1 is used for classifying, in terms of numerical values, the Web sites on the basis of their information and entertainment properties. This survey was conducted with a sample of 31 respondents. Each respondent examined three randomly assigned sites out of the 20 Web sites[11] listed in Table 1. After discarding some incomplete forms, there were 89 responses, which were used for the classification of Web sites. The average of information and entertainment properties (on a scale of 1 to 5) of each Web site is presented in Table 2, and their relative positions are shown in Figure 2.

We then compared the positions of the sites in Table 1 and Figure 2 and selected the sites, which were common to both for a particular quadrant. Therefore, we selected www.rediff.com, www.indiainfoline.com, www.allindia.com, and www.nazara.com for further analysis. We selected two additional Web sites (www.mapsofindia.com and www.indiafm.com) closer to the mean for better analysis of the differences between the sites' evaluations. The brief overviews and screenshots of some short-listed sites are shown in Appendix 2.

Table 2. Site scores on information and entertainment properties

S. No.	Name of Web Sites	Information Average	Entertainment Average
1	www.rediff.com	4.37	3.65
2	www.123india.com	3.92	3.65
3	www.indiainfo.com	3.88	3.33
4	www.indiatimes.com	3.90	3.90
5	www.indya.com	3.72	3.65
6	www.webindia.com	3.67	2.88
7	www.mapsofindia.com	3.92	3.28
8	www.timesofindia.com	4.18	3.60
9	www.naukri.com	3.71	2.88
10	www.indiainfoline.com	4.13	3.13
11	www.allindia.com	3.38	2.69
12	www.dgreetings.com	3.87	3.70
13	www.theholidayspot.com	3.47	3.88
14	www.khel.com	3.96	3.40
15	www.smashits.com	2.86	3.02
16	www.indiafm.com	3.62	3.65
17	www.nazara.com	3.44	3.84
18	www.paheli.com	3.37	3.73
	Mean	3.75	3.43

Figure 2. Relative positions of Web sites on the basis of information and entertainment scores

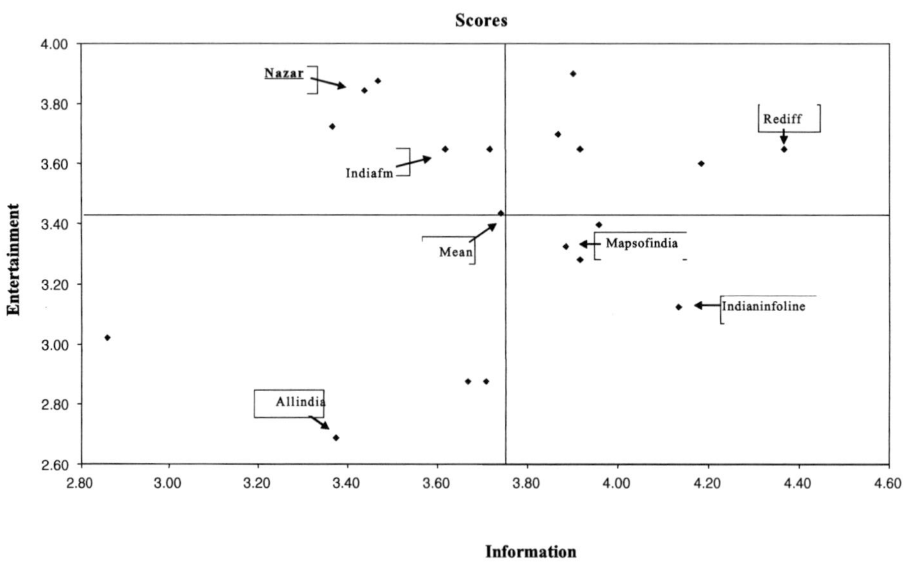

Survey 2: Measurement of Involvement

Survey 2 is used for measuring the involvement and positive affect of the respondents toward a Web site. This survey was conducted on a sample of 37 respondents. The sample included all the respondents who had participated in Survey 1 and six additional respondents. Most respondents (33 out of 37) in the sample were assigned two Web sites to examine, while a few (4 out of 37) were assigned four Web sites. Thus, this survey resulted in 82 responses. The sites were assigned randomly to respondents. This survey was conducted in the following manner.

First, an in-class survey was conducted which was concerned with the individual characteristics pertaining to information (e.g., information-seeking tendency) and entertainment (e.g., sensation-seeking tendency) profiles of the respondents. Then the respondents were told the names of the Web sites randomly assigned to them 1 week before filling out the questionnaires related to utilitarian and hedonic evaluations of involvement and positive affect. They were instructed to visit the assigned sites as many times as they could over that period. One week later, they were asked to fill out the questionnaires in the computer systems laboratory.

Survey 3: Effect of Time on Involvement

In Survey 3, we investigate the effect of time on the involvement of Web users at a one-week interval for three weeks. We appointed a panel of 14 respondents for this study. Half of the respondents were new respondents, while the rest had participated in the earlier two surveys. Based on the possible levels of an individual's profiles (high × low, information × entertainment), which he/she filled in the first session, we analyzed four types of respondents in this study. For the entire period of this analysis, the respondents were assigned a specific Web site out of the four possible Web sites classified in the above fashion.

Results and Analysis

We performed statistical analyses using STATISTICA software on the collected data from various surveys.

Reliability of the Constructs

The following Cronbach alpha values were found for the various constructs:

Scale	Cronbach alpha
Information-seeking tendency	0.62
Individual specific focused attention	0.64
Sensation-seeking tendency	0.55
Mood variability	0.68
Site information profile	0.79
Site entertainment profile	0.70
Utilitarian evaluation of involvement	
Need	0.88
Value	0.90
Hedonic evaluation of involvement	
Interest	0.83
Appeal	0.81
Positive affect	0.77

With the exception of sensation-seeking tendency scale, the other scales show reasonable values of Cronbach's alpha. In case of sensation-seeking tendency scale, it is possible that some respondents were not able to relate well with some scale items such as "I sometimes like to do things that are a little frightening" or "I would not like to be hypnotized." This could be attributed to the language or cultural barriers hindering the correct interpretation of terms "hypnotized" or "frightening."

Analyses and Interpretation of Results

Results Related to Main Effects

Overall Results

For hypotheses testing, we use multiple regression technique. The results of individual specific main effects are shown in Table 3(A) and the results of moderator effects are shown in Table 3(B). All hypotheses, except Hypothesis 2(A), were supported at 95% level. Hypothesis 2(A) on the relationship between

Table 3(A). Overall results of main effects

Dependent Variable	Utilitarian Evaluation of Involvement		Hedonic Evaluation of Involvement		Positive Affect	
Independent Variable	Information-Seeking Tendency	Individual Specific Focused Attention	Sensation-Seeking Tendency	Mood Variability	Utilitarian Evaluation of Involvement	Hedonic Evaluation of Involvement
	α_1 (*t*-statistic)	α_2 (*t*-statistic)	β_1 (*t*-statistic)	β_2 (*t*-statistic)	γ_1 (*t*-statistic)	γ_2 (*t*-statistic)
	0.65 (4.94)	0.33 (2.52)	0.14 (1.79)	0.82 (10.31)	0.42 (4.60)	0.58 (6.40)

Table 3(B). Site-specific results of main effects

Dependent Variable	Utilitarian Evaluation of Involvement		Hedonic Evaluation of Involvement		Positive Affect	
Independent Variable	Information-Seeking Tendency	Focused Attention	Sensation-Seeking Tendency	Mood Variability	Utilitarian Evaluation of Involvement	Hedonic Evaluation of Involvement
Name of Web Site	α_1 (*t*-statistic)	α_2 (*t*-statistic)	β_1 (*t*-statistic)	β_2 (*t*-statistic)	γ_1 (*t*-statistic)	γ_2 (*t*-statistic)
Rediff (High-High)*	0.94 (2.91)	0.04 (0.12)	0.16 (0.71)	0.79 (3.60)	0.66 (3.34)	0.33 (1.65)
Mapsofindia (High-Low)	0.66 (4.25)	0.34 (2.15)	0.24 (1.58)	0.75 (4.97)	0.71 (4.33)	0.29 (1.79)
Indiainfoline (High-Low)	0.87 (2.35)	0.12 (0.32)	0.03 (0.24)	0.95 (7.43)	0.63 (2.73)	0.37 (1.58)
Allindia (Low-Low)	0.29 (0.67)	0.70 (1.65)	-1.76 (-1.80)	2.60 (2.67)	0.77 (1.73)	0.23 (0.52)
Indiafm (Low-High)	0.81 (2.26)	0.15 (0.42)	0.10 (0.80)	0.89 (7.16)	0.28 (1.34)	0.71 (3.36)
Nazara (Low-High)	0.32 (0.96)	0.66 (1.96)	0.23 (1.06)	0.72 (3.28)	0.39 (1.50)	0.60 (2.27)

** Represents that the Web site is high in information properties and high in entertainment properties. Note: Cells with significant effects are shaded.*

hedonic evaluation of involvement and sensation-seeking tendency could not be supported, possibly due to the measurement-related problems mentioned earlier in connection with the sensation-seeking tendency variable.

The overall results, shown in Table 3(A), suggest that utilitarian evaluation of involvement is significantly affected by the two factors, individual information-seeking tendency ($\alpha_1 = 0.65, t = 4.94$) and individual specific focused attention ($\alpha_2 = 0.33, t = 2.52$). Hence Hypotheses 1(A) and 1(B) are supported. Similarly, the hedonic evaluation of involvement is affected by the two factors, individual specific sensation-seeking tendency and individual specific mood variability. Both factors are positive but only one factor (mood variability) is significant (β_1 = 0.82, t = 10.31). Hence, it supports Hypothesis 2(B) but does not provide enough support for Hypothesis 2(A).

The last result of Table 3A suggests that positive affect is also affected by two factors, utilitarian ($\gamma_1 = 0.42$, $t = 4.6$) and hedonic ($\gamma_2 = 0.58$, $t = 6.4$) evaluation of involvement. Since both the independent variables are positive and significant, the results support Hypotheses 3(A) and 3(B).

Site-Specific Results

In order to generate more insights regarding site-specific effects of various factors, we perform the regressions separately for each Web site. For example, in case of a site that is high in information but low in entertainment (e.g., mapsofindia.com), consistent with our hypotheses, we would expect the coefficients of regression of utilitarian evaluation of involvement on information profile variables to be more significant than those of hedonic evaluation of involvement on entertainment profile variables. Moreover, the coefficient of regression of affect on utilitarian evaluation would be more significant than on hedonic evaluation of involvement for such a site. Similar results for other sites would provide greater support to our hypotheses testing results. We show these results in Table 3(B) and make the following observations:

(i) *rediff.com* (high information and high entertainment): The individual specific information seeking tendency appears to affect utilitarian evaluation of involvement ($a_1 = 0.79$, $t = 3.60$), and individual specific mood variability appears to affect hedonic evaluation of involvement ($b_2 = 0.95$, $t = 7.43$). For positive affect, only utilitarian evaluation of involvement is significant ($g_1 = 0.66$, $t = 3.34$). Thus, even though this site was classified as high on both information and entertainment aspects, the respondents relied mainly on the utilitarian aspects while evaluating this site.

(ii) *mapsofindia.com* (high information and low entertainment): Both individual specific information-seeking tendency ($a_1 = 0.66$, $t = 4.25$) and individual specific focused attention ($a_2 = 0.34$, $t = 2.15$) affect utilitarian evaluation of involvement. Again, individual specific mood variability affects hedonic evaluation of involvement ($b_2 = 0.75$, $t = 4.97$), and as expected, only utilitarian evaluation of involvement affects positive affect ($g_1 = 0.71$, $t = 4.33$).

(iii) *indiainfoline.com* (high information and low entertainment): Individual specific information-seeking tendency seems to affect utilitarian evaluation of involvement ($a_1 = 0.87$, $t = 2.35$). Individual specific mood variability seems to affect hedonic evaluation of involvement ($b_2 = 0.95$, $t = 7.43$). As expected, only utilitarian evaluation of involvement affects positive affect ($g_1 = 0.63$, $t = 2.73$).

(iv) *allindia.com* (low information and low entertainment): Both individual specific information-seeking tendency and focused attention are not significant for utilitarian evaluation of involvement. The effect of mood variability is significant ($b_2 = 2.6, t = 2.67$) for hedonic evaluation of involvement. For positive affect, both utilitarian and hedonic evaluations of involvement are not significant.

(v) *indiafm.com* (low information and high entertainment): Individual specific information-seeking tendency affects utilitarian evaluation of involvement ($a_1 = 0.81, t = 2.26$) even for this high entertainment site, which seems to suggest that some respondents might have been interpreting some entertainment-specific details (e.g., results from box office, movie review, cine awards, and interview of celebrities) as "relevant information." Again, for hedonic evaluation of involvement, individual specific mood variability is significant ($b_2 = 0.89, t = 7.16$), and as expected, only hedonic evaluation of involvement affects positive affect ($g_2 = 0.71, t = 3.36$).

(vi) *nazara.com* (low information and high entertainment): Individual specific focused attention affects utilitarian evaluation of involvement ($a_2 = 0.66, t = 1.96$), which can be expected as even a high entertainment site may contain some amount of information, which requires focused attention for entertainment-prone individuals. For hedonic evaluation of involvement, only individual specific mood variability is significant ($b_2 = 0.72, t = 3.28$). As expected, only hedonic evaluation of involvement is significant for positive affect ($g_2 = 0.6, t = 2.27$).

Results Related to Moderator Relationship

Hypotheses 4(A) to 6(B) are related to moderator relationship. For analysis regarding Hypotheses 4 and 6A (i.e., information profile of a Web site), we pool the observations of high and low information sites (HI vs. LI) separately. The Chow test for comparing the regressions of HI and LI sites of utilitarian evaluation of involvement on information-seeking tendency and focused attention results in the value of F-statistic = 6.31, which is greater than the critical F-value of 3.13 at 5% confidence level and degrees of freedom 2 and 78. Thus, Hypothesis 4 is supported. In other words, the positive impact of an individual's information profile on utilitarian evaluation of involvement appears to be greater when the information profile of the site assigned is better. Similarly, the Chow test for comparing the regression of positive affect on utilitarian evaluation of involvement results in the value of F-statistic = 12.66, which is greater than the critical F-value of 3.98 at 5% confidence level and degrees of freedom 1 and 80. Thus, the utilitarian evaluation appears to lead to more positive affect for better information sites.

For analysis regarding Hypotheses 5 and 6B (i.e., entertainment profile of a Web site), we pool the observations of high and low entertainment sites (HE vs. LE) separately. The Chow test for comparing the regressions of HE and LE sites of hedonic evaluation of involvement on sensations-seeking tendency and mood variability, and positive affect on hedonic evaluation of involvement, result in the values of F-statistic lower than the critical F-value at 5% confidence level. Thus, Hypotheses 5 and 6B are not supported. This could be due to small sample size in the case of individual sites or lower reliabilities of entertainment profile measures.[12]

Summary of Results

All the hypotheses, except hypothesis 2(A) on the relationship between hedonic evaluation of involvement and sensation-seeking tendency, are supported. In general, the site-specific results are in the direction that makes intuitive sense. For example, an individual's information profile factors, information-seeking tendency, and focused attention appear to affect significantly the utilitarian evaluations of high information sites (e.g., rediff.com, indiainfoline.com, or mapsofindia.com). Similarly, an individual's entertainment profile factor, mood variability, is important for hedonic evaluation of high entertainment sites (e.g., allindia.com, indiafm.com, or nazara.com). Further, in general, utilitarian evaluation is more significant in generating positive affect in high information sites, whereas hedonic evaluation is more significant in generating positive affect in high entertainment sites.

An interesting result obtained is that for some high entertainment sites (e.g., indiafm.com), the individual information profile factors, such as information-seeking tendency, are also significant for utilitarian evaluation of involvement. This could be attributed to the nature of information available at these sites. Moreover, for all of the high information sites, the individual entertainment profile factor, mood variability, was found highly significant in explaining hedonic evaluation. It is also possible that some of the short-listed Web sites were interpreted as both informative and entertaining. This could particularly be the case with the sites that provide relevant "information" about "entertaining" Indian movie industry.

Results of Effect of Time on Involvement

Since the concept of involvement has long-term implications, it is useful to study the effect of time on involvement (Richins & Bloch, 1991). Previous researchers have also differentiated between situational involvement (primarily dealt with in this paper) and enduring involvement (a long-term measure of involvement, which has time-based implications) (Bearden & Netemeyer, 1992). It is expected that the involvement of a visitor would increase in the case of a match between the site profile and the user profile, and vice versa. We present some representative results of this site-user analysis in Figure 3.

When a high information and high entertainment profile respondent is "matched" with a site of high information and high entertainment profile (e.g., rediff.com), the utilitarian as well as hedonic evaluation of a person (high on information as well as entertainment profile) increases as time passes (see Figure 3(A)). In case of a match of a high information and low entertainment profile respondent with a high information but low entertainment profile site (e.g., indiainfoline.com), the utilitarian evaluation of the respondent increases, but hedonic evaluation of involvement does not show any trend with the passage of time (see Figure 3(B)).

In case of a mismatch of a low information and high entertainment profile respondent with a high information but low entertainment profile site (e.g., indiainfoline.com), as expected, both utilitarian and hedonic evaluations show generally decreasing trend (see Figure 3(C)). Interestingly, in case of a match

Figure 3. Time-based measurement of involvement

(A) High – high respondent, high– high site (Rediff.com)

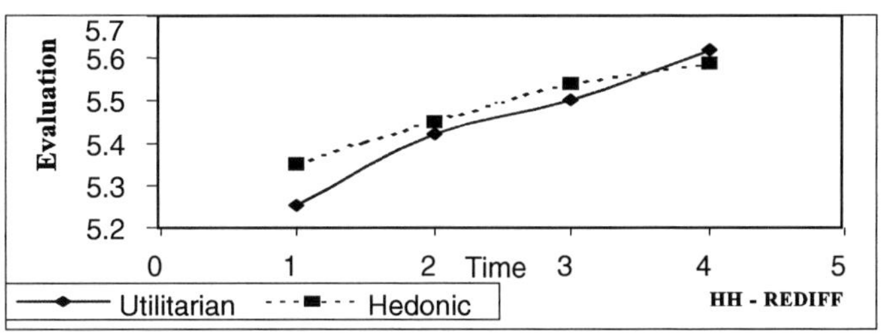

(B) High – Low Respondent, High– Low Site (Indiainfoline.com)

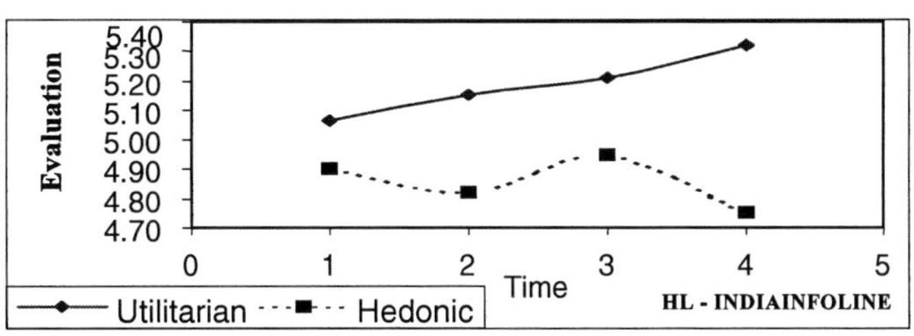

Figure 3. Time-based measurement of involvement

(C) Low – High Respondent, High – Low Site (Indiainfoline.com)

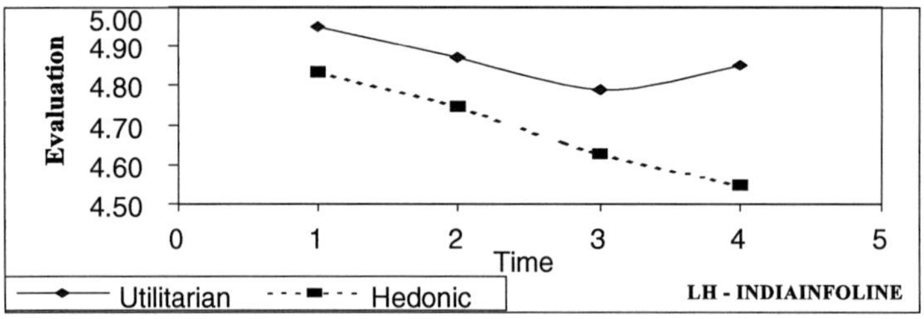

(D) Low – Low Respondent, Low – Low Site (Allindia.com)

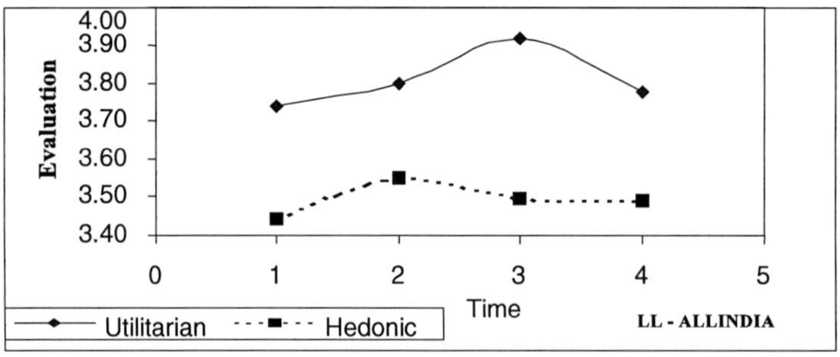

of a low-low respondent with a low-low site, the evaluations do not show any trend as time passes (see Figure 3(D)). The result is interesting as it indicates that the sites that provide low levels of information or entertainment may not be able to involve a person who is low in seeking information or entertainment. These results are encouraging, and future research should examine such time-based evaluations of involvement in greater detail.

Conclusions, Limitations, and Directions for Future Reseach

The importance of Internet-based commerce to the global economy has long been recognized (Henry et al., 1999). However, as the competition in this environment intensifies, Web marketers increasingly need to understand factors that engage consumers in order to fulfill their marketing objectives in terms of visit durations, repeat visits, and online purchase. We propose the current framework as an important early step in developing the understanding and use of factors affecting consumer involvement toward Web sites.

At a broad level, the major contribution of this line of research is to conceptualize the factors that lead a consumer to visit a Web site more frequently and to illustrate how the individual difference in Web site involvement can be explained and measured in terms of the different constructs. Our results show that the components of consumer's information (e.g., information-seeking tendency, focused attention) and entertainment (e.g., mood variability) profiles significantly affect utilitarian (need, value) and hedonic (interest, appeal) evaluations of involvement, respectively, to generate positive affect toward the Web site. Web site factors such as informativeness and organization further enhance these relationships.

Our findings imply that a good Web site is one that delivers relevant and well-organized information in an engaging manner. At a basic level, the major managerial implications of our work are that if a site has high information providing elements, then it must target high information-seeking visitors. Conversely, for a given segment profile, our methodology can help in editing and design decisions by studying the impact of modifying the site's content according to the involvement level of the target segment.

Since the proposed framework involves stable individual difference factors (e.g., information- or sensation-seeking tendencies), the approach can be used to compare the online consumer behavior from diverse backgrounds, nationalities, and cultures for the benefit of global sites such as amazon.com or yahoo.com. The consumer behavior differences can also be compared for traditional versus electronic media. Further, understanding differences in people's behavior could also aid the development, design, and evaluation of commercial Web sites, online retail stores, search engines, and other information products and services. The culmination of the proposed framework in a quantitative model of online consumer behavior will help generate a priori predictions about the effectiveness of different Web site designs and promotional strategies. There might also be a higher dimension to the concept of involvement in online environments. For example, there might be a greater possibility of involvement of online consumers who are more techno-ready (see Parasuraman, 2000, and Parasuraman & Colby, 2001, for the concept of techno-readiness).

Our study has some limitations, which could be addressed by future research. The survey involved student respondents who tended to be younger, better educated, and more informed than the general Internet population. It is possible that these individuals have greater ability to use and develop affect toward a Web site; thus, their responses would overstate the true evaluation of Web site for all consumers. On the other hand, it is plausible that these individuals would also have higher expectations regarding information and the market strategies of Web sites, and thus might be more critical of Web sites. Further, it is possible that some subjects who viewed more than one Web site may have carried their evaluations from one Web site to another. Future researchers should examine a larger sample without repeated measures. Another refinement could be an experiment that also examines interactions. Such an experiment could be 2×2×2×2 type, in which the first two combinations refer to the individual's and the last two combinations refer to the site's information and entertainment properties.

In the present framework, we have included only information and entertainment profiles of an individual. Some other personality or demographic characteristics, such as skill, Web usage, and playfulness, should also be included in future research. Further research on the Web site involvement model could also include additional variables, which we may have omitted in the interest of parsimony and tractability. For example, the investigation of the role of prior expectation to enjoyment, based on advertising and word of mouth, could play a role in determining actual enjoyment. Another variable that could be included in this framework is that of techno-readiness of a consumer (Parasuraman, 2000). A hypothesis worth examining in this context could be that more techno-ready consumers of the Web show greater levels of involvement than those by novices.

Our model is essentially a static model in which we took individual constructs as stable over time, although some construct may change during the consumption experience. Therefore, another research direction would be to extend this framework to take into account the dynamic nature of different constructs. Another attractive future research direction would be to extend the model for measuring the customer's involvement for those consumers who purchased from Web sites.

References

Baron, R. M., & Kenny, D. A. (1986). The moderator-mediator variable distinction in social psychological research: Conceptual, strategic and statistical considerations. *Journal of Personality and Social Psychology, 51*(6), 1173–1182.

Batra, R., & Stayman, D. M. (1990). The role of mood in advertising effectiveness. *Journal of Consumer Research, 17*, 203–214.

Baumgartner, H., & Steenkmap, J.-B. E.M. (1996). Exploratory consumer buying behavior: Conceptualization and measurement. *International Journal of Research in Marketing, 13*, 121–137.

Bearden, W., & Netemeyer, R. (1992). The effect of enduring, situational, and response involvement on preference stability in the context of voting behavior. *Psychology and Marketing, 9*(2), 143–156.

Bezos, J. (1999, July 20). *Setting the standard with Jeff Bezos.* Internet Summit 99, Dana Point, CA.

Buss, A. H., & Plomin, R. (1975). *A temperament theory of personality development.* New York: Wiley.

Chen, Q., & Wells, W. D. (1999). Attitude towards the site. *Journal of Advertising Research, 39*(5), 27–38.

Childers, T. L., Carr, C. L., Peck, J., & Carson, S. (2001). Hedonic and utilitarian motivations for online retail shopping behavior. *Journal of Retailing, 77,* 511–535.

Chow, G. C. (1960). Tests of equality between sets of coefficients in two linear regressions. *Econometrika, 28*(July), 591–605

Cognitiative. (1999). E-commerce and the evolution of retail shopping behavior. *Pulse of the Customer, 1*(2).

Costley, C. (1988). Meta analysis of involvement research. *Advances in Consumer Research, 15,* 554–562.

Csikszentmihalyi, M. (1977). *Beyond boredom and anxiety.* San Francisco: Jossey-Bass.

Csikszentmihalyi, M. (1990). *Flow: The psychology of optimal experience.* New York: Harper & Row.

D'Ambra, J., & Rice, R. E. (2001). Emerging factors in user evaluation of the World Wide Web. *Information & Management, 38,* 373–384.

Day, E., Stafford, M., & Camacho, A. (1995). Opportunities for involvement research: A scale development approach. *Journal of Advertising, 24*(3), 69–75.

Dayal, S., Landesberg, H., & Zeisser, M. (2000). Building digital brands. *The McKinsey Quarterly, 2,* 43–51.

Dholakia, U., & Bagozzi, R. P. (2001). Consumer behavior in digital environments. In J. Wind & V. Mahajan (Eds.), *Digital marketing: Global strategies from world's leading experts.* New York: John Wiley & Sons.

Eighmey, J. (1997). Profiling user responses to commercial websites. *Journal of Advertising Research, 37,* 59–66.

Eliashberg, J., & Sawhney, M. S. (1994). Modeling goes to Hollywood: Predicting individual differences in movie enjoyment. *Management Science, 40*(9), 1151–1173.

Forrester Research. (2001, January 5). Digital marketing will reach $63 billion in the US, while online advertising alone will rise to $42 billion worldwide by 2005. Retrieved March 10, 2004, from *www.forrester.com/ER/Press/Release/0,1769,485,00.html*

Forrester Research B. V. (2001, July 23). Online shopping is alive, and European retailers will reap 103 billion Euros in gross profits through 2006. Retrieved March 10, 2004, from *www.forrester.com/ER/Press/Release/0,1769,600, 00.html*

Hammond, K., McWilliam, G., & Diaz, A. N. (1998). Fun and work on the Web: Difference in attitudes between novices and experienced users. *Advances in Consumer Research, 25*, 372–378.

Hanson, W. (2000). *Principles of internet marketing*. South–Western College Publishing.

Harvard Management Communication Letter. (2000, August 3–5). *Communicating with your customers on the Web.*

Haubl, G., & Trifts, V. (2000). Consumer decision making in online shopping environments: The effects of interactive decision aids. *Marketing Science, 19*(1), 4–21.

Henry, D., Cooke, S., Buckley, P., Dumagan, J., Gill, G., Pastore, D. et al. (1999). *The emerging digital economy II.* Washington, DC: United States Department of Commerce.

Hirschman, E. C., & Holbrook, M. B. (1982). Hedonic consumption: Emerging concepts, methods and propositions. *Journal of Marketing, 46,* 92–101.

Hoffman, D. L., & Novak, T. P. (1996a). Marketing in hypermedia computer–mediated environments: Conceptual foundations. *Journal of Marketing, 60*(July), 50–68.

Hoffman, D. L., & Novak, T. P. (1996b). A new marketing paradigm for electronic commerce. *Information Society, 13*(January–March), 43–54.

Holbrook, M. B., & Hirschman, E. C. (1982). The experiential aspects of consumption: Consumer fantasies, feeling and fun. *Journal of Consumer Research, 9,* 132–140.

Hoque, A. Y., & Lohse, G. L. (1999). An information search cost perspective for designing interfaces for electronic commerce. *Journal of Marketing Research, 36*(3), 387–394.

Isen, A. M. (1984). Toward understanding the role of affect in cognition. In R. S.Wyer & T. K. Srull (Eds.), *Handbook of social cognition* (pp. 179–236). Hillsdale, NJ: Lawrence Erlbaum.

Kolakata, R., & Whinston, A. B. (2000). *Frontiers of electronic commerce.* Singapore: Addison Wesley Longman.

Korgaonkar, P. K., & Wolin, L. D. (1999). A multivariate analysis of Web usage. *Journal of Advertising Research, 39*(2), 53–68.

Krishnamurthy, S. (2002). *E-commerce management: Text and cases*. Southwestern College Publishing.

Loiacono, E. T., Watson, R. T., & Goodhue, D. L. (2002). WebQual: A measure of website quality. *AMA Winter Proceedings*, 432–438.

Mahajan, V., Srinivasan, R., & Wind, J. (2002). The dot-com retail failures of 2000: Were there any winners? *Journal of Academy of Marketing Science, 30*(4).

Mannell, R. C., Zuzanek, J., & Larson, R. (1988). Leisure states and 'flow' experiences: Testing perceived freedom and intrinsic motivation hypotheses. *Journal of Leisure Research, 20*(4), 289–304.

Mano, H., & Oliver, R. (1993). Assessing the dimensionality and structure of the consumption experience: Evaluation, feeling, and satisfaction. *Journal of Consumer Research, 20*, 451–466.

Mathews, A. W. (2001, March 26). Creating the buzz: The movie tomcats opens this week, the Web promotion began long before that. *Wall Street Journal*, p. R13.

Moldovan, S. E. (1984). Copy factors related to persuasions scores. *Journal of Advertising Research, 24*(6), 16–22.

Nielsen, J. (1996). Top ten mistakes in Web design. Retrieved March 10, 2004, from *www.useit.com*

Nielsen, J. (1999a). *Why people shop in the Web?* Retrieved March 10, 2004, from *www.useit.com*.

Nielsen, J. (1999b). *Ten good deeds in Web design.* Retrieved March 10, 2004, from *www.useit.com*

Novak, T. P., Hoffman, D. L., & Yung, Y.-F. (2000). Measuring the customer experience in online environments: A structural modeling approach. *Marketing Science, 19*(1), 22–42.

Nvision. (1999). 4 out of 5 users never re-visit the average Web site. *CyberAtlas*. Retrieved October 21, 1999, from *http://cyberatlas.Internet.com/bigpicture/demographics/article/0,1323.5931_212071,00.html*

Parasuraman, A. (2000). Technology Readiness Index (TRI): A multiple-item scale to measure readiness to embrace new technologies. *Journal of Service Research, 2*(4), 307–321

Parasuraman, A., & Colby, C. L. (2001). *Technoready marketing: How and why your customers adopt technology*. New York: The Free Press.

Raju, P. S. (1980). Optimum stimulation level: Its relationship to personality, demographics and exploratory behavior. *Journal of Consumer Research, 7*(December) 272–282.

Reddy, A. C., & Iyer, R. (2002). Creating and maintaining effective e-commerce websites. *Journal of Internet Marketing, 2*(1).

Reibstein, D. J. (2001). The Internet buyer. In J. Wind & V. Mahajan (Eds.), *Digital marketing: Global strategies from world's leading experts* (pp. 201-225). New York: John Wiley & Sons.

Richins, M. L., & Bloch, P. H. (1991). Post-purchase product satisfaction: Incorporating the effects of involvement and times. *Journal of Business Research, 23*, 145–158.

Rothbart, M. K., & Derryberry, D. (1981). Development of individual differences in temperament. In M. E. Lamb & A. L. Brown (Eds.), *Advances in development psychology* (Volume I). Hillsdale, NJ: Lawrence Erlbaum.

Schilinger, M. J. (1979). A profile of responses to commercials. *Journal of Advertising Research, 19*(2), 37–46.

Stakes are high for Amazon.com CEO. (1999, December 20). *Star Tribune* (Minneapolis, MN), p. D8.

Underwood, B., & Froming, W. J. (1980). The mood survey: A personality measure of happy and sad moods. *Journal of Personality Assessment, 44*, 404–414.

van Schaik, P., & Ling, J. (2003). Using on-line surveys to measure three key constructs of the quality of human-computer-interaction in Web sites: Psychometric properties and implications. *International Journal of Human-Computer Studies, 59*, 545–567.

Varianini, V., & Vaturi, D. (2000). Marketing lessons from e-failures. *The McKinsey Quarterly, 4*, 86–97.

Weber, J. (1999, August 2–9). The bottom line. *The Industry Standard, 5*, p.

Webster, J., Trevino, L. K., & Ryan, L. (1993). The dimensionality and correlates of flow in human-computer interactions. *Computers in Human Behavior, 9*(4), 411–426.

Wells, W. D., Leavitt, C., & McConville, M. (1971). A reaction profile for TV commercials. *Journal of Advertising Research, 11*(6), 11–17.

Wolfinbarger, M., & Gilly, M. C. (2001). Shopping online for freedom, control, and fun. *California Management Review, 43*(2), 34–55.

Zaichkowsky, J. L. (1985). Measuring the involvement construct. *Journal of Consumer Research, 12*, 341–352.

Zaichkowsky, J. L. (1994). The personal involvement inventory: Reduction, revision, and application to advertising. *Journal of Advertising, 23*(4), 59–70.

Zeithaml, V. A., Parasuraman, A., & Malhotra, A. (2000). *E-service quality: Definition, dimensions, and conceptual model* (Working paper). Cambridge, MA: Marketing Science Institute.

Zeithaml, V. A., Parasuraman, A., & Malhotra, A. (2002). Service quality delivery through Web sites: A critical review of extant knowledge. *Journal of Academy of Marketing Science, 30*(4), 362–375.

Zhang, P., & Li, N. (2004). An assessment of human-computer interaction research in management information systems: Topics and methods. *Computers in Human Behavior, 20*(2), 125–147.

Zuckerman, M. (1979). *Sensation seeking: Beyond the optimal level of arousal.* Hillsdale, NJ: Lawrence Erlbaum.

Endnotes

1 Corresponding author. Assistant Professor, Department of Industrial and Management Engineering, 3rd Floor, Faculty Building, Indian Institute of Technology, Kanpur-208 016 UP INDIA, Tel: +91-512-2597460, Fax: +91-512-2597553, 2590260, E-mail: sswami@iitk.ac.in.

2 Sanjeev Swami is Assistant Professor, Department of Industrial and Management Engineering, Indian Institute of Technology, Kanpur, and Ram Krishna is Systems Engineer with Tata Consultancy Services, India. The authors thank the anonymous reviewer, and Professors Josh Eliashberg, Barbara Kahn, Ashok Mittal, and A.K. Sharma for their helpful comments.

3 Recently, some studies in the Human–Computer Interaction (HCI) literature have included the issues of involvement in their research (van Schaik & Ling, 2003; Zhang & Li, 2004). However, the focus of this literature is on user–analyst differences, interactions, and involvement, and not on online consumer behavior.

4 Our conceptualization of consumer involvement with a Web site is based on consumers' preference or liking for a Web site, and does not differentiate between whether the preference is formed as a result of fewer visits of longer duration, or a greater number of visits of shorter duration.

5 Dholakia and Bagozzi (2001) state that "flow may be viewed as a zenith of positive experience when navigating in the DE, experienced only when everything comes together: . . . when task characteristics are right (fast connections, *engrossing web sites,* encounter with new challenges, etc.)" (p. 167, emphasis added).

[6] Varianini and Vaturi (2000) propose similar ideas of "profiling" a consumer in the context of digital marketing.

[7] There are some similarities between the information-seeking tendency and the *exploratory behavior* (Baumgartner & Steenkamp, 1996; Novak, Hoffman, & Yung, 2000) or *exploratory mind-set* (Dholakia & Bagozzi, 2001). However, these constructs refer to consumers' general orientation to encounter new or unfamiliar experiences. The information-seeking tendency construct in this study is a modification of the above constructs to specifically reflect consumers' orientation toward acquiring timely and valuable new information.

[8] Underwood and Froming (1980) note that "certain individuals report several mood experiences each day so that their moods are continually changing. In contrast, other people have mood shifts only now and again" (p. 405). They propose a *reactivity* construct that measures long-term variability in moods across individuals. The proposed moodiness parameter is similar to Underwood and Froming's reactivity construct.

[9] A pool of 79 Web sites collected at this stage is available from the authors.

[10] We added two more Web sites, www.nazara.com and www.paheli.com, which did not appear in the Top 50 list, but were found to be popular among the local respondent population.

In the above-mentioned 20 Web sites, two Web sites (www.indiaserver.com and www.ciol.com) were not rated adequately by any respondent. Therefore, we discarded them from our further study.

[11] Recognizing the less significant effect of sensation-seeking tendency in overall results, the Chow test was performed for the effect of hedonic evaluation of involvement on mood variability alone. This analysis resulted in the value of F-statistic = 3.48, which is still lower than the critical F-value of 3.98.

Appendix 1: Scales Used in Different Surveys

Scale	Variable Name	Scale Items
CONSUMER INFORMATION PROFILE		
Information-Seeking Tendency	IST1	Even though there are thousands of different sources of information, I tend to use the same type of sources. (R)
	IST2	When I hear about new information/news, I am eager to check it out.
	IST3	Searching various sources of information is a waste of time. (R)
	IST4	I like to search for and find out about the latest sources of information.
	IST5	I value new information a lot.
	IST6	I try to update my knowledge from various media.
Individual Specific Focused Attention	FA1	When visiting a Web site, I am not absorbed intently. (R)
	FA2	When visiting a Web site, I am deeply engrossed.
	FA3	When visiting a Web site, my attention is focused.
	FA4	When visiting a Web site, I do not concentrate fully. (R)
SITE INFORMATION PROFILE		
Informativeness	IT1	Informative
	IT2	Intelligent content
	IT3	Knowledgeable
	IT4	Resourceful
	IT5	Up-to-date
Organization of Information Elements	O1	When I use the Web site there is very little waiting time between my actions and the computer's response.
	O2	Interacting with the Web site is slow and tedious. (R)
	O3	Pages on the Web site I visit usually load quickly.
	O4	I find this Web site not messy to use.
	O5	I find this Web site cumbersome to use. (R)
	O6	I find this Web site not confusing to use.
	O7	I find this Web site irritating to use. (R)
UTILITARIAN EVALUATION OF INVOLVEMENT		
Need	N1	Vital/Superfluous
	N2	Needed/Not Needed
	N3	Essential/Nonessential
	N4	Fundamental/Trivial
	N5	Beneficial/Not Beneficial
	N6	Useful/Useless
Value	V1	Important/Unimportant
	V2	Means a lot to me/Means nothing to me
	V3	Relevant/Irrelevant
	V4	Valuable/Worthless
	V5	Matters to me/Does not matter to me
	V6	Of concern to me/Of no concern to me
	V7	Significant/Insignificant

Appendix 1: (cont.)

Scale	Variable Name	Scale Items
CONSUMER ENTERTAINMENT PROFILE		
Sensation-Seeking Tendency	SST1	I would like a job that requires a lot of traveling. I would prefer a job in one location.
	SST2	I would prefer living in an ideal society in which everyone is safe, secure, and happy. I would prefer living in exciting settings.
	SST3	I sometimes like to do things that are a little frightening. I avoid activities that are dangerous.
	SST4	I would not like to be hypnotized. I would like to be hypnotized.
	SST5	The most important goal in life is to live it to the fullest and experience as much as possible. The most important goal in life is to find peace and happiness.
	SST6	When I go on vacation, I prefer the comfort of a good room and bed. When I go on vacation, I prefer the frequent change of accommodations.
Mood Variability	MV1	I may change from being happy to sad and back again several times a week.
	MV2	Compared to my friends, I am less up and down in my moods. (R)
	MV3	Sometimes my mood swings back and forth very rapidly.
	MV4	My moods are quite consistent; they almost never vary. (R)
	MV5	I am not as moody as most people I know. (R)
SITE ENTERTAINMENT PROFILE		
Entertainment Properties	EP1	This Web site is fun to visit.
	EP2	This Web site is not exciting. (R)
	EP3	This Web site is cool.
	EP4	This Web site is not imaginative. (R)
	EP5	This Web site is flashy.
Organization of Entertainment Elements	OE1	This Web site has animation elements.
	OE2	The use of colors in this Web site is not good. (R)
	OE3	This Web site has enough graphics/pictures.
HEDONIC EVALUATION OF INVOLVEMENT		
Interest	I1	Exciting/Unexciting
	I2	Interesting/Boring
	I3	Fascinating/Ordinary
Appeal	A1	Appealing/Unappealing
	A2	Desirable/Undesirable
POSITIVE AFFECT		
Affect	PA1	After visiting the Web site I feel unhappy. (R)
	PA2	After visiting the Web site I feel pleased.
	PA3	After visiting the Web site I feel dissatisfied. (R)
	PA4	After visiting the Web site I feel content.

Appendix 2: Brief Overview of Short-Listed Web Sites

Screen-Shots

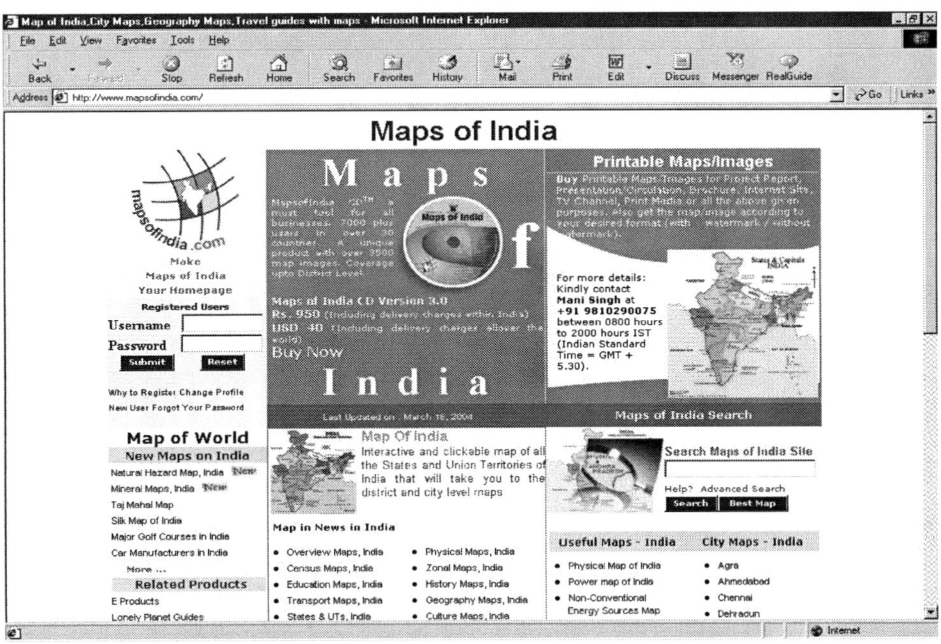

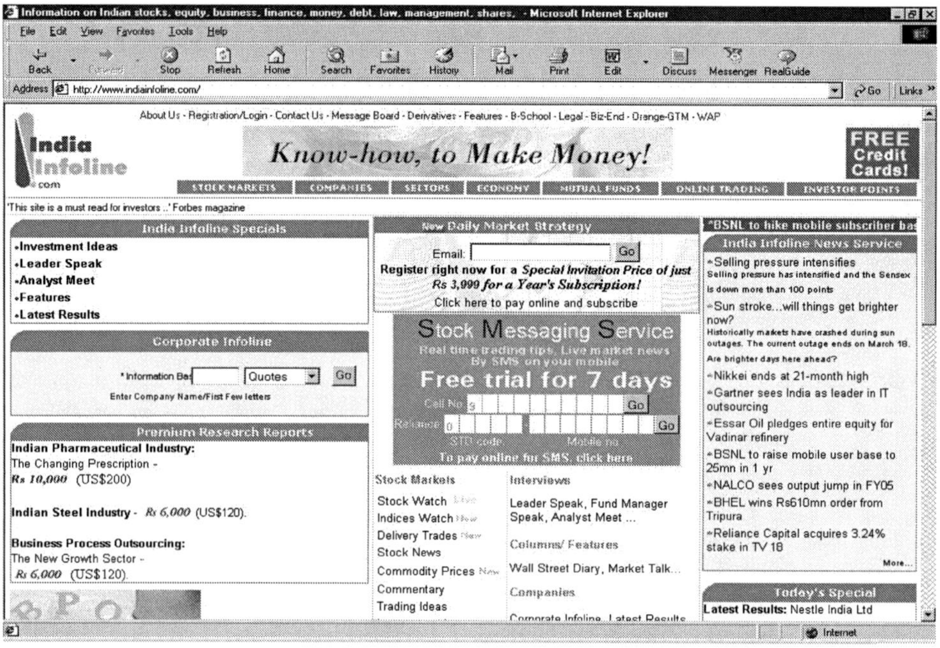
Information on Indian stocks, equity, business, finance, money, debt, law, management, shares. - Microsoft Internet Explorer
File Edit View Favorites Tools Help
Back Forward Stop Refresh Home Search Favorites History Mail Print Edit Discuss Messenger RealGuide
Address http://www.indiainfoline.com/
Go Links
About Us - Registration/Login - Contact Us - Message Board - Derivatives - Features - B-School - Legal - Biz-End - Orange-GTM - WAP
India Infoline .com
Know-how, to Make Money!
FREE Credit Cards!
STOCK MARKETS COMPANIES SECTORS ECONOMY MUTUAL FUNDS ONLINE TRADING INVESTOR POINTS
'This site is a must read for investors ..' Forbes magazine
India Infoline Specials
•Investment Ideas
•Leader Speak
•Analyst Meet
•Features
•Latest Results
Corporate Infoline
Information Base Quotes Go
Enter Company Name/First Few letters
Premium Research Reports
Indian Pharmaceutical Industry:
The Changing Prescription -
Rs 10,000 (US$200)
Indian Steel Industry - Rs 6,000 (US$120).
Business Process Outsourcing:
The New Growth Sector -
Rs 6,000 (US$120)
Daily Market Strategy
Email: Go
Register right now for a Special Invitation Price of just Rs 3,999 for a Year's Subscription!
Click here to pay online and subscribe
Stock Messaging Service
Real time trading tips, Live market news By SMS on your mobile
Free trial for 7 days
Cell No Go
Reliance Go
STD code Mobile no
To pay online for SMS, click here
Stock Markets
Stock Watch
Indices Watch
Delivery Trades
Stock News
Commodity Prices
Commentary
Trading Ideas
Interviews
Leader Speak, Fund Manager Speak, Analyst Meet ...
Columns/ Features
Wall Street Diary, Market Talk...
Companies
"BSNL to hike mobile subscriber ba
India Infoline News Service
•Selling pressure intensifies
Selling pressure has intensified and the Sensex is down more than 100 points
•Sun stroke...will things get brighter now?
Historically markets have crashed during sun outages. The current outage ends on March 18. Are brighter days here ahead?
•Nikkei ends at 21-month high
•Gartner sees India as leader in IT outsourcing
•Essar Oil pledges entire equity for Vadinar refinery
•BSNL to raise mobile user base to 25mn in 1 yr
•NALCO sees output jump in FY05
•BHEL wins Rs610mn order from Tripura
•Reliance Capital acquires 3.24% stake in TV 18
More...
Today's Special
Latest Results: Nestle India Ltd
Internet

Allindia Technologies Limited, providers of internet solutions,ecommerce solutions,internet adv - Microsoft Internet Explorer
File Edit View Favorites Tools Help
Back Forward Stop Refresh Home Search Favorites History Mail Print Edit Discuss Messenger RealGuide
Address http://www.allindia.com/
Go Links
Allindia Technologies
Pioneering internet solutions
COMPANY INFO SERVICES SUCCESS STORIES CONTACT CAREERS TAKE A TOUR
Pioneering internet solutions
VeriSign Trust Network
batchmates.
allindia Shop
June 30, 2003
United Bank of India, the bank with "Unique Banking Ideas" relaunches its corporate site, powered by Allindia Technologies.
December 29, 2003
Uttorayon - Joint venture of Bengal Ambuja Housing Development Limited and Luxmi Township Limited at the Chandmoni Tea Estate, Siliguri. In association with The Government of West Bengal.
January 10, 2004
Grameen Sanchar Society, commonly known as GRASSO launches its portal. Its mission is to transform the resourceful unemployed but enthusiastic rural youth into a successful network through many innovative and uniquely thought out self-employment schemes.
Company Info | Services | Success Stories | Contact | Careers | Take a Tour | Home
© 2004 Allindia Technologies Limited. Phone: 91-33-24754136, Fax: 91-33-24852196. webmaster
Internet

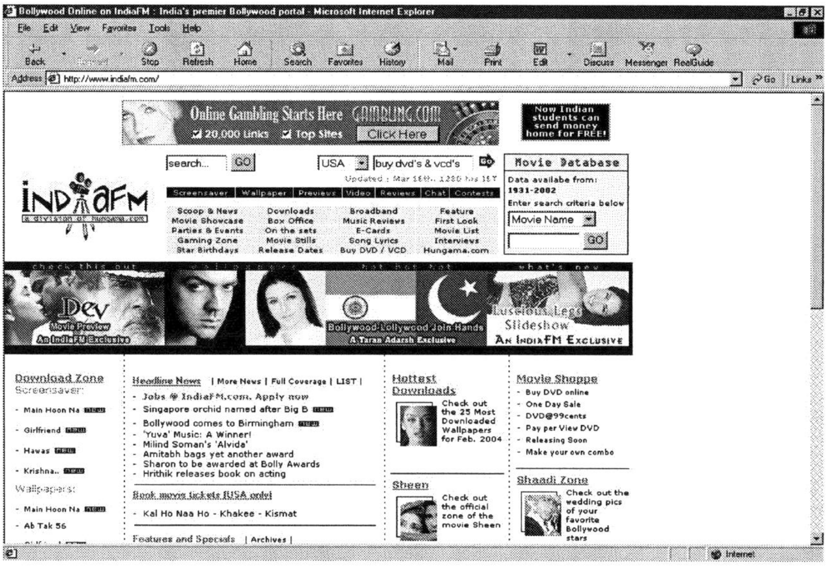

Description

Rediff.com is a portal that specializes in providing both *information* (news, weather, stock market, tickets, career tips, and IT education) and *entertainment* (e-mail, fun, humor, latest movies, and sports news).

MapsofIndia.com is an *information* provider of maps of all the major sectors in the country including infrastructure and transport, railway, road *and* tourism maps, states and union territories, *district- and city-specific maps.*

IndiaInfoline.com is the premier site about *information* on business, investment, and finance, and it offers content ranging from stock markets, mutual funds, and personal finance to law, taxation, and economy.

Allindia.com conceptualizes and creates software and Internet solutions for a diverse mix of corporate clients. This site is located in the *low information–low entertainment* quadrant because of its perceived low relevance to the engineering student population.

Indiafm.com provides *entertainment* information about movie reviews, release dates, concert listings, box office results, celebrity interviews, and cine awards.

Nazara.com provides *entertainment* information related to Hollywood as well as Bollywood (India's movie industry) movies, television, and theater. In the movie section, it provides information related to awards, reviews, child snippets, features, nostalgia, news and stuff, download, now showing, profiles, star of the month, interviews, regional spice, and photo gallery. (Note: Currently, this site no longer exists and its domain name has been acquired by another company.)

Chapter II

An Examination of Consumer Behavior on eBay Motors

Mark P. Sena, Xavier University, USA

Gerald Braun, Xavier University, USA

Abstract

With annual sales of $7.5 billion, eBay Motors has become one of the most important online marketplaces. For several years, researchers have used eBay transactions as a mechanism for examining consumer behavior and economic relationships in Internet auctions. As automobiles have emerged as the leading product category on eBay, research focused specifically on eBay Motors is an important extension to this line of research. This study builds on past research by examining research questions using a sample of 126 eBay Motors exchanges along with benchmark pricing data from Kelley Blue Book. The findings of the study suggest that, within selected data ranges, such factors as seller feedback ratings, number of pictures in item description, and seller type (dealer vs. individual) may affect the percentage of retail value that sellers are able to earn in eBay Motors auctions.

Introduction

What product generates the most revenue for eBay? Many people are surprised to learn that the answer is automobiles. It may seem ironic that a product that requires such a substantial investment and carries such a great degree of risk could be traded using a site originally developed for trading Pez dispensers. Nonetheless, not only has eBay become a legitimate channel for automobile sales, it has, in fact, become the world's largest automobile marketplace.

Ever since the emergence of eBay as a phenomenon of the Internet age, academic researchers from various disciplines have collected eBay data to examine consumer behavior in Internet auctions. Most of these studies have examined standardized products (such as computers and disk drives) or collectibles (such as coins and stamps). In recent years, businesses of all sizes have recognized the potential of using eBay as a channel for products of various types. As the focus of eBay has expanded beyond a collectables trading site, it becomes an even more valuable source for e-business researchers.

Previous research has examined the relationship between user reputation (using eBay's feedback ratings) and auction pricing (Dellarocas, 2003). This study will examine these relationships as they pertain to automobile pricing. We also examine some additional relationships particular to automobile auctions, including the impact of seller type (dealer or individual), age of automobile, and the number of digital images included in the auction listing. The results of this study will extend the knowledge of consumer behavior in Internet auctions using an important emerging product type. The remainder of this paper is organized according to the following sections. We briefly describe eBay Motors' rating system and listing functions, provide background information on the use of the Internet as a channel for auto sales, and summarize previous research on auction pricing and reputation. Next, we describe the study's methodology, providing a description of variables and hypotheses. We then provide statistical analyses and discussion based on a sample of 126 auction listings. Finally, we provide conclusions and describe future directions for this line of research.

Background and Literature Review

eBay Feedback and Listings

Using the same reputation system as eBay's traditional site, users of eBay Motors have official reputations represented by a "feedback profile." After a transaction has been completed, eBay trading partners have the opportunity to rate their partner by leaving either a positive, negative, or neutral rating, along with a comment of up to 80 characters in length (see Figure 1). As a member accumulates feedback, a user rating is calculated with each positive comment earning +1 points, each neutral comment earns +0 points, and each negative comment earns –1 points (eBay Feedback Forum, 2004). This rating and the percentage of feedback rated positively are prominently displayed next to the user's ID (see Figure 2). Though not required, participation levels at eBay are remarkably high as buyers leave feedback on sellers 52.1% of the time and sellers on buyers 60.6% of the time (Dellarocas, 2003). Once left, a comment cannot be edited and becomes a permanent part of the feedback profile. Thus,

Figure 1. eBay feedback form

Figure 2. eBay feedback rating

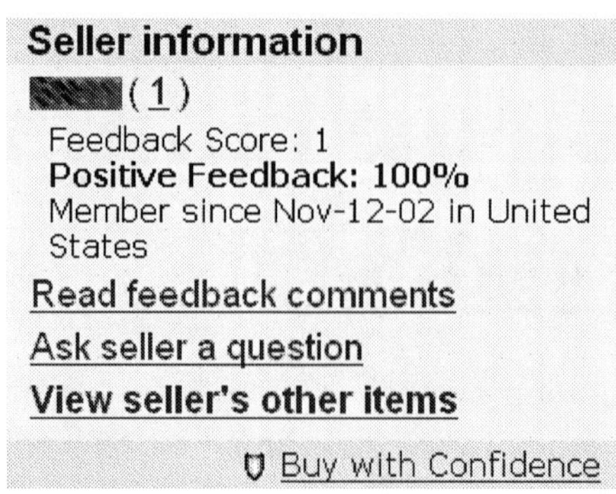

a negative or even a neutral rating can be detrimental to the user's ability to sell in the eBay community in the future.

eBay Motors auction listings contain fundamental bidding data such as the winning bid, ending date and time, number of bids, and so forth. The listings also allow sellers to provide a formatted Web page that describes the vehicle and displays multiple pictures that can be enlarged to show details. The description and pictures of the vehicle are very important in overcoming the limitations of an online automobile marketplace. A previous study (Sena, Heath, & Webb, 2004) suggests that the quality of an auction's description might impact the final winning price of the auction.

It is important to note that, like traditional eBay auctions, eBay Motors utilizes proxy bidding (users specify their highest price and the system automatically increases the winning bid when necessary), which means that the final bid price is typically determined by the second highest bidder. For example, if the winning bidder listed $10,000 as the highest amount willing to pay and (ultimately) the second-highest bidder placed a bid of, say, $9,500, then the winning bid price would be $9,600 (the second place amount plus an increment of $100). In other auction listings, the winning price could be determined by a "buy it now" price set by the seller which, if selected by a bidder, ends the auction immediately.

Research on Internet Auctions

With the success of eBay, a number of studies have examined various measures of reputation on the likelihood of successful sales occurring, and in particular, on the final prices for goods sold at online auctions (Sena et al., 2004). Table 1 summarizes the results of various studies that have examined the impact of feedback on ratings. Such studies have yielded conflicting results as to the relationship between reputation and winning bid prices on eBay. For details on prior research, see Dellarocas (2003).

The Internet Auto Market

eBay Motors (2004), a division of the online auction site, introduced used car buyers and sellers to their bidding process with a category dedicated to cars in 1999. eBay Motors was started as a separate division in April 2000, with sales of $1.5 billion in cars and parts in its first full year (Wingfield & Lundegaard, 2003). In 2002, it sold 300,000 vehicles, while attracting more than 6.1 million unique visitors in the month of February. Total sales for 2002 represented 25% of eBay's gross merchandise (Cuneo, 2003a). Sales volume increased to 500,000

Table 1. Prior research on impact of eBay feedback on winning bid price (Adapted from Sena et al., 2004)

		Negative Feedback Effect on Winning Bid Price			
		Increases	**No Effect**	**Reduces**	**Not Tested**
Positive Feedback Effect on Winning Bid Price	**Increases**		Ba & Pavlou (2002) – music, software, electronics Bajari & Hortacsu (2003) – coins	Houser & Wooders (2000) – computer chips Kalyanam & McIntyre (2001) – PDAs Lucking-Reiley, Bryan, Prasa, & Reeves (2000) – coins Melnik & Alm (2002) – gold coins Standifird (2001) – PDAs	Livingston (2002) – golf clubs
	No Effect	Kauffman & Wood (2000) – coins	Resnick & Zeckhauser (2002) – MP3 players, Beanie Babies		
	Reduces				
	Not Tested			Eaton (2002) – electric guitars Lee, Im, & Lee (2000) – computer equipment (though only for used)	
Net score increases price			Cabral & Hortacsu (2003) – coins, Beanie Babies, and laptop computers Dewan & Hsu (2001) – stamps McDonald & Slawson (2002) – dolls Sena, Heath, & Webb (2004) – designer watches and DVDs		

per month by 2003 and was expected to reach 1 million per month by 2004. Revenues have been forecast to reach $3 billion for 2005, potentially qualifying eBay Motors for Fortune 500 status (Verma, 2003). While initial listings concentrated more on exotic and high-end vehicles, according to Simon Rothman, originator of eBay Motors and vice president of eBay's U.S. operations, cars such as the Ford Taurus and Honda Accord top the sales list (Cuneo, 2003b).

While eBay Motors has emerged as the leader in Internet car sales, AutoByTel (2004) introduced online car buying to the general public in 1995. While initially focusing on new car sales along with CarsDirect (2004), they have both more recently entered the used car market. AutoTrader (2004) began exclusively as an online used car dealer as AutoConnect in 1998. It now lists more than 2 million used vehicles from private owners and dealers. Cars.com (2004) also launched in 1998 by pulling used "vehicle listings from thousands of dealer inventories and classified ads nationwide."

Selling cars on the Internet also has its drawbacks. Online sellers have to contend with frugal buyers searching for a bargain, possibly leading to a lower sale price. While this lower revenue may be offset by reduced costs for dealers, along with quicker sales for both dealers and private owners, according to estimates by the Goldman Sachs Group, only "about 30% of auto listings on eBay close with a winning bid" (Wingfield & Lundegaard, 2003).

Chip Perry, president of AutoTrader, notes that his company research shows that online used car sales "are inherently limited by the fact that consumers are reluctant to make purchases sight unseen" (Cuneo, 2003a). His site has recently entered the auction car sales market as direct competitor to eBay, and offers a "conditional bidding" process where the winning bidder is not obligated to buy until the car's condition has been verified by an inspector. eBay also makes a special effort to "build trust, confidence and support to both buyers and sellers," by insisting on ethical behavior. Feedback about both the seller and buyer are readily available, and a strict set of "rules" govern transactions. For instance, "eBay will throw out a seller who regularly receives negative feedback" (Piszczalski, 2003). Most vehicles on eBay come with protections such as purchase insurance at no extra cost. Cars that are never delivered or misrepresented are insured for up to $20,000. These extra efforts by online marketers seem to have had an influence on the car-buying public. While many shoppers still choose to buy locally, three-quarters of all car sales on eBay involve out-of-state transactions (Wingfield & Lundegaard, 2003).

For the buyer, online vehicle sales seems to be a shopper's mecca. At any given moment, a shopper may find 20,000 cars listed just on eBay Motors (Fahey, 2003). Hundreds of choices for a given car model, such as Honda Accord, may be available at any given time. With multiple search options, buyers have the ultimate flexibility in comparison shopping. They also have a wealth of information about the vehicle immediately available, and may contact the seller for further details for clarification.

Still, as with used car buying in general, some shoppers are happy and some are not. Reports of misrepresentation and fraud occur for online sales as well as for the stereotypical used car lot. Some dealers who have tried online sales have also been disappointed and Internet car sales have not yet had a serious impact on traditional sales. Although a few dealers are changing their way of business, moving from the traditional car lot to exclusive online sales, only 0.6% of the 43 million used cars sold annually are sold on eBay Motors (Wingfield & Lundegaard, 2003).

Research Questions and Methodology

From February through August of 2004, 126 observations were collected from completed eBay Motors auctions. Our data include only auctions offering Honda

Accords made between 1992 and 2003 with winning bid prices between $4,000 and $20,000. Data were only collected on completed auctions in which the "reserve price" (minimum seller is willing to accept) was met and in which the automobile is described as being in good condition. Autos that had been damaged, salvaged, or customized were not considered.

Using the data (model type, year, mileage, options, etc.) from each auction listing, "blue book" values were collected for each vehicle using the *Kelley Blue Book* (2004) Web site (kbb.com). If the necessary data were not included in the listing (model type, options, etc.), the observation was not included in the data set (see Figure 4 for an example of a *Kelley Blue Book* retail price listing).

Since our study involved vehicles with varying model types (e.g., DX, LX, EX), mileage, and options, the price ratio is the primary dependent variable of interest. This ratio serves as percentage of retail value that an auction listing achieved. For example, if an auction's winning bid price was $7,000 and the automobile's retail value (as determined by using the *Kelley Blue Book* price) was $10,000, the price ratio would be 70%.

Based on the variables shown in Table 2, some interesting research questions emerge. Many of these research questions help to explore the role of risk in eBay Motors auctions. In some eBay markets, more expensive items could sell for a lower percentage of retail value. For example, Sena et al. (2004) found that the retail value of DVDs was negatively correlated with the price ratio (percent of retail value). However, in the case of automobiles, given a fixed model type (Honda Accords), more expensive (or newer) models may be considered less risky and thus may realize a higher price ratio.

Table 2. Description of variables

Winning Bid Price – Includes only completed auctions where bid price exceeds "reserve price" (the minimum price specified by the seller)
Blue Book Value – Retail value of automobile as listed by *Kelley Blue Book* (kbb.com)
Price Ratio – The ratio of (Winning Bid Price/*Kelley Blue Book* Value)
Year – Model year of the automobile
Seller's Feedback Rating – Number of completed auctions in which seller was rated as positive (serves as an estimate of seller experience)
Seller's Percent Positive – Number of positive feedback ratings divided by the total number of feedback ratings (positive, negative, and neutral)
Buyer's Feedback Rating - Number of completed auctions in which buyer was rated as positive (serves as an estimate of buyer experience)
Number of Pictures – Number of unique images that users can access within the auction listing (commonly presented as "thumbnail" photos that can be enlarged to show detail)
Dealer – Whether the listing indicates that the seller is an automobile dealership or an individual seller
Bids – Number of bids placed during the auction (a "1" bid auction may indicate a "buy it now" auction; eBay uses "proxy bidding" in which bids are automatically submitted by the system when a bid exceeds the current price but is below a prior bidder's maximum price)

To examine these factors from different perspectives, we have focused on nine specific research questions as shown in Table 3. Questions 1–3 focus on the relationship between price ratios and winning bid prices, retail values, and the age (model year) of the autos. Research question 4 focuses on the impact of automobile dealerships on bid prices. Beyond the perception that dealers may be less likely to commit fraud (perhaps because users have a name, address, etc.), they may also have the ability to offer services, warranties, and so forth, that may entice buyers to offer higher bids.

Research question 5 explores the relationship between the number of bids at an auction and the winning bid price while research question 6 examines whether listings that include more pictures realize higher prices. This research question builds on a finding from Sena et al. (2004) that higher quality descriptions (for designer watches and DVDs) resulted in higher bid prices (see Figure 3 for an example of a listing with 28 thumbnail photos).

Prior research has indicated, with some exceptions, that seller feedback correlates positively with winning bid prices. As described in Table 2, two seller reputation variables were collected from eBay listings: seller percent positive and seller feedback rating. The feedback rating serves as a measure of the seller's experience, as estimated by the seller's number of previous feedback responses. These variables are generally the only measures of seller reputation that eBay buyers observe as they are displayed on the main auction listing. Research questions 7 and 8 examine whether seller feedback ratings have an impact on winning bid prices. It is important to reiterate that our sample includes only completed auctions, excluding auctions where bid prices did not exceed the seller's reserve value. Thus, it is possible that seller feedback plays an important

Table 3. Research questions

Research Question 1: Do autos with higher winning bid prices sell for a higher percentage of retail value?
Research Question 2: Do more expensive autos (those with higher blue book values) sell for a higher percentage of retail value?
Research Question 3: Do autos with more recent model years sell for a higher percentage of retail value?
Research Question 4: Do autos listed by dealerships sell for a higher percentage of retail value (as compared with those listed by individual sellers)?
Research Question 5a: Do auctions with more bids sell for a higher percentage of retail value? **Research Question 5b:** Do auctions with one bid (i.e., "buy it now" auctions) sell for a higher percentage of retail value?
Research Question 6: Do auction listings that contain a greater number of pictures sell for a higher percentage of retail value?
Research Question 7: Do autos listed by sellers with higher feedback scores (i.e., more experienced eBay users) sell for a higher percentage of retail value?
Research Question 8: Do autos listed by sellers with higher percent positive feedback sell for a higher percentage of retail value?
Research Question 9: Do autos purchased by winning buyers with higher feedback scores (i.e., more experienced eBay users) sell for a lower percentage of retail value?

Figure 3. Example of "thumbnail" photos in eBay Motors listing

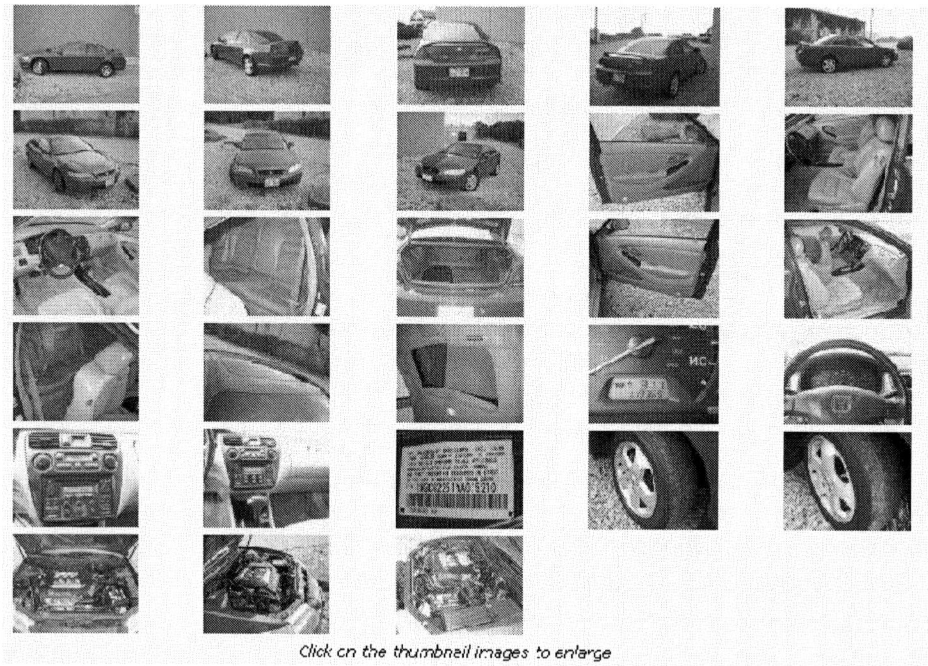

Figure 4. Example of Kelley Blue Book listing

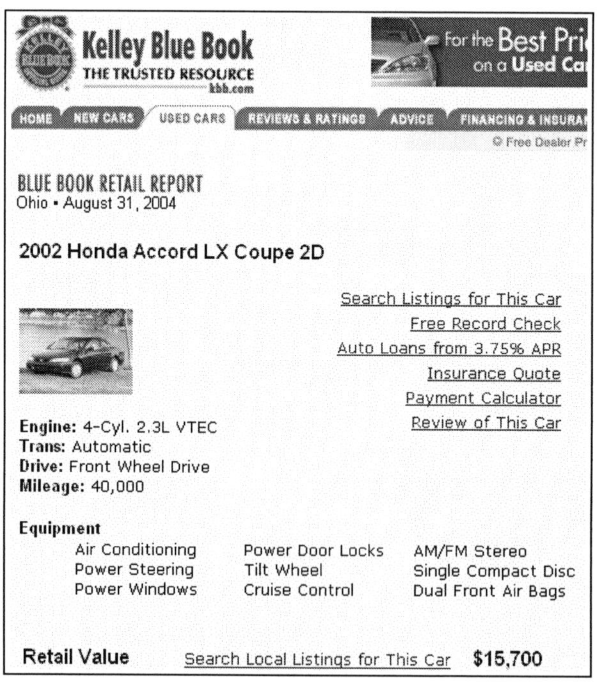

role beyond what our study captures. For instance, the seller feedback (or lack thereof) may result in fewer or lower bids that fail to meet the seller's minimum acceptable price.

Finally, research question 9 examines the role of feedback ratings for the buyer rather than the seller. The seller feedback is an estimate of buyer experience with eBay. From our anecdotal observations, it appears that many buyers purchase multiple vehicles on eBay Motors, presumably with the intention of reselling. This variable, if significant, would likely be negatively related to price ratio, as one would expect more experienced users to recognize better deals (and thus realize lower price ratios).

Statistical Analyses and Findings

Descriptive Statistics

To begin our analysis, we examine the descriptive results of our data set. As shown in Table 4, the mean winning bid price for the 126 automobiles in our sample was $8,765, while the mean retail value of these automobiles was $12,092, resulting in a mean price ratio of just over 72%. The authors collected data for listings with model years ranging from 1992 to 2003 with a mean year of 1998.75.

Compared with other eBay marketplaces, buyers and sellers seem to have fewer feedback ratings. Buyers in our sample have an average of 17.83 feedback ratings while sellers have an average of 177.49. Like other eBay markets, feedback tends to be heavily positive with sellers in our sample having a mean positive feedback percentage of 97.43%. It is important to note that eBay combines all feedback into one rating regardless of whether the user was a buyer or seller and whether the item was sold on eBay Motors or another eBay listing. Thus, feedback scores and percent positive ratings can occasionally be misleading (e.g., a rating based on Beanie Baby purchases rather than auto sales).

Given the limitations of using eBay Motors for such an important purchase, the auction listing plays an important role in marketing the auto and conveying the important information that potential buyers require. Thus, it is not surprising that sellers provide numerous digital images in most listings. In our sample, the mean number of pictures provided was 18.59. Automobiles offered by dealerships may be considered less risky by some eBay users. In our sample, 71% of the sellers were deemed to be automobile dealerships based on the item description. The number of bids on automobile auction may vary depending on the starting

Table 4. Descriptive statistics (n=126)

Variable	Minimum	Maximum	Mean	Std. Dev
Winning Bid Price	$4,050	$18,900	$8,765.50	3421.31
Blue Book Value	$5,775	$21,175	$12,091.83	3946.19
Price Ratio	48.2%	96.2%	72.1%	0.11
Year	1992	2003	1998.75	2.48
Buyer's Feedback Rating	0	475	17.83	51.92
Seller's Feedback Rating	0	8856	177.49	802.01
Seller's Percent Positive [1]	80%	100%	97.43%	4.00
Number of Pictures	2	75	18.59	11.36
Dealer	0	1	0.71	0.46
Bids	1	72	19.84	15.25

[1] Excludes six observations with zero feedback ratings

Table 5. Correlation between price and age of auto and price ratio

Variable	Correlation With Price Ratio
Winning Bid Price	.482***
Blue Book Value	.120
Year	.066

*** *significant at p<=.01;* ** *significant at p<=.05;* * *significant at p<=.10*

(minimum) bid price, the reserve price, and whether the seller offers a "buy it now" option. In our sample, auctions had a mean of 19.84 bids, with 13 auctions ending after just one bid.

Research Questions 1-3

As shown in Table 5, the correlation between price ratio and the winning bid price is very strong while the correlations between price ratio and blue book value and year are positive but insignificant in our sample. However, as shown in Table 6, a test of mean differences at selected values show that there may still be some relationship between these variables. This suggests that perhaps the relationships are not linear. For example, in the case of model year, perhaps buyers are willing to pay a higher percentage of retail for a recent (and presumably more trouble-free and less risky) car, but the relationship fails to hold once cars reach a certain age.

Table 6. Mean differences among price and age of auto and price ratio

Variable	Mean Price Ratio
Winning Bid Price >= $9,000 (n=52)	76.3%
Winning Bid Price < $9,000 (n=74)	69.1%***
Blue Book Value >= $14,000 (n=40)	74.9%
Blue Book Value < $14,000 (n=86)	70.8%**
Year >= 2001 (n=36)	76.3%
Year < 2001 (n=90)	70.3%*

*** significant at $p<=.01$; ** significant at $p<=.05$; * significant at $p<=.10$

Table 7. Relationship between auto dealerships and price ratio

Variable	Correlation With Price Ratio
Dealer	.098
Variable	**Mean Price Ratio**
Dealership (n=89)	72.8%
Individual Seller (n=37)	70.4%

Research Question 4

The results in Table 7 are somewhat surprising. While the sample data indicate that dealerships earn a moderately greater percentage of retail value than individual sellers (72.8% vs. 70.4%), the results are not statistically significant. Perhaps as dealers gain more experience in using eBay these differences will become greater. It may also be possible that buyers may have more confidence in private sellers and are willing to pay a higher price under certain circumstances.

Research Question 5

As shown in Table 8, there was zero correlation between the number of bids and the percentage of retail value earned in our sample. The data seem to indicate that perhaps auctions with a single bid (indicating the likelihood of a "buy it now" purchase) result in higher price ratios. However, given the small sample size, this difference in means is not statistically significant, leaving this as an item for future study.

Table 8. Relationship between number of bids and price ratio

Variable	Correlation With Price Ratio
Number of Bids	.000
Variable	**Mean Price Ratio**
Number of Bids =1 (n=13)	74.2%
Number of Bids >=2 (n=113)	71.8%

Table 9. Relationship between number of pictures and price ratio

Variable	Correlation With Price Ratio
Number of Pictures	.160*
Variable	**Mean Price Ratio**
Number of Pictures >=13 (n=66)	74.9%
Number of Pictures <=12 (n=60)	69.0%*

**** significant at p<=.01; ** significant at p<=.05; * significant at p<=.10*

Research Question 6

Table 9 reveals, in our opinion, the most interesting finding of this study. While the correlation between the number of pictures and price ratio is somewhat weak (with a p-value of .07), one would expect that this relationship would probably not follow a linear pattern. That is, if an auction includes very few pictures, this may increase the perceived risk and result in a lower price. However, at some point, additional pictures probably do not return the same marginal benefit. In our sample, there was a large number of listing that included 12 pictures (perhaps from a template offered by eBay). These listings and those that included fewer pictures earned on average nearly 6% less of retail value compared with listings that include 13 or more pictures. It is very likely in the near future that multimedia presentations with video or panoramic images will become common on eBay Motors and other sites demonstrating used vehicles.

Research Questions 7-9

In our initial analysis, as shown in Table 10, it is somewhat surprising that feedback does not play a substantial role in determining price ratios. None of the correlations between feedback variables and price ratio were statistically significant. While Table 11 shows some moderate differences in mean price ratio

Table 10. Correlation between price and age of auto and price ratio

Variable	Correlation With Price Ratio
Seller's Feedback	.078
Seller's Percent Positive	-.003
Buyer's Feedback	-.028

Table 11. Mean differences among price and age of auto and price ratio

Variable	Mean Price Ratio
Seller's Feedback >= 20 (n=78)	72.8%
Seller's Feedback < 20 (n=48)	70.9%
Seller's Percent Positive >= 98% (n=75)	72.5%
Seller's Percent Positive < 98% (n=45)	71.3%
Buyer's Feedback >=25 (n=21)	70.3%
Buyer's Feedback < 25 (n=105)	72.4%

Table 12. Relationship between percent positive and price ratio: Limited to auctions listed by sellers with a minimum of 25 feedback ratings

Variable	Correlation With Price Ratio
Seller's Percent Positive (n=74)	.125
Variable	**Mean Price Ratio**
Seller's Percent Positive >= 98% (n=43)	74.7%
Seller's Percent Positive < 98% (n=31)	69.1%**

**** significant at p<=.01; ** significant at p<=.05; * significant at p<=.10*

among selected subsections of the data, these are also not statistically significant. Of course, feedback may still play an important role in a buyer's decision to bid on a particular vehicle or on vehicles that fail to result in a sufficient bid price to meet the seller's minimum (reserve) price. However, our data set fails to show substantial relationships between eBay's feedback and winning bid prices (as compared with the respective retail value).

In an attempt to further explore the role of seller feedback (in particular, the percent positive variable), we selected a subset of the data using only observation in which the seller had been rated at least 25 times. In sellers with very few feedback details, the percent positive is likely not as meaningful to prospective buyers. The results presented in Table 12 show that perhaps when buyers observe an adequate number of feedback ratings, then the percent positive rating does play a role in the amount they are willing to bid for an automobile. Although the correlation is still not statistically significant in this subset, a comparison of means among subgroups with greater than 98% positive feedback ratings versus those with less than 98% positive feedback shows a statistically significant difference in price ratio.

Conclusion

The principal findings of our study may be of interest to both practitioners and scholars of various disciplines. Our results provide an empirical basis for future studies and reveal several research questions that can be probed in greater detail using additional methodologies and more extensive data sets.

While numerous studies have analyzed eBay exchanges, this study has the potential to be among the most significant because of the importance of automobiles in our economy. While our data set was limited, it captured over $1.1 million worth of transactions. The results provide a starting point for academic assessment of this exciting and important market.

The results of this analysis promote an understanding of the factors that impact bid prices of automobiles in Internet auctions. For example, our findings reveal that the price of the automobile and the inclusion of numerous pictures may play an important role in predicting the percent of retail value that an auction listing will achieve.

The study also adds to the growing body of literature focused on the impact of Internet-based reputation systems. While the relationships between feedback ratings and price ratios in our data set were not statistically significant (contrary to some past studies), more studies are needed to further explore this relationship. Our analysis does point out that the relationships between the variables in our study may not follow a linear pattern. Thus, there is an opportunity for researchers to conduct more robust statistical analyses on data sets of this nature.

Although the market for automobiles on the Internet, particularly on eBay Motors, has exploded in the past year, the marketplace is still in its infancy. Consumer habits are likely to adjust over time as sellers learn to use the medium more effectively and buyers become more comfortable with the marketplace. Similarly, advancements in technology and new business ventures will undoubtedly continue to play a role in these exchanges. This study provides a cursory analysis of the eBay Motors marketplace as it currently exists for the data we collected. Clearly, further research focusing on eBay Motors and other Internet-based automobile marketplaces is needed to clarify the relationships examined in this research.

References

AutoByTel. (2004). Retrieved August 15, 2004, from *www.autobytel.com*

AutoTrader. (2004). Retrieved August15, 2004, from *www.autotrader.com*

Ba, S., & Pavlou, P.A. (2002). Evidence of the effect of trust building technology in electronic markets: Price premiums and buyer behavior. *MIS Quarterly, 26*(3).

Bajari, P., & Hortescu, A. (2003). Winner's curse, reserve prices and endogenous entry: Empirical insights from eBay auctions. *Rand Journal of Economics, 34*(2).

Cabral, L. M. B., & Hortacsu, A. (2003). *The dynamics of seller reputation: Theory and evidence from eBay.* (Working paper). New York: Stern School of Business, New York University. Retrieved from *http://pages.stern.nyu.edu/~lcabral/papers/ebay.pdf*

Cars.com. (2004). Retrieved August 15, 2004, from *www.cars.com*

CarsDirect. (2004). Retrieved August 15, 2004, from *www.carsdirect.com*

Cuneo, A. Z. (2003a). eBay bids to remake $372B used-car biz; Ads pitch service that "nationalizes" local industry. *Advertising Age, 74*(19), 1.

Cuneo, A. Z. (2003b). eBay unleashes used-car campaign. *Automotive News, 77*, 16.

Dellarocas, C. (2003). The digitization of word-of-mouth: Promises and challenges of online feedback mechanisms. *Management Science, 49*(10), .

Dewan, S., & Hsu, V. (2002). *Price discovery in generalist versus specialty online auctions.* (Working paper). Irvine: Graduate School of Management, University of California. Retrieved from *http://databases.si.umich.edu/reputations/bib/papers/Dewan&Hsu.doc*

Eaton, D. H. (2002). *Valuing information: Evidence from guitar auctions on eBay.* (Working paper). Murray, KY: Murray State University. Retrieved from *http://campus.murraystate.edu/academic/faculty/david.eaton/workpaper0201.pdf*

eBay Feedback FAQs. (2004). Retrieved August 15, 2004, from *http://pages.eBay.com/help/new/feedback_faqs.html*

eBay Feedback Forum. (2004). Retrieved August 15, 2004, from *http://pages.eBay.com/services/forum/feedback.html*

eBay Motors. (2004). Retrieved August 15, 2004, from *www.motors.ebay.com*

Houser, D., & Wooder, J. (2003). Reputation in auctions: Theory, and evidence from eBay. Under review at *Journal of Economics and Management Science* (*http://w3.arizona.edu/~econ/working_papers/Internet_Auctions.pdf*).

Kalyanam, K., & McIntyre, S. (2001). Returns to reputation in online auction markets. (Working paper W-RW01-02). Santa Clara, CA: Santa Clara University. Retrieved from *http://business.scu.edu/faculty/research/working_papers/pdf/kalyanam_mcintyre_wp10.pdf*

Kauffman, R. J., & Wood, C. (2000, August). Running up the bid: Modeling seller opportunism in Internet auctions. *Proceedings of the Americas Conference on Information Systems (AMCIS)*, Long Beach, CA.

Kelley Blue Book. (2004). Retrieved August 15, 2004, from *www.kbb.com*

Lee, Z., Im, I., & Lee (2000). The effect of negative buyer feedback on prices in Internet auction markets. *Proceedings of the 21st International Conference on Information Systems*, Brisbane, Australia.

Livingston, J. (2002, October). How valuable is a good reputation? A sample selection model of Internet auctions. *Proceedings of the International Atlantic Economic Society Meetings*, Washington, DC.

Lucking-Reily, D., Bryan, D., Prasa, N., & Reeves, D. (2000). Pennies from eBay: The determinants of price in online auctions. (Working paper). Nashville, TN: Department of Economics, Vanderbilt University. Retrieved from *www.vanderbilt.edu/econ/reiley/papers/PenniesFromEBay.pdf*

McDonald, C. G., & Slawson, V. C. Jr. (2002). Reputation in an Internet auction market. *Economic Inquiry*, *40*(3), 633–650.

Melnik, M. I., & Alm, J. (2002). Does a seller's reputation matter? Evidence from eBay auctions. *Journal of Industrial Economics*, *50*(3), 337–349.

Piszczalski, M. (2003). eBay & autos: A new model? *Automotive Design & Production*, *115*(3), 16.

Resnick, P., & Zeckhauser, R. (2002). Trust among strangers in Internet transactions: Empirical analysis of eBay's reputation system. In M. R. Baye (Ed.), *The economics of the Internet and e-commerce*. Greenwich, CT: JAI Press.

Sena, M., Heath, E., & Webb, M. (2004). The impact of eBay ratings and item descriptions on auction prices: A comparison of designer watches and

DVDs. In S. Krishnamurthy (Ed.), *Contemporary research in e-marketing, vol. 1.* Hershey, PA: Idea Group.

Standifird, S. (2001). Reputation and e-commerce: eBay auctions and the asymmetrical impact of positive and negative ratings. *Journal of Management*, 27.

Verma, M. (2003). Click-drive: eBay motors zooms, zooms, zooms. Local dealers in first gear. *Greater Baton Route Business Report, 21*(26), 36.

Wingfield, N., & Lundegaard, K. (2003, February 7). Improbably, eBay emerges as a giant in used-car sales. *Wall Street Journal Online.*

Chapter III

Job Search at Naukri.com: Case Study of a Successful Dot-Com Venture in India

Sanjeev Swami, Indian Institute of Technology, Kanpur, India[1]

Abstract

This chapter presents the case study of a successful dot-com venture in India, Naukri.com, in the job search market. We begin by providing an overview of job search methods in both general and the specific Indian contexts. The advent and growth of the e-recruitment market is also discussed. We then provide background information for Naukri.com by focusing on its business model, growth, organizational structure and human resource management. The product/service offerings of Naukri.com for recruiters and job-seekers are discussed next. We then provide a critical analysis of the consumers of the company and its competitors. We conclude by assessing Naukri.com's marketing strategy during initial (1997-2000) and recent (2001-2004) time periods.

Introduction

Until 1997, job seekers in India would wait the whole week for the weekly supplements of various newspapers or sundry employment journals and gazettes to learn about vacancies and job openings in the industry. Then came the Internet and threatened to push the days of white envelopes to oblivion. In India, a forerunner in ushering in the change in the way one looks at job hunting today is a relatively small, but rapidly growing company, Naukri.com. Today, it is regarded as one of the most resourceful destinations for job seekers, ranging from a seasoned professional to a recent graduate. According to the CEO of Naukri.com, the major challenge that the organization currently faces is the management of growth. The company had steadily grown from Rs. 40 lacs to Rs. 1 crore to a Rs. 20 crore company in the year 2004. The next year's target is Rs. 45 crores.[2] Management of such rapid growth in such a short period of time requires effective strategies not only to attract talent but also to retain it. Therefore, in the middle of 2004, the challenges facing Naukri.com involved the issues related to organizing its e-business and the proper management of its growth.

Job Search Methods and the Advent of E-Recruitment

Job Search Methods: General Approaches

Several methods have been recognized as the standard methods of job search in the United States and other parts of the world (www.bls.gov/oco/oco20042.htm). A representative list of these methods, along with their comparative description, is provided below:

1. *Personal contacts/Networking:* In this method, family, friends, and acquaintances of the job seeker offer one of the most effective ways to find a job. They may help the candidate directly or put him/her in touch with someone else who can. Such *networking* can lead to information about specific job openings, many of which may not be publicly posted. Networking, or referrals, has emerged as one of the most productive ways to find a job in recent years, and has been loosely defined as follows—*When you let others know that you are looking for a job, and they let someone else know, and so on.*

2. *Executive Search Firms:* The job seeker may contact firms that specialize in searching executives for their clients with a certain background and qualification. However, an executive search firm's primary function is usually to find "stars" for their clients, and they place less emphasis on placing outplaced or unemployed candidates.
3. *Business Directories/Company Sites:* A relatively recent approach toward job search is to visit various companies' sites on the Internet which are in the area of expertise of the candidate. A list of major companies in a specific field may be available at sites such as Hoovers.com. At a company's site, links such as *Employment Opportunities*, *Careers*, *Join Us*, and so on, are provided. E-mail addresses are usually provided so that the interested candidates could mail their résumés electronically. Alternatively, the candidate may directly contact the company by getting its contact information from business directories.
4. *Employment Agencies and Career Consultants:* Most of the employment agencies operate on a commission basis, with the fee dependent upon a percentage of the salary paid by a successful applicant, paid either by the candidate or the hiring company. Although employment agencies can help save time and contact employers, the commission costs may sometimes outweigh the benefits. There are other agencies that usually specialize in jobs for secretaries, administrative assistants, clerks, and other clerical workers. They may sometimes test the prospective candidates in typing, Word, Excel, Access, PowerPoint, or other skills, and may even provide training for the same.
5. *Job Fairs:* Many companies send representatives to job fairs for the purpose of recruiting new candidates. These fairs are generally held at large convention or outplacement career centers, and promoted in local newspapers or on the Internet. These events provide great networking opportunities with prospective employers.
6. *School Career Planning and Placement Offices:* College/university placement offices help their students and alumni find jobs. They set up appointments and allow recruiters to use their facilities for interviews. Placement offices may also have lists of jobs for on-campus, regional, nonprofit, and government organizations. Students can receive career counseling and testing and job search advice. At career resource centers, students may attend workshops on such topics as job search strategy, résumé writing, letter writing, and effective interviewing; critique drafts of résumés and watch videotapes of mock interviews; explore files of résumés and references; and attend job fairs conducted by the placement office. These remain one of the easiest and most attractive methods of finding a job.

7. *Classified Ads:* The "Wanted" ads in newspapers is one of the most traditional methods of recruitment. However, one must realize that not all job openings are listed in these ads. Also, classified ads sometimes do not give all of the important information. They may offer little or no description of the job, working conditions, or pay. Some ads do not identify the employer, and only provide a post office box number to which the candidate can mail his/her résumé, thus making follow-up inquiries very difficult. Some ads offer out-of-town jobs; others advertise employment agencies rather than actual employment opportunities. Usually the Sunday or weekend editions of newspapers carry the most listings. Other outlets for these ads are in the form of business magazine ads and employment news bulletins.
8. *Internet Networks and Resources:* The Internet provides a variety of information, including job listings and job search resources and techniques. Several sites have emerged in this category; examples include Naukri.com in India, and monster.com in the United States. The job listings are generally posted by the field or discipline, and a search using keywords is recommended for such sites. Some Web sites provide national or local classified listings and allow job seekers to post their résumés online. Others offer advice on how to search for a job, prepare for an interview, or write résumés. These sites allow candidates to send their résumé to an employer by e-mail or to post it online.
9. *Government/State Employment Service Offices:* The state employment service, sometimes called Job Service, operates in countries such as the United States in coordination with the U.S. Department of Labor's Employment and Training Administration. Local offices, found nationwide, help job seekers find jobs and help employers find qualified workers at almost no cost to either. These also sponsor database services, such as *America's Job Bank* (www.ajb.org, sponsored by the U.S. Department of Labor), which is an Internet site that provides a database of over one million jobs nationwide, creates and posts résumés online, and sets up an automated job search. The state employment offices also provide services for special groups, such as veterans, dislocated workers, military personnel, and youth. Information on obtaining a position with the Federal Government is also through telephone-based systems.
10. *Professional Associations:* Many professions have associations that offer employment information, including career planning, educational programs, job listings, and job placement. The associations' services are generally available to only the members of the association.
11. *Labor Unions:* Labor unions provide various employment services to members, including apprenticeship programs that teach a specific trade or skill.

12. *Community Agencies:* Many nonprofit organizations, including religious institutions and vocational rehabilitation agencies, offer counseling, career development, and job placement services, generally targeted to a particular group, such as women, youth, minorities, ex-offenders, or older workers.

Job Search Methods: Indian Scenario

In the Indian context, job search methods have not been as elaborate as listed above. The methods also varied according to the graduation degree of the candidate. While private companies were quite willing to visit the campuses of engineering and business schools throughout the country, they were not so eager to recruit from the colleges of nonprofessional degree courses such as arts, education, humanities, and so on. Consequently, school placement offices (method (vi) above) were the most popular option for business and engineering graduates. For other types of candidates, the classified ads option (method (vii) above) was one of the predominant ones. Another attractive option was to prepare for the competitive examinations for clerical or executive positions in public sector banks, government jobs, administrative services, and so on. Although not widely documented, it was generally believed that the networking or referral option (method (i) above) also worked reasonably well in the Indian environment. Some employment agencies and career consultants (method (iv) above) were also present in India, but their role was restricted to only a very small percentage of the job seeking population. Lately, however, the role of placement consultants and some newer methods in job search had increased with the advent of Internet, outsourcing, proliferation of software firms, and entry of multinational and global corporations in India. The newer methods included executive search (method (ii)), Internet resources (method (viii)), and professional associations (method (x)). Other options, such as job fairs (method (v)), state employment offices (method (ix)), labor unions (method (xi)), and community agencies (method (xii)), were either dysfunctional or virtually nonexistent in India.

The communication methods of prospective employers with job seekers had also adapted to the advancement of technology. Initial communication methods predominantly involved print media ads such as those in newspapers and magazines. In addition, a local gazette, *Employment Bulletin*, carried the major advertisements on a periodic basis. As radio was one of the most affordable means of entertainment and information gathering, a radio program, *Employment News*, also gave relevant information about jobs. Subsequently, with the diffusion of television in the market, some job-related information also started appearing on national and regional networks. The latest occurrence in this trend has been that of e-recruitment job search option. The promise of instant delivery, paperless transaction, lower cost, and access to a large amount of information made this a really attractive option.

E-Recruitment Market in India

Similar to the software industry, the e-recruitment industry also performed reasonably well from 2002 onward. The market witnessed a healthy growth rate of 80%–100%. Growing at approximately 100%, the players, which have emerged as the clear winners are Naukri.com, JobsAhead.com, Jobstreet.com, and Monster.com. The online job market is expected to grow faster than the conventional recruitment market, and is likely to capture sizable share of traditional channels such as newspaper recruitment advertising. From an estimated Rs 25 crore in 2002, the online job market was expected to reach Rs 45 crore in the year 2004. This promised to be a phenomenal progress, which would defy the trends of the dot-com washout. Arun Tadanki, president of Monster Asia, agrees: "The economy is very strong and the recruitment market is booming. The jobs market is one of the best in recent years."[3] Tadanki estimates India's online recruitment sector will clock revenues of between Rs 750–800 million during 2004, which is about 12% of the total recruitment market. "In two years' time it could shoot up to 25%," Tadanki says. Stuart McKelvey, Monster's Group president for Asia-Pacific, was also quite optimistic about e-recruitment market and estimated that the online opportunity for hiring in India is growing at 80% to 90% each year.

Background of Naukri.com

Historical Perspective

The vision of Naukri.com is "To create a platform where, in 20 years' time, every Indian who is looking for a job can find one." In March 1997, as the influence of the Internet was beginning to grow in India, Naukri.com was launched as a floorless employment exchange. It was conceived as a platform for employers and job seekers to meet and exchange information. The site was launched with databases of jobs, résumés, and placement consultants. In October 1997, the service went commercial. By then, more than 50 companies had tried out the services offered by Naukri.com and were satisfied with the response they received. Since then, the client list has increased to over 7,500 companies.

Info Edge, the holding company of Naukri.com, started in 1989 and became Info Edge (India) Private Limited on May 1, 1995. It was in the business of selling reports and project marketing-related consulting services to its clients. Info Edge also provided management consulting services to a number of clients in India and abroad. In 1991, the Department of Telecommunications (DoT) of the Government of India began to experiment with Videotex services. Info Edge put in its application as information providers—people who would run a database. The mechanism proposed involved a central server in one place. Several databases would reside on the server. Each database would be accessed by the public through terminals in different telephone exchanges on payment of a fee. Consequently, Info Edge advertised for information providers. The complete project concept was called "Jobnet." The Videotex pilot project of the DoT, however, did not take off and Info Edge was eventually forced to abandon its plans for this service. Over the next few years, Info Edge evaluated the idea of providing job information to the public independently, but was unable to identify a financially viable technology backbone until the Internet entered India.

Today, Naukri.com aims to provide Indians with Indian qualifications the maximum opportunity for their career growth. It has also been promoted in all parts of the globe, where Indian qualifications are acceptable, and clients have

Table 1. Financial performance of Naukri.com (1999–2003)

	1999	2000	2001	2002	2003
Revenue	21.14	37.64	96.44	379.00	907.00
Costs Incurred	1.90	4.12	20.69	28.98	130.96
Gross Profit	**19.24**	**33.52**	**75.75**	**350.02**	**776.04**
Selling/ General/Administrative Expense	15.40	29.93	265.85	402.15	620.32
Depreciation/Amortization	0.80	1.90	18.13	46.00	55.00
Other Expenses	0.37	0.50	3.52	16.35	20.70
Total Operating Expense	**16.57**	**32.33**	**287.50**	**464.50**	**696.02**
Operating Income	2.67	1.19	(211.75)	(114.48)	80.02
Income Before Tax	**2.67**	**1.19**	**(211.75)**	**(114.48)**	**80.02**

(All figures are in Lacs of rupees.)

been enlisted. Over 10% of its current corporate client list consists of companies located in the United States, Africa, Middle East, and Far East. Similarly, about 5% of the job seekers approaching Naukri.com are nonresident Indians wanting to return to India. The financial performance of Naukri.com from 1999 to 2003 is given in Table 1.

Naukri.com planned to rake in Rs 450 million in sales in the fiscal year ending March 31, 2005, on increasing online traffic.[4] Despite the recent merger of its two major competitors, JobsAhead.com and Monsterindia.com, Naukri.com said it was well poised to achieve 100% sales growth in the current fiscal over the previous year's Rs 220 million. Naukri.com claimed it had emerged as the fastest-growing recruitment site in the Indian market with 10,500 clients, offices in 18 locations across the country, over 64,000 live job listings, and a rapidly expanding résumé database.

Business-to-Business or Business-to-Consumer Site?

Since Naukri.com has both job seekers and corporates as its customers, there is some confusion as to whether it is a business-to-business (B2B) or business-to-consumer (B2C) site. According to Sanjeev Bikhchandani, it is both B2B and B2C. It is essentially a medium where Naukri.com enables handshakes between corporate and prospective employees. They are able to meet on the Naukri.com Web site.

Business Model of Naukri.com

Naukri.com has had a clear revenue model from the beginning. As with any other business, there has to be a direct inflow of revenue for services rendered. While it has a select few services that are free to both job seekers and job providers, the majority of its services are paid for by one of the two segments. Ninety percent of Naukri.com's revenues come from corporate clients, and the remaining 10% of the revenue comes from job seekers. Naukri.com is open to the idea of secondary revenue sources such as advertisements on its site. However, as Naukri.com's entire focus was on providing recruitment solutions, such a mode of revenue generation was not vigorously pursued. Sanjeev Bikhchandani (CEO, Naukri.com) says, on secondary sources of revenue, "If somebody pops in with an advertisement, we don't refuse him." A brief description of the services provided by Naukri.com, both paid and free, is provided in a later section. As Naukri.com has grown, it has been conscious of controlling expenses, especially advertising, which has been one of the pitfalls of many a dot-com businesses. A

Figure 1. Business model of Naukri.com

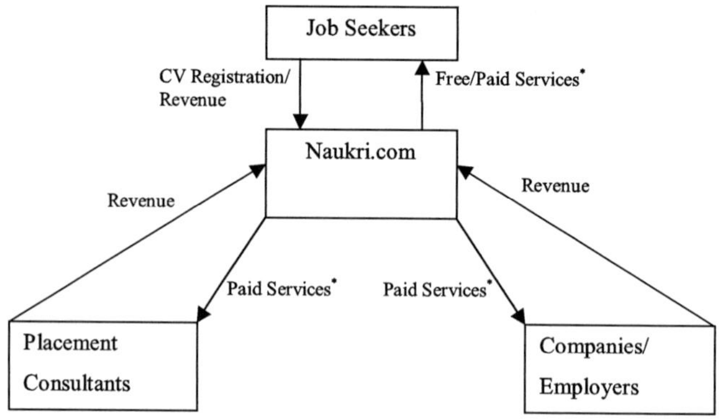

** Description of services referred here is provided in a later section.*

diagrammatic representation of the business model of Naukri.com is presented in Figure 1.

Tracing the Growth of Naukri.com

One of the most important factors that made Naukri.com profitable was the founder's tight leash on the expenses. Started with self-funding in 1997, Naukri.com did not have deep pockets to begin with. Naukri.com did not face many problems procuring finances, human resources, and the entire infrastructure. This was primarily because the parent company, Info Edge, was already in the business of preparing reports and databases. It employed three data entry operators and asked them to put some jobs into the database structure. The technology person, who was a part-time employee, was then asked to convert this into a Web site. The name "Naukri.com" was thought of and registered. To begin with, finances were not a problem because the staff consisted of three data entry operators and a part-time technology person. The Web site was served out of a hired server in the United States. The hiring cost of the server was US$25 per month. Slowly, as business began to pick up, Info Edge closed down all other business and put all of its staff to work on the Naukri.com business. Sanjeev Bikhchandani says, "And before we knew it, the thing just kept growing and growing and expanding. And we had to slowly close the other businesses and put all the staff here and this thing began to make money."

The investment in the first 3 years was to the tune of Rs 25 lacs. The company kept its overheads low, refused to splurge on advertising and promotions, and sailed through the dot-com bust with little problem. According to Bikhchandani,

"We had a small team and a lot of our marketing was done via word of mouth and some ads in print." It was only after Bikhchandani was certain in his mind that there was a huge market for e-recruitment in India that he decided to invest more in expansion. In mid-2000, the company approached ICICI Bank, which picked up a stake in the venture, providing it with the capital needed to spread its wings.

From just one office in Delhi in the year 2000, the company then crossed state borders to have 15 offices in 13 cities nationwide. Naukri.com now covers cities such as Noida, Gurgaon, Chandigarh, Mumbai, Pune, Ahmedabad, Baroda, Indore, Chennai, Hyderabad, Bangalore, Cochin, Coimbatore, and Kolkata. There is one office in California, United States, which looks after overseas operations.

The Brain Wave

Sanjeev Bikhchandani, CEO, is not just another netpreneur. He is an Indian Institute of Management (IIM) Ahmedabad graduate who left his cushy job at SmithKline Beecham to try his luck in the topsy-turvy world of Internet marketing. Bikhchandani, during his IIM Ahmedabad days, got placed in SmithKline Beecham before the regular placements season began at IIM Ahmedabad. Therefore, he was drafted in a voluntary position into the placement office to help out the companies visiting the campus. It was here that he noticed that two blue chip companies, Citibank and Hindustan Lever Limited, literally coming to blows over talent. He realized then that companies would go to any length for talent and expressed in his own words, "When I saw this, I realized that, listen, there is literally a war for talent; I saw it first hand."

This war for talent registered in Bikhchandani's mind but took a back seat, and in 1989 he joined SmithKline Beecham as a brand manager for the brand for the kids' health drink Horlicks. He and all his colleagues used to sit in an open hall. When the latest issue of the business magazine *Business India* would come in the office, all his colleagues would start reading it from the back because the appointment advertisements were at the back. The interesting thing that he observed here was that all the people who were flipping through appointment advertisements were not hunting for a job. This led Bikhchandani to realize that probably jobs were a very high-interest category and even if one is not searching for a job, he/she looks at the list of opportunities. Finally, one more thing that Bikhchandani noticed was that almost every day, his colleagues used to receive calls from placement consultants. Even though his colleagues were not interested in taking up a new job, they would take the calls and talk to those placement consultants.

These observations helped Bikhchandani figure out that there is a huge fragmented database of jobs with different placement consultants and jobs are a high-interest category. If someone could consolidate the database of live jobs and put it in one place and continuously update it, that would be a very powerful product and money could be made out of this. Bikhchandani realized this by the end of 1989 and early 1990. He quit his job in October 1990 and along with a partner started the company Info Edge (India) Private Limited. This company was initially into databases, trademark searching services, report writing, and so on. But the jobs database idea remained dormant in his mind.

Why the Name Naukri.com?

While there are many factors that contributed to making Naukri.com a success story, part of the credit goes to its unique nomenclature. The Naukri.com team had intentions of giving the Web site an English name. A number of names were thought of, such as, jobsindia, indiajobs, employindia, indiaemploy, careerindia, careersindia, indiacareers, employmentIndia, and recruitmentindia. To their disappointment, however, all these names were already registered. Therefore, a compromise had to be made and a decision was made to name the Web site Naukri. Opponents of this name said that this name was down market and had the connotation of "servitude" *(naukar)* attached to it. But the name was retained because of its memorability and uniqueness. Interestingly, Sanjeev Bikhchandani considers the brand name to be an asset for his company. Bikhchandani says, "It's turned out to be a great asset for us. At that time, I thought it would be a handicap." Moreover, he did not believe that the Hindi name would be a handicap in the southern part of India for the simple reason that Hindi movies are released in south India and they are avidly watched there.

Why Naukri.com was not Affected by the Dot-Com Meltdown

The parent company of Naukri.com is 14 years old. It launched Naukri.com in March 1997 and operated for 3 years without venture capital. Since venture capital funding was not taken upfront, the company had to make money in order to survive. Dot-coms themselves are just about 7 years old and were not fashionable at the time when Naukri.com was launched. Therefore, by the time dot-coms became popular, Naukri.com was already profitable and without venture capital funding too. Venture capital funding was taken merely to scale up an existing profitable model.

Bikhchandani claims the dot-com bust in fact helped Naukri.com. When competitors came to India, they had a high cost model and did not know how to make money because of their unfamiliarity with the market. Naukri.com, on the other hand, was already making money. Naukri.com did not spend its money on advertising. It just put it in a bank, put feet on the street, hired salespeople, built client relationships, and opened new offices. When the meltdown actually happened, competitors could not get a second round of funding whereas Naukri.com did not need a second round of funding. This helped Naukri.com in beating competition.

During the meltdown, foreign competitors such as monster, jobstreet, and jobsdb, came to India with the promise of sending Indian technical manpower abroad. The meltdown resulted in a reduced demand for Indian technical manpower. The foreign portals then lost interest in the Indian market. There was additional pressure on them in the United States. Bikhchandani says, "We used the last 4 years of meltdown very, very profitably in consolidating our business, building our brand, moving in a planned manner, not spending our money foolishly, and really strengthening our position. So the meltdown actually helped us because it really killed our competition."

Organizational Structure

The organization chart of Naukri.com is presented in Figure 2.

Figure 2. Organization chart of Naukri.com

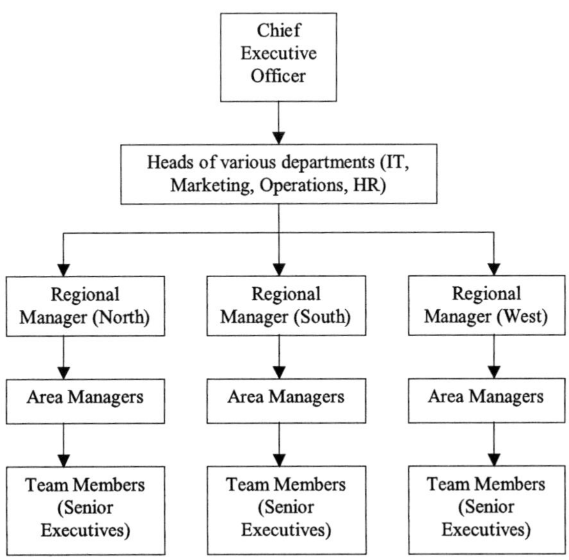

Human Resource Management at Naukri.com

The profiles of various management personnel at Naukri.com is presented in Appendix 1. It is clear from the management profiles that Naukri.com has a fairly sophisticated pool of talent in its management. The work environment at Naukri.com is also very open and friendly. According to the HR manager, problems are resolved by discussions. Even if it is an interdepartmental issue, appointments are not required for discussions with the personnel of the other department. For instance, if the marketing team was working on product development, it would need to work in close coordination with technology because technology is ultimately going to deploy the product over the net. If the marketing people have any queries, then they can straight away walk up to the technology people and get the issue resolved.

People at Naukri.com are given opportunities to learn even at the cost of making mistakes. In the words of the HR manager, "People here get a lot of opportunity to learn by making mistakes, I would say. Because a lot of responsibility is given and space is given, that you try out things and try to learn on your own." The management at Naukri.com also encourages idea generation. When a new member joins a team, he/she is only assigned a task. How to accomplish the task is his/her prerogative. This prompts the new team member to formulate new ideas to do the assigned task in the best possible way. Since organizational issues are recognized as one of the major challenge areas that Naukri.com is facing, during recruitment, attention is paid to ensure that the selected candidate has the right kind of attitude that would help him/her fit into the system. Says the HR manager, "If the attitude is right, people will always learn the skills of doing the task." The regional offices themselves hire employees from campus recruitment for the regional offices, while the head office helps the regional offices when lateral recruitment is to be done. This assistance is provided to them in terms of short-listing the candidates and conducting telephone interviews. The regional offices themselves proceed with the final interview and selection process.

Product/Service Offerings of Naukri.com

The products offered by Naukri.com are aimed at two broad groups of customers: (1) recruiters and (2) job seekers. The products for each group are explained below.

Products for Recruiters

Naukri.com offers a range of services to recruiters. A brief description of each product/service follows:

a. *Best Places to Work:* An exclusive section for top companies, this is the first section that appears on the Naukri.com home page. Naukri.com develops a career micro-site for the customer company with a link from the home page. This ensures maximum branding and visibility to a company's recruitment requirements. This package provides the Web-enabled Response Management Software, and e-Apps, free of charge.
b. *Job Gallery:* A listing in this section makes the client company directly accessible from the Naukri.com home page. Vacancy listings may be customized like the vacancies in a newspaper. Client company is seen with other quality organizations and vacancies are highlighted.
c. *Hot Vacancies:* This is the premium job listing service provided by Naukri.com to its clients. This gives the client companies' vacancies greater visibility in a less cluttered space and they get listed with other quality jobs. Their listing gets covered in the Classifieds section, where free Job Alerts are done for the client companies' vacancies and a logo is included on listings.
d. *Classifieds:* Designed to be brief and to the point, the format ensures easy access of information. Vacancies are listed in specific and relevant categories, thereby ensuring a higher degree of relevant response.
e. *Résumé Database Access:* RESDEX, for short, this product makes the client company's recruitment exercise simple, targeted, and focused as an "in your hands" solution. The client may search profiles that are specific to the client's requirements and access fresh and active job seekers anytime from anywhere. RESDEX contains the highest quality résumés available in India today.
f. *Electronic Application:* This product is also referred to as e-Apps. The e-Apps Response Management System reduces time spent on managing applications by 80%. CVs are collected in a database format, which can be used to filter out relevant candidates from a large pool in a matter of minutes.

The first four services are job-posting services. The point to note here is that all of the above services/products offered by Naukri.com to employers are paid products/services.

Products for Job Seekers

Naukri.com offers a range of services to job seekers. A brief description of each product/service follows.

a. *Résumé Flash:* Naukri.com has a database of 1,000 leading placement consultants in India. For the requisite fee, Naukri.com sends the job seeker's résumé to 800 or 1,000 placement consultants. The choice of the number of consultants to whom the job seeker wants to have his/her résumé sent is entirely his/hers.

b. *Résumé Development:* Naukri.com's experts help the job seeker to develop a powerful and effective résumé. This service is also rendered for a fee.

c. *Job Mail:* All the jobs posted on the site are first matched with a job seeker's profile and if there is a fit, the job listing is e-mailed to the prospective employee. This service may be subscribed to for a 3- or 6-month period.

d. *Job Alert:* All the vacancies that Naukri.com receives are mailed to the job seeker. This is a free service.

e. *Résumé Display:* In the Paid Résumé Display option, the job seeker's CV is visible to all recruiters/HR Managers/Placement Consultants who visit Naukri.com looking for candidates free of charge to them. This service may be subscribed to for a period from 6 months to 1 year.

f. *Résumé Manager:* This is a free service in which the job seeker's CV is visible only to Naukri.com's clients who have purchased the RESDEX product from Naukri.com.

In addition to the above products/services, Naukri.com also offers certain services such as short-listing candidates and organizing walk-in interviews which no other medium does. This makes Naukri.com an end-to-end recruitment solutions provider.

Technology Involved

Because the services offered by Naukri.com are deployed over the Internet, it requires a very sound technological backup. The organization has a 20-strong team of technology persons, out of which 16 are on the software development side. This team is entrusted with the responsibility of continuously improving and upgrading existing products and adding new products.

Naukri.com has 10 servers in a server farm in the United States. The technology team in India manages those servers. The Web site is served from the servers in the United States. The head office has about 250–300 personal computers, which are used for daily operations. The operating system used is Linux, the Web servers used are Apache, the RDBMS software used is MySQL, and the programming language employed is PHP. According to Sanjeev Bikhchandani, not much data mining is done at Naukri.com.

Product and Service Pricing Strategy

The basic strategy of Naukri.com is to be present at every price point in the market—right from Rs 500 to Rs 9 lacs. Presence at all the price points enables Naukri.com to service low-budget customers, and at the same time, have high-end customers. The low-priced services are there to basically enable penetration. To quote Sanjeev Bikhchandani, "Essentially our old strategy is penetration—to make the medium popular." There is also grading in the price charged within a product. For example, for one of the products, RESDEX, the price can range anywhere between Rs 15,000 and Rs 1.5 lacs, depending on how many logins the customer wants, and whether the customer wants it for 1 month, 3 months, or 1 year. Similarly, there are a number of other pricing options available.

Consumer Segments

The key segments in a B2B sense that Naukri.com serves are recruitment consultants and corporates. Within the placement consultant segment, it was found that consultants catering to different industries are different from each other in terms of their recruitment solution requirements. For instance, placement consultants serving the IT sector would be quite different from the other placement consultants. Within the corporate segment, the segmentation is by the verticals, that is, by the industry type. Segmentation is also done according to the size of the companies. In some cases, segmentation is also done geographically.

Naukri.com serves all these segments and is a leader in all the segments. Naukri.com has been able to achieve a position of leadership in all these segments primarily because of the fact that it was the first mover in the online recruitment market. "I think one of the best-kept secrets of most market leaders is being the first mover. The fact that we moved three years before anybody else really helped us because we understood the customer, we understood the recruiter, we understood the medium, we understood the technology that has to work in order to make money," informs Sanjeev Bikhchandani. Also, because

Naukri.com's knowledge of the Indian customer went a long way in contributing to the overwhelming success of Naukri.com, Bikhchandani believes that foreign companies had to adapt their pricing strategy and their business model and there they floundered.

Competition

Naukri.com's two closest competitors are Jobstreet.com and JobsAhead.com in the Indian market. However, some big multinational competitors, such as Monster.com, have also set up their Indian operations, namely, Monsterindia.com. The screens shots of the Web sites of various competitors are provided in Appendix 2. The details of these Web sites are presented in the following.

Jobstreet.com

Launched in 1995, JobStreet.com has also grown rapidly to become one of the leading Internet recruitment Web sites in the Asia-Pacific. JobStreet.com offers a comprehensive suite of interactive recruitment services. International and local Asian corporations recruit from JobStreet.com's pool of talent and manage their recruitment process through uniquely developed software applications via the Internet. The Web site has 2.5 million users and has country-specific Web sites for Singapore, Malaysia, India, and the Philippines. It has the following products and services on offer:

a. *Online Job Posting*
   - Employers can post jobs at their India site
   - E-mail notification to suitable candidates through automated job alerts
   - Browsing candidates are able to apply online immediately to posted job advertisements
   - SiVA (JobStreet's online recruitment management system) Résumé Management Application to zero-in on the right candidate

b. *JobStreet SELECT*
   - Screen applications and conduct first round interviews

c. *JobStreet IMPACT*
   - Employer career Web site management

- Access to candidate database
- Integrate all candidate data in SiVA to the company's HR system

d. *Other Services*

- Online testing – Employers can evaluate applicants with customizable online tests
- Targeted banners
- Newsprint ads – Candidates apply online to employers' newsprint ads and process them with SiVA

In addition to the above-mentioned products, JobStreet also has secondary sources of revenue, such as the facility given to clients to advertise on their Web site.

JobsAhead.com

JobsAhead has a team of over 125 personnel spread across eight metropolitan cities in India. It has the unique distinction of powering the job section of India's largest horizontal portals such as Yahoo!. Recently, in May 2004, U.S.-based global leader in online jobs, Monster Worldwide Inc., announced that it has acquired JobsAhead.com for consideration of Rs 40 crores.[5] The Web site receives around 5.5 million unique visitors every month and has 2.7 million résumés posted on it. It has close to 5,000 corporates as its clients.

The deal involved acquisition of a company named Webneuron Services, which runs JobsAhead.com. JobsAhead.com was among early entrants in India's e-recruitment space, where it competes primarily with Naukri.com. "India is an important and strategic market with vast pool of skilled manpower. We set eyes on India as it has one of fastest growing recruitment markets," says Stuart McKelvey, Monster Worldwide Group president (Asia-Pacific). The original promoters of JobsAhead.com, which include Chairman Puneet Dalmia and Vice Chairman Alok Mittal, will continue to play their respective roles in the new entity. They will benefit monetarily from acquisition besides venture capitalist ChrysCapital, which invested around Rs 25 crore in the company.

Prior to the merger with Monster, JobsAhead.com offered the following products/services to job seekers:

a. *Right Résumé:* Résumé writing service
b. *Résumé Blaster:* Sends résumés of job seekers to placement consultants all over the country and to the Middle East (for an extra fee)

c. *Résumé Highlighter:* Highlights the posted résumé of job seeker so that it may easily catch the attention of the recruiter/placement consultant
d. *Placement Directory:* Complete directory of top placement consultants across India and abroad
e. *Career Booster:* A package providing all the services listed above

For employers, JobsAhead offers the following products/services:

a. *Database Access:* Paid access to the database of job seekers.
b. *Job Listings:* Employers can advertise their jobs on JobsAhead and let their jobs viewed by over one million job seekers
c. *Stingers:* Employers' jobs can be directly delivered into job seekers' mail boxes or the job seeker can be called for a walk-in interview

This online job company has also been the only player globally to develop role-based matching techniques (MarksMan), which in conjunction with text-based résumé search (TextStar), has significantly improved customer experience. MarksMan allows corporates to search for candidates by their current job role or designation. It defines the job requirement in a single phrase thereby reducing the cumbersome filling of search forms. A single click search, MarksMan classifies the recruitment market into 23 categories and 600 roles that users can easily understand. Users can further refine their search based on industry, experience, location, and key skills. TextStar works for the employers' company by allowing the user to perform a search on all contents of a candidate's résumé. This tool is similar to Google in its functionality. JobsAhead claims that the use of this tool makes any recruitment effort "100% more accurate."

Monsterindia.com

Monsterindia.com is a flagship brand of Monster Worldwide (NASDAQ: MNST), which is a leading online global careers network and hiring management resource. It was founded in 1994 by Chief Monster, Jeff Taylor, and at present, has sites in 20 countries around the world.

As part of its India strategy, Monster Worldwide Inc, the parent of job site Monster.com, has bought Indian Web site JobsAhead.com as a part of a global acquisition drive to boost revenues.[6] The deal, worth about Rs 400 million ($9.6 million), is Monster's fourth acquisition in less than 3 months and is the first buyout in India, which is Asia's third-largest economy and home to booming software and telecom industries. JobsAhead.com, which focuses on IT and BPO recruitment, will now be fully owned by Monster India. Monster Asia President and Managing Director Arun Tadanki said that the combined entity will have close to 3,500 clients from across the industry and companies of various sizes. "The new entity will also have data base of 25 lacs job applications and unduplicated traffic of 55 lacs job seekers, which is twice as large as our nearest competitor," with an obvious reference to Naukri.com.

It offers products/services to three consumer segments: (1) job seekers, (2) employers, and (3) movers. Job seekers can search for jobs, build and post their résumés, and access a number of pages of career information and advice. It also offers regular e-recruitment facilities, such as résumé registration and e-mail alerts. Job seekers can also use the Monster site as a networking platform. The products for employers include searching candidates in Monster's Résumé Database tool, building the company's own private candidate database with the tool Career Site Hosting, leveraging the company's brand by letting candidates learn more about the company with the tool Employer Profiles, and streamlining the hiring process with the Hiring Tools, Applicant Tracking, and Candidate Screening products. In addition, Monster also provides unique solutions to the large workforce moving from one location to another. To this segment, it offers services such as finding a local real estate agent, getting instant mortgage rates, and planning the move within a short period of time. These services are provided on Monstermoving.com, positioned as "Your One-Stop Moving Resource."

Comparison of Competitors

The business models of the competitors are largely similar to each other's. Except for the moving services offered by Monster.com, all of the models involve a mixture of services for both employers and job seekers. Job seekers are usually allowed free posting of résumés and employers are charged to access the database.

There was considerable confusion as to which company was the market leader in online jobs marketspace in India. According to some estimates, JobsAhead.com has a 40% share of the online jobs market, while monster.com has another 25%. "Together, we will be almost twice as large as the next player [Naukri.com]," Dalmia of JobsAhead.com added.[7] According to comScore MediaMetrix, which is an international company that independently tracks traffic on the Internet, Monster and JobsAhead together received 55 lacs unduplicated (i.e., unique) visitors in April 2004 compared with 26 lacs for the nearest competitor. Despite the recent merger of its two competitors, JobsAhead.com and Monster, Naukri.com said it was well poised to achieve 100% sales growth in the current fiscal over the previous year's Rs 220 million. On the merger of JobsAhead.com with Monster, Sanjeev Bikhchandani, CEO of Naukri.com, claimed, "We are ahead of both JobsAhead.com and Monster combined in terms of traffic, daily additions, résumé database, and client base. . . . Postmerger, even clients are realizing the power of Naukri.com as a unified force credibly offering services and targeting sales of between Rs 400 million and Rs 450 million over sales of Rs 220 million in 2003–04."[8]

Marketing Strategy of Naukri.com

Initial Marketing Strategy (1997–2000)

The initial marketing strategy was geared toward fulfilling two objectives. The first objective was to get the companies and placement consultants to list their jobs on the Web site and the second one was to get job seekers to visit the site. Toward achieving the first objective, an intensive search exercise was carried out. The team went through the previous issues of several newspapers and magazines, went to libraries, scanned Yellow Pages, and built a mailing list that contained names and addresses of approximately 24,000 companies and placement consultants who had placed an advertisement for jobs in the last 5 years. Letters were mailed out to them with information about the service. At the same time, another list of newspapers and magazines was compiled. Letters were also sent to these newspapers and magazines informing them of the introduction of this unique service. Advertising was also done but on a very small scale. It was restricted to small-classified displays in newspapers. In effect, initially, the marketing strategy of Naukri.com was based on direct mailing and it was actually a very low cost one.

Current Marketing Strategy (2001–2004)

The marketing strategy currently being followed by Naukri.com is a "two-pronged" one, in the words of its marketing manager, Ayesha Kapur. Naukri.com reaches out to two segments primarily—job seekers and employers. To reach out to recruiters, Naukri.com has a 130–140-strong sales force across the country that goes around and meets clients face-to-face, introduces them to the products, and explains them. The mechanism adopted to reach out to the other segment, that is, job seekers, is aggressive advertising. Aggressive advertising has kept momentum only during the last year (2003–2004). Naukri.com has been advertising on television and the print media and is now exploring radio as a medium for advertising its services and products. Advertisement on television has included promotion during the India–Australia cricket game series telecast on the national television network, *Doordarshan,* in the year 2001.

Such aggressive advertising is a new feature of Naukri.com. Earlier, when the company was a start-up and revenue was not as much as it is today, advertising was done on a much smaller scale. Says Ayesha Kapur, "So 2 years ago, when our revenues were about Rs 4 crores, accordingly the ad budget was something smaller than what it was last year. This year we are targeting Rs 20 crores. Accordingly our ad budgets have also grown."

For the year 2004, the marketing budget of Naukri.com is close to Rs 4–5 crores. The figure of how much to spend on advertising is arrived at by taking into consideration a number of factors such as what needs to be done in north, south, east, or west India, which media to use for advertising, and so on. Also, the company is now looking at advertising as more of an investment rather than an expense.

Sanjeev Bikhchandani is of the opinion that a service should be advertised only if advertising is producing results. According to him, Naukri.com did not advertise aggressively earlier because it "did not have the wherewithal to take advantage of advertising." Now that the market is booming, management at Naukri.com believes that this is the right time to advertise. Therefore, when Naukri.com was a start-up, focus was on development of business, growing products, and increasing product offerings. Once venture capital funding was taken, a conscious decision was taken to shift focus to grow business, invest in infrastructure, develop offices all over the country, and advertise.

Alliances with Other Organizations

Media alliances with various media houses such as *Hindustan Times*, *New Indian Express*, and *The Telegraph*, also form a part of the marketing strategy of Naukri.com. The management says that it also considers itself a media company. It has a certain reach and the newspapers have their own reach. Therefore, there are always some people that Naukri.com manages to reach and some people that the newspaper houses manage to reach. The deals thus sealed require the newspapers to provide some advertising space to Naukri.com. Naukri.com, on its part, promotes these newspapers on its Web site, in a bartering kind of arrangement. These alliances, thus, give the company frequent advertising and also save the company a lot of money.

Advertising over the Internet is primarily accomplished by means of alliances with established sites such as MSN and Yahoo!. In these deals, MSN or Yahoo!

places a banner or a text link on their site. Depending on the number of click-throughs, number of CV registrations, and number of banner impressions, payment is made to MSN and Yahoo!. There is no revenue-sharing arrangement between Naukri.com and MSN or Yahoo!. The objectives of online advertising are similar to that of television and print advertising—drive CV registration. But promotion over television and print has the additional objective of branding, which is not there in Internet advertising.

Positioning of Naukri.com

The services of Naukri.com are positioned in a different fashion for job seekers and employers. The positioning for employers is end-to-end recruitment solutions. For some key clients, Naukri.com has done first round of short-listing, and organized walk-in interviews, but those types of services are rendered to only key accounts.

For job seekers, the positioning is essentially in terms of the largest database of jobs that Naukri.com claims to have in its possession. It also claims to have jobs in its database that are of much superior quality as compared to the jobs in the database of the competitors. Value proposition is also a part of the positioning. Naukri.com promises the following advantages to its customers, both job seekers and employers:

- National and global reach
- Recruitment costs reduced by 80%
- Hiring cycle time reduced by over 60%
- Reduced junk and irrelevant responses
- Confidentiality
- Several options to suit varying recruitment needs
- Management of responses through Naukri.com's e-recruitment software application

Product/Service Development at Naukri.com

The sales force of Naukri.com is in constant touch with its clients. The sales team brings back feedback on a daily basis. This forms the major source of intelligence and is one of the main inputs that go into new product development. The needs of HR managers in various sectors are studied thoroughly to determine the features that may be incorporated into the new product. Other modes of intelligence gathering include looking at competitors' Web sites and products, and analyzing what the market is demanding. This is then followed by discussion with the technology team. They determine the best way in which the new product may be deployed over the Internet. Other departments such as finance and operations play their respective roles in new product development.

Interestingly, no formal marketing research is done for intelligence gathering purposes. Most of the information is what the clients give to the sales people of Naukri.com. The marketing team at Naukri.com believes that the clients would be honest while revealing information because business here is primarily based on relationships that develop over a period of time. Says Ayesha Kapur, "It is not a question of making a sale once and not seeing them again. It is not like, say for instance, advertising in print, where there is not that hand holding, being in touch with clients." The product development team adds two to three features to its products on a daily basis based on the feedback it receives through the sales team. The marketing team dispatches a lot of corporate communication to its clients to make the clients aware of the small improvements that have been made to existing products. But most of the talking is still done by the sales team.

Co-Branding

Naukri.com is very clear in this regard. It will not indulge in any sort of promotion that dilutes its brand. As mentioned earlier, several alliances have been forged with media houses such as *Hindustan Times*, and so forth, but none of them can be strictly called a co-branding exercise. Naukri.com did a co-branded section with *Business Today* called "Jobs Today." But in that venture, too, according to the marketing manager of Naukri.com, *Business Today* stood on its own strength and Naukri.com stood on its own strength. The section "Jobs Today" no longer appears in *Business Today* as it has been discontinued.

Innovative Mailing

Instead of sending out plain brochures to corporate clients, the marketing team at Naukri.com has an innovative theme-based direct mailing. For instance, it created a "Stress Ball" campaign, the theme of which was "Squeeze the Stress Out of Recruiting." Then, for the response management team, a puzzle was created with the theme "Take the Puzzle Out of Recruiting." This, according to Ayesha Kapur, is helping because "everyone gets a brochure every now and then through a courier but if you get something that's interesting, you look at it, it's got a theme around it, you can squeeze it, play around with it. It's a little bit more interesting."

Off-Line Presence

Naukri.com brought out a magazine that had all the jobs listed and was sold at newsstands. But that has taken a back seat lately. This magazine was brought out with the intention of catering to those people who did not have access to the Internet or those who did not have the time to navigate through the site and find relevant jobs. The magazine was intended to be a ready reckoner with the top 1,500 jobs listed. The jobs were classified in terms of different functional areas, different levels in terms of seniority—senior level, middle level, junior level, freshers, and so on. However, at the moment, it appears that the reason why it has taken a back seat is because the online business is doing very well. Therefore, the management is just focusing on the online business in terms of all their resources of management, technology, operations, and personnel.

The Future of Naukri.com

Naukri.com has elaborate market expansion plans for the future. It plans to take its existing products to new markets outside India. The markets that are being eyed include the United States and the Middle East. If there is a requirement for Indian talent in those markets, then Naukri.com wants to be in a position to satisfy those demands by allowing recruiters there to come in contact with the talent in India. The ultimate goal of Naukri.com is to be a global hub for Indian talent.

As far as mergers and acquisitions are concerned, Sanjeev Bikhchandani does not see a need for it in the foreseeable future. He says, "We do not need mergers. We are doing well in the current state. And, at least in the foreseeable future, we know we don't need to merge. As far as acquisitions are concerned, we are growing so fast without acquisition, we feel we don't need an acquisition." Also, Naukri.com is not contemplating an initial public offer (IPO) in the near future because, according to Sanjeev Bikhchandani, companies go for IPOs in order to raise money and since Naukri.com is internally generating all the money it needs, he does not feel that there is a need for an IPO.

Are those viewpoints likely to change with the merger of Monster.com and JobsAhead.com?

Endnotes

1 Corresponding Author: Assistant Professor, Department of Industrial and Management Engineering, Indian Institute of Technology Kanpur, India, E-mail: *sswami@iitk.ac.in*. The author thanks the following MBA students for their work on this case: Neelabhro Deb, Sudhir Nagle, Sreejith Ummathiriyan, and Bindumadhavi P.

2 US$ 1 = Rs 45 (approx.); Units conversions: 1 lacs = 0.1 million, 1 crore = 0.1 billion

3 "Monster Worldwide buys India's JobsAhead.com for $9.6 mn." Retrieved May 25, 2004, from www.expressindia.com/fullstory.php?newsid=31796#compstory

4 "Naukri.com to generate Rs.450 mn in sales in 2004–05." Retrieve June 8, 2004, from www.keralanext.com/news/index.asp?id=38521

5 Monster India buys JobsAhead.com. Retrieved May 26, 2004, from www.deccanherald.com/deccanherald/may262004/b1.asp

6 Monster Worldwide buys India's JobsAhead.com for $9.6 mn. Retrieved May 26, 2004, from www.expressindia.com/fullstory.php?newsid=31796

7 Monster acquires JobsAhead. Retrieved May 26, 2004, from http://autofeed.msn.co.in/pandoraV2/output/30C606E3-C4D6-4B25-BDD3-8A0CBCD359EB.asp

8 India News. Naukri.com to generate Rs 450 mn in sales in 2004–05. Retrieved June 8, 2004, from www.keralanext.com/news/index.asp?id=38521

Appendix 1

Profiles of Management Personnel of Naukri.com

Sanjeev Bikhchandani (CEO): He is 38 years old. He graduated from St. Stephen's College Delhi with a BA in economics. Subsequently, he completed an MBA from the Indian Institute of Management (IIM) Ahmedabad. He has been associated with multinational corporations such as SmithKline Beecham and Lintas. IIM Ahmedabad, IMT Ghaziabad, Times School of Marketing, and Delhi School of Communication have invited him as a guest lecturer in the functional area of marketing. He was the former editor of *Careers*—the career supplement of *Pioneer*—and has coauthored two books on job hunting and careers. He is also a member of the Editorial Advisory Board, Encyclopedia Britannica India, student's edition.

V. N. Saroja (COO): She is 33 years old. She graduated with a degree in mathematics from Hindu College in 1988 and followed it up with an MBA from the Indian Institute of Ahmedabad in 1990. After a 5-month stint at IFCI, she began freelance consulting and preparation of multi-client reports. Clients included NASSCOM, Vedika Software, HTA, Trikaya Grey, Garware, Wallropes, Salora, and some NRIs amongst others. She has been a visiting faculty at IMT Ghaziabad and the National Institute of Advertising and has been associated with Info Edge since 1991. She has been with Naukri.com ever since its inception.

Ambrish Raghuvanshi (CFO & Head–HR): He is 40 years old. He holds a bachelor's degree in commerce, is a chartered accountant and an MBA from XLRI, Jamshedpur. He has worked with multinational corporation banks such as HSBC, Standard Chartered, and Bank of America, where he was vice president of Corporate and Investment Banking.

Simeryn Jeyadev (Head, Operations): She is 38 years old. She started her career in 1985 with ABC Placement Consultants and moved to NIIT Ltd. in 1988, where she held various responsibilities including sales, center administration, training, coordination, and corporate communications.

Hitesh Oberoi (Head–Sales and Marketing): He is 30 years old. He is a computer science engineer from IIT Delhi and an MBA from IIM Bangalore. He was formerly with Hindustan Lever Limited.

Anil Lall (Head of Technology): He is 37 years old and has 14 years experience in software development. He graduated in commerce from Bhagat Singh College in 1986.

Vivek Khare (General Manager–Technology): He is 30 years old. He did his MSc (Physics) from IIT Kanpur and MBA from Birla Institute of Management Technology, New Delhi. Previously, he was employed at FIITJEE.

Sharad Malik (Adviser): He is 38 years old and is an electrical engineer from IIT Delhi. He did MS and PhD in computer science from the University of California, Berkeley, in 1987 and 1990, respectively. Currently he is a professor in the Department of Electrical Engineering, Princeton University, and also serves as a consultant to a number of companies in Silicon Valley technology companies.

Sushil Bikhchandani (Head–U.S. Operations): He is 45 years old. He did his BTech (computer science–1978) at IIT Delhi. He did his MBA at IIM Ahmedabad. In 1986, he completed his PhD in economics at Stanford University. Currently, he is a professor at the Anderson Graduate School of Business at the University of California, Los Angeles.

Surabhi Motihar (Head–Product Development): She is 36 years old and did her degree in economics from St. Stephen's College, Delhi, in 1986. In 1989, she finished her MBA from the Indian Institute of Management Ahmedabad. She worked as a marketing executive in Nestlé India Limited, where she was responsible for product management (Maggi noodles).

Appendix 2

Screen Shots of Different Web Sites Referred to in the Chapter

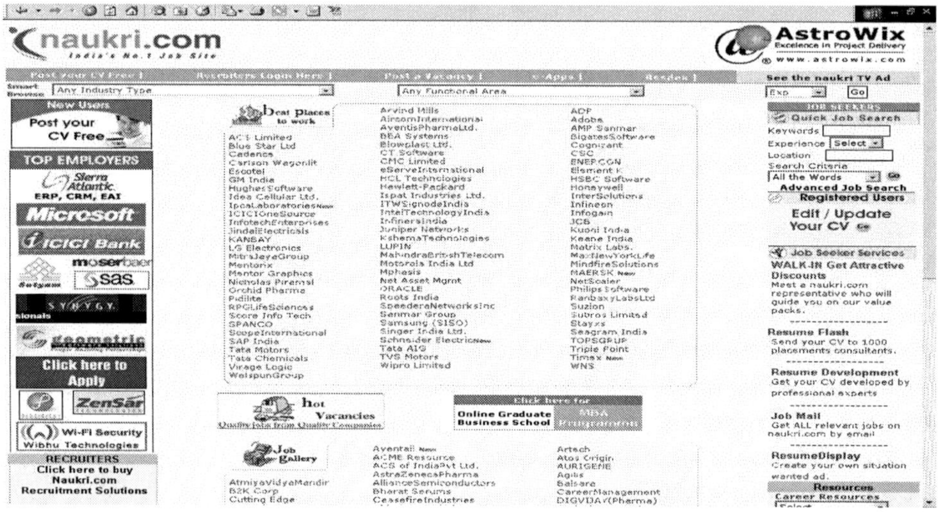

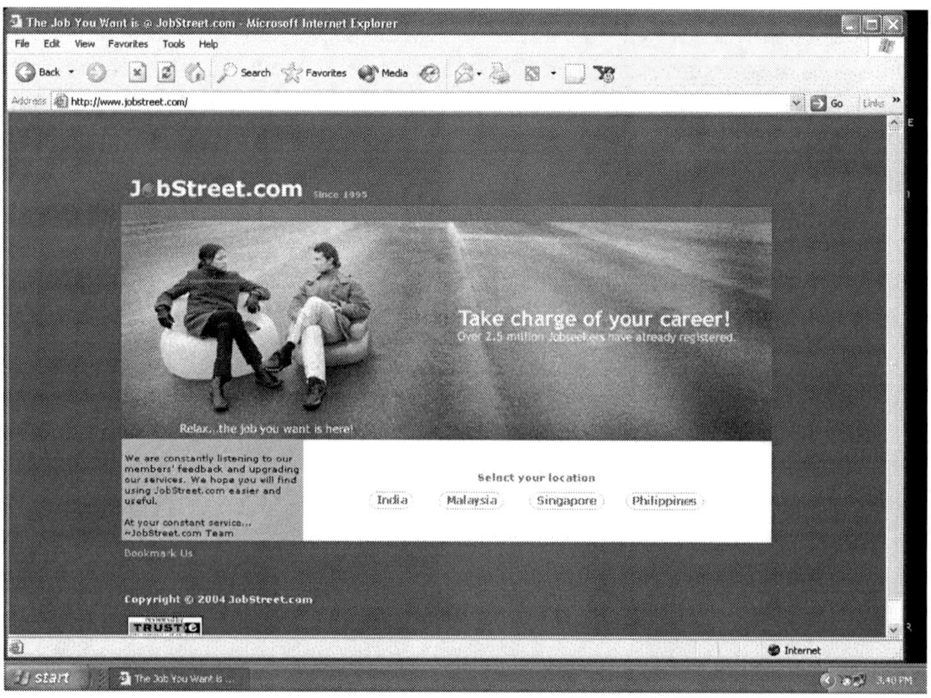

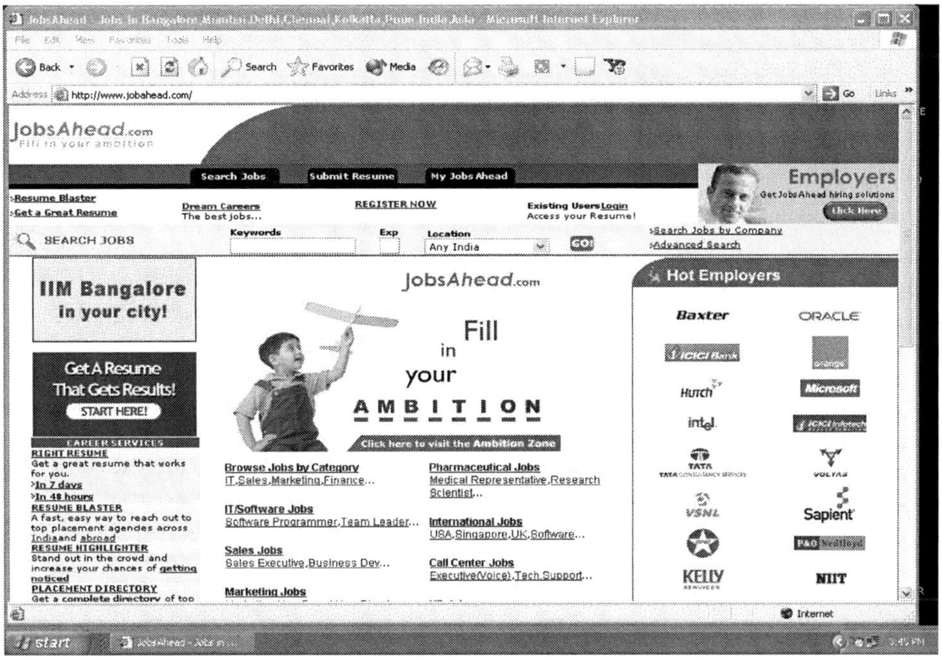
http://www.jobahead.com/
JobsAhead.com
Search Jobs
Submit Resume
My Jobs Ahead
Employers
Resume Blaster
Get a Great Resume
Dream Careers
The best jobs...
REGISTER NOW
Existing Users Login
Access your Resume!
SEARCH JOBS
Keywords
Exp
Location
Any India
GO!
Search Jobs by Company
Advanced Search
IIM Bangalore in your city!
Get A Resume That Gets Results!
START HERE!
Fill in your AMBITION
Click here to visit the Ambition Zone
Hot Employers
Baxter
ORACLE
Hutch
Microsoft
intel
TATA
VOLTAS
VSNL
Sapient
KELLY
NIIT
CAREER SERVICES
RIGHT RESUME
Get a great resume that works for you.
In 7 days
In 48 hours
RESUME BLASTER
A fast, easy way to reach out to top placement agencies across India and abroad
RESUME HIGHLIGHTER
Stand out in the crowd and increase your chances of getting noticed
PLACEMENT DIRECTORY
Browse Jobs by Category
IT,Sales,Marketing,Finance...
IT/Software Jobs
Software Programmer,Team Leader...
Sales Jobs
Sales Executive,Business Dev...
Marketing Jobs
Pharmaceutical Jobs
Medical Representative,Research Scientist...
International Jobs
USA,Singapore,UK,Software...
Call Center Jobs
Executive(Voice),Tech Support...
Internet

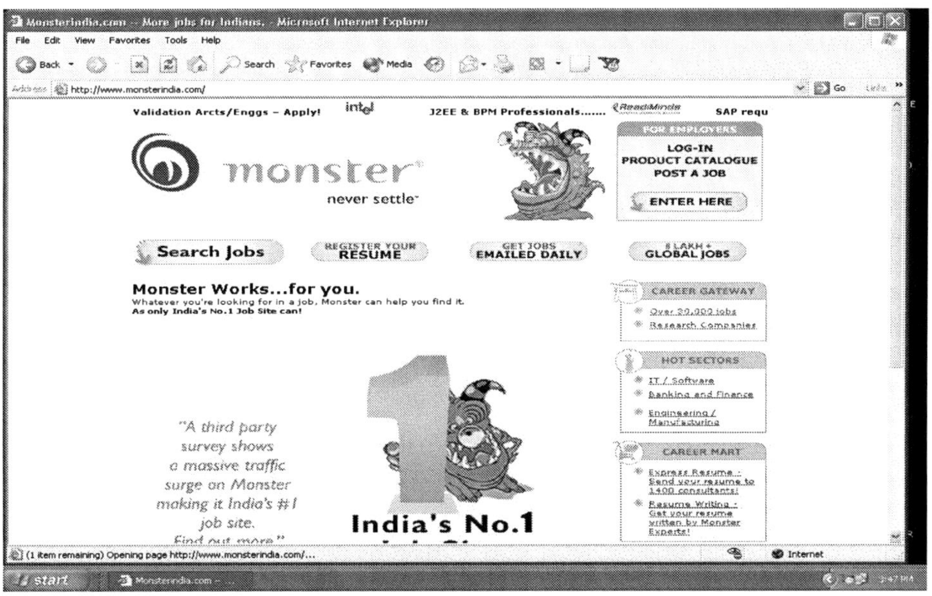
Monsterindia.com -- More jobs for Indians. - Microsoft Internet Explorer
http://www.monsterindia.com/
Validation Arcts/Enggs – Apply!
J2EE & BPM Professionals......
SAP requ
monster
never settle
FOR EMPLOYERS
LOG-IN
PRODUCT CATALOGUE
POST A JOB
ENTER HERE
Search Jobs
REGISTER YOUR RESUME
GET JOBS EMAILED DAILY
8 LAKH + GLOBAL JOBS
Monster Works...for you.
Whatever you're looking for in a job, Monster can help you find it.
As only India's No.1 Job Site can!
CAREER GATEWAY
Over 30,000 jobs
Research Companies
HOT SECTORS
IT / Software
Banking and Finance
Engineering / Manufacturing
CAREER MART
Express Resume - Send your resume to 1400 consultants!
Resume Writing - Get your resume written by Monster Experts!
"A third party survey shows a massive traffic surge on Monster making it India's #1 job site.
India's No.1
Internet

Chapter IV

User-Centered Design and Marketing: Online Customer Value

Thomas W. Porter, University of North Carolina Wilmington, USA

Abstract

The purpose of this chapter is to help Web marketers better understand the basis for the development of more customer-focused, value-enhanced Web sites. To help address this issue, this chapter integrates theory and research from user-centered design with theory and research from marketing on value and goal-directed behavior to develop and support a model of online customer value. The model based on means-end theory provides a theoretical explanation for linking Web site features and functions to perceptions of value by consumers.

Introduction

To compete in today's turbulent business environment firms are being directed to focus efforts on increasing value delivered to customers (Vandermerwe, 2000). This focus on enhancing customer value is also at the cornerstone of many high-profile e-commerce books (Seybold, 1998; Tapscott, Ticoll, & Lowy, 2000).

The consensus from these sources is that the firm's Web marketing efforts will only be successful if the Web site offers something of value to the site visitor. Research on value creation (Day, 1990; Naumann, 1995) further emphasizes the importance of creating value for customers as a means of competing more effectively in the marketplace. Research on delivering customer value is consistent with the notion that firms need to be increasingly market oriented (Kohli & Jaworski, 1990; Narver & Slater, 1990). Unfortunately many Web sites fail to deliver on the opportunity that the Internet provides for enhancing value to customers. Thus the purpose of this chapter is to help Web marketers better understand the basis for the development of more customer-focused, value-enhanced Web sites.

In order to better understand the nature of value online, this chapter integrates theory and research from Human–Computer Interaction (HCI), marketing, and psychology. I begin by reviewing the principles of user-centered design (UCD) and highlighting the commonalities between UCD and consumer behavior (CB). Second, I review a variety of value-related concepts and perspectives from the marketing and HCI literature in order to propose a definition of online value. Next, I present and support a model customer value that links Web site features to perceptions of value (see Figure 1). Finally, I discuss some key implications of the model.

User-Centered Design and Consumer Behavior

There has been considerable attention paid to the issue of how to develop more useful, more user-friendly systems in the field of user-centered design (Karat & Karat, 2003; Maguire, 2001b). UCD is an approach to the design of user interfaces that includes continuous and early focus on the consumer's tasks and goals. UCD emerged from researchers and practitioners of HCI. HCI is an interdisciplinary field made up of researchers from numerous fields including psychology, cognitive science, engineering, and information systems. HCI researchers and practitioners are focused on creating more usable systems by ensuring that technology matches people's needs and supports the tasks that people would like to perform.

UCD is a design process that aims to improve the "quality in use" of a system. While the marketing literature focuses on customers or consumers, the UCD literature emphasizes the importance of the "user" as the focal point of the design effort. The term "user" refers to the general population of individuals who are expected to make use of the system. At the heart of UCD is the core philosophy that the best way to design a system is by focusing on the user and their activities. Focusing on users is critical in design because systems appropriate for one user group may be completely inappropriate for another set of users. For example, an information system developed for data professionals that allows a high degree of flexibility in structuring queries against a database would likely be incredibly frustrating to managers with minimal database expertise. By emphasizing users and their tasks, UCD aims to create systems that provide the appropriate functionality and are easier to use.

CB and UCD have a great deal in common. The two fields have followed parallel paths in their development and share an emphasis on human beings as part of their core philosophy. UCD was developed as an alternative to a technology-centered approach to design (Henneman, 1999). The technology-centered approach to design involves first identifying the functionality that a system should support and then designing a system that will support that functionality. The problem with this approach is that it overlooks the central role of the users of the system. Ultimately, the philosophical shift from technology-centered design to user-centered design in information systems mirrors the philosophical shift from sales orientation (product focused) to market orientation (customer focused) in the marketing literature.

While the emphasis placed on understanding and serving human needs is part of each discipline's core philosophy, the fundamental purposes of each field have led to differences in how human behavior is studied and understood. Marketing's purpose—to sell products—results in an emphasis on the exchange process. The human studied is the consumer or customer and the goal of the research is to understand the internal and external factors that affect the consumer during product consideration, acquisition, and consumption. In contrast, UCD's purpose—to design better systems—leads to a focus on the usage of the product or system. The human studied is the user and the goal of the research is to understand the individual, task, and contextual factors that affect the user as he/she carries out his/her work. These differences in orientation have led to a subtle but distinct difference in marketing's "customer" and UCD's "user."

Marketing, heavily indebted to the field of psychology, frequently emphasizes the human as a "black box" that needs to be understood. As a result, a significant body of customer-based research is designed to understand things such as consumer decision processes, attitudes, and learning. Likewise the extant "tools" of marketing (television, print, and radio advertising) have helped shape the types of research questions most relevant to marketers. Research in marketing has often focused on the consumer as a receiver of the marketer's message. The marketer's challenge is to capture the consumer's attention in order to effectively communicate the marketing message. In this model the marketer is the protagonist, actively seeking out consumers in order to communicate the message—a message which may or may not be relevant to the receivers of the message.

In contrast, the emphasis in UCD is much more on the "human as a doer." Work is performed in context and to accomplish a task. The dominant research methodology that underlies UCD is contextual inquiry, an approach grounded in activity theory (Nardi, 1996). In activity theory, the basic unit of analysis is human work (or activities). Activities are driven by certain needs where people wish to achieve a certain purpose. This activity is usually mediated by one or more instruments or tools. System designers have found activity theory to be particularly useful as a framework for understanding user needs for a couple of reasons. First, activity theory helps understand system requirements at the most basic level—the tasks and activities the system should support. Second, activity theory is useful for understanding the broader social context of key stakeholders in an activity.

The UCD literature is particularly relevant for understanding consumer behavior online where the traditional roles between marketer and customer are reversed. Online, the consumer becomes the protagonist, actively seeking out personally relevant information and performing personally relevant tasks. In this role reversal, consumers have greater control. They deliberately choose to visit a Web site and they choose when to exit the site. Wolfinbarger and Gilly (2001) report that most online shopping is goal oriented—with 71% of their sample reporting that their online purchase was planned. However, even most unplanned, online behavior can be characterized as purposeful. For example, Hoffman and Novak (1996) suggest that experiential behavior involves a person going online to *do* things such as to learn about a product, to be entertained, or to interact with other people. Thus experiential behavior *is* goal directed; it is just that the consumption goals are more hedonic in nature.

The marketer must understand the consumer's purpose for being on the site and provide the tools necessary for the consumer to accomplish his/her goals. The traditional consumer behavior literature with its emphasis on the exchange process is less suited to understanding online consumer behavior than research from UCD with its emphasis on product usage. The philosophical orientation in the UCD literature of "human as doer" is particularly relevant for understanding how to develop more usable Web sites that provide value to customers.

Despite the many similarities between CB and UCD, there has been remarkably little cross-pollination between the two literatures. The common core philosophies, concepts, and parallel developmental paths are noteworthy and provide a common ground for researchers in each field to come together. However, ultimately it is the differences ("human as black box" vs. "human as user," "marketer as protagonist" vs. "consumer/user as protagonist") that should make

UCD interesting to marketers. The integration of the literature on CB with that of UCD is a key contribution of this chapter.

Limitations of the Traditional Benefit vs. Cost Model of Customer Value

While the need for providing customers value online is well appreciated, the more practical question of how to deliver that value is less well understood. One reason for this is the significant differences that exist between what value means to a consumer online versus off-line. Much of the research on value in marketing and consumer behavior (Zeithaml, 1988; Ravald & Gronroos, 1996) has emphasized how customers perceive and evaluate a "product's" value. The traditional conceptualization of value highlights a key consumption goal which can be described as "value in exchange." Value in exchange is derived as the consequence of product acquisition. It represents a favorable ratio between what one receives in the form of benefits versus what one gives up during product acquisition. Price plays a key role in most conceptualizations of value. For example, if a consumer is able to find identical products for sale in two stores, with all other factors being equal (e.g., service, support, etc.), the product with the lower price would be considered a better value. However, because there is usually not a price associated with using a commercial Web site, these models are not effective at explaining value online.

Researchers have indicated that consumers derive value from other consumption activities as well. Woodruff and Gardial (1996) identify two additional types of value that occur as a result of product consumption—"value in use" and "value in possession." The value-in-use perspective emphasizes the instrumentality of products in achieving the consumer's goals. For example, coffee might be consumed to help a customer wake up in the morning. As a result, value in use involves an evaluation of the effectiveness of a product within a particular usage context. The value-in-possession perspective highlights the notion that product possession can provide important symbolic or self-expressive meaning to consumers. Products such as family heirlooms may have great value in possession but limited value in use or value in exchange.

Of the three dimensions of consumer value—value in exchange, value in use, and value in possession—only value in use appears highly relevant to commercial Web sites. While a Web site may be *used* to facilitate acquisition of another product or service, the value in exchange relates to the acquired product not the Web site. For example, a book bought from Amazon.com for 50% off might be considered a good value. In this case, the Web site would have value as well, but the relevant form of value is the Web site's *value in use* in allowing the consumer to purchase a book at a favorable price. The concept of value in exchange can have meaning in the context of subscription-based services, fee-based services, or the purchase of digital products online where a consumer is paying for services received on the Web site. However, because the ability to access and use a commercial Web site is for the most part free, the value-in-exchange concept is largely irrelevant. Likewise, because commercial Web sites exist in the public domain for use by potential customers, the value-in-possession component of value seems to have limited applicability.

Interestingly this discussion on value in use helps to make the concept of online value look a lot like the concept of usability from the literature on UCD. In the next section, I review three value-related concepts (usability from the UCD literature, Holbrook's theory of value, and Woodroff's means-end theory of customer value). This is not intended to be a thorough review of the literature on value (see Payne & Holt, 2001 for such a review); such a review is beyond the scope of this chapter. Rather, this literature is introduced because it offers the potential for helping to better understand the concept of online value as well as the factors that may be important in determining value.

Usability: If the fundamental purpose of marketing activity is to create value for the customer, the corresponding goal of UCD is to create usability for the user of the system. Usability refers to the efficiency with which users are able to complete their tasks with the system, and their overall satisfaction with that process. Henneman (1999) suggests that usability exists when the design of the system matches what the intended end users need and want.

How important is usability to the success of a Web site? Perhaps the best evidence is anecdotal with IBM's Web site providing a vivid example (Van Duyne, Landay, & Hong, 2003). IBM found its Web site was not designed well for its customers. The Web site was very confusing and visitors had a very difficult time finding their way to the products and information they were looking for. The most utilized features on the Web site were the search feature and the help link. As a result of the difficulties encountered by customers, IBM redesigned its Web site from the ground up with the goal of enhancing the usability of the site. When the redesigned site was launched, the utilization of the search and help links dropped dramatically and online sales increased 400%.

In addition to the benefits that firms can receive from developing more usable systems, users benefit in numerous ways. Maguire (2001) identifies five key benefits of designing a usable system: (1) increased productivity by allowing the user to focus on the task rather than the tool; (2) reduced errors by making the interface more straightforward; (3) reduced training and support; (4) improved acceptance by users who prefer a system that is easy to use; and (5) enhanced reputation in the marketplace. Furthermore, by taking users into account when developing a Web site, UCD may actually lower the costs of design by minimizing the number and severity of problems that are only discovered after the system has been developed. Just as important, early detection of problems provides value to users by reducing system downtime and expensive maintenance costs.

The concept of *context of use* is fundamental to understanding usability. For example, a marketer may claim to have a very usable Web site. In fact, it may only be usable in a certain range of contexts. Consider a Web site that allows travelers to quickly check flight availabilities and book frequently traveled routes with a single click. The Web site might be extremely usable for a business traveler who flies regularly but extremely unusable for a consumer wanting to plan a personal vacation. The context of use provides the frame of reference that allows the user to evaluate the usability or value of the system.

Maguire (1999) argues that understanding the context in which a product is going to be used is essential to assessing the product's usability. The importance of context in understanding usability is reflected in the International Standards community by defining usability in terms of context. The ISO 9241 (ISO, 1997) standard defines usability as being "the extent to which a product can be used by specified users to achieve specified goals with effectiveness, efficiency and satisfaction in a specified context of use."

When it comes to assessing usability, users evaluate the effectiveness of the system in helping them accomplish their goals. However, even though the usability definition suggests a narrowly defined range of users and usage situations individual differences in user goals, expectations, and experiences are inevitable. As a result, usability perceptions are inherently subjective. Agarwal and Venkatesh (2002) argue that "usability is not intrinsically objective in nature, but rather is closely intertwined with an evaluator's personal interpretation of the artifact and his or her interaction with it" (p. 170).

Holbrook's Theory of Consumer Value: The conceptual work on consumer value by Holbrook (1994) provides an alternative to the traditional cost-versus-benefits approach. Holbrook defines consumer value as "an interactive relativistic preference experience." He further suggests that consumer value refers to the *evaluation* of some *object* (product, service, event, etc.) by some *subject,* usually a consumer. The four facets of Holbrook's definition (interactive, relativistic, preference, and experience) make his theory of value broadly applicable and remarkably relevant to understanding value online. The interactive nature of value indicates that value is neither entirely subjective (in the eye of the beholder) nor entirely objective (imbued in the physical attributes of a product). Rather, value involves the interaction of an individual who appreciates the physical attributes of a product that can potentially create value. The relativistic nature of value suggests that consumer value is not absolute; rather, it depends on things such as the usage situation, the individual, and the competitive products with which value is assessed. The preferential nature of value highlights the notion that consumer value occurs as the result of an evaluative judgment the consumer makes of particular object. The experiential nature of value suggests that value resides not in the product itself but rather in the consumption experience derived from the product.

The relativistic nature of consumer value provides a possible clue to understanding how consumers may make value judgments online where the price of use is not a factor. Expanding on Holbrook's theory of value, Oliver (1999) suggests that value assessments can involve either intraproduct (benefits of product A compared to costs of product A) or interproduct (benefits of product A compared to benefits of product B). Intraproduct comparisons are consistent with the traditional costs compared to benefits judgment most commonly used in the marketing literature. Interproduct comparisons involve a comparison between an alternative and some referent. The referent can be an existing product or even an ideal prototype for the product category. The interproduct comparison approach appears to hold the key to understanding customer value in an online setting. Consumer's value assessments for Web sites are likely to be made based on comparisons with experiences they have had using other Web sites that allow customers to accomplish similar goals.

Holbrook's definition appears to capture the most important characteristics of online value: it is a subjective judgment, based on an individual's goals and use situation. Thus, Holbrook's perspective recognizes the importance of context in assessing value. From a theoretical perspective Holbrook's theory of value appears to be an important foundation in which to conceptualize online value.

Woodruff's Means-End Model of Customer Value: Means-end theory has been traditionally used to help explain how consumers understand and evaluate the physical attributes of the products they purchase (the means) to create desired consequences that help them achieve valued outcomes (the ends) (Gutman, 1982). The theory and its associated laddering methodology have typically been used to develop a better understanding of the factors influencing consumer choice or decision-making behavior (Mulvey, Olson, Celsi, & Walker, 1994; Klenosky, Gengler, & Mulvey, 1993).

While Gutman's (1982) work on means-end theory linked product attributes to higher order "values," Woodruff adapted the theory to explain consumers' perceptions of "value.". Woodruff proposed a customer value hierarchy model in the form of a means-end chain. Woodruff (1997) defined customer value as "a customer's perceived preference for and evaluation of those product attributes, attribute performances, and consequences arising from use that facilitate (or block) achieving the customer's goals and purposes in use situations" (p.

142). A key aspect of this definition is the contextual nature of value perceptions. Value is perceived in the context of how the consumer would like use the product or service.

In Woodruff's model, value perceptions can occur either before or after a consumption experience. The value desired by consumers is rooted in a means-end way of thinking. Consumers form preferences for product features and attributes based on their ability to help consumers achieve desired consequences. Likewise, consumers form preferences for certain consequences based on their desire to achieve their higher-order goals. Following a consumption experience, consumers assess *received value* using the same type of analysis. If product consumption facilitates goal accomplishment, then the product is viewed as delivering value. For example, a consumer takes a breath mint to relieve bad breath. The value of the breath mint is evaluated in the context of how effective it was in accomplishing the consumer's goal of relieving the offensive odor. In addition, goals also provide the context that allows consumers to ultimately evaluate a product's features and attributes. For example, based on the effectiveness of the breath mint, the consumer can form a judgment about the importance of the product attribute "retsin."

In addition, Woodruff also describes how *value in use* can be integrated into a disconfirmation model of customer satisfaction. The value desired by a consumer prior to product consumption evokes a set of expectations and hence a comparison standard against which the received value is evaluated. If the value received exceeds the value desired, then a positive disconfirmation occurs and the result is a positive impact on feelings of satisfaction.

Online Customer Value: A Proposed Definition and Theoretical Model

The objective of this section is to introduce and support a theoretical model and definition of online customer value that recognizes the "human as doer" nature of consumer behavior online. The different perspectives on value and usability provide a basis for understanding and defining the meaning of "online value" among goal-directed customers. To help address this issue, it is appropriate to revisit the definitions of usability and value offered by the ISO (1997), Holbrook (1994), and Woodruff (1997). These definitions are included in Table 1 to allow for easier comparison. A key commonality among these definitions is that value/usability is derived as a result of a customer/user achieving his/her goals. Thus, these definitions appear to be grounded in the *value-in-use* model in which value resides not in the product but occurs as a result of product usage. Another similarity is that value is inherently related to the usage context. This is explicit

Table 1.

	Definition
Usability (ISO, 1997)	"The extent to which a product can be used by specified users to achieve specified goals with effectiveness, efficiency and satisfaction in a specified context of use" (ISO 9241-11 – Part 11).
Value (Woodruff, 1997)	"A customer's perceived preference for and evaluation of those product attributes, attribute performances, and consequences arising from use that facilitate (or block) achieving the customer's goals and purposes in use situations" (p. 142).
Value (Holbrook, 1994)	"An interactive relativistic preference experience" (p. 5).

in both the ISO and Woodruff's definitions and is a key aspect to the relativistic nature of value highlighted by Holbrook.

Integrating these various perspectives and building on the work of Woodruff, online value is defined as "a customer's perceived preference for and evaluation of those Web site features and functions that facilitate (or block) the performance of the tasks that are instrumental in achieving the customer's goals and purposes associated with the Web site visit." Conceptualizing online customer value as a means-end model provides a theoretical explanation for linking Web site features and functions to perceptions of value by consumers. The means-end model of online customer value (see Figure 1) indicates that consumers' value perceptions are based on the extent to which the Web site facilitates the accomplishment of specific usage goals and tasks. Likewise, customers' goals

Figure 1. Customer perceived value for goal-directed behavior

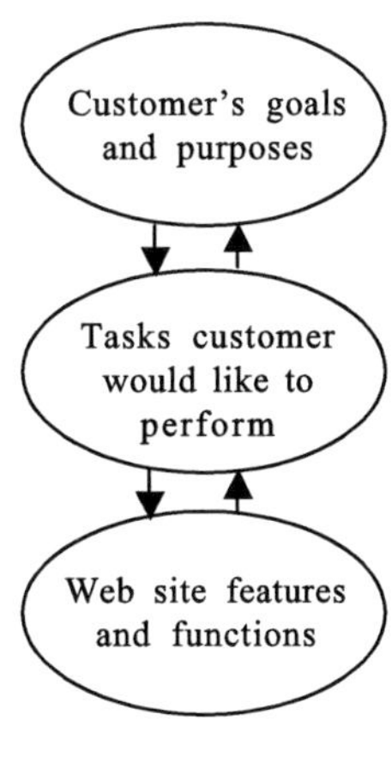

and tasks provide the context in which the Web site features, content, and functionality are assessed. Just as Woodruff's definition links goals to product attributes, this definition links goals to Web site features. The only difference is the critical role that tasks play in the online environment. The next sections highlight the key elements of the model: goals, tasks, and Web site features.

Goals and Tasks: The means-end model of online value integrates the concepts of goals from the CB literature and tasks from the UCD literature within a unified framework. Goals and tasks are clearly related concepts and each serves a similar purpose. While the consumer behavior literature describes consumers motivated by goals, the UCD literature focuses on users motivated to accomplish tasks. The challenge in relating and differentiating these concepts is the inconsistency in how the term "goal" is used in the UCD literature. Sometimes researchers in the field of UCD distinguish between tasks and goals. For example, Maguire (2001) indicates that "Tasks are the activities undertaken to achieve a goal." However, it is not uncommon for the terms "task" and "goal" to be used interchangeably. For example, Van Duyne, Landay, and Hong (2003) recognize that tasks such as "I want to find the best digital camera for under $500 and buy it" are referred to as goals by some authors.

Research on goal hierarchies (Bagozzi & Dholakia, 1999; Bettman, 1979) provides a way to distinguish between goals and tasks. Goal hierarchies are conceptually related to means-end chains. In fact, Gutman (1997) in an effort to integrate these concepts define a means-end chain as a hierarchy of goals. Goal hierarchies are useful for understanding the relationship between goals that occur at different levels of abstraction.

A goal hierarchy is essentially an interrelated sequence of goals that allows consumer to break up a complex problem into a series of smaller problems. For example, a consumer's goal to lose weight can be broken down into multiple subgoals such as to join a gym and eat a healthier diet. Each subgoal can in turn be broken down further into action steps. Thus the subgoal of joining a gym may lead the customer to conduct an online information search in order to find a gym that is appropriate for his/her needs.

These lower-level goals or "action steps" are clearly related to the concept of a task in the UCD literature. By characterizing a task as an action step undertaken to achieve a higher-order goal, we are able to integrate and position the concept of a task into theory from CB on the structure of goals. The UCD literature suggests that tasks can also be represented hierarchically based on their level of abstraction. The hierarchical nature of tasks is clearly illustrated in the design methodology of task analysis (Richardson, Ormerod, & Shepherd, 1998) in which the requirements for a system are assessed by evaluating the procedures, actions, and decisions that must be achieved to reach the user's goal.

The task analysis is carried out by decomposing tasks into lower-level tasks, or subtasks, in order to better understand the actions taken to accomplish the goal and the features and functionality necessary to support the user in their completion of the task.

To understand how a consumer wants to use a Web site to accomplish a personally meaningful goal, it is necessary to understand the specific tasks that the consumer would want to carry out in order to accomplish the goal. For example, a consumer might go to his/her online banking Web site in order to ensure that he/she has enough money in his/her checking account. In order to successfully complete this goal, he/she will perform several tasks, such as (1) to check the savings account balance, (2) to check the checking account balance, and (3) to transfer funds between the savings account and the checking account.

The model suggests that online value is assessed in a means-end way based on the extent to which a Web site supports the accomplishment of the consumer's goals. Thus, the fit between the customer's goal relevant tasks and the features, functions, and content of the Web site becomes an important concept. When the fit is positive, meaning that from the customer's judgment the Web site effectively supports the tasks necessary to accomplish his/her goal, then the perceived online value will increase. Likewise, when the fit is poor, the consumer will assess the level of online value as low.

P1: Online value is positively related to the fit between the consumer's goal and the Web site's ability to support the tasks necessary to accomplish the goal.

Web Site Features: At the lowest level of the means-end model are Web site features that include the specific content and functionality a consumer uses to complete a task. Internet researchers (Ghosh, 1998; Zott, Amitb, & Donlevya, 2000) emphasize the importance of Web site features and services as a means of creating value online. The challenge for Web marketers in building high-value Web sites is that there are a wide variety of potential features and functions that can be offered (Rayport & Jaworski, 2001; Saeed, Hwang, & Grover, 2003). Web site features such as virtual communities or Web site personalization are viewed as tools that can be offered online as a means of enhancing the value of the Web site and promoting longer visit durations and a greater likelihood of repeat visits.

The nature of the Web as a tool that is used to accomplish a task rather than as a "product" has implications in terms of how features are evaluated. Rather than evaluating the Web site in a bottom-up approach as some combination of its various features, consumers are likely to evaluate the instrumentality of the Web site and its features in allowing the consumer to accomplish his/her tasks. This is consistent with research in consumer behavior (Park & Smith, 1989) which indicates that when a goal is available, consumers construct decision criteria in a top-down approach from the goal. Thus, two consumers arriving at a Web site for a bed and breakfast with two different goals "find a unique place to stay" versus "make a reservation" may view the same Web site features but reach completely different conclusions about the importance of the features.

This discussion also highlights the notion that Web site features may or may not provide value to Web site users. Ultimately Web site features provide benefits to consumers only when the consumer has a need that a particular feature can help address. To help explain this situational relationship between features and functions, Ratneshwar, Shocker, Cotte, and Srivastava (1999) propose an intervening construct termed an "affordance." They defined an affordance as "the potential benefits and disadvantages of a product (or a set of complementary products) in relation to a particular person" (p.). Features designed into a product only "afford" benefits when an individual has the motivation and ability to take advantage of the potential benefits. For example, Yahoo! may afford Web site personalization, but only to an individual with the interest in making use of the benefits. This discussion suggests the following:

P2: For a goal-driven consumer, the Web site features perceived as most important will be those related to task accomplishment.

Testing the Model: The model presented here represents efforts to build a foundation for the systematic development of a theory of online customer value. Much work remains to be done in terms of developing suitable measures of online value and empirically testing the predictions of the model. One way the model can be tested is with an experimental design. A key prediction of the model is that consumer value perceptions are related to the degree to which the Web site supports the accomplishment of the consumer's task. This prediction may be tested empirically by manipulating the tasks assigned to subjects. Some subjects may be assigned to tasks that the Web site is well suited to support; others may be assigned tasks that the Web site is not well designed to support. Following completion of the online task post hoc, subjects could be asked to evaluate the Web site, including perceived value of the Web site, satisfaction, usability, and the satisfaction with various Web site features.

Another experimental option could involve a task requiring the comparison of two Web sites. Web sites could be selected so that Web site A is a good fit for the customer's task but has few additional features, while Web site B is a poor fit for the consumer's task but has many features that are not essential to the task. Subjects could be assigned to one of two groups, a task performing group and a control group that is not given a specific task. After a visit to each of the two sites, subjects in each group could be asked to evaluate each Web site for factors such as perceived value, satisfaction, usability, and the satisfaction with various Web site features. A pattern of results that showed that the task performing group perceived the value of Web site A to be superior to Web site B, while the control group perceived the value of Web site B to be superior to Web site A would provide support for the model.

An alternative approach to testing the model involves using Web site usage statistics. Third-party vendors, such as Web Trends, offer packages that aggregate log file data into managerially relevant statistics and information. These data provide an abundance of information useful to Web marketers including the number of unique site visitors, the number of return visitors, the average Web site visit duration, the average number of pages viewed per visit, the most frequently traveled paths traveled within the site, and many other statistics. Site statistics such as visit duration and repeat visits provide a behavioral measure of the value a Web site provides to site visitors. If a Web site engenders longer visits and more repeat traffic, it suggests that the Web site at least partially meets the requirements of site visitors. Likewise, it suggests a good fit between the Web site's features and the site visitor's requirements. Web sites could be evaluated for how well the Web site supports common customer goals. A positive relationship between goal-Web site fit and important value relevant to online behaviors (visit duration, repeat visits, etc.) would provide support for the model.

Summary

In summary, the model presented here conceptualizes consumer value in computer-mediated environments as a means-end chain in which the customer's goals (or desired usage) of a Web site provides the context that allows value to be assessed. The goal-directed nature of consumer behavior online has significant implications for Internet marketers. By understanding the consumer's online goals and related tasks, the Web marketer is in a position to understand the various contexts in which the consumer would like to use the Web site. Furthermore, a failure to deliver a Web site that enables customers to accomplish their goals and tasks is likely to result in dissatisfaction and defection to other more useful Web sites. At the bottom of the means-end chain are Web site features. The model suggests that Web site features and content are evaluated by the consumer in the context of their goals and tasks. Thus determining which features and content are relevant begins with an understanding of the consumer's goals.

An important contribution of this chapter is the introduction of research on UCD from the field of HCI into the discourse on value and marketing. There has been and continues to be a significant body of research in these areas dealing with how to improve the user experience when working with computer systems. Unfortunately, theories and findings from the HCI literature have been largely ignored by marketing academicians. Thus a key contribution of this chapter is to transfer some of the knowledge developed in these fields into the marketing literature. The model developed in this chapter integrates insights from both disciplines. The means-end model used as an integrative framework is well established in the consumer behavior literature and has been used to explain consumer value (Woodruff, 1997). However, the constructs used in the model (usability/value, tasks/goals, and Web site features) reflect the influence of UCD theory and practice.

Woodruff (1997) argue that if organizations are to become better at competing on superior customer value delivery, they will need a corresponding set of "tools of customer value." The field of UCD provides a wealth of tools and techniques for understanding users and their tasks. Tools such as customer personas, customer scenarios, and tasks analysis all based on the "human as doer" model hold significant promise for Web marketers as practical means of developing Web sites that provide value to customers.

References

Agarwal, R., & Venkatesh, V. (2002). Assessing a firm's Web presence: A heuristic evaluation procedure for the measurement of usability. *Information Systems Research, 13*, 168–186.

Bagozzi, R. P., & Dholakia, U. (1999). Goal setting and goal striving in consumer behavior. *Journal of Marketing, 63*(4), 19–33.

Bettman, J. R. (1979). *An information processing theory of consumer choice*. Reading, MA: Addison-Wesley.

Day, G. S. (1990). *Market driven strategy: Processes for creating value*. New York: The Free Press.

Ghosh, S. (1998). Making business sense of the Internet. *Harvard Business Review, 76*(2), 126–135.

Gutman, J. (1982). A means-end chain model based on consumer categorization processes. *Journal of Marketing, 46*(Spring), 60–72.

Gutman, J. (1997). Means-end chains as goal hierarchies. *Psychology & Marketing, 14*, 545–560.

Henneman, R. L. (1999). Design for usability: Process, skills, and tools. *Information Knowledge Systems Management, 1*, 133–144.

Hoffman, D. L., & Novak, T. P. (1996). Marketing in hypermedia computer-mediated environments: Conceptual foundations. *Journal of Marketing, 60*(3), 50–68.

Holbrook, M. B. (1994). The nature of customer value. In R. T. Rust & R. L. Oliver (Eds.), *Service quality: New directions in theory and practice*. Newbury Park, CA: Sage.

Holbrook, M. B. (1999). Introduction to consumer value. In M. B. Holbrook (Ed.), *Consumer value* (pp. 1–27). London: Routledge.

Huffman, C., & Houston, M. J. (1993). Goal-oriented experience and the development of knowledge. *Journal of Consumer Research, 20*(September), 190–207.

International Organization for Standardization (ISO). (1997). *ISO 9241-11 – Part 11 - Guidelines for specifying and measuring usability*. Geneva, Switzerland: Author.

Karat, J., & Karat, C. M. (2003). The evolution of user-centered focus in the human-computer interaction field. *IBM Systems Journal, 42*, 532–541.

Klenosky, D. B., Gengler, C. E., & Mulvey, M. S. (1993). Understanding the factors influencing ski destination choice: A means-end analytic approach. *Journal of Leisure Research, 25*, 362–379.

Kohli, A. K., & Jaworski, B. J. (1990). Market orientation: The construct, research propositions, and managerial implications. *Journal of Marketing, 54*(April), 1–18.

Kortge, G. D., & Okonkwo, P. A. (1993). Perceived value approach to pricing. *Industrial Marketing Management, 22*, 133–140.

Maguire, M. (2001a). Context of use within usability activities. *International Journal of Human-Computer Studies, 55*, 453–583.

Maguire, M. (2001b). Methods to support human-centered design. *International Journal of Human-Computer Studies, 55*, 587–634.

Mulvey, M. S., Olson, J. C., Celsi, R. L., & Walker, B. A. (1994). Exploring the relationship between means-end knowledge and involvement. *Advances in Consumer Research, 21*, 1–7.

Nardi, B. A. (1996). Activity theory and human computer interaction. In B. A. Nardi (Ed.), *Context and consciousness: Activity theory and human-computer interaction* (pp. 7–16). Cambridge, MA: MIT Press.

Naumann, E. (1995). *Creating customer value: The path to sustainable competitive advantage*. Cincinnati, OH: Thompson Executive Press.

Naver, J., & Slater, S. (1990). The effects of a market orientation on business profitability. *Journal of Marketing, 54*(October), 20–25.

Oliver, R. L. (1977). *Satisfaction: A behavioral perspective on the consumer*. New York: McGraw-Hill.

Oliver, R. L. (1999). Value as excellence in the consumption experience. In M. B. Holbrook (Ed.), *Consumer value* (pp. 43–62). London: Routledge.

Park, C. W., & Smith, D. C. (1989). Product-level choice: A top-down or bottom-up process? *Journal of Consumer Research, 16*, 289–300.

Pieters, R., Baumgartner, H., & Allen, D. (1995). A means-end chain approach to consumer goal structures. *International Journal of Research in Marketing, 12*, 227–244.

Ravald, A., & Gronroos, C. (1996). The value concept and relationship marketing. *European Journal of Marketing, 30*.

Rayport, J. F., & Jaworski, B. J. (2001). *E-commerce*. New York: McGraw Hill/ Irwin.

Richardson, J., Ormerod, T. C., & Shepherd, A. (1998). The role of task analysis in capturing requirements for the interface design. *Interacting with Computers, 9*, 367–384.

Saeed, K. A., Hwang, Y., & Grover, V. (2003). Investigating the impact of website value and advertising on firm performance in electronic commerce. *International Journal of Electronic Commerce, 7*(2), 119–141.

Seybold, P. B. (1988). *Customers.com: How to create a profitable business strategy for the Internet and beyond.* New York: Times Business.

Tapscott, D., Ticoll, D., & Lowy, A. (2000). *Digital capital: Harnessing the power of business webs*. Boston: Harvard Business School Press.

Van Duyne, D. K., Landay, J. A., & Long, J. I. (2003). *The design of sites: Patterns, principles, and processes for crafting a customer-centered web experience.* Boston: Addison-Wesley.

Vandermerwe, S. (2000). How increasing value to customers improves business results. *Sloan Management Review, 42*(Fall), 27–37.

Wolfinbarger, M., & Gilly, M. C. (2001). Shopping online for freedom, control and fun. *California Management Review, 43*(2), 34–55.

Woodruff, R. B. (1997). Customer value: The next source for competitive advantage. *Journal of the Academy of Marketing Science, 25*(2), 139–153.

Woodruff, R. B., & Gardial, S. F. (1996). *Know your customer: New approaches to understanding customer value and satisfaction.* Malden, MA: Blackwell.

Zeithaml, V. A. (1988). Consumer perceptions of price, quality, and value: A means-end model and synthesis of evidence. *Journal of Marketing, 52*(July), 2–22.

Zott, C., Amitb, R., & Donlevya, J. (2000). Strategies for value creation in e-commerce: Best practice in Europe. *European Management Journal, 18*, 463–475.

Chapter V

A Synthesis and Analysis of Behavioral and Policy Issues in Electronic Marketing Communications

Merrill Warkentin, Mississippi State University, USA

Robert S. Moore, Mississippi State University, USA

Melissa Moore, Mississippi State University, USA

Abstract

Marketers now use numerous electronic communication vehicles in which the collection and use of personal information can influence the development of relationships between firms and individual consumers. However, the level of acceptance of the collection and use of personal information varies among consumers, and many consumers are unaware of the details of this process. This chapter provides an interdisciplinary synthesis of recent research concerning emerging electronic marketing communications. An overview of relationship marketing is followed by an exploration of how different levels of marketing information acquisition and integration impact consumer perceptions and behaviors. Then a discussion of recent legal and policy issues related to online privacy is followed by implications of electronic marketing communications and online privacy concerns on perceptions and subsequent customer relationships.

Introduction

Within the span of only a few years, marketers have witnessed an explosion in the number of available electronic communication vehicles. These new media channels include the firm's Web site, directed online advertisements placed on Web pages, commercially oriented e-mails, text messaging, and direct communication to mobile devices (i.e., smart phones and personal digital assistants [PDAs]). In each of these communication medium, the collection and use of personal information can influence the development of relationships between firms and individual consumers. Firms that seek to differentiate themselves from the competition and better target their messages must collect and use personal information.

However, a consumer's level of acceptance of the collection and use of information falls along what has been called an intrusion continuum (Petty, 2003), with some individuals advocating a right to privacy and are strongly opposed to any information collection processes while others appreciate that personal information use is a prerequisite for improved service and value. Firms tend toward the latter perspective and consider consumer information as a resource to be used not only internally but also to be shared with third parties. Internal use allows integration of seemingly disparate customer information into meaningful user profiles, which are used to develop highly personalized communications. Businesses collect information with consumers knowingly providing the information (i.e., through filling out online forms) or unknowingly (i.e., online behavior tracking, use of store loyalty cards) providing information to businesses. Yet individuals are often unaware of how the information is to be used, how accurate the information is, and who will have access to the information.

In this chapter, we provide an interdisciplinary synthesis of recent research concerning emerging electronic marketing communications (i.e., Internet and mobile device enabled). First, we present an overview of relationship marketing, emphasizing how trust, a key antecedent of successful relationships, is influenced by marketing communications. Next, we explore how different levels of information acquisition and integration used in electronic marketing communications impact consumer perceptions and behaviors. Third, we provide a discussion of recent legal and policy issues related to online privacy. Last, we provide an analysis of the extant literature and suggest implications of electronic marketing communications and online privacy concerns on perceptions and subsequent customer relationships.

Background on Relationship Marketing

Over the past 20 years, researchers in the field of marketing have adopted a relationship-based philosophy toward marketplace interactions. Firms have moved from generic mass-marketing communications toward highly individualized targeted communications. Figure 1 provides a general illustration of marketing communications' effect in the relationship marketing process. The ultimate purpose of targeted communications is the formation of relationship commitment (loyalty) from customers. As individuals become committed to a firm, they are more likely to stay with the firm, speak positively to others about the firm, and disclose further information about their likes and dislikes to the firm, leading to even more targeted communications.

Trust is generally accepted to be essential in the development of successful relationships (Garbarino & Johnson, 1999; Morgan & Hunt, 1994). With electronic communications overall, developing trust is seen as an important step in the relationship-building process (Lee & Turban, 2001). Trust leads an individual to believe that the company will "perform actions that will result in positive outcomes ... as well as not take unexpected actions that result in negative outcomes" (Anderson & Narus, 1990, p. 45). In marketplace interactions, trust is necessary before one is willing to share personal information. However, in the case of the Internet, because it is a relatively new means for engaging in

Figure 1. Marketing communications' role in building relationships

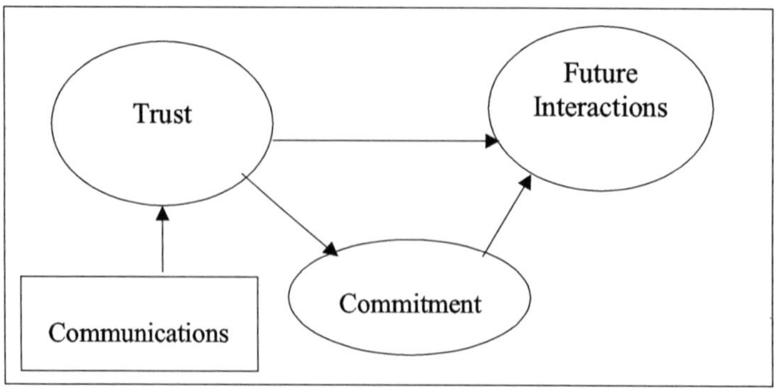

commercial and communication activity, uncertainty and risk are often noted as reasons for an individual's reluctance to provide information (Suh & Han, 2003).

Role of Communication in Relationship Marketing

Communication is a necessary and important antecedent of trust in relationship marketing (Morgan & Hunt, 1994). The role of communication in developing trust is through information exchanges between the partners (Anderson & Narus, 1990). Generally speaking, marketing communications in the electronic environment are viewed as any action that results in electronically based information being shared between an individual and a firm. Therefore, electronic communication is more than just firm-created communications and encompasses individual actions with the electronic communication vehicle such as visiting a firm's Web site, sending a firm e-mail, receiving opt-in newsletters, filling out forms, engaging in text messaging with service personnel, tracking a package, or responding to a short messaging service (SMS) offer. Such a broad definition allows any electronically enabled interaction between the firm and an individual to be viewed as a communication act.

Information Integration and Marketing Communications

The integration of information is a powerful tool for enhancing customer relationships through the development of personalized marketing communications and customized offers (Peltier, Schibrowsky, Schultz, & Davis, 2002).

Figure 2. Information used to create personalized marketing communications

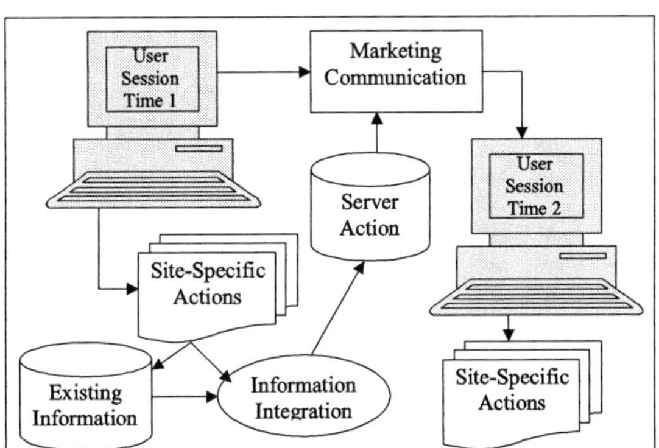

Information integration is a technology-based approach that assimilates relevant data from internal and external sources to develop a valuable application for the firm (Jhingran, Mattos, & Pirahesh, 2002). Figure 2 illustrates the information integration process. For example, as an Internet user begins his/her session, information is collected based on current actions and previously stored information. This information is then integrated to offer a targeted marketing communication to the user. The user's response is collected to be used to calibrate and modify future communications (Gatarski, 2002; Sherman & Deighton, 2001). Each of these components is briefly described.

- *Existing Information:* Existing information encompasses any information that has been collected previously about or from a particular user. An individual firm may possess or have access to data not only on a user's purchasing history, demographics, or financial status, but it may also have access to data about the user's previous usage patterns on the Internet (Bhat, Bevans, & Sengupta, 2002), as well as communications that the user may have had either directly with the company through telephone conversations, e-mails, online comments (Romano, Donovan, Chen, & Nunamaker, 2003), responses to previous wireless communication, or from contracted secondary sources.
- *Site-Specific Information:* Beyond the obvious collection of information related to a specific purchase (e.g., name, address, payment method, and items purchased), Web sites and partnered third parties utilize technological tools to obtain real-time information about a user. The use of client- and server-side technologies allows the specific actions in a current Internet session to be tracked and recorded.

The most prevalent client-side technology, which resides on the user's computer, is the cookie. Cookies are small text files that are capable of tracking and recording information such as the specific visited Web page URLs and information provided to such Web sites. Server-side technologies are under the control of a Web site's owner. Log files keep track of items such as which Web pages are called and how long a page is kept open. Web bugs combine the capabilities of server log files and cookies by tracking users across participating Web sites. Web bugs are especially interesting because they not only track behavior on a single Web site but can also be used to analyze behaviors across different Web sites over time.

- *Information Integration:* The ability to efficiently and systematically combine information from many sources is no small task (Somani, Choy, &

Kleewein, 2002). The amount of potential information available about an individual user is staggering. However, the ability of firms to integrate and extract situation-specific data and apply them in a targeted marketing communication is a valuable asset which, if used effectively, can provide the firm with a strategic competitive advantage (Roth, Wolfson, Kleewein, & Nelin, 2002).

- *Server Actions:* In terms of Internet marketing communications, the information integration process utilizes information resources to have the server react differently for each customer. The degree to which the server reacts differently is driven by the amount of information integration used to form a profile (Wiedmann, Buxel, & Walsh, 2002).

Peltier, Schibrowsky, Schultz, and Davis (2002) suggest that to effectively segment customers into prospects requires integrating informational elements beyond just demographic data into a profile. They note that psychographic information (information such as values, motivations, beliefs, attitudes, and lifestyles) can be used in the creation of profiles for specific relational segments of customers. For each profiled segment, cross-selling opportunities and marketing communications can be developed to match the purchasing needs of that segment. This type of integration was implemented by a financial services firm to determine current customers' probability of purchasing supplemental services by combining their transaction history with competitors' products and service information (Kamakura, Weddel, de Rosa, & Mazzon, 2003).

- *Marketing Communications:* The use of technology to integrate individual information for marketing purposes has been generally available to marketers since the early 1990s (Blattberg & Deighton, 1991). Firms at that time were using proprietary customer data as the basis for determining new product sales based on previous purchasing patterns.

Today, most electronic marketing communication efforts of firms are matched with some aspect of the individual (Raghu, Kannan, Rao, & Whinston, 2001). These efforts include both asynchronous and synchronous communication formats. Asynchronous formats are exemplified by brand-building Web sites (i.e., Sony.com, Disney.com, or Kelloggs.com) in which the visitor interacts with the brand itself (McAllister & Turrow, 2002), online advertisements (i.e., banners, popups, or interstitials), which are ads placed on content sites (Zhou & Bao, 2002), and commercially oriented e-mails, which may be requested by recipients (Krishnamurthy, 2001a) or unsolicited "spam." Most recently, synchronous formats of communication have emerged, such as wireless communication technologies which include instant messaging (IM) also known as text messaging, and communication to mobile devices, such as smart phones and PDAs. Integration technologies are viewed as essential tools to assist in the development of targeted communications. The communications themselves, personalized and customized based on personal information represent an important building block in the firm–consumer relationship. However, the degree in which these communications are accepted by users and contribute to a relationship depends on whether the individual has given the marketer permission to use information (Godin, 1999; Krishnamurthy, 2001b).

Permission marketing refers to a marketing communication technique that suggests users will be more accepting of a message if they agreed to receive it (Godin, 1999). Krishnamurthy (2001b) built on this premise and coined the term *permission intensity*—a combination of a user's willingness to receive a message and the leeway he/she allows the marketer to use personal information.

Recent Legal and Policy Issues Concerning Online Privacy

The preceding discussion concerning relationship marketing, trust, and marketing communications clearly illustrate that firms need personal information. However, a very real problem with using technology to create personalized communications is that individuals may not necessarily want their personal information collected or used. Consider the following events:

- April 1991 – Lotus Development Corporation withdraws its *MarketPlace: Households* software program from the market after widespread public concern. The $695 product had a searchable database of 120 million Americans, containing their names, addresses, estimated incomes, consumer preferences, and other personal details (Culnan, 1993).
- April 2000 – The Federal Trade Commission (FTC) places the Children's Online Privacy Protection Act (COPPA) of 1998 into full effect. The Act contains specific guidelines on data collection and use concerning children under the age of 13.
- May 2000 – Toysmart.com, facing bankruptcy, attempts to sell off its database of customer information as an asset even though its privacy policy explicitly stated that information would not be shared with third parties (Eisenbach, 2001).

- May 2000 – The FTC recommends that Congress take action to create legislation for all commercially oriented Web sites to comply with "the fair information practice principles—consisting of notice, choice, access and security" on the collection and usage of personal information (FTC, 2000).
- January 2002 – Eli Lily and Company settles with the FTC after an e-mail containing the e-mail addresses of all 669 subscribers to its Prozac medication reminder service was sent to the entire list inadvertently in the "To:" field (FTC, 2002).
- August 2002 – DoubleClick Inc., the nation's leading Internet advertising service settles with 10 states for $450,000 over its privacy practices of tracking online behavior through cookies and Web bugs (Culberg & Reilly, 2002).
- February 2003 – The largest fine ever assessed by the FTC was on Mrs. Fields Cookies and Hershey Foods Corporation ($185,000) for collecting personal information from children without parental consent in violation of COPPA (FTC, 2003).
- July 2003 – Google search engine feature provides personal information (such as name, address, and maps to address) to any publicly listed telephone number (Saranow, 2003).

As the above anecdotes reveal, the clash between personal information and business use of technology is not new. What *is* new is that technological improvements have made it much easier and cheaper for virtually any firm to collect or acquire personal information (Rust, Kannan, & Peng, 2002). For many consumers, there is a constant trade-off between personalization, the value which it provides, and personal privacy (Foxman & Kilcoyne, 1993).

Privacy is the extent to which personal information is not known by others (Rust et al., 2002) and the amount of control that is kept by the individual over how the information is used (Foxman & Kilcoyne, 1993). However, most Americans do not know what information is collected about them, how it is used, or how it is transferred between parties (Milne & Rohm, 2000; Turow, 2003).

A key influencer of why an individual is willing to give information is the reputation of the firm (Andrade, Kalcheva, & Weitz, 2002). The more reputable a firm is perceived to be, the less concern an individual has over the collection of personal information. Additionally, the more complete a firm's privacy policy, the less concern an individual has over information collection and use (Culnan, 2000; Milne & Culnan, 2002; Miyazaki & Fernandez, 2000). Unfortunately, the content of privacy policies of even the most popular Web sites are difficult to comprehend, which may affect the policy's usefulness (Graber, D'Alessandro, & Johnson-West, 2002; Milne & Culnan, 2002).

A potential means of increasing consumer trust in a firm's privacy standards is through the use of seals of approval. Seals of approval from trusted third parties may lead to increased trust in an Internet firm's operation (Miyazaki & Krishnamurthy, 2002); however, users must be aware of the legitimacy of the seal. Internet-based seals of approval are not well known by users and one study found that even if they are aware of the seal's legitimacy, less than half reported that the seal affects their purchasing decisions (Head & Hassanein, 2002). However, seals of approval do have varying levels of importance in different stages of the purchasing cycle. In particular, seals of approval were most beneficial in the establishment of a relationship with a firm and third party seals have been shown to reduce concerns to disclose personal information, especially for those that view Internet purchases as risky (Miyazaki & Krishnamurthy, 2002). Therefore, there appears to be a limited role in using third-party seals to allay an individual's privacy concerns.

Others feel that most privacy tools are consumer controlled such as a consumer's willingness to accept cookies or to read policy statements (Turner & Dasgupta, 2003). A specific mechanism that could potentially improve user trust is the widespread adoption of the World Wide Web consortium's Platform for Privacy Preferences (P3P). P3P allows a user's stated privacy preferences to be compared with a Web site's information collection practices. When the firm wants more information than the individual has stated as preferences, the user would be notified (Powell, 2002).

Conclusion

The preceding sections have synthesized recent literature concerning the integration of electronic communications in the development of customer–firm relationships. We have discussed the importance of marketing communications for firms as they attempt to build trust and acquire long-term (repeat) customers. Firms want positive relationships with customers since these customers are likely to speak positively about the firm, purchase again from the firm, and trust the firm enough to share valuable personal information.

On the individual level, our discussion of the privacy literature notes that an individual's level of concern for privacy is likely to influence his/her acceptance of personalized and highly targeted communications. Additionally, the level of privacy intrusion that is unacceptable is likely to be more pronounced with the sharing of traditionally sensitive personal information, such as medical or financial information, than it may be with less sensitive areas such as purchasing patterns and electronic behavior. However, with the availability of seamless, real-time information integration, most individuals do not know how, who, or when their personal information is being shared between parties or is being used to create marketing communications. As consumers learn that their personal information is being collected without their knowledge and is being used in the development of electronic communications, especially when the communication uses personal information and is intrusive, there is potential for a backlash against the message sponsor and even against the technology itself.

The 21st century is likely to witness new and unforeseen convergences of electronic devices. For example, the physical locations of technology to track and record information is moving away from the firm and toward the individual as illustrated by the U.S. Food and Drug Administration's (FDA's) approval in October 2004 of an implantable chip that could contain an individual's medical history. The use of radio frequency identification (RFID) chips to track the movement of individual products is yet another example of this shift. Convergences and applications such as these may require individuals, businesses, and governments to take proactive positions on acceptable circumstances for personal information use and perhaps even on the question of who owns personal information.

References

Anderson, J. C., & Narus, J. A. (1990). A model of distributor firm and manufacturer firm and manufacturer firm working partnerships. *Journal of Marketing*, *54*(1), 42–58.

Andrade, E. B., Kaltcheva, V., & Weitz, B. (2002). Self-disclosure on the Web: The impact of privacy policy, reward, and company reputation. *Advances in Consumer Research*, *29*(1), 350–353.

Bhat, S., Bevans, M., & Sengupta, S. (2002). Measuring users' Web activity to evaluate and enhance advertising effectiveness. *Journal of Advertising*, *31*(Fall), 97–106.

Blattberg, R. C., & Deighton, J. (1991). Interactive marketing: Exploiting the age of addressability. *Sloan Management Review*, *33*(1), 5–14.

Culberg, K., & Reilly, B. (2002). DoubleClick settles: Implements greater transparency procedures in data collection, agrees to pay settlement of $450,000. *Journal of Internet Law*, *6*(3), 25–26.

Culnan, M. J. (1993). H*ow did they get my name? An exploratory investigation of consumer attitudes toward secondary information use. MIS Quarterly*, *17*(3), 341–363.

Culnan, M. J. (2000). Protecting privacy online: Is self-regulation working? *Journal of Public Policy & Marketing*, *19*(Spring), 20–27.

Eisenbach III, R. L. (2001). The Internet company's customer list: Asset or liability? *Computer & Internet Lawyer*, *18*(8), 25–31.

Federal Trade Commission (FTC). (2000). Privacy online: Fair information practices in the electronic marketplace. Retrieved November 4, 2003, from *www.ftc.gov/reports/index.htm#2000*

Federal Trade Commission (FTC). (2001). Eli Lilly settles FTC charges concerning security breach. Retrieved November 4, 2003, from *www.ftc.gov/opa/2002/01/elililly.htm*

Federal Trade Commission (FTC). (2003). FTC receives largest COPPA civil penalties to date in settlements with Mrs. Fields Cookies and Hershey Foods. Retrieved November 4, 2003, from *www.ftc.gov/opa/2003/02/hersheyfield.htm*

Foxman, E. R., & Kilcoyne, P. (1993). Information technology, marketing practice and consumer privacy: Ethical issues. *Journal of Public Policy & Marketing*, *12*(Spring), 106–119.

Garbarino, E., & Johnson, M. S. (1999). The different roles of satisfaction, trust, and commitment in customer relationships. *Journal of Marketing*, *63*(2), 70–87.

Gatarski, R. (2002). Breed better banners: Design automation through on-line interaction. *Journal of Interactive Marketing*, *16*(Winter), 2–14.

Godin, S. (1999). Permission marketing: The way to make advertising work again. *Direct Marketing*, *62*(2), 60–63.

Graber, M. A., D'Alessandro, D. M., & Johnson-West, J. (2002). Reading level of privacy policies on internet health web sites. *Journal of Family Practice*, *51*(July), 642–645.

Head, M. M., & Hassanein, K. (2002). Trust in E-commerce. *Quarterly Journal of Electronic Commerce*, *3*(3), 307–325.

Jhingran, A. D., Mattos, N., & Pirahesh, H. (2002). Information integration: A research agenda. *IBM Systems Journal*, *41*(4), 555–562.

Kamakura, W. A., Wedel, M., de Rosa, F., & Mazzon, J. A. (2003). Cross-selling through database marketing: A mixed data factor analyzer for data augmentation and prediction. *International Journal of Research in Marketing*, *20*(1), 45–65.

Krishnamurthy, S. (2001a). An empirical study of the causal antecedents of customer confidence in e-tailers. *First Monday*, *6*(January). Retrieved November 4, 2003, from *http://firstmonday.org/issues/issue6_1/krishnamurthy/index.html*

Krishnamurthy, S. (2001b). A comprehensive analysis of permission marketing. *Journal of Computer-Mediated Communication*, *6*(2). Retrieved from *www.ascusc.org/jcmc/vol6/issue2/krishnamurthy.html*

Lee, M. K. O., & Turban, E. (2001). A trust model for consumer internet shopping. *International Journal of Electronic Commerce*, *6*(1), 75–91.

McAllister, M. P., & Turow, J. (2002). New media and the commercial sphere: Two intersecting trends, five categories of concern. *Journal of Broadcasting & Electronic Media*, *46*(4), 505–514.

Milne, G. R., & Culnan, M. J. (2002). Using the content of online privacy notices to inform public policy: A longitudinal analysis of the 1998–2001 U.S. Web surveys. *Information Society*, *18*(October), 345–360.

Milne, G. R., & Rohm, A. J. (2000). Consumer privacy and name removal across direct marketing channels: Exploring opt-in and opt-out alternatives. *Journal of Public Policy & Marketing*, *19*(Fall), 238–250.

Miyazaki, A. D., & Fernandez, A. (2000). Internet privacy and security: An examination of online retailer disclosures. *Journal of Public Policy & Marketing*, *19*(Spring), 54–61.

Miyazaki, A. D., & Krishnamurthy, S. (2002). Internet seals of approval: Effects on Online privacy policies and consumer perceptions. *Journal of Consumer Affairs*, *36*(Summer), 28–49.

Morgan, R. M., & Hunt, S. D. (1994). The commitment-trust theory of relationship marketing. *Journal of Marketing*, *58*(3), 20–38.

Peltier, J. W., Schibrowsky, J. A., Schultz, D., & Davis, J. (2002). Interactive psychographics: Cross-selling in the banking industry. *Journal of Advertising Research*, *42*(2), 7–22.

Petty, R. D. (2000). Marketing without consent: Consumer choice and costs, privacy, and public policy. *Journal of Public Policy & Marketing*, *19*(Spring), 42–53.

Powell, T. (2002). P3P plan. *Network World*, *19*(39), 41–42.

Raghu, T. S., Kannan, P. K., Rao, H. R., & Whinston, A. B. (2001). Dynamic profiling of consumers for customized offerings over the Internet: A model and analysis. *Decision Support Systems*, *32*(2), 117–133.

Romano Jr., N. C., Donovan, C., Chen, H., & Nunamaker Jr., J. F. (2003). A methodology for analyzing Web-based qualitative data. *Journal of Management Information Systems*, *19*(4), 213–246.

Roth, M. A., Wolfson, D. C., Kleewein, J. C., & Nelin, C. J. (2002). Information integration: A new generation of information technology. *IBM Systems Journal, 41*(4), 563–577.

Rust, R. T., Kannan, P. K., & Peng, N. (2002). The customer economics of Internet privacy. *Journal of the Academy of Marketing Science, 30*(Fall), 455–464.

Saranow, J. (2003, July 29). More privacy on the Web. *Wall Street Journal–Eastern Edition*, p. D1.

Sherman, L., & Deighton, J. (2001). Banner advertising: Measuring effectiveness and optimizing placement. *Journal of Interactive Marketing, 15*(Spring), 60–65.

Somani, A., Choy, D., and Kleewein, J. C. (2002). Bringing together content and data management systems: Challenges and opportunities. *IBM Systems Journal, 41*(4), 686–696.

Suh, B., & Han, I. (2003). The impact of customer trust and perception of security control on the acceptance of Electronic commerce. *International Journal of Electronic Commerce, 7*(Spring), 135–161.

Turner, E. C., & Dasgupta, S. (2003). Privacy on the Web: An examination of user concerns, technology, and implications for business organizations and individuals. *Information Systems Management, 20*(Winter), 8–18.

Turow, J. (2003). Americans and online privacy: The system is broken. Annenburg Public Policy Center at the University of Pennsylvania. Retrieved November 4, 2003, from *www.appcpenn.org*

Wiedmann, K., Buxel, H., & Walsh, G. (2002). Customer profiling in e-commerce: Methodological aspects and challenges. *Journal of Database Marketing, 9*(2), 170–184.

Zhou, Z., & Bao, Y. (2002). Users' attitudes toward Web advertising: Effects of Internet motivation and Internet ability. *Advances in Consumer Research, 29*(1), 71–78.

Chapter VI

Providing Value to Customers in E-Commerce Environments: The Customer's Perspective

Shailey Minocha, The Open University, UK

Liisa H. Dawson, The Open University, UK

Ann Blandford, University College London Interaction Centre, UK

Nicola Millard, British Telecommunications PLC, UK

Abstract

Effective advertising, good usability, and creating value are important in an e-commerce environment to attract and retain customers. In the human–computer interaction (HCI) literature, research into the success or failure of business to consumer (B2C) e-commerce sites has primarily focussed on usability. While increasing usability is important, even if an e-commerce Web site conforms to the Web design heuristics and usability guidelines, it might not always generate a positive total customer experience (TCE). Therefore, it is important that along with usability heuristics, customer relationship management (CRM) strategies are integrated into the design of the e-commerce environments for developing robust and long-term online customer–organisation relationships. We report on a project that is part of an ongoing cross-disciplinary research programme at the Open University, United Kingdom, which aims to integrate HCI and CRM strategies into the design and evaluation of e-commerce environments. In this project, we examined the customer's interaction with e-commerce environments and how a B2C relationship can be effectively supported from a customer's perspective. Based on intensive research that involved collecting data from naturalistic observations of customers shopping on e-tailing environments, interviews, group interviews, and by identifying the negative incidents or obstacles that mar the customer's TCE, we have developed E-SEQUAL (E-SErvice QUALity), a framework for online service quality. E-SEQUAL is an evaluation instrument consisting of e-CRM (CRM for e-economy) or customer relationship-enhancing heuristics and HCI heuristics which can be applied to integrate customers' perceived dimensions of service quality into the design and development of e-commerce environments. E-SEQUAL can provide guidance to e-businesses regarding integration of front- and back-end business processes, and across different customer touch points such as phone, fax, e-mail, and so on. It can be applied by Web designers, marketing professionals, and developers to come up with requirements for integrating customers' expectations, and perceptions of service quality and value into the design of e-commerce Web sites. Furthermore, it can be used as an evaluation instrument by usability professionals for evaluating the conformance of an e-commerce environment against HCI (usability) and e-CRM heuristics.

Introduction

Online retail will grow from $95.7 million in 2003 to $229.9 billion in 2008, according to a report from Forrester Research (Forrester, 2003). More significantly, online retail sales are expected to account for 10% of total U.S. retail sales by 2008. In the United Kingdom, online sales already make up 4% of the total retail sales. Despite the growth in online retail sales, statistics show that 67% of transactions on the Web are never completed (Cohen, 1999). Only 36% of customers are satisfied by electronic transactions and this bad experience tends to drive customers to other channels (Chatham, 2002). Of the transactions that are not completed, 53% of abandoned transactions require a phone call to the customer services or an off-line action. Consequently, call centre costs increase due to call volumes rising—with a reported rate of increase in volume of up to 65% as Internet use increases (Millard, 2001).

Evidently, while there are growing numbers of e-customers, such statistics suggest customers' dissatisfaction with e-commerce. Customers are not being supported in the completion of their transactions, and the defection rates are consequently high. With increasing competition in the e-marketplace and with a choice of off-line business channels (e.g., physical stores and mail order), it is difficult for e-businesses to first attract and then retain customers.

Customer retention and loyalty affect profit and growth to a significant extent. Depending on the industry, increasing the percentage of loyal customers by as little as 5% can increase the profitability by 30% or even 85% (Reichheld & Sasser, 1990)—a ratio estimated to be even higher on the Web than through traditional retail channels (Reichheld & Schefter, 2000). This reflects an important challenge to e-commerce to shift the focus from *customer acquisition* to *customer retention.*

To retain customers, it is necessary to ensure that the customer perceives value from the experience with an e-business (Weinstein & Johnson, 1999). *Value* from a customer perspective may be defined in terms of satisfaction with, and perceived quality of, the service received in the course of the e-commerce experience. A positive perception of value (when customers' experiences meet or exceed their expectations) will exhibit great influence in persuading a customer to return to the site. Therefore, generating a positive customer experience, and then continuously providing one, is important for (B2C) e-businesses to attract and retain customers (Seybold, 2001).

In the HCI literature (e.g., Spool, Scanlon, Schroeder, Synder, & De Angelo, 1999; Nielsen, Molich, Snyder, & Farrell, 2001; Vividence, 2002), research into the success or failure of E-Commerce environments has primarily focused on the usability of the core Web site. Central to this has been how design criteria or heuristics such as ease of navigation and optimal response time can be managed to create usable customer-focused e-commerce sites. However, it is evident from the relationship marketing literature (e.g., Payne, Christopher, Clark, & Peck, 1995) and the CRM literature (e.g., Dyche, 2002) that such a unidimensional focus on Web design features and usability of an e-commerce site ignores the broader service delivery system within which the virtual customer–organisation interaction occurs.

CRM or *relationship marketing* is a set of business strategies designed to add value to customer interactions by providing service quality that exceeds the customers' expectations (Minocha, 2000b). *Service quality* is the customer's subjective assessment of the service he/she is receiving compared to the service he/she expects (Gefen, 2002). The essence of service quality is, therefore, the ability to deliver what the customer needs and expects. If the service quality of the customer's experiences with an e-business exceeds his/her expectations, he/she would be willing to come back and conduct further business with the vendor.

Conversely, customers who experience low service quality will be more inclined to move to other vendors because they are not getting what they expect.

The relationship marketing literature suggests that a customer assesses the service quality at every point in which he/she may interact with a business (each different point is called a *touch point*). In addition to the Web site of the e-business, a customer may interact with an e-business across other touch points for tasks not fully supported by the Web site. For example, a customer may call up the support hot line, or send an e-mail to inquire about a delayed order, or receive an e-mail about a special offer or promotion, or receive an e-mail confirming an order. It is, therefore, limiting to consider e-commerce purely in terms of its Web site, as this only represents one touch point of the e-business.

In this paper we have employed the term *e-commerce environment* to imply not only the front-end of the e-commerce, which is the Web site, but also the back-office systems such as credit card handling, delivery of products/services, pre- and post-sales support, and customer services. A customer's interaction with an e-commerce environment therefore extends beyond the transaction on the Web site, and can occur via other touch points such as e-mail, phone, or fax.

In the cross-disciplinary research presented here, we have been examining the integration of CRM and HCI strategies into the design and usability of e-commerce environments so as to engender customer retention, trust, and loyalty. We have performed a study to understand customers' requirements and perceptions about service quality from e-tailing (retail) environments. From this, we have developed a framework called E-SEQUAL (E-SErvice QUALity). E-SEQUAL consists of HCI and e-CRM (CRM for e-economy) or customer-relationship enhancing heuristics which can be applied to integrate customers' perceived dimensions of service quality in the design and usability evaluations of e-commerce environments.

In this paper we first outline the terminology and research concepts related to the customer's interaction with e-commerce. This is followed by a description of the techniques that we applied to capture genuine customer experiences of interacting with e-commerce, and then we discuss how this study led to the development of E-SEQUAL. Finally, we present a comparison of E-SEQUAL with a range of other service quality frameworks for (B2C) e-commerce from the HCI and marketing literature.

Terminology and Research Concepts

Figure 1 illustrates the different stages of a customer's purchasing behaviour within an e-commerce environment. Stage 1 is *expectations setting*. During this stage the customer draws upon a number of social, organizational, and individual influences from which he/she will create a personal benchmark of service quality expectations. These influences include his/her motivations, his/her needs along with the benefits and costs of using e-commerce, recommendations, word of mouth, advertising, brand, his/her own experiences of interacting with off-line business channels of that and other organisations, and so on. These influences play a vital role in his/her decision about which Web site to visit and whether to make a purchase on that site.

The next three stages (2–4 in Figure 1) of a customer's interaction with an e-commerce environment constitute a *service encounter* (Gabbott & Hogg, 1998; Dawson, Minocha, & Petre, 2003a): a prepurchase stage; an e-purchase stage; and finally a postpurchase stage. During the prepurchase stage, the customer chooses a Web site, searches for a product or service and makes a decision about whether to make a purchase. This decision is based on the usability of the home page and other Web pages of this site, information provided about the product or service, the price, the credibility of the Web site, the delivery mechanisms and refunds policy, and so forth. During the e-purchase stage, the customer selects the product or service and completes the transaction; a bricks-and-mortar store analogy of this would be putting the product into the shopping cart and moving to the checkout in order to pay for the item. In online environments, this usually involves entering personal details, billing and delivery information, and credit card details. Finally, the postpurchase stage involves tracking the order and

Figure 1. The purchase and consumption cycle with an e-commerce environment

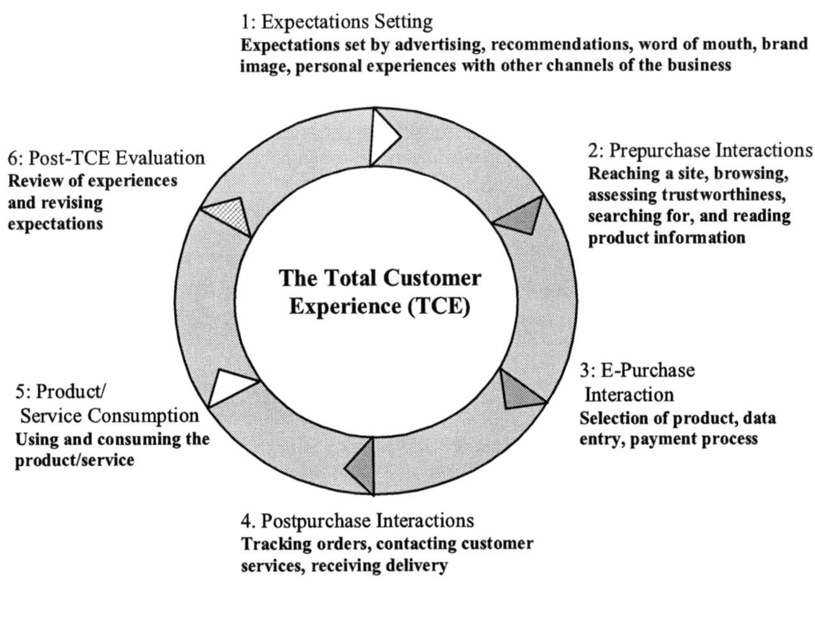

receiving the delivery of products/services. During this stage of the service encounter the customer may need to query an order, complain about the state of the delivery, or question his/her credit card handling, and he/she is likely to contact the organisation at touch points other than the Web site. If the customer is also the consumer, he/she will consume the products/services (stage 5). We have referred to the customer's holistic experience over stages 1–5 as the *total customer experience* (TCE).

Finally, the customer will review his/her experiences of conducting business with the e-commerce environment (stage 6). During this stage, the customer compares the overall experience with the benchmark of expectations set during stage 1, and assesses whether he/she has received value from his/her experience. Unpleasant or unsatisfactory experiences across any of these stages and/or during the consumption stage may render a negative TCE, despite the e-commerce Web site being usable. If the evaluation of the TCE during stage 6 results in the customer perceiving that he/she has not received value, it is unlikely that the customer will return to the site for future business.

Investigating the Service Encounter

The aim of the research which led to E-SEQUAL was to capture the customer's expectations of desired service quality. During our study we focused on those situations in which the expectations of service quality across the service encounter (stages 2–4 in Figure 1) were not met. We elicited customers' perceptions for those negative incidents and this led to our understanding of customers' service quality expectations. These negative incidents or *obstacles* were seen to mar a customer's TCE.

We define *obstacles* as those aspects of an e-commerce environment which made it unpleasant, onerous, inefficient, or impossible for the customer to achieve a positive TCE. These are situations when customer's experiences with an e-commerce environment fall below his/her expectations. Obstacles could be as follows:

- Usability problems with the site such as use of ambiguous terminology, or use of flashy features that look good but only work for those customers with high-speed Internet access.
- Situations that could adversely influence, or even erode, the customer–organisation relationship. Examples of such obstacles are hidden costs, such as shipping costs, taxes or tariffs, return information being unclear or not easily accessible, or pop-up surveys that appear at inopportune moments.

Obstacles can often cause breakdowns in the customer–organisation relationship. A *breakdown* is a "deal breaker," for example, when the customer abandons shopping on a site and moves to a competitor's site, or when the customer may not want to return for a repeat purchase or visit. Examples of breakdowns and obstacles that cause them are presented below.

- A break in the smooth course of a customer's interaction with the front-end of the e-commerce environment, that is, with the Web site. Here, the obstacles are the usability problems with the site such as animations or images that cause computers to crash, or a customer not being able to find a product/service because of ineffective search mechanisms, or a mismatch of cultural requirements and expectations.
- A break in the customer's interactions with other aspects of the e-commerce environment such as during presales support, with the security in credit card handling, or the delivery of products/services. Examples of obstacles causing such breakdowns include asking a customer to register before the customer has decided to shop on the Web site, automatic newsletter registration after a purchase from which it is difficult to unsubscribe, or unsupportive customer services.

However, not all obstacles cause breakdowns. Even spelling errors on the Web site or in an e-mail, a discourteous or not-so-helpful reply to a query, or not receiving a prompt response to an e-mail from the customer services can become obstacles in the customer–organisation relationship.

Each obstacle identified in our study was documented on an obstacle card (described in the next section) and analysed in its context including the stage of the service encounter in which it occurred, a consequence of the obstacle—whether a breakdown occurred—and the customer's response to the situation which arose as a result of the obstacle. In addition, we suggested requirements and design solutions that could resolve the obstacle. We have termed the description of an occurrence of an obstacle and its context as a *sociological account* (Minocha, Dawson, Blandford, & Roberts, 2003b).

Through an understanding of obstacles, our aim was to propose e-CRM and HCI heuristics for the design and usability of e-commerce environments that would prevent such obstacles from occurring, and hence generate a positive TCE.

Exploring Obstacles to the TCE

The study that we conducted focussed on understanding the customer's experience across the service encounter (stages 2–4 in Figure 1), but data about stages 1, 5, and 6 also emerged, providing us with an understanding of the customer's TCE. Since one technique may not be able to capture genuine customer experiences across all these stages, we employed a range of complementary techniques to evaluate the TCE.

During the *first phase* of a *three-phase study,* we conducted naturalistic observations of 12 users carrying out genuine self-motivated tasks with e-tailing sites, which we had been invited to observe. Eight out of the 12 users were female and four were male. Ten out of the 12 users were academics; one was a project engineer and one was a sales representative in the manufacturing industry. The group was culturally diverse including six nationalities and four nonnative English speakers. However, all of the participants had been living in the United Kingdom for 5 years or more. All were already Internet and e-commerce users. Whilst we recognised that the group may not be representative of the broadest, multicultural e-commerce user population, the aim of this study was to identify factors that prevented a positive TCE, and for this initial demonstration, it was sufficient to have a group selected on a pragmatic basis. Future work will attempt to identify appropriate demographic variables for group selection and to extend the work reported here.

The users were volunteers who were planning to carry out some form of business with e-commerce. Therefore the tasks that they carried out were completely dictated by the volunteers themselves and involved a wide range of different sites. Such in situ observations of authentic interactions had the potential to uncover obstacles not predicted—or possibly not attended to—by typical HCI techniques such as controlled task-based user observations (observing users performing "set" tasks on "preset" sites), task analysis or other analytical evaluation techniques (Preece, Rogers, & Sharp, 2002), nor by using techniques that would only capture reflective or nonsituated data such as focus groups and interviews. The naturalistic observations also helped to capture the customer's complete interaction environment: its physical, social, and cultural constituents.

The observations enabled us to capture data about the pre- and e-purchase stage of the service encounter, in which the customer would find a product, make a decision about whether to make a purchase and then carry out the purchase. Following each observation session, we conducted an interview with the customer and discussed issues from our observations regarding the expectations-setting and prepurchase stages (see Figure 1). These issues included motivation for choosing to conduct business with e-commerce and also with a particular e-commerce site; had they used the site before, how did they know of the site and what had made them stay on the site once they reached it? For example, a customer's motivation to use e-commerce over other business channels was seen as convenient and time saving. One customer who bought her dog's food from a particular site that offered free delivery said, "I suppose it would be just as easy to go and get Monty's [the dog] food, but when you can sit at home for two minutes and have it delivered the next day and not have to carry about big heavy bags of dog food . . ." Also, in the postsession interviews we are able to expand our knowledge of the obstacles that we had observed.

In the *second phase* of the study we conducted a number of group-interview sessions with between six to eight regular customers of e-commerce environments who had not been involved in the first phase of the study. During the group interviews, the participants were encouraged to discuss their good and bad experiences with e-commerce, including their motivations for using e-commerce. The group interviews helped to elicit customers' reflective and subjective experiences of the postpurchase and post-TCE evaluation stages (stages 4 and 6, respectively, in Figure 1) of the service encounter.

In order to encourage participation during the group interviews, we employed an approach of writing questions that we wanted to discuss about e-commerce experiences onto cards (Minocha, Dawson, Petre, & Modi, 2003a). These were then dealt out between the participants. Each participant would read out a question from one of his/her cards and initiate the discussion that would address the question. This gave the participants ownership of the discussions, encouraging everyone to become involved at least at some point during the group interviews.

During the third and final phase of our study, we returned to the customers whom we had originally observed shopping in the first phase and conducted semistructured interviews in order to elicit their experiences of the postpurchase stage, the product or service consumption stage, and the post-TCE evaluation stage of their encounters with e-commerce environments (stages 4, 5, and 6, respectively, in Figure 1). We asked questions about whether the products arrived on time, the state of paperwork such as invoices, whether there was any need to contact customer services, if they will go back to that e-commerce environment for repeat business, and so forth.

The data collected during this three-phase study encompassed the entire TCE and supported the identification of obstacles during data analysis. Each obstacle elicited from the data was considered within its context and was detailed on an *obstacle card* (see Table 1 for an example of an obstacle card). We derived the obstacle card from the critical incident technique (Bitner, Booms, & Tetreault, 1990; Minocha, 2000a). Each obstacle card contained details about the events leading up to the obstacle, the cause and consequence of the obstacle, the customer's response to the situation which arose as a result of the obstacle, how the sociological account concluded, and whether the obstacle resulted in a breakdown. Finally, for each obstacle, requirements and design solutions were proposed that would resolve the obstacle. In total 196 obstacle cards were extracted from this three-phase study spanning the customer's purchase and consumption cycle (Figure 1).

Table 1. Example of an obstacle card

User 5 / DM		5I
1. Events leading up to an obstacle		DM clicks on a site and spends a few seconds looking for something that would tell her that the site is trustworthy, such as links to familiar companies, recognisable and credible logos, user comments, reviews, and so forth. She finds none.
2. Obstacle situation		For DM to use a Web site for shopping, she must have a level of trust in the site. Here she cannot find any cues that would lead her to think the site is trustworthy.
3. Obstacle (the cause of a diminished TCE)		There are no cues to ensure that the site is credible.
Obstacle Consequence	4a. How did the obstacle affect the customer?	There is no notion of trust that has been built.
	4b. What did the customer do in response?	DM leaves the site.
5. How did the sociological account conclude?		DM now searches again to go to another site.
6. Did the obstacle result in a breakdown (from the business perspective)?		Yes
7. Requirements and design solutions		Introduce signs of credibility and trustworthiness on the home page, such as seals of approval accreditations, certification, customers' reviews, and so on.

While analysing the obstacle data, which proved to be rich and insightful (Minocha, Dawson, Blandford, & Roberts, 2003b), we were able to identify patterns or "themes" of obstacles which could then be developed into a catalogue of obstacles. The catalogue encompassed issues such as individual customers' expectations, and social, cultural, and organisational obstacles that influence a customer's perception of value and experience with an e-tailing environment. The catalogue consisted of 18 obstacle categories, with each category comprising a number of subcategories (for a complete list of the obstacle categories, refer to Dawson, Minocha, & Petre, 2003b). Examples of the obstacle categories were mismatch between existing shopping experiences; cues that diminish trustworthiness; asynchronous match between different business processes; problematic user interface elements; and so on.

The catalogue then helped to structure the process of developing E-SEQUAL. Heuristics and subheuristics of E-SEQUAL were developed by working through each category and subcategory of the catalogue of obstacles and examining all of the requirements and design solutions from the obstacle cards.

Developing E-SEQUAL

The heuristics and subheuristics in E-SEQUAL represent those requirements or solutions that either resolve or avoid specific obstacles that were observed to diminish a customer's perception of value during our study. By avoiding such obstacle situations and positively encouraging characteristics that will enhance the customer's perception of value received from their interaction with e-commerce environments, customer loyalty and retention will be promoted.

For example, to resolve the obstacle category of "failure of e-commerce experience to match with customer's existing shopping references," the heuristic "match existing shopping experiences" was developed. Subheuristics helped provide further clarity. For example, "match existing shopping experiences" was elaborated as:

- Provide a similar range of products or services on the Web site to that of other off-line shopping channels.
- Ensure that functionality matches with that of leading e-commerce sites.
- Provide similar incentives as those that may be found in off-line channels.

The derived heuristics and subheuristics demonstrated the importance of integrating CRM and HCI strategies in the design and usability of e-commerce environments. For example, each of the subheuristics in the above example is a CRM strategy. Similarly, HCI issues emerged as heuristics and subheuristics. For example, the heuristic "support the customer interface experience (home page level)" has the following sub-heuristics:

- Clearly state the purpose of the Web site on the home page in order to avoid confusion about what the site offers.
- Consider home page presentation and avoid cluttering the display with distracting, annoying, and excessive visual graphics, advertising, and pop-ups.
- Provide a variety of different ways to search for a product or service.
- Ensure that all textual labels are meaningful, well placed, and are consistent throughout the Web site.

The E-SEQUAL heuristics embody both usability issues that concern the customer's interaction with the Web site and the issues that arise due to the expectations of service quality customers bring to the e-commerce interaction. E-SEQUAL, therefore, integrates both e-CRM and HCI strategies and provides explicit guidance in terms of heuristics and subheuristics which can be applied by Web designers, marketing professionals, and developers to integrate customers' perceived dimensions of service quality and value into the design and development of e-commerce environments. E-SEQUAL can be used by usability professionals as a checklist for evaluating the conformance of an e-commerce environment against the HCI (usability) and e-CRM heuristics.

In Table 2, examples of the E-SEQUAL heuristics and subheuristics that illustrate the coverage across the TCE are presented. At the end of each subheuristic, there is a code indicated in brackets, such as {2G}, which occurs at the end of sub-heuristic A2 (see Table 2); the number in this code represents the user number and the letter G represents the individual obstacle that was

Table 2. Example of E-SEQUAL heuristics and sub-heuristics

A. MATCH EXISTING SHOPPING EXPERIENCES	A1. Match the ranges of products available on the Web site with other shopping channels {1V} A2. Ensure that functionality matches that of similar or competitor sites {2G} A3. Provide similar incentives as those that may be found in other shopping channels {PO-5C} A4. Avoid overuse of the shopping metaphor, for example, use of terminology such as aisles, shelves {3H}
B. SUPPORT THE CUSTOMER INTERFACE EXPERIENCE	B1. Provide a variety of different ways to search for a product or service {8L} B2. Ensure that the Web site is localised in terms of prices in local currency, time settings, metric system, size charts, and so forth {8E} B3. Ensure that labels and icons are meaningful, and are used consistently throughout the Web site {1R} B4. Allow the customer to type the first letter(s) of his/her country of residence in a drop-down box {4I}
C. GIVE CUES TO ENHANCE TRUSTWORTHINESS	C1. Keep sites up to date {5F} C2. Have signs of credibility on the home page {5I} C3. Provide complete contact details and different mechanisms for contact {5D} C4. Avoid hiding extra costs, for example, for credit card use or for delivery {10F, 6C, 11B}
E. PROVIDE QUALITY INFORMATION	E1. Consider how the customer may want to view the product/service information {5L} E2. Provide links to or prompt for related products or services, such as accessories to products, especially when such related products enhance the performance of a product {8O} E3. Ensure that measurement information such as size charts of shoes, clothing, and so forth, is accurate and consistent {1N} E4. If specifying product IDs or other identifiers for products/services, ensure that these identifiers are recognised and used consistently throughout the site {8P, 7K}
K. PROVIDE A RELIABLE CUSTOMER SERVICE	K1. Provide a sympathetic and helpful customer service {PO-5E, 11E} K2. Have personalised correspondence with the customer {PO-6A} K3. Ensure that e-mails sent to customers that concern critical problems with an order, either request a reply or are flagged to provide evidence that the customer has received the e-mail {PO-10B} K4. Ensure quick responses to customers' queries {PO-7F, PO-1G}

identified from user 2's data. The code {PO-5C} implies that this obstacles was elicited during the third phase of our study when we returned to the customers whom we had originally observed (PO: Postobservation session) shopping in the first phase; 5 is the user number and C is one of the obstacles that was identified in user's 5 data. These codes provide a unique identifier for each obstacle card. Therefore, if further clarity is required while applying E-SEQUAL, the obstacle card can be easily accessed.

Evaluating E-SEQUAL

After developing E-SEQUAL, we decided to have it evaluated by usability practitioners in the area of e-services for determining its usefulness and usability. For these evaluations, each usability practitioner was given £30 to make a purchase from one of the three e-commerce sites that we had specified. Whilst making the purchase of their choice, they were asked to apply E-SEQUAL for evaluating customer's TCE with the e-commerce environment. Through these evaluations, the usability practitioners were able to assess how the heuristics of E-SEQUAL supported the evaluation of a customer's TCE across the entire service encounter. Each practitioner was asked to complete a questionnaire to elicit his/her views regarding the usefulness and usability of E-SEQUAL. The feedback from these evaluations was very encouraging. On the whole, they considered the heuristics to be useful. They commented on the sequence in which the heuristics were presented and the phrasing of some of the heuristics which they felt required clarity. Their feedback was fed into the next iteration of E-SEQUAL. Due to space restrictions, the entire set of heuristics is not presented here, but the authors will be happy to provide it to interested colleagues.

Extracting Positive Accounts

At this point we returned to the data of our three-phase study and began to extract the positive accounts in which the customers' TCE had specifically been enhanced. One example of these positive accounts involved an instance in which a customer's perception of value was restored despite an obstacle having occurred. This customer had had to call customer services to complain about a missing item from an order that had arrived. To compensate for this obstacle, the e-business sent the item to her in the return post as well as including a letter of apology and a free gift. This e-business had not only resolved the problem of the missing item in an efficient manner, but it had also shown that if problems were to occur, it would resolve them quickly and sincerely. Another positive account involved delivery, which had also been identified as an obstacle by some customers during our study. On one of the e-business sites, there were customer-definable options of delivery dates and times, thereby giving the customer some control over the delivery. The customer was happy with this flexibility and was satisfied with his experiences in the e-purchase stage. Once these positive accounts had been extracted from the data, the corresponding heuristics were also incorporated into E-SEQUAL.

Comparing E-SEQUAL with Other Online Service Quality Frameworks

In order to further understand the challenge of customer retention in e-commerce, we carried out a comprehensive review of the extant literature related to the provision of service quality to customers of e-commerce environments. Because of the multidisciplinary nature of this research area, we looked at a range of frameworks from both the HCI and the marketing disciplines: e-SERVQUAL (Zeithaml, Parasuraman, & Malhotra, 2000, 2002) from the service marketing literature; WebQual (Barnes, Liu, & Vidgen, 2001; Barnes & Vidgen, 2000) from the management information systems literature; and Zhang and von Dran's Web site quality model (2002) from the HCI literature.

We compared these frameworks with E-SEQUAL by assessing each of them against a set of dimensions. These dimensions involve (see Table 3) the application of the framework (how it can be used), the e-commerce domain(s) that was investigated to develop the framework, and whether the framework is generic to e-commerce, or is it specific to particular domains of e-commerce (rows 2, 3, and 4 of Table 3); influences from other models, or the theoretical basis, and the research method used to develop the framework (rows 5 and 6 in Table 3); the coverage of the framework with respect to the service encounter and Web site quality (row 7 in Table 3); and finally, the coverage of the framework with respect to the usability issues of customer–Web site interaction (row 8 in Table 3). In the following sections, we present a comparison of each of these dimensions.

Application of the Framework

E-commerce is a vast domain involving e-tailing, e-finance, e-banking, e-travel, e-government, and so on. It is likely that customers have different service quality expectations from e-commerce environments of different domains. In this section for each of the frameworks, we first discuss the different domains that

Table 3. Comparison dimensions of four frameworks of service quality in e-commerce

Comparison Dimension	E-SEQUAL (Dawson et al., 2003b)	Web site Quality Model (Zhang & von Dran, 2002)	e-SERVQUAL (Zeithaml et al. 2002)	WebQual (Barnes & Vidgen, 2000)
1. Discipline it pertains to	**HCI and Relationship marketing (CRM)**	**HCI**	**Service Marketing**	**Management Information Systems**
2. Usage (how can the framework be used?)	**Evaluation instrument of CRM and HCI heuristics to guide the design and usability of E-Commerce environments**	**Web site design quality features in a checklist form, which can be used as usability heuristics**	**Conceptual model of on-line Service quality**	**Questionnaire of Web site quality**
3. Generic/Domain-Specific (Can it be applied only to specific domain(s)?)	**Specific to E-Tailing; Intention to develop a generic set of heuristics with domain-specific add-ons**	**Categorises common Web design features and domain-specific features of Web site quality**	**Specific to E-Tailing**	**Attempt to make it a generic instrument for assessment of E-Commerce Web site quality**
4. Domain in which it has been applied or derived from	**E- Tailing**	**E-Education E-Tailing E-Government E-Finance E-Medicine E-Entertainment**	**E-Tailing**	**E-Auction E-Tailing E-Education**
5. Influences (Has it been derived from another model?)	**Based on observations of customers experiences with E-Commerce (empirically-grounded)**	**Kano Model of quality**	**Based on SERVQUAL**	**Communication theory and information quality literature**
6. Research method (Techniques)	**Naturalistic customer observations, group interviews, semi-structured interviews, critical incident technique**	**Questionnaires, surveys, and checklist approach – prioritisation of the Web site design features in order of importance for Web site quality**	**Focus groups / Surveys**	**Quality workshops to elicit customer perceptions, questionnaires, surveys**
7. Focus on Web site quality / Service encounter	**Service encounter and the TCE**	**Web site quality**	**E-purchase and post-purchase of the service encounter**	**Limited notion of a service encounter; main emphasis is on the E-Purchase stage**
8.Focus on Usability of customer-Web site interaction	**Explicit usability heuristics based on HCI and cognitive psychology literature for the practitioners**	**Checklist approach to usability and engagement of an E-Commerce Web site**	**Ambiguous (HCI) terminology and no explicit guidance to practitioners in terms of heuristics or guidelines**	**Ambiguous (HCI) terminology and no explicit guidance to practitioners**

each framework has been developed in, or can be applied to. We also discuss how each of the frameworks may be used by a Web site designer or a marketing manager.

E-SEQUAL

E-SEQUAL, as discussed in this chapter and in Dawson, Minocha, and Petre (2003b), is a service quality framework that is empirically grounded and integrates e-CRM and HCI strategies for the effective design and development of e-tailing environments. E-SEQUAL can provide guidance to e-businesses regarding integration of front- and back-end business processes, and across different customer touch points such as phone, fax, e-mail, and so on. It can be applied as an evaluation instrument to guide Web designers, marketing professionals, developers, and usability professionals to come up with requirements for integrating customers' expectations of service quality, value, and usability into the design of e-tailing environments.

We are currently performing similar studies in e-travel and e-banking environments to find out how customers' expectations of service quality and their perceptions vary across domains. Based on our results, we aim to enhance E-SEQUAL to develop it into a "generic" service quality framework comprising service quality characteristics that are common to a variety of e-commerce domains, and it will be supported by some heuristics (as add-ons) that are specific to the particular domain to which E-SEQUAL is being applied for assessing the service quality.

Zhang and von Dran's Web Site Quality Model

Zhang and von Dran's Web site quality model (Zhang & von Dran, 2002) can be used as a checklist of quality factors of Web site design by Web designers and evaluators for six e-commerce domains, including retail, education, government, finance, medicine, and entertainment. In their framework, the Web site quality factors are divided into categories and features, where each feature is like a heuristic and guides the incorporation of customer's quality expectations into the design of Web sites. For example, for the category C8 Navigation, the features supporting this are F8-1 indication of user's location within the Web site, F8-2 navigation aids, and F8-3 directions for navigating the Web site.

Zhang and von Dran argue that customers of an e-commerce domain do not regard all quality factors as equally important. Their results also show that rankings of important quality factors differ from one e-commerce domain to another. For example, the educational and medical domains require *comprehen-*

siveness of information, a feature not ranked on the five most-important lists in the other four domains.

e-SERVQUAL

e-SERVQUAL (Zeithaml, Parasuraman, & Malhotra, 2002) is a conceptual model of service quality for e-tailing environments, and has the following characteristics: efficiency, reliability, privacy, responsiveness, contact, compensation, and fulfilment. These characteristics represent the criteria customers use to evaluate online services. For example, the characteristic *responsiveness* has the criteria *ability to get answers to questions, quick delivery,* and *updates on status of order.* E-SERVQUAL can be used as a framework by marketing managers to assess the service quality of e-tailing environments.

WebQUAL

WebQUAL (Barnes, Liu, & Vidgen, 2001) is an online questionnaire which is applied to assess customers' perceptions of the quality of Web sites. The questionnaire is completed by customers and the qualitative customer assessments are converted into quantitative metrics that are useful for management decision making. WebQUAL allows comparisons to be made between e-commerce environments in the same domain, or for the same e-commerce environment over time.

WebQUAL has been iteratively developed through its application to a number of domains, from university Web sites through to auction sites, book store Web sites, and even wireless application protocol (WAP) sites on mobile phones. One of the major influences in its development has been the communications theory, and therefore, WebQUAL is particularly suited for assessing the information quality of information-intensive e-commerce environments. The WebQUAL instrument is being iteratively refined by applying and adapting it to a variety of e-commerce domains.

Theoretical Basis and Research Method

In this section, we discuss the theoretical bases and models that have influenced each of these frameworks, and the research methodology used to develop these frameworks.

E-SEQUAL

E-SEQUAL, as we have discussed earlier in this chapter, has been developed from a study of e-tailing environments. E-SEQUAL is not based on an existing model of service quality but has been developed from empirical data collection and analysis. We employed a range of complementary techniques to capture customers' expectations, experiences, and perceptions of service quality over the purchase and consumption process of customers with an e-commerce environment. These techniques were naturalistic observations, group interviews and semistructured interviews for data collection, and critical incident technique for documenting and analysing the obstacles. E-SEQUAL has been refined by practitioner testing. Each heuristic and subheuristic of E-SEQUAL can be traced back to the raw data of obstacles from which it was derived, and so traceability is supported.

Zhang and von Dran's Web Site Quality Model

Zhang and von Dran (2002) have concluded that customers' preferences, requirements, and expectations of service quality vary across different e-commerce domains, and that these quality expectations change over time. They first used a marketing model, the Kano quality model (Kano, Serku, Takahash, & Tsuji, 1984), as a framework in an exploratory investigation of customers' expected quality factors for a specific type of site (CNN.com) in order to develop a Web site quality model. They employed questionnaires and surveys to validate and extend the Web site quality model, and to rank the quality factors in six e-commerce domains: education, retail, government, finance, medicine, and entertainment.

WebQUAL

WebQUAL is based on quality function deployment (QFD) (Bossert, 1991) and is based on three characteristics of customers' perceived quality: information quality derived from the communications theory from the information systems literature; interaction quality based on SERVQUAL (Parasuraman, Zeithaml, & Berry, 1994); and Web site design quality from the usability literature. It has been derived from these theoretical influences, and through elicitation of customers' perceptions of service quality via quality workshops, questionnaires, and surveys.

e-SERVQUAL

e-SERVQUAL, on the other hand, is a conceptual model of online service quality for e-tailing environments. It is based on the traditional (off-line) service quality framework called SERVQUAL (Parasuraman et al., 1994) and has been derived from an exploratory research involving focus groups and two phases of empirical data collection and analysis. This process produced seven service quality characteristics: efficiency, reliability, fulfilment, privacy, responsiveness, compensation, and contact.

Supporting the Service Encounter Versus the Web Site Experience

The focus of our study, as reported in this chapter, was to investigate the service encounter (stages 2–4 of the purchase and consumption cycle) (see Figure 1). However, when we were eliciting data, we were also able to capture some data for other stages (stages 1, 5, and 6) of this cycle. Though the heuristics and subheuristics of E-SEQUAL encompass all six stages, the heuristics for the customer's service encounter with an e-commerce environment (stages 2–4) are far more comprehensive than for stages 1, 5, and 6. Stages 1, 5, and 6 need further investigation by application of other techniques such as card sorting, laddering interviews, and projective techniques to elicit factors such as customers' attitudes, beliefs, values, and associations with brands, and so forth, which attract and retain customers. Investigation of these factors will be done in the next stage of our research programme.

In order to compare E-SEQUAL with other service quality frameworks, we have, in Table 4, listed the service quality factors of the different frameworks against the three stages of the service encounter: prepurchase, e-purchase, and postpurchase. Some duplication occurred as a result of this, as some dimensions were relevant to more than one stage of the service encounter. The duplication is indicated by an asterisk after the relevant dimension (see Table 4). Table 4 helps in comparing how and to what extent each of the other three frameworks—Zhang and von Dran's Web site quality model, e-SERVQUAL, and WebQUAL—contributes toward understanding of customers' quality expectations across different stages of the service encounter.

E-SEQUAL

E-SEQUAL consists of heuristics (see Table 4) and subheuristics (not shown in Table 4) for all three stages of the service encounter. These heuristics provide

Table 4. Comparison across the service encounter of four frameworks of service quality in ecommerce

	E-SEQUAL (Dawson et al., 2003b)	Web site Quality Model (Zhang & von Dran 2002)	e-SERVQUAL (Zeithaml et al., 2002)	WebQual (Barnes & Vidgen, 2000)
Pre-Purchase	Match existing shopping experiences Support the novice customers Match customers' expectations from on-line experience Give cues to enhance trustworthiness Support the customer interface experience * Ensure ease of navigation* Provide quality information Cater for different technologies*	Credibility {Reputation external recognition} Information content Organisation of information content Impartiality {unbiased / engendered information} Visual displays* Navigation* User empowerment {user control of speed and sequence of interaction}* Enjoyment* Technical support {system loading; browser support}*	Efficiency {getting to the Web site, simple to use, finding relevant information,}* Reliability {Technical functioning}*	Reputation Attractive appearance Site easy to learn Design is appropriate to the type of site Site conveys competency Clear and understandable interaction* Easy navigation * Easy to use* Conveys a sense of community* Site creates a positive experience* Information {Accurate, Believable, Timely, Relevant, Easy to understand, Information at the right level of detail and Appropriate format of information} Conveys a sense of community Site creates a positive experience
E-Purchase	Support the customer interface experience Ensure ease of navigation Ensure that information required from the customer is explained upfront Ensure customers are in control Cater for different technologies	Visual displays Navigation Cognitive outcomes {learned new skills/knowledge} Enjoyment Privacy {data encryption; access requirements} User empowerment {user control of speed and sequence of interaction} Technical support {system loading; browser support}	Efficiency* {easy to complete transaction} Security / Privacy {not sharing information; security of data; etc} Reliability {Technical functioning}	Clear and understandable interaction Easy navigation Easy to use Feeling of safety in completing transaction Secure personal information Personalisation
Post-Purchase	Integrate front-end and back-end processes Provide a reliable customer service Provide a reliable delivery service Maintain continuity across touch points Ensure Customers are in control Match the provided service to the service intended		Responsiveness {provision of appropriate information to resolve/explain problems; etc.} Contact {provision for customers to speak to a live customer service agent} Compensation {Money-backs; returning shipping and handling costs} Fulfilment {accuracy of service promise; products in stock; delivery; etc.}	Easy to communicate with organisation Good feeling of confidence about delivery

guidance for supporting the customer not only in his/her interaction with the Web site particularly during the e-purchase stage, but across all of the touch points via which a customer may interact with an e-business during the service encounter.

Zhang and von Dran's Web Site Quality Model

As indicated in Table 4, Zhang and von Dran's Web site quality model is primarily concerned with the user interface of the Web site. In addition to usability and ease-of-use features, that reflect their HCI background, Zhang and von Dran identify Web site quality factors such as the credibility of the organisation as reflected by cues on the Web site, and customers' affective, intellectual, and aesthetic needs. For example, they have factors such as enjoyment and cognitive outcomes (learnability) in their model. However, their model fails to address service quality characteristics of the service encounter which are beyond the user interface design of the Web site and customer–Web site interaction. For example, their model (see Table 4) does not provide any quality factors for the postpurchase stage of the service encounter. As we have indicated earlier, the quality provided by the Web site becomes insignificant if the service quality expectations are not met elsewhere in the service encounter, for example, receiving inadequate information when customer service is contacted to inquire about a delayed order generates a negative TCE.

e-SERVQUAL and WebQUAL

Both e-SERVQUAL and WebQUAL cover aspects of all three stages of the service encounter (see Table 4). As compared to E-SEQUAL, both e-SERVQUAL and WebQUAL have high-level quality factors, and do not provide guidance to the level of heuristics and subheuristics provided by E-SEQUAL (see Table 2). e-SERVQUAL has a particular emphasis on the postpurchase stage in which a customer is most likely to interact with touch points other than the Web site. From our studies, we have found this to be a particularly important stage of the service encounter and if obstacles occur here, they are at least as likely to prevent a positive customer's perception as the obstacles that occur with the Web site interaction during the prepurchase and the e-purchase stages.

WebQUAL, on the other hand, emphasises the prepurchase stage in which a customer makes his/her decision whether to make a purchase. Again, this is a very important challenge for e-commerce and plays a large role in changing browsing or potential customers into customers who are willing to make a purchase. WebQUAL additionally emphasises issues of reputation and attractive appearance. These factors relate to the expectations-setting and prepurchase stages of the purchase and consumption cycle (Figure 1) in which a customer builds his/her expectations about the interaction with the Web site. WebQUAL does not include fulfilment as a dimension in the postpurchase stage. It, therefore, does not capture the customer's experiences over the entire service encounter.

Supporting the Usability of the Customer–Web Site Interaction

We have seen that customers consider both Web site design quality and service quality of the e-commerce experience when they are evaluating their experiences with an e-commerce environment. The usability of the customer–Web site interaction is one of the main Web site design quality factors that influences the customer's TCE during the purchase and consumption cycle (Figure 1) with an e-commerce environment. In this section, we compare the different frameworks in terms of the guidance they provide toward designing and evaluating the customer–Web site interaction.

E-SEQUAL

The HCI heuristics in E-SEQUAL are from the HCI and cognitive psychology literature. Although E-SEQUAL is based on actual customer observations, we were not able to capture a wide range of HCI or usability issues of Web site design and interaction in the study. In addition, E-SEQUAL does not cover accessibility (for users with special needs) issues of the TCE. Therefore, we propose that E-SEQUAL be used in conjunction with a usability evaluation instrument, which is more comprehensive than the list of HCI heuristics in E-SEQUAL, and an accessibility checklist.

Zhang and von Dran's Web Site Quality Model

Zhang and von Dran's quality model is particularly oriented toward the design and usability of the Web site. In addition, it has quality factors such as enjoyment and cognitive outcomes which indicate its focus on the customer–Web site interaction.

e-SERVQUAL

e-SERVQUAL has emerged from the marketing discipline and does not cover aspects of usability as comprehensively as Zhang and von Dran do in their framework. Even when e-SERVQUAL covers some aspects of usability of Web sites, its use of HCI terminology is quite general (e.g., ease of use, efficiency). Another example is that one of the characteristics during the e-purchase stage is *easy to complete transaction*: e-SERVQUAL does not provide guidance on how the process of transaction should be designed to make it "easy" for the customer.

WebQUAL

WebQUAL has twelve quality characteristics: informational fit to task, interaction, trust, response time, design, intuitiveness, visual appeal, innovativeness, flow (emotional appeal), integrated communication, business processes, and substitutability. Overall, it focuses on helping Web designers to better design Web sites as most of its quality characteristics relate to the usability of the customer–Web site interaction. However, these top-level usability characteristics do not provide enough detail and guidance to the designer on how a characteristic can be applied while designing an e-commerce environment.

Summary of the Comparison

While the frameworks discussed here conceptualise service quality, there are significant differences in their contributions toward improving the service quality of e-commerce environments. Zhang and von Dran focus on the technical quality of the Web site itself rather than the service quality provided to customers through the Web site and other touch points of the e-commerce environment. The characteristics in WebQUAL are also limited to the customer's interaction with the site. e-SERVQUAL focuses more on service quality through efficiency, reliability, fulfilment, compensation, and so on, and less on the interaction with the Web site. E-SEQUAL consists of both HCI and e-CRM heuristics and, therefore, encompasses characteristics of *both* Web site design and service quality across all the three stages of the service encounter.

E-SEQUAL is the only framework (as compared to the other three discussed here) that provides a prescriptive set of heuristics and lower-level subheuristics that can be applied for the design and evaluation of e-tailing environments. The other frameworks list the characteristics but do not elaborate them to an extent to provide explicit guidance to Web designers or marketing managers. For example, whilst Zhang and von Dran's features could be used as the basis upon which heuristics could be built, their categories and features are presented as a checklist. Despite providing a useful profile of e-commerce quality, WebQUAL does not provide prescriptive advice concerning how an organisation might improve its e-commerce offering. WebQUAL is an online questionnaire and is aimed at the customer rather than the designer.

e-SERVQUAL represents a high-level model of service quality and so it does not provide systematic guidance for its application, which E-SEQUAL provides. Some of the characteristics in E-SERVQUAL, which have been derived from focus groups, are in some cases subjective comments. For example, the criteria that read *easy to find what I need, good user interface, not too many graphics that take time to download,* and so forth, leave the designer questioning what a "good" interface is? What is meant by "too many graphics"? The characteristic of *efficiency* has criteria such as *simple to use, getting to the Web site doesn't require me to input a lot of information,* and *easy to complete transaction.* Each of these criteria is dependent upon the individual's judgement of what "a lot of information entry" is, or what "simple to use" means for the individual. In a practical sense, such characteristics and high-level criteria of service quality do not provide explicit guidance to the Web site designer involved in designing and developing e-tailing environments.

E-SEQUAL consists of heuristics that cover all three stages of the service encounter. The other frameworks' coverage is focussed on one or two of the stages of the service encounter. WebQUAL and e-SERVQUAL emphasise the need for providing service quality at different stages of the service encounter, illustrating the need for e-businesses to look beyond the Web site. However, e-SERVQUAL has a particular focus toward the postpurchase stage while WebQUAL's characteristics are more concentrated in the prepurchase stage. Zhang and von Dran's focus on the Web design, and hence, do not provide any guidance for the postpurchase stage.

Finally, the E-SEQUAL heuristics have come directly from, and can be easily traced back to, the elicitation of customers' experiences by applying a variety of data elicitation techniques. E-SEQUAL is, therefore, grounded in the customer's perceptions of service quality. In comparison, the derivation of each of the other three frameworks has been via customer workshops, surveys, questionnaires, focus groups, or literature review. Whilst such data elicitation is credible, the most obvious limitations with these types of data elicitation techniques is the inability to collect real-world situated data, therefore limiting the data collection to reflective or nonsituated data.

Conclusions

As e-commerce proliferates, e-tailers are realising that the key determinants of success and failure are not merely a usable Web site or low price but rather the provision of service quality that exceeds customers' expectations. To encourage repeat purchases and build customer loyalty, organisations should shift their focus from *e-commerce* (the transactions) to *e-service*, providing a positive TCE before, during, and after transactions. Marketing managers need to understand what are the service quality characteristics of an e-tailing environment that will help meet the customers' expectations, and what actions need to be taken to deliver value and superior service quality to customers. In this chapter, we have begun to address these questions.

We have reported a study that involved investigating a wide range of obstacles that mar a customer's TCE. During our study, we elicited the criteria customers use in evaluating the service quality of e-tailing sites. We have seen that in addition to having a usable site, other CRM characteristics such as cues of trustworthiness on the Web site, consistent service across different touch points and business channels of the organisation, assurances of privacy and security, and so forth, are clearly important factors that cannot be overlooked for attracting and retaining customers. In order to provide value to the customer and meet his/her service quality expectations, it is therefore necessary to look beyond the usability of the Web site. Our study has led to the development of a framework—E-SEQUAL.

E-SEQUAL is a service quality framework that is empirically grounded in customers' perceptions of real experiences with e-tailing environments. Through conducting observations of genuine customers carrying out self-defined and self-motivated tasks in their natural environments, obstacles that can diminish the service quality have been identified. Customers' experiences are embodied directly into E-SEQUAL in terms of e-CRM and HCI strategies for the effective design, development, and evaluation of e-commerce environments.

In contrast, other frameworks from both the HCI and the marketing domains that endeavour to support the understanding of service quality and Web site quality of (B2C) e-commerce environments *fail to* address all stages of the service encounter, provide explicit guidance for the Web designer or marketing manager, ground their research in real occurrences of customer experiences, and formalise subjective statements into meaningful and objective service quality characteristics.

Acknowledgments

The research project in CRM and service quality reported in this chapter is a part of an ongoing research programme in e-service quality being carried out by the User Experience Strategy group in the Department of Computing of the Open

University (OU). This research programme was first initiated in 2001 as part of a Shailey Minocha's British Telecommunications PLC (BT), and was supported by BT Exact (2001–2002). It has since then been supported by the EPSRC Grant No. GR/R60867/01 (2002–2004), BT (2003–2004), and the Research Development Fund of the OU (2003–2006).

We are grateful to all the participants who gave time to contribute to this study. We thank Dr. Marian Petre of the User Experience Strategy group, OU, UK, Dr. Gordon Rugg of Keele University, UK, and Mr. Dave Roberts of IBM, UK, for their advice and support to this research.

References

Barnes, S., & Vidgen, R. (2000, July 3–5). *WebQual: An exploration of Website quality*. Proceedings of the Eighth European Conference on Information Systems, Vienna, Austria.

Barnes, S., Liu, K., & Vidgen, R. (2001, June). *Evaluating WAP news sites: The WebQual/M approach*. Proceedings of the Ninth European Conference on Information Systems, Bled, Slovenia.

Bitner, M. J., Booms, B. H., & Tetreault, M. S. (1990). The service encounter: Diagnosing favorable and unfavorable incidents. *Journal of Marketing, 54*, 71–85.

Bossert, J. L. (1991). *Quality function deployment: A practitioner's approach*. Milwaukee, WI: ASQC Quality Press.

Chatham, B. (2002). Exposing customer experience flaws. *Forrester Tech Strategy Report*.

Cohen, J. (1999, October). The Grinch cometh. *Neteffect*.

Dawson, L. H., Minocha, S., & Petre, M. (2003a). Social and cultural obstacles to the (B2C) e-commerce experience. *Proceedings of BCS-HCI 2003* (pp. 225–241).

Dawson, L. H., Minocha, S., & Petre, M. (2003b). E-SEQUAL: Evaluating (B2C) e-commerce environments across the service encounter. Paper presented in *Workshop 6–Exploring the total customer experience: Usability evaluations of (B2C) e-commerce environments*.

Dyche, J. (2002). *The CRM handbook: A business guide to customer relationship management*. Addison-Wesley.

Forrester. (2003). US eCommerce to hit nearly $230 billion in 2003. Retrieved March 14, 2004, from *www.forrester.com/ER/Press/Release/0,1769,823,00.html*

Gabbott, M., & Hogg, G. (1998). *Consumers and services*. Chichester, UK: John Wiley & Sons.

Gefen, D. (2002). Customer loyalty in e-commerce. *Journal of the Association for Information Systems, 3*, 27–51.

Kano, N., Seraku, N., Takahashi, F., & Tsuji, S. (1984). Attractive and normal quality. *Quality, 14*.

Millard, N. J. (2001). Creating the customer experience: Holistic interaction from Website to call centre and beyond. *Proceedings of HCI International 2001* (Vol. 2, pp. 134–136).

Minocha, S. (2000a). Causal analysis: A technique to explore breakdowns in usage scenarios. *Proceedings of HCI International 2000, 2*, 27–28.

Minocha, S. (2000b). Design of e-business sites for effective customer relationship management. *Proceedings of the Australian Conference on Computer-Human Interaction OzCHI 2000* (pp. 68–69).

Minocha, S., Dawson, L. H., Blandford, A., & Roberts, D. (2003b). The customer's perspective: Sociological accounts of e-commerce encounters. *Proceedings of the IADIS International Conference WWW/ Internet 2003* (Vol. 1, pp. 69–76).

Minocha, S., Dawson, L. H., Petre, M., & Modi, S. (2003a). *Usability evaluations of (B2C) e-commerce environments*. Paper presented in Workshop 6 – Exploring the Total Customer Experience: Usability Evaluations of (B2C) E-Commerce Environments, Interact 2003.

Nielsen, J., Molich, R., Snyder, C., & Farrell, S. (2001). *E-commerce user experience*. Fremont, CA: Nielsen Norman Group.

Parasuraman, A., Zeithaml, V. A., & Berry, L. L. (1994). Reassessment of expectations as a comparison standard in measuring service quality: Implications for further research. *Journal of Marketing, 58*, 111–124.

Payne, M., Christopher, M., Clark, M., & Peck, H. (1995). *Relationship marketing for competitive advantage: Winning and keeping customers*. Butterworth-Heinemann.

Preece, J., Rogers, Y., & Sharp, H. (2002). *Interaction design: Beyond human-computer interaction*. John Wiley & Sons.

Reichheld, F. F., & Sasser, W. E. J. (1990). Zero defections: Quality comes to services. *Harvard Business Review, 68*, 105–111.

Reichheld, F. F. & Schefter, P. E. (2000). Loyalty: Your secret weapon on the Web. *Harvard Business Review, 78*, 105–113.

Seybold, P. B. (2001). *The customer revolution.* Random House.

Spool, J. M., Scanlon, T., Schroeder, W., Synder, C., & De Angelo (1999). *Web site usability: A designer's guide.* Morgan Kaufmann.

Vividence White Paper. (2002). Stop losing customers on the Web. Retrieved March 14, 2004, from *www.vividence.com*

Weinstein, A., & Johnson, W. C. (1999). *Designing and delivering superior customer value.* CRC Press.

Zeithaml, V. A., Parasuraman, A., & Malhotra, A. (2000). *A conceptual framework for understanding e-service quality: Implications for future research and managerial practice.* (Working paper, report no. 00-115). Marketing Science Institute.

Zeithaml, V. A., Parasuraman, A., & Malhotra, A. (2002). Service quality delivery through Web sites: A critical review of extant knowledge. *Journal of the Academy of Marketing Science, 30*, 362–375.

Zhang, P., & von Dran, G. M. (2002). User expectations and rankings of quality factors in different Web site domains. *International Journal of Electronic Commerce, 6*, 9–33.

Chapter VII

Key Success Requirements for Online Brand Management

Subir Bandyopadhyay, Indiana University Northwest, USA

Rosemary Serjak, Graduate Student, University of Ottawa, Canada

Abstract

In recent years, many online brands (or e-brands) have emerged. For a brick-and-mortar brand to excel in the online environment, the brand manager must appreciate some of the key features of the Internet and make adjustments to the traditional brand management strategy. For example, the control of communication in case of online brand management lies with both the brand manager and the consumer, whereas from the traditional branding perspective, the control by and large rests with the brand manager only. We highlight the differences between traditional brand management and online brand management. We then focus on several key success factors in building a successful online brand, which we believe will help guide the brand manager through a series of steps leading to successful online branding.

Introduction

Consumer enthusiasm for online shopping is on the rise. This underlines the dichotomy of supply side and demand side of the online business. Today's online consumers demand more—they do not like limited selection, slow downloads, and inadequate navigation. The e-tailers who are unable to meet rising customer expectations are destined to fail. To operate successfully, e-tailers need a clear competitive advantage based on an attractive offering, a viable business model, and a dedicated brand management team. Success also depends on loyal customers who keep on buying products and, more importantly, bring in more loyal customers through positive word-of-mouth communication. Because the Internet is in a continuous dynamic state, firms need to follow a flexible e-brand management policy. Recent trends indicate that one viable business model could encompass both a physical brick-and-mortar presence and an Internet presence.

Marketing over the Internet implies a whole new dimension in which to engage, retain, and transact with the consumer. The future looks bright for the brand manager because the number of potential customers seems boundless. It was projected that (1) the number of computers connected to the Internet grew from 2.2 million to over 43 million worldwide between January 1994 and January 1999 and (2) the number of Internet users was over 160 million as of March 1999, with over 90% of these users having joined in the last 5 years (Hanson, 2000). A recent report showed that all of these projections have been greatly exceeded; as of December 2002, there are 580 million Internet users worldwide (Nielsen-NetRatings, 2003).

Today's most successful companies, along with companies that desire to meet with financial success, are quite aware of the power of the Internet (such as economy of scale, direct communication with the consumer across the globe, etc.). However, it is still considered a relatively new mechanism with respect to the opportunity for online brand development. Due to the relative newness of the Internet and its unknown potentials, many companies do not have a results-driven path toward developing a brand on the Internet. A preliminary step includes dissecting what brand management entails for the online marketer. Although a number of recent books (see, for example, Braunstein & Levin, 2000; Carpenter, 2000; Kania, 2000; Ries & Ries, 2000) and articles (see, for example, Aaker, 2002; McWilliam, 2000; Murphy, Raffa, & Mizerski, 2003; Sealy, 1999) have addressed the issue of e-branding, no one has articulated the critical differences between traditional and online brand management. For a brand manager, it is imperative to appreciate these differences. It is natural for a brand manager to apply his/her off-line brand experience to online branding. While this approach will work to some extent, it will fail to appreciate some of the unique features of the Internet. For example, the control of communication in case of online brand management lies with both the brand manager and the consumer, whereas from the traditional branding perspective, the control mainly rests with the brand manager only.

In the following paragraphs, we will highlight two brands—one traditional off-line brand foraying into online branding, and the other a purely online brand—to show how online branding differs from traditional branding. The first brand is Procter & Gamble's Pampers diaper. Similar to many name brands, Procter & Gamble struggles to differentiate its Pampers from its competitors'. Fortunately, its Web site (www.pampers.com) has enabled Pampers to augment its core product in a variety of ways. The notable online strategies are as follows: (1) the popular "Vantastic Sweepstakes" offered a Chrysler van full of diapers; (2) a "gift pack" provided a convenient way to send a supply of Pampers along with a Fisher-Price toy to a friend; (3) a playing center, a sharing center, and a learning center offer visitors an opportunity to explore a plethora of practical issues; and (4) the Parenting Institute offers advice from experts on a myriad of issues such as health, development, and child care (see Aaker, 2002, for more details). These unique features have made the Pampers Web site the second most popular baby-care products. It is important to note that all the strategies mentioned above are unique to the Web and are difficult to duplicate in the traditional brick-and-mortar business.

The second brand we are going to highlight is Amazon.com—a brand built primarily on the Web. Amazon.com has utilized many techniques that are unique to the Web to catch the imagination of so many people. Some of the important features of Amazon's brand management strategy are as follows (see Dayal, Landesburg, & Zeisser, 2000; and Roberts, 2003 for more details):

- *Personalization*: Amazon has developed a comprehensive database customer purchase history and buying interests. As a result, it can reach a single customer with a customized offer. Customers have the control to customize their own page and also to make recommendations directly to the company.
- *Collaboration*: Amazon collaborated with Gary Trudeau, the creator of the "Doonesbury" cartoon strip to organize a contest on the Web. First, Trudeau posted the first set of a Doonesbury strip and invited visitors to the site to complete the cartoon. Each day Trudeau would evaluate each posting and selected a winner. Trudeau finally created the last section and the 11-section cartoon was completed.
- *Self-service option*: Amazon offers a variety of self-service options in its "My Account" page. These services range from reviewing personal account transaction to changing personal information.

- *Streamlined purchase process*: Amazon offers the unique "1-Click" system that stores payment information for customers so that they do not have to fill in an order form every time they make a purchase.
- *Dynamic pricing*: Amazon offers an auction page where site visitors can observe the price variations of a product and bid for it. In the off-line world, a customer can learn about the price variations only if he/she takes the trouble to check out the prices in retail stores in the neighborhood.

It is evident that the strategies outlined above are unique to the Web. An online brand manager must appreciate the strength of these innovative tools in brand building. To that extent, a brand like Pampers, which has both an off-line and an online presence, must blend the best of off-line and online techniques to build strong brands on the Web. Online brand managers must learn to select the best technique for the branding task at hand. Unfortunately, very few studies have articulated these critical differences in off-line (or traditional) and online branding techniques.

Our paper intends to fill this important void in the online branding literature. First, we outline the importance of, and challenges to, online brand management. Next we summarize the critical differences between online and traditional brand management. Finally, we present a set of critical success factors in building a successful online brand.

The Importance of Online Brand Management

We cannot overemphasize the importance of online brand management to an online company. According to Carpenter (2000), there are a variety of differences between online and off-line branding. Carpenter states: "In the online world, distribution has emerged as being even more important than more traditional brand-building tools. If you don't have Web allies that can get your brand in front of large numbers of people at a reasonable cost, it's unlikely that your business will thrive." One must also keep account of the market momentum, or the "Mo Factor" (Carpenter, 2000). He emphasizes the need to communicate a constant sense of momentum. Smart online marketers are aware that by having momentum behind them, the barriers to business success get dissolved. Along with the sharply focused marketer will come the strategic partner eager to develop an alliance. As a result, potential competitors will think twice about entering the category. Customers will see this particular company as a winner, which in turn, strengthens the perceived quality of the brand. Hence, momentum is a critical factor to the success of an online brand.

For an existing brand, the Internet can provide a central organizing platform for integrating marketing communication functions of a company. Instead of looking at the Internet as another medium for information and transaction, firms must take a broader view for the brand-building process with the Internet being a critical element of the process (Aaker, 2002). The brand manager should think about joint strategy that will leverage the reach and power of the Internet to boost the sales of an online as well as an off-line brand.

Challenges to Online Brand Management

The following are challenges faced by online brand managers:

1. *Insufficient use of Internet tools*: Online marketers have yet to utilize the available online tools to an optimal level. For example, according to a business media expert, in 2003, only 5% of a company's online marketing budget is spent on permission-based e-mail, which is generally considered to be a very effective method of reaching the consumer (Ottawa Business Journal, 2003). There is also not sufficient investment in customer-friendly tools that reduce operating costs. Banks are an exception in this respect where ATMs along with online banking and telephone banking have reduced the labor cost to service customers.
2. *Price- and service-sensitive customers:* Many retailers worry that a large percentage of price-sensitive customers shop online to hunt for bargains. This can cause problems for them because they are forced to compete on the basis of price, making them vulnerable to bankruptcy. In addition, studies indicate that a common complaint related to online shopping is that the product the consumer wants is out of stock. Other complaints include the following:

    - The customer did not want to pay for shipping and handling
    - The site performed too slowly
    - The customer was uncomfortable submitting credit card information online (security concerns)
    - The customer was concerned about ability to return items

3. *Lack of understanding customer expectation*: One reason that many dot-com companies fail is due to their negligence toward recognizing their customers' expectations. A static Web site or a site that is inaccessible due to the construction of the site will at the very least annoy the potential customer, hence lowering the chances of a return visit. In addition, many users become comfortable with the layout of the Web site and drastic changes to the appearance and navigation of the Web site may make customers uncomfortable and require that users "relearn" how to use the site.
4. *Use of inaccurate performance metrics*: Another recurring problem lies in the inability for e-tailers to sustain their customers. An organization can count the number of "eyeballs" that its site receives; however, the actual number of returns is unquestionably more important and more difficult to determine. The trick is to determine if your target customers are likely to visit your site and not how many "eyeballs" your site receives.
5. *Misperception about the appropriate online branding strategy*: A final problem with online brand management is the marketer's perception that an entire shift of marketing priorities is in order. Knowledge of traditional marketing should not be shelved. As of 2004, we are still in a transition mode. It is a combination of print, television, radio, and electronic advertising that will strengthen a brand. Advertising and promotional communications should be within the context of the investment of your customers. For example, some customers do not see the need in upgrading their Pentium III processor to a Pentium IV processor, or changing the mode of their cellphone from analogue to the improved digital mode. Instead, they want new products to be interchangeable with their existing medium of technology. What should be emphasized and promoted here is the *loyalty* and *trust* of the customer. Brand managers should adhere to keeping their online customers, along with their non-Internet customers, aware of their brand, and satisfied with the goods or services they receive. Hence, it is important that online marketers realize that the Internet is not the only medium and that some Internet users are not on the "cutting edge" of technology.

Given the problems faced by online brand managers, it is clear that most of these problems are attributable to a lack of understanding of the online brand management. Specifically, brand managers often assume erroneously that a successful off-line or traditional branding strategy will also work for online branding.

Brand Management: Traditional Versus Online

What we have been implying is summed up in the following: there exists a knowledge gap between the traditional marketing approach of a brand and this new and dynamic method of e-branding on the Internet. For example, many brand managers assume erroneously that a successful off-line or traditional branding strategy will also work for online branding. Conversely, many other managers believe in a complete overhaul of the traditional brand management. It is clear from the foregoing discussion that the online brand managers are not clear about the differences, if any between traditional and online brand management. Therefore, it is important for the marketer to be aware of some of the issues regarding the differences between traditional and online brand management. Exhibit 1 below outlines these key differences.

Focus

Traditional brand management primarily focuses on the product and its relationship with the consumer. Kapferer (1992) posits that the strength of a brand is reflected by the number of its customers who are brand sensitive. He charac-

Exhibit 1. Differences between traditional and online brand management

Criterion	Traditional Brand Management	Online Brand Management
1. Focus	Predominantly on product and profit	Predominantly on customer relationship
2. Scope	Mostly a line of product	Mostly corporate branding
3. Management structure	Retail managers	New breed of technomanagers
4. Control of communication	Rests with the brand manager	Rests with both the brand manager and the customer
5. Targeting	Mostly one-to-many	One-to-one
6. Scope of creating brand personality	Through noninteractive television and print ads	Through interactive online chat rooms and communities

terizes brand sensitivity in terms of the relationship among brands for a given consumer for a given product category. The marketing strategy, therefore, draws more attention to the general makeup of the product. The product is marketed to better appeal to the consumer, resulting in increased sensitivity and ultimately, to better profitability.

Online brand management, on the other hand, focuses principally on better customer relations. Building a relationship with the customer through personal profiles, e-mail, video, and knowledge of their journeys on the Internet is the key to the online brand manager (Kania, 2000). Introducing a brand online requires great commitment and organization. The online brand manager is better positioned to creatively meet the needs of the customer faster and more efficiently due to the speed and the personal service option that the Internet provides. The online brand manager can also attempt to influence customers without overt marketing by utilizing customer personalization. The relationship building process allows the brand manager to get to know the likes and dislikes of his/her customer; therefore, "suggestion" advertising or guiding the customer can be possible. Amazon.com is a great example of personalized service. Once a customer has purchased a book from its Web site, Amazon.com keeps a record of the purchase. When that same customer returns to the site for another purchase, suggestions are given regarding similar literature (dependent on the previous purchase and the profile of the individual) available through its Web site. One-stop shopping is also very attractive to the average consumer who ideally wants to be able to do his/her purchasing at one time, on one site, with someone he/she knows and trusts, and save money on shipping. The brand manager has the ability to design the Web site to meet the need of the average customer. This gives the online brand manager the opportunity to retain customers and increase site visitation. Simplifying the customer's life is what the aim of a virtual store should be, and therefore one-stop shopping is a popular trend that must be addressed.

Online brand management involves branding a Web site not as an actual product, but rather as a service. Since a majority of online purchases involve the same product, online brand management needs to creatively position its Web site over its competitors' who are selling the same product. Online brand management can be more complex than traditional brand management because online purchasers are much more price sensitive. For example, Proctor & Gamble (P&G) has proven to be very effective at creating brands such as Tide and Downy. P&G is able to distinguish its brand based on physical characteristics such as how well it cleans, how nice it smells, and so forth. On the other hand, Web sites distinguish themselves by their level of service (ease of use, personalization, security) and price rather than through product characteristics.

Scope

The traditional brand manager is primarily involved in the marketing of one particular line of product that accommodates concentrated efforts at planning new product campaigns, promotional activities, and advertising. Although branding is done at different levels of brand hierarchy, such as corporate brand, family brand, and product brand, product branding is the more common approach to brand management where each product requires individual branding.

Corporate branding, as opposed to product branding, is more prevalent in online brand management, especially for the click-and-mortar companies. It is beneficial to the brand manager, not only for centering of branding efforts onto one brand but also for the clarification of the organization's position in the mind of the consumer. The Internet has produced corporate brands such as CD Now, E*trade, Yahoo!, eBay, and Autobytel. These corporate brands are challenging traditional brands for the customer's top-of-mind awareness. The classic example is the online competition between BarnesandNoble.com and Amazon.com. Studies have consistently ranked Amazon higher than BarnesandNoble.com in brand awareness. We believe this is because Amazon has successfully created an online corporate brand while Barnes and Noble has not been able to create this type of online brand recognition.

It is true that many famous brands (such as Tide, Ivory, and Vicks) have Web sites of their own. However, the link with other brands in the same corporate family remains strong in brand-specific Web sites. For example, the Web site of Tide, a P&G product, heavily cross-promotes the fabric softeners made by P&G such as Downy, Bounce, Febreze, Dreft, and Dryel.

Famous corporate brands such as GE and Kraft leverage the Web even more to augment the corporate brand. For example, GE outlines its entire product line in the Web site (ge.com) under two broad categories: home products and business products. Under the home products category, GE lists its products in such diverse product lines as appliances, lighting, consumer electronics, television programs, home comfort, and safety. GE's business products include its brands in aviation, automobiles, energy, healthcare, retail, and transportation. Similarly, Kraft lists its product line under five major food categories: beverages (e.g., Maxwell House coffee and Kool-Aid), convenient meals (Oscar Meyer bacon and Digiorno frozen pizza), cheese (e.g., Philadelphia cream cheese and Kraft grated cheese), grocery (e.g., Grey Poupon condiments and Post cereals), and snacks (Chips Ahoy! cookies).

Management

In traditional brand management, retailers work in collaboration with brand managers to make pricing and merchandising decisions. Manufacturers introduce their products to the public through stores such as Wal-Mart or Target. These retail stores sell products purchased from many manufacturers along with their store brands or private labels. Retail managers think of a marketing strategy to persuade consumers to purchase goods from their establishment. For example, Wal-Mart's marketing strategy demonstrates that it will always have lower prices than its competitors.

Online brand management demands a diverse form of management. Unlike traditional brand managers, this new breed of technomanagers must execute duties pertaining to their corporate Web site. An online brand manager's duties consist of measuring Web site traffic, purchases, and frequency of guest visits. The information gathered on visitors' preferences is utilized to develop future marketing strategies. In addition, the online brand manger is responsible for finding out why users do not complete a transaction and correct the problem if there is one. Dot-com businesses started with an intimate knowledge of Internet technology and Web audience. Online brands are marketed by people who are technically savvy, and are adept in using interactive dialogue to bring together the user and the brands.

Successful online brands are managed by individuals who consider brand management as management of values. These brand managers view their role as that of conductors, providing brand leadership but leaving the community of customers to jointly define the brand personality (de Chernatony, 2000).

Control of Communication

The brand manager controls the unidirectional communication process in the traditional brand management. This allows the manager to decide what message is more appealing to the customers. And then the message is presented to the general public through television, radio, newspapers, or magazines. If customers desire to express their thoughts and opinions about a particular product, they can call a toll-free number, or go to the retail store to fill out a comment or suggestion card.

Conversely, customers are in control of communications online. The bidirectional nature of online communication allows the customer to control communication by leaving comments at a site. This is more direct and effective than leaving comments at a retail store. This can help the brand manager create a one-to-one relationship with the customer by showing that the company cares about each and every consumer and responds to each comment. Furthermore, comments and suggestions help online managers develop Web sites that promote increased one-to-one customer communication.

Targeting

Marketers traditionally identify segments within a broader market and design brand messages to these selected segments or target markets. While there is a distinct trend toward targeting smaller segments or niches, there is a logical limit to how small a target market can become. Cost of design, manufacturing, promotion, and distribution restrict the number of product lines. Thus, targeting is done on one-to-many basis in traditional brand management. The company wants to expand its product to a large magnitude of customers. Currently, there is no way to successfully create a close relationship with customers when products are being sold in large retail stores such as Wal-Mart. These types of stores cater to large groups of people to make purchases, and hence cannot customize their offerings according to each customer's likes and preferences.

On the Web, segmentation can be even more precise because online brand managers routinely collect information on customer profiles and their online behavior patterns. For example, Amazon.com keeps preferences of previous customers. When a customer returns to the Web site, suggestions for new books are displayed on the Web page based on criteria from the past visit or purchase. This helps the customer feel like the company knows what he/she wants. All of this can be accomplished with the use of sophisticated Internet tools available to the online brand manager.

In fact, some online companies even go one step further and target individuals. This strategy of one-to-one marketing is possible when a message or product can be targeted to one individual. The Internet makes this possible by allowing the company to address each of its customers individually. Unique Web features such as e-mail, an online community, chat, Web conferencing, auctions, and cookies help in one-to-one marketing. Many sites feature elements of one-to-one marketing. For example, Dell makes custom computers as per the specification supplied by its customers. Also, CNN allows its registered users to personalize their site, MyCNN, to include news of their choice.

The ability to interact and chat with the customer one-on-one enables a brand to customize and even personalize its offerings (Travis, 2001). The online environment enables the customer to customize his/her choice of product attributes from the list of options offered by the manufacturer on its Web site. However, that is not the end—the customer may decide to become a co-creator of the product by collaborating with the brand to develop the exact product he/she needs. This is quite common for the business-to-business customers. Engineers representing suppliers and customers often collaborate intimately to produce a piece of software or hardware specially designed for the customer. The advantage of such personalization is that the customer tends to stay with the manufacturer because he/she does not want to repeat the process with another supplier.

Scope of Creating Brand Personality

Online branding offers a broader scope of creating a brand personality. Researchers found that the exposure to the brand Web site increases the brand personality (Muller & Chandon, 2003). They also found that the brand is perceived younger and more modern, as well as more sincere and trustworthy, when a visitor has a more positive attitude toward the Web site. Moreover, they found that the effect of exposure to a Web site depends on the product category: for functional/utilitarian products (such as mobile phones), the effect of exposure on youthfulness and modernity is superior than for autoexpressive products (such as luxury clothes). These results clearly indicate that the Internet offers unique opportunity to the brand manager to augment online brand personality.

Traditionally, a company tries to create a unique personality for its brand so that a customer can identify or associate with the brand. This gives a reason for the customer to return to the site over and over again. Online brands can create electronic chat rooms for discussions where actual customers represent the personalities of the brands. Interactions between customers or between customer and company produce a much more potent association than a print or television ad that uses a model to represent the target audience. In fact, there is empirical evidence to show that online communities increase repeat site visits and time spent in a given site (Kania, 2000).

But there is much more to creating a brand personality than purely offering Internet features; customers want a balance between online and off-line features. Everything that a company does and does not do contributes to its brand personality. The way it treats its employees is reflected by the way they treat the customers. Customers also see how the item the company sells is packaged, what type of delivery trucks the company uses, what events the company sponsors, and the way the company handles problems (Zyman, 2002).

Key Success Factors in Building Brands Online

The Internet offers the potential to gain new customers by generating product awareness, increasing market penetration, and gaining offshore customers through its global reach. In order to gain these brand-building benefits offered by the Internet, a few conditions (we call them the success factors) must be satisfied. These success factors are outlined below. Note that a number of these conditions are true for traditional (or off-line) brand building as well. We emphasize, however, on their relevance for online brand building.

Create brand recognition. This is the key step to building an online brand. The first and most critical step for a pure Internet company is to develop a name that stands out in customers' minds and relates to the item that it is selling. This may sound very much like a brick-and-mortar requirement, but it is even more important for a click-and-mortar company. Since pure click-and-mortar companies do not have a physical location that customers can drive past, creating a simple but memorable name is critical. If the Web site name is too long or complicated, potential customers will become frustrated and never check out the Web site.

One of the most often cited companies for creating a short but memorable name is Amazon.com. In addition, Amazon.com created a tag line to compliment its name: "The World's Largest Bookstore." This tag line explains why Amazon.com is a fitting name for this Web site: the Amazon River is the largest in the world and Amazon.com touts its selection of books as being the largest in the world.

There are a number of ways to create brand recognition. As we mentioned above, the company needs to develop a unique name that is easy to remember and spell. Perhaps a catchy logo or phrase will make the Web site stand out in customers' minds. Some companies even create a mascot or catchy "jingle" for the company. It is also important to have promotions and to advertise the special features of the Web site, such as speedy customer service. These last two factors, promotions and special/unique features, will be addressed later.

Protect the domain name. An online brand must steadfastly protect its domain name from unrelated firms or individuals. It is quite simple to register similar domain names and variations thereof that can confuse online consumers (Murphy et al., 2003). Usually, individuals register famous brand names to attract consumers to their sites or sell them to the highest bidder. There are two types of sites that are most harmful: gripe sites and parasites (Nemes, 2000). Gripe sites include a derogatory word to the domain name such as fordsucks.com. Parasites, on the other hand, capitalize on user typing errors (such as untied.com instead of united.com for United Airlines) to score hits. A successful online company should register all possible variations to its domain name that are vulnerable to abuse. For example, Exxon registered exxonsucks.com to preempt any possible battle with a cybersquatter.

Murphy, Raffa, and Mizerski (2003) have explored the domain name registration strategies by the world's top 75 brands. The results of their study indicate that top brands of the world are aware of the importance of global and national domain name registration. However, they are not very adept in monitoring gripe sites and parasites.

Differentiate the brand. Critical success factors differ between organizations, but it is critical that online e-tailers differentiate their brand from the crowd. This can be accomplished in a variety of ways:

- Give a good first impression on the site accompanied by good navigational tools.
- Use a domain name that is easy to remember and is globally sensitive. The aim should be to attract the right customer to the site.
- Make the Web site simple yet attractive. Design the navigational tools with this in mind.
- Make the site a one-stop shop. For example, if the Web site sells coffee, offer a variety of mugs, coffee tables, picture frames, and other amenities that would complement the product and keep the consumer and his/her money at the site.
- Offer prizes. There are some consumers who are attracted by online contests and prizes. Continuing with the above example, offer a customer the chance to win a coffee table.

E-mail is at the core of a good marketing mix. Permission-based e-mail is a key element in a profitable Internet business marketing mix. Among online purchasers, 73% claim that this is their most preferred method of learning about new products, services, and promotions from online retailers (Ottawa Business Journal, 2003). This method outranks traditional distribution channels such as TV, print, direct mail, telemarketing, and direct sales. The study conducted by FloNetwork Inc. asked online buyers how they learned about Internet merchants' goods and services. Six out of 10 respondents replied that permission-based e-mail was how they usually found out about new products, services, and/or promotions. This figure is two times more than that for banner ads, and eleven times more than that of magazines and TV combined. Additionally, 7 out of 10 online buyers divulged that they click through to a company's Web site as a result of permission-based e-mail newsletters and 61% report having made an online purchase as a result of permission-based e-mail.

Get to know who is coming to the site. Investigate how and why customers visit the Web site; then create unique ways to retain the right type of customers. There are some customers who are "thrift" shoppers and are not the "ideal" customers because they only purchase items that are on sale. These customers should not constitute the target market and hence the Web site may not want to attract only these types of customers. According to Gutzman (2000), it is actually a bad thing to get the wrong people to come to a site. The problem with having the wrong people come to a site is the confusion as to who are the real customers. This will make the brand manager's task of retaining customers even harder. In short, he/she should not focus too much on statistics and should focus more on attracting the right clientele.

The long-term goal of a Web site should be to create loyal customers who are loyal to its brand. It may be necessary to attract customers through the use of price promotions in the short-run, but in the long-run these types of promotions cannot be maintained if the Web site is losing money on each and every sale, as many of the dot-com companies discovered during the recent shakeout phase.

Encourage brand loyalty. This involves satisfying the customer over and over again. Consumer satisfaction occurs when the performance of the product exceeds expectation. The online brand manager should aim for this. Do not promise service that cannot be delivered. Offer long-term warranties, if possible, because warranties add value to the product and also increase its perceived quality. The convenience of shopping on the Internet should include a convenient service or pickup for the product. Delivery should be made in a reasonable amount of time and the product should be easily returnable, if necessary.

In addition, some customers may feel more comfortable actually speaking with a "real" person. Therefore, it is important to provide customer service through other channels besides the Internet. Consider providing a toll-free phone number, fax number, online chat sessions, and other channels preferred by customers. Do not limit the brand to being a purely Internet brand; the company should strive to create a proper balance between online and off-line presence.

Finally, loyalty programs that reward the customer for repeat purchases can be advantageous as well. For example, the brand manager could offer his/her customers a 10% discount after five purchases. By using such a program, he/she can encourage his/her customers to come back and make future purchases.

Address the privacy issue readily and openly. Given that the almost immediate concern of customers is the privacy factor involving the information they share with the company, one way to win and keep customer's loyalty is to give them more control over how their personal information is used. To ensure a better reception from customers regarding the exchange of information, Merkow (2000) recommends the adoption of the P3P in addition to posting "human-readable" privacy policies. The P3P allows customers to control how their personal identifying information is used. It is an embedded technology in the user's browser that confirms whether a site's privacy practices meets the user's predefined privacy preferences. Another popular electronic transfer system (EFT) is i-Escrow (Greenspan, 2000). The i-Escrow holds the customer's credit card funds in a trust account and the funds are not released to the seller until the customer has received the product and is satisfied with its condition. This is also an effective way to establish customer trust and provide good customer service. Another money transfer system, PayPal, has been popularized by eBay. By using PayPal, a buyer with an e-mail address can send money to a seller who has an e-mail address.

In general, the company must offer alternatives to customers in providing sensitive financial information. Some customers may prefer to give their credit card number, while others prefer to mail a check. Let the customer pay in the manner he/she feels the most comfortable with, be it by credit card, debit card, bank transfer, money order, or personal check.

Utilize cross-selling and cross-promotion to gain competitive advantage. The notion of cross-selling entails attracting customers to the site and then marketing products that are related in some way to the primary product. When the Web site is attracting the wrong customer base, cross-selling suffers. If the Web site is selling some products at a loss in hopes of cross-selling the profitable products and it hits upon price-sensitive shoppers who will buy only at the lowest price, then the company might find that all cross-selling efforts may be in vain.

In addition, a brand manager must try to develop online media relations with other Web sites. For example, hyperlinks to areas in his/her site on other Web pages can be very useful. Combine this with the use of meta-tagging. This entails including keywords in the pages describing the content of his/her site. Words used should be related to his/her business and help guide consumers to his/her Web site. Essentially, this is how a brand manager can drive traffic to his/her site. Other key elements for online promotions include submissions to online awards, online media relations, content-focused e-mail, and online contests.

In addition to these online promotions, it is important to create an off-line presence through promotions. Customers do not learn about new companies and/or products solely through the Internet. Customers live in a dynamic environment and therefore learn about new companies/Web sites through various types of media, including television, newspaper, magazines, and other media. Therefore, be sure to incorporate well-balanced promotions to attract as many new customers as possible.

Use online and traditional means to develop and manage your brand. Having an online and off-line presence can be an important factor for all brands, both established brands and start-ups. However, it is especially important that start-ups with limited resources be firm with their advertising dollars. Besides the usual online advertising opportunities such as banner ads, pop-up ads, and so forth, a company should also target off-line buyers by using advertising such as radio in a select group of cities and/or cable television. The mix of online and off-line media is essential to established organizations. Schwab, now a successful online brokerage house, still has 250 branches in the United States, and 70% of the American population is within 10 miles of a Schwab office. However, Schwab and e-Schwab have now become one organization due to their success online (Hanson, 2000).

Measure brand performance. In all industries and in all types of markets, it has been acknowledged that from strong brand equity flows customer loyalty and profits. The world's strongest brands share similar attributes regarding their success at branding. The foremost quality an organization should truly understand and focus on is the notion that its brand excels at providing the consumer with what he/she truly desires. A product that has been construed in a manner that complements the particular attributes the brand manager wishes to convey is going to be the winner. The attributes combined with the brand's image, the service, and other tangible and intangible components will create a complete and presentable product.

Performance Metrics

The brand manager needs to determine what his/her short-term and long-term objectives are and how he/she is going to measure the success or failure of his/her initiatives. In the rush to brand online, many companies failed to measure their Web site's performance accurately. It did not seem to matter if the company was losing money. Companies were pouring money down the drain because they failed to create metrics for performance.

The number of "eyeballs" that visit a site is measured differently depending on the company objective. How it is measured is interwoven in the online branding strategy. Some companies may choose not to measure the number of visitors because that number may be meaningless. It may be more important to measure the number of repeat visitors.

Therefore, it is essential to create specific, measurable performance metrics. For example, a brand manager may want 10% of his/her current customers to reorder within 2 weeks, and 20% to reorder within 2 months, and 50% to reorder within 1 year. He/she needs to create short-run metrics to ensure that his/her company is going to reach its long-term goals during the required time frame.

Follow a consistent brand strategy. Keeping the branding strategy consistent is essential to long-term growth and perhaps survival. There is a need to find a balance between continuity in the marketing activities and the innovation that is required to keep the product "fresh" in consumers' mind. The brand manager should not confuse his/her customer by changing or modifying his/her logo or his/her marketing message in hopes of gaining new customers, since what might happen instead is that he/she loses his/her current customers without any guarantee of attracting and retaining a larger percentage of new clients. Michelob provides a good example of what can happen when a brand endures numerous repositioning. It moved from an "It's Michelob" slogan in the 1970s to "Weekends Were Made for Michelob," and from "Put a Little Weekend in Your Week" to yet another campaign in the mid-1980s with "The Night Belongs to Michelob." This resulted in an unstoppable slide in sales. In 1994, another ad campaign titled, "Some Days Are Better Than Others" was introduced. It was designed to make the point that "a special day requires a special beer." The slogan was yet again modified to "Some Days Were Made for Michelob." As a result of continuous changes in the slogan, the average consumer was left dazed and confused as to when and where Michelob should be consumed. This was reflected in the sales performance of Michelob. In 1994, sales were 2.3 million barrels, as compared to 8.1 million barrels in 1980 (Hanson, 2000).

Some Questions Still Remain Unanswered

Given the great amount of research proclaiming the power of the Internet, we can safely assume that online communication of any type is not a trend that is soon going to disappear. However, we can admit to some fault finding in the quest to brand online. As advertising via television commercials has been experiencing difficulties in retaining the attention of viewers for quite some time, advertising and promoting on the Web is now wrestling with this same problem. How does one impress a potential online customer today? How dynamic does one's Web site have to be? What type of graphics will attract one's target market? Concurrently, the issue of customer "stickiness" or loyalty to a Web site is one that is difficult to read. How does one know if online brand management is the catalyst for an increase or a decrease in online popularity and/or sales?

The following issues also deserve some attention:

- Profiles of your customers cannot all be verified for accuracy, thereby creating a problem as to how you can define your customer and then market to them accordingly.

- How can you get online shoppers to reveal their true identity in order to serve them better and to develop a relationship of trust?
- There is an unknown time investment related to spending on advertisements and promotions via the Web.
- How do you know when to stop pouring money into your online site?
- The positioning of your brand in the mind of the consumer is often unknown to the brand manager. Thus the importance of online brand management is difficult to weigh with respect to a potential repositioning of the brand—if it is in question.

Acknowledgments

We thank Soumita Banerjee for research support and Maggie Madden, Julie Wolfe, and Jerome Cockburn for editorial support. The first author gratefully acknowledges the financial support of the School of Business and Economics, Indiana University Northwest, and the Research and University Graduate School of Indiana University.

Conclusion

Online brand management presents a twist on traditional brand management. In order to compete in today's marketplace, it asks the brand manager not to discard his/her knowledge of traditional brand management, but rather to shift his/her priorities toward the issues and contingencies regarding online brand management. Customer satisfaction must become priority. It could in fact become the company's defining competitive advantage, given that the battle for product differentiation is stronger than ever in today's marketplace. Granted that the brand manager has more opportunity than ever before to combine technology and marketing know-how to brand a product, the online world presents many challenges. As such, the brand manager must take advantage of the Internet's global reach to perpetuate his/her company's brand.

Creating an online brand can be a very difficult and time-consuming project. But remember, the most critical steps to creating an online brand are creating name recognition, providing a unique product and/or exceptional customer service, and advertising through a variety of media. It may be easy to think of these steps as a pyramid, but each of these requirements must be met to reach the ultimate goal: customer loyalty.

Online retailing has room for growth, and this gives the brand manager more reason to hone his/her brand management skills to take advantage of the increasing number of Web-savvy customers. By adhering to the issues that most affect the brand manager and ultimately the consumer, certain routes to failure can be avoided. The brand manager can use the key success factors outlined in this paper, as a strategic guide to aid in engaging, retaining, transacting, and sustaining new customers every day.

References

Aaker, D. A. (2002). The Internet as integrator: Fast brand building in slow growth market. *Strategy+Business, 28*, 48–57.

Amazon 2002 Annual Report. *www.amazon.com*

Amazon.com. (1998). Gary Trudeau and Amazon.com launch "The People's Doonesbury @ Amazon.com." Press Release Archive.

Braunstein, M., & Levin, E. H. (2000). *Deep branding on the Internet: Applying heat and pressure online to ensure a lasting brand.* Roseville, CA: Prima Venture.

Carpenter, P. (2000). *E-brands: Building an Internet business at breakneck speed.* Boston: Harvard Business School Press.

Dayal, S., Landesberg, H., & Zeisser, M. (2000). Building digital brands. *McKinsey Quarterly, 2*, 3.

de Chernatory, L. (2001). Succeeding with brands on the Internet. *Brand Management, 8*(3), 186–195.

Greenspan, R. (2000). Be seen and get paid. http://Internet_com's Electronic Commerce Guide – EC Tips.

Gutzman, A. D. (2000). Unconventional wisdom: Traffic is overrated. Retrieved from *http://ecommerce.Internet.com/solutions/tech_advisor/article/html*

Hanson, W. (2000). *Principles of Internet marketing.* Cincinnati, OH: South-western College Publishing.

Kania, D. (2000). *Branding.com: Online branding for marketing success.* Chicago: NTC Business Books, American Marketing Association.

Kapferer, J.-N. (1992). *Strategic brand management.* London: Kogan-Page.

Keller, K. L. (2002). *Strategic brand management: Building, measuring, and managing brand equity* (2nd ed.). Upper Saddle River, NJ: Prentice Hall.

McWilliam, G. (2000). Building strong brands through online communities. *Sloan Management Review, Spring*, 43–54.

Merkow, M. (2000). Inside the Platform for Privacy Preferences (P3P). http://Internet_com's Electronic Commerce Guide – EC Outlook.

Muller, B., & Chandon, J.-L. (2003). The impact of visiting a brand website on brand personality. *Electronic Markets, 13*, 210–221.

Murphy, J., Raffa, L., & Mizerski, R. (2003). The use of domain names in e-branding by the world's top brands. *Electronic Markets, 13*(3), 30–40.

Nemes, J. (2000). Domain names have brand impact. *B to B Chicago, 85*(12), 20–22.

Nielsen-NetRatings. (2003, February 20). Global Internet population grows an average of four percent year-over-year.

Ries, A., & Ries, L. (2000). *The 11 immutable laws of Internet branding*. New York: HarperCollins.

Roberts, M. L. (2003). *Internet marketing: Integrating online and offline strategies*. New York: McGraw-Hill Irwin.

Sealy, P. (1999). How e-commerce will trump brand management. *Harvard Business Review,* July–August, 171–176.

Travis, D. (2001). Branding in the digital age. *Journal of Business Strategy, 22*(3), 14–18.

Wilson, P. (2000, July 4). Canadians hot for net but slow to buy online. Retrieved from *www.ottawacitizen.com*

Zyman, S. (2002). *The end of advertising as we know it.* Hoboken, NJ: John Wiley & Sons.

Chapter VIII

The Evolution of the Theory and Practice of Marketing in Light of Information Technology

Daniela Andreini, University of Bergamo, Italy

Abstract

Marketing is a discipline that concentrates on the process of exchange between two market groups, and for this reason, it has been immediately involved with developments in the Internet—understood as a suitable phenomenon for discovering new opportunities and possible threats to modern business management (Burke, 1996) and as a commercial business tool (Alba et al., 1997; Quelch & Klein, 1996). The aim of this chapter is to highlight the marketing elements that, according to an accurate review of international literature, have been involved in the development of new information technology and, in particular, the Internet. The investigation concerns in particular

- *customers: the buying behavior of Internet users compared to traditional behavior;*
- *relations and communication: in this section we try to understand what are the barriers to the development of these relations: trust, safety, and manipulation are some of the obstacles examined;*

- *marketing research: an accurate review of international scientific literature highlights the online research techniques and tools that are of greater use to companies;*
- *marketing management: products, prices, place (distribution), and promotion are unequivocally decided by the company but may become an area of negotiation between companies and customers thanks to new multimedia tools; and*
- *marketing performance: this section illustrates what are the best performance indicators for measuring the activities carried out by an e-commerce project.*

Introduction

Marketing is a discipline that has become well-established within companies. It concerns the "social and managerial process by which a person, or group, obtains that which is the object of their desire, creating, offering and exchanging products and values with others" (Kotler, 1984, p.). It is because this discipline concentrates on the process of exchange between two market groups that is has been immediately impacted by new technologies such as the Internet. New terms have been coined within this discipline to describe the impact of technology, among which are interactive marketing (Deighton, 1996; Iacobucci, 1998; Webster, 1996), real-time marketing (McKenna, 1997), one-to-one marketing (Peppers & Rogers, 1997), and digital marketing (Parson, Zeisser, & Waitman, 1998). The problems arising from the recession of the "new economy," however, has made it necessary to carefully rethink and reposition some of the theories about the impact of the Internet on marketing.

The aim of this chapter is not to bring about a new interpretation of the marketing evolution in light of new technology but to highlight the marketing elements that, according to an accurate review of international literature, have been involved in the development of new information technology and, in particular, the Internet.[1] The investigation will focus on the following:

- relations and communication
- customers
- marketing research
- marketing management
- marketing performance

Evolution of the Theories of Internet Marketing

The study of marketing in the Web era has developed in different ways based on the value given to the new interacting technology. Four different schools of thought have emerged (Coviello & Milley, 2001):

> The first school, founded by Hoffman and Novak (1997), introduces the theory of a new level of marketing created by the effects of intrinsic interactivity of information technology. Venkataraman (2000, p. 15), for example, claims that the "Internet changes everything." The same reflections are made by Kotler (1999), who declares that "In the next ten years marketing will be restructured from A to Z" (p. 259). Webster[2] (1996) also argues that both strategic marketing and traditional-type operative marketing must radically evolve and change or otherwise disappear.
>
> The second school of thought, developed by authors such as Levin (1996) and Carter (1996), consider interactive technology as a potential component of the marketing mix. A practical example of this is the use of databases for the development of traditional and nontraditional advertising, sales promotions, and price discounts (Burke, 1997) and to improve sales staff activities (Blattberg & Deighton, 1991). This school of thought comes very close to the debates originating in the Harvard Business School concerning the future development of interactive marketing.

These two schools of thought consider marketing to be strongly influenced by new technology, both in its strategic and operative form. From this, one can deduce that new technology can expand and modify the makeup of the marketing mix. In contrast, the schools described below, consider new technology as a tool, targeted exclusively for supporting more operative marketing without, however, fundamentally modifying the strategic aspects.

> The third school of thought claims that new technology is only a new sales channel for the market (Ghosh, 1998; Quinn, 1999). Similarly, Peterson, Balasubramanian, and Bronnenberg (1997) suggests that the channel and the traditional market are complementary channels to distribute the product.
>
> The fourth and last school of thought, instead, supports a relativist relationship between the Internet and marketing (Haeckel, 1998), claiming that new technology can be used in different ways by different

companies. Some use new technology to completely restructure their company, while others use it exclusively to improve the performance of certain marketing activities (e.g., e-mail marketing, online advertising, online catalogs, etc.).

The position of this chapter is very close to the fourth school of thought. In this point of view, the Internet is considered, therefore, as a potentially revolutionary tool or opportunity. Its real potentiality shall be greater or less according to the inclination of the company itself to use it to develop business opportunities with customers, the market, and partners. The personal position of this author "supports" a vision that considers new technology as capable of modifying the role of the customer at both a strategic level and an operative level. I propose moving from considering customers as a passive group to thinking of them as an active group. This is neither trivial nor is it easier to carry out. This position is supported by recent theoretical trends which will be dealt with in the next paragraphs (Wind & Mahajan, 2002; O'Connor & O'Keefe, 2000). These consider the Internet able to modify operative and strategic company marketing models, only if integrated with more traditional tools and only if supported by precise managerial planning.

The Study Subject Matter

The aspects that feel the influence of new technology to the greatest extent concern fundamental variables of marketing activity such as advertising, distribution, services, customer care, and so forth. The Internet, in fact, allows business transformations within marketing strategies and operations as well as the same within behaviors and relations between enterprise and customer. This chapter looks at the following four elements (Figure 1):

- *customers:* it is well known that new technology has greatly contributed to improving the knowledge of consumers and has also changed their buying process. This section of the chapter concentrates on the buying behavior of online users as opposed to off-line users. In particular, the way in which they may actively participate in the commercial creation of goods and services is different. The aim of this contribution is to find consistent buying behavior models.
- *relations and communication:* can information technology change the nature of communication between company and stakeholders? Can these new and more direct forms of communication change the nature of commercial relations between people? In this section we try to understand

Figure 1. Internet fields of influence on marketing

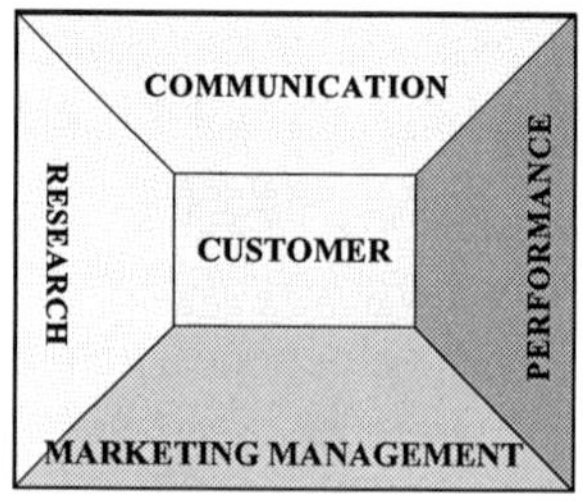

what are the barriers to the development of these relations: trust, safety, and manipulation are some of the obstacles that are examined.

- *marketing research*: this function has a key role in the development of marketing strategies. It is well known that no strategic plan can exist without first examining and researching the environment inside and outside the company. The Internet, however, has quantitatively and qualitatively improved data available to management who often have difficulty in managing and interpreting it. On one hand, an accurate review of international scientific literature highlights the online research techniques and tools that are of greater use to companies; and on the other hand, it highlights how the Internet has a natural tendency to autorationalization (e.g., autosegmentation).
- *marketing management*: starting from the 4Ps,[3] it is shown how the Internet has changed the strategy and operative impact of marketing on company activity. Products, prices, place (distribution), and promotion are unequivocally decided by the company, but may become an area of negotiation between companies and customers thanks to new multimedia tools.
- *marketing performance*: in this section I focus upon the best performance indicators for measuring the activities carried out by an e-commerce project.

The Impact of the Internet on Customers

Introduction

As seen in the first paragraph, marketing is defined as a process that enables different people to obtain that which is object of their desire through commercial exchange. The people involved in company activity, therefore, may be many, some of whom are the suppliers, the state, employees, customer, and financiers. But the fundamental person for the accumulation of value is, without doubt the customer, who permits survival and profitability of the enterprise (Grönroos, 1996).

The customer[4] becomes, for all intents and purposes, the key agent in the new approach to marketing developed at an academic level; the indispensable reference for this are the theories belonging to relationship marketing of the Scandinavian School and the theory on American value (Grönroos, 1994; Porter, 1985). Both, in fact, consider the customer at the center of company activities, in order to create economic and social value even for the enterprises. On the one hand, the theories of relationship marketing consider relationships a suitable activity for creating value, and on the other hand, the value theory claims that the main company processes create value for both sides. Both, however, consider marketing the main activity suitable for the creation and perception of value on the part of the customer and company.

Berthon, Holbrook, and Hulbert (2000) claim to this effect that "the type of modern marketing evolution depends on two distinctive keys or dimensions: one lower or one higher level of market power owned alternatively by the consumer or the producer." These same authors explain, in fact, that after the era of customer supremacy, induced by different factors, among which is hypercompetition, overproduction, and the opening of international commerce, the era of "strong interaction using paradigms of emerging information" is reached. This means that companies must participate in the formation of traditional and virtual market relationships which must be increasingly more intense and well constructed, to satisfy not only the final customer, but also the company stakeholders.

It is fundamental to first consider the company: it decides in which stage of the commercial relationship and in what way the customer may actively participate in the creation and commercialization of goods or services, and only afterward may the customer decide for him-/herself if and how to actuate such a transaction, according to his/her maturity and tendency to use new technology. The clash between these two "cultures" leads to the development of new relationships which can create alternative forms of interaction, based not only on the use of a single or prevalent communication tool, but also on the integration of different tools of consumer marketing. So, for example, in the area of online customer care, communications through e-mail can be integrated by a toll-free number, fax, telephone, and other forms of company communication.

The Behavior of the Modern Consumer

The customer, as shown above, is the center of marketing activities, and his/her satisfaction is the principle key to the success of the company. The Internet represents, in this respect, an extremely efficient tool. It facilitates the interaction between customer and company, allowing the company not only to satisfy the customer's requirements, but also to understand the needs and habits of its users more clearly, quickly, and cheaply. This cognitive process leads to a better structuring of both the company supply and networks with suppliers, and internal organization by the company.

In order to improve the ability of the company to understand in-depth and construct supply suitable for the customer's requirements, Leeflang and Wittink (2000) maintain that the market quota must be replaced by the "customer quota" and that the brand manager should be replaced by the "customer manager" and finally, the profitability of the product must be replaced by the profitability of the customer. These activities have been established for many years in industrial sectors since the number of industrial customers is less and nominally they account for a major part of turnover. However, the use of the Internet now also allows similar analysis and monitoring processes to be applied to vast numbers.

In particular, the study of customer behavior on the Internet is strongly related to certain marketing variables (Hoffman, Novak, & Yung, 2000) of fundamental importance for the support of managerial activity and particularly for the following:

- Creating communication and relationships with the customer
- Stimulating buying and contact with the company
- Checking the degree of online customer satisfaction
- Understanding the role of online company brand names
- Construction of interactive and attractive Internet sites

The theories of online buying behavior are divided into different tendencies: Wind (2001) has underlined the urgency to completely modify business strategies in light of new technology available to consumers of the new millennium. Mahajan (2001) concluded, on the contrary, that many aspects of the behavior of the final consumer and marketing remain the same, and he advises customer managers instead to go into the human features of buying behavior more deeply.

A third theory has risen from these two theories, known as the "hybrid consumer" by Wind and Mahajan (2002). This describes the consumer/user as one who uses different media and combines human needs with highly rational behavior. The modern consumer is not yet the cybernetic agent, super computerized, and already informed, as described in the first theories of Internet marketing (Cronin, 1994), but he/she is neither a more traditional consumer as described in the first marketing manuals (Kotler, 1984). The new concept consumer has been classified a "centaur," an image that indicates the upper part of the centaur as the more rational aspect of the buying process, and the lower part as the more irrational and impulsive aspect of the buyer. This representation depicts a subject that, although having mastered new technology, is still guided by very human desires. He/she is the humoral consumer, that is, he/she shows the behavior of unpredictable consumption; but it is essential for companies to be present at all the relevant points of contact and interaction with him/her.

The arrival of the Internet and the recent development of new communication and interaction tools (Web TV, mobile phone, satellite, etc.) have not ousted the common use of traditional tools, not even within the buying process of a customer who is totally open to online transactions. There is, in fact, the idea that online and off-line customers are completely different from one another, and that the two categories must be approached by companies in totally different ways (O'Connor & O'Keefe, 2000). But this, as we will see, is not always possible.

With respect to the consumer described in traditional marketing models, the modern consumer accesses a greater amount of information, has more sophisticated means of making contact with the global market and has different media available for avoiding advertising and traditional communication systems. But this does not mean that the online customer is more rational or less emotional than the off-line consumer. In short, modern buying activity conforms to a more dynamic model, where sensorial and emotional involvement transforms the buying process into a "buying experience."[5]

Alongside the daily increase in information and computerization, interest for what cannot be identified as rational is placed: namely, the set of perceptions, beliefs, and sensorial activities of the consumer that in the examination of final consumer behavior certainly cannot be ignored.

All this coincides with the vision of modern markets, in which

- information is not always available (Simon, 1957). One just has to think that with a single research engine only just over 50% of the significant pages on a specific topic are identified and this percentage rises to 90% if one uses at least six different research engines (Bradlow & Schmittlein, 2000);
- decisions are taken according to limited rationality, seeking the most satisfying but not the best solution (Simon, 1957); and

- it is not true that the choice of market subjects are always directed toward opportunist aims (Adler & Kwon, 2002; Yli-Renko et al., 2001). Behavior and adaptive learning should in fact be considered, that is, the so-called phenomenon of "path dependency" (Bell & Pavitt, 1993; Nelson & Winter, 1982; Rosenberg, 1995).

For this reason, analysis of consumers by the company should be characterized, on the one hand, by usefulness and functionality, and that they develop new technological tools during online purchases, and on the other, by the examination of perceptive and sensorial behavior of the traditional buying process integrated with new systems of communication and transaction.

Internet and new technology are not able today to replace the pleasure of certain segments of clientele of going into a perfume shop, testing the cosmetics personally, trying different fragrances, and exchanging opinions on the experience with sales staff and friends. With this image, one can conclude that although new technology has brought more tools of information and rationality into the buying process, it cannot replace the human pleasures of personal and sensory interaction, an aspect that must be strongly monitored by the company.

Differences Between the Online Buying Process and the Traditional Buying Process

In the past, in order to better understand the distinction between the behavior of the online customer and the off-line customer, a traditional process of buying was proposed in which the major differences between virtual buying and traditional buying were highlighted. Although this model is useful to schematize different commercial behavior according to the transaction tool used, this does not mean that the customers behave unequivocally or use only one buying tool. They, in fact, may sway from one side to another, sometimes combining traditional activities with virtual ones in order to buy only one item. The starting point for the study of this behavior came from the work of O'Connor and O'Keefe (2000), which compares online and off-line buying situations in the buying process of final goods by a consumer.

As we can see from Table 1, the online consumer seems to adopt a more rational behavior thanks to the use of computerized and informative tools, but in reality, the buying process is currently a combination of the two models shown above. An online buyer may, in fact, perceive a need for a particular product from the mass media, seek information and evaluate the products on the Internet, exchange opinions with persons he/she knows and trusts, buy in a physical shop and then evaluate the performance of the product in an online community. Even

Table 1. Comparison between the online and off-line buying process of the consumer (Adapted from O'Connor & O'Keefe, 2000)

BEHAVIOR	OFF-LINE MODEL	ONLINE BEHAVIOR
Recognition of the need	Recognition of the need can originate from an internal stimulus (physiological and psychological need) or an external stimulus, some of which include: • advertising and promotion; • points of sale and visual merchandising; • emulation; • social requirements, and so forth Companies stimulate demand using advertising presented in such a way that is strategically in favor of the company offer	Online advertising is available at the discretion of the user (e.g., pop-up, banner). This does not change the fact that all other influences are the same whether online or off-line
Information research	The perception of the risk levels for buying and the risk of use of the product determine the amount of energy used by the user when searching for information and for evaluation before buying	The costs of searching for information are reduced or eliminated, thereby simplifying the comparisons between competing companies. Buying experiences and third-party buying are easily accessible even within news groups
Evaluation of the alternatives	Evaluation of the alternatives may occur in different ways by • evaluation of the attributes; • experience of other consumers; • expected personal value; and • preference of a brand name. In particular, the research carries out a significant role when too much information is available or when there is a need to acquire a "status symbol"	On the Internet, automatic compensatory decisional techniques have developed (research engines[1]) which are unconnected to the brand and to testing. In this case, the Internet assists in the evaluation of the attributes and in preference of a brand name News groups and online forums have a significant role in the exchange of opinions on buying experiences of consumers
Buying	The decision to buy is taken based on different factors, including • brand name; • buying point; • quantity; • moment of purchase; and • method of payment	The Internet requires very little interaction and any bargaining of the buying conditions is limited
Postpurchase evaluation	The postpurchase experience influences the attitude toward the brand name, the probability of buying again, and the positive passing of information by word of mouth to others[20]	Information by word of mouth spreads quickly within discussion groups resulting in an accelerated diffusion curve

within one buying phase the person may show hybrid behavior. So, for example, the decision to buy may involve the Internet, using online auctions, wireless systems such as the mobile phone, from which he/she can receive a message that the auction has finished, and traditional systems, if the buyer decides to collect the products at a physical location. This leads enterprises to examine the behavior of the modern consumption completely and drives them to develop different methods of communication and interaction. Therefore if, on the one hand, a business must understand when and how the Internet intervenes in the buying process of its customers, on the other hand, this analysis must be backed up by examination of the real benefits that virtual connection can bring to the customer.

In conclusion to this mapping of the buying process, the following will be identified:

a) Which consumers are more inclined to use different interaction tools to start, develop, and conclude the buying process for a particular product and service.
b) Which are the multimedia tools and what usefulness they will have.
c) How many potential users are prepared to use any of the multimedia tools.
d) The investment in interaction systems compared to the number and economic potential of each segment, that is, the return on investments in information technology.

All these data can be also used by a business to segment the market in order to better address its technological integration in the buying process of its customers.

Moreover, the use of different online and off-line interaction and information tools does not only respond to functional benefits but must also take into account the emotional and social benefits involved in the buying process. In this case we do not talk of the buying process but of the *buying experience.* This term involves qualitative elements which concern entertainment, culture, information and enjoyment. Each type of product will involve a different type or level of experience. There are various aspects involved in this area, which may be physiological, behavioral, and sociological, whose value is often of great importance. Some of these concern the components of value according to Holbrook (1999), in particular

- the desire for excellence: that is, to take the most effective and efficient decision possible;
- social status;
- the esteem of the community;
- ethics—this applies mainly to ecological products or products from underdeveloped economies;
- social need;

- amusement; and
- aesthetics.

These are only some of the components that make up a buying experience and they are often difficult to measure as personal perceptions cannot be unequivocally connected to one event. Something, for example, which amuses and entertains one consumer may bore another. For this reason, customers should be studied segmented also by their lifestyles or by more qualitative variables concerning their sensorial perception of the buying experience.

The Impact of the Internet on Online Business Communication and Relations

Online Communication

The Internet modifies two fundamental marketing components: communication and relations. It has, in fact, been shown to be a fundamental tool of communication that integrates with, but does not replace, traditional commercial channels and tools. This is due to its intrinsic communicative features and, in particular,

- the ability to store at low cost vast quantities of information in different virtual areas (Peterson et al., 1997);
- the availability of powerful and economic tools for search, organization, and diffusion of information (Peterson et al., 1997);
- personalization of communication (Quelch & Klein, 1996);
- the possibility of taking advantage of informative experiences is much greater than that provided by a printed catalog (Peterson et al., 1997); and
- the temporal synchronicity that changes the method of traditional company communication "to one way" (McKenna, 1997).

The new paradigms of communication introduced by the Internet are not unknown to communication science; the definitions of one-to-one, one-to-many, many-to-one, and many-to-many communication (Hoffman & Novak, 1996) can also be applied to the usual forms of communication such as the telephone, direct advertising, and cultural events sponsoring. In reality it is the speed of message exchange that is changed by Internet as well as the development of contact opportunities. All the theories and mass communication models for commercial use, which are based on more interactive communication systems and which were difficult to put into practice due to the enormous cost of implementation, can finally be developed a low cost on the Internet. In particular, examples of theories developed in light of interactivity, such as relationship marketing (Grönroos, 1996) and company network systems (Johanisson, 1987; Powell, 1990; Rullani, 1993), can now be realized in practice due to the existence of the Internet.

Online, one can use all communication models theorized and practiced traditionally (Hoffman, Novak, & Yung, 1996). A paradigmatic example is the contemporary use of *broadcasting* models, whose standard messages are broadcast to many subjects, and *narrowcasting* models, whose targeted messages are spread to a limited number of people. On the Internet even the methods of communication are many: both *push* and *pull* methods work together. The push method consists of an essentially passive recipient receiving messages that are not requested; on the contrary, with the pull method, it is the customer who requests and makes sure he/she receives the message.

Another fundamental aspect of communication in the Internet is by word of mouth, a form of communication that cannot be controlled by the business, the so-called "gossip" (Grönroos, 1999). Traditionally, when a business planned its company communication activities, it did not worry in the least about information that circulated amongst consumers, as the occasions for meeting were limited. Only during market research did the levels of satisfaction and the perceptions of consumers emerge and were taken into consideration and analyzed so that the offer could be improved. On the Internet this is not possible. Communication by word of mouth has become even more powerful, the discussion groups on the Internet are extremely numerous and opinions and buying experiences are freely exchanged and are outside the company's control. One of the main interests of today's enterprises should be nonstructured communication, that is, communication that was not possible before the advent of the Internet. At this point, the enterprise should monitor its position within these discussion groups, without attempting to manipulate the opinions of the consumer and so introducing communication that is free from commercial conventions. Unfortunately, in commercial practice, certain cases of incorrect behavior by companies have been observed. They have attempted to influence the opinions of online discussion groups, concealing their true identity. Many of the news groups and online forums have codes of ethics that forbid, for example, advertising by companies. These codes of ethics should be respected; if not, the online community would be slowly abandoned due to lack of trust by the participants. At this point, the enterprise would not even receive the benefits of its online monitoring.

Communication over the Internet is therefore fast, direct, and above all, interactive. Businesses must radically change their position and start to listen and seriously communicate with their customers and potential customers.

Online Business Relations

Good online communication leads to good interaction with the customer, which may then transform into a stable and continuing relationship. This last aspect is fundamental for carrying out the company's marketing targets, which, as highlighted in the introduction, concern the following in particular (Kotler, 1984):

- The efficiency of exchange activity
- The satisfaction of the target market

In order to further understand the dynamics of exchange, we can refer to the Scandinavian theory of relationship marketing in which marketing activities shift from a mere attraction of the consumer to activities concerning the relationship, and in particular, the care of the needs and expectations of the customers over time (Ravald & Grönroos, 1996). The concept of interaction develops according to those activities that allow mutual influence between the different people involved in the communication. Specifically, online interaction is less expensive and can be developed more rapidly with respect to traditional interaction, but it can also be more easily broken down.

The relationship is instead a much deeper notion: it is the bond that unites two or more people over a long period of time. The creation of a relationship with customers and other horizontal and vertical actors in the market allows businesses to gather better commercial information with the aim of improving the ability to answer unexpected changes in the market. The relationship, therefore, requires listening on the part of the enterprise and above all the ability to reply immediately and in a personalized way. According to this theory, interaction and communication to be developed with the company stakeholders are two of the key processes of marketing strategy for recognizing, analyzing, and finally, satisfying the needs of the customer (Grönroos, 1999).[6] In particular, the ability to satisfy the requirements of the customer allows an exchange between the company and the customer to take place (Grönroos, 1999). The processes that occur between enterprise and customer and, particularly, relationship, mutual satisfaction of requirements, and commercial exchange, can be developed thanks to the existence of different channels of communication, which must answer to the requirements of flexibility, speed, and integration.

We can deduce, therefore, how important new information and communication technology is for creating profitable relationships which are continuous over time with the different market operators. The Internet is a very powerful tool for this type of relationship, but taken on its own, it cannot enjoy the status of sufficient and necessary condition for the concept of relationship as such. In fact, communication, interaction, and relationships must be consistent with one another, especially if they come from different company communications channels (cross-channel). This implies that all communication tools used by an enterprise, whether more or less innovative, must extend to integrated and uniform communication with the customer. Often, we hear of information that differs between Internet sites, the call center, or the same company representative. Customers do not find consistency between communications and relationships that they try to establish online and those that develop from other company channels.

The activities of communication and interaction must be planned so that the customer trusts the company, and considers it an organization capable of "relating" to his/her needs, so that a long-lasting and continuous relationship in different places and situations can be established. In order to achieve this, the enterprise must create

- a company organization in which the different channels of communication are used as an opportunity and not as businesses in conflict with one another;
- customer relationship management (CRM) systems integrated within all company departments;
- integrated databases that allow data to be shared by all people within the company; and
- measuring system for evaluating the commerce results which can also measure the economic contribution of all cross-channel and cross-device activities.

The enterprise must therefore be able to create a consistency in content, relationships, participation, and sharing with the customer using different company communication tools (cross-device), in different place, and even with different people. This consistency is the basis for creating trust between the business and customer.

Trust and the Internet

Relationships and interactivity can only and exclusively be achieved when there is cooperation from the customer. If he/she does not collaborate in the exchange of information, essential for the personalization of products and services, a relationship can never be established. The fundamental prerequisite for creating this exchange of information between company and customer is *trust*.

Moreover, also in the marketing literature, trust is considered a fundamental variable in establishing any relationship with the consumer and to develop a commercial relationship over time. Trust is one of the mainstays in economic relationships that, if present, allows significant innovation using new technology, and if absent, becomes a barrier to development and evolution of business.

Because of its virtuality, Internet trust earns a peculiar position of value because of the following features:

a) *Overabundance of information*: contrary to what one may think, this feature causes the greatest disorientation amongst users, who, because of their overexposure to information, need operators and middlemen to clarify their ideas, by the construction of informative content.

b) *Telepresence*: anthropological and economic studies have shown that trust is created by continuous relationships, and physical and cognitive vicinity. All this leads to a "paradox of online trust" (Ugolini, 1999) in which relationships come from the rather original context of physical and temporal distance and without concrete human contact.

It is, therefore, necessary to first investigate, study, and understand how one can act using the Internet to create an environment that inspires trust and empathy. If not, it will be very difficult and practically impossible to establish any type of relationship with customers and in particular with prospective customers.

Initially, trust must be understood in economic terms: it consists of a cognitive system of predicting the behavior of other people, which is created by the request of confirmation of what has already been experimented in terms of other people's behavior. In particular, according to Whitener, Brodt, Korsgaard, and Werner (1998), trust consists of three peculiarities: in the first place, by the expectations and conviction that the actions of the opposite party are carried out in good faith; second, by the conviction that the opposite party cannot force or control this conviction; and last, by the perception that his/her own performance depends on the actions of the opposite party (reciprocity principle).

Trust, therefore, is a cognitive process based on reciprocity, which may be more or less conscious, that is established between two or more people interacting with each other. The perception that one of the two is not in good faith, or that one of the two has a greater position of force in the relationship, causes a lack of trust. This is based on the perception that one of the two subjects will behave dishonestly for his/her own advantage and not for the common good of the established relationship.

If trust exists, instead,

a) the uncertainties and times of the decisional process are reduced, because it allows the decider to take less information into consideration, turning to experiences that have already been experimented with in the past. This occurs when the brand is used as a synthesis of the qualitative expectations established by the customer;
b) there is an increased tendency to give out information, as the person is sure that the information will be correctly used; and
c) the use of information supplied by interacting people increases as they are considered reliable sources of information.

A recent study has verified that the following six factors create online trust (Cheskin Research, 2000). It should be noted that these elements have a similarity with off-line company reality.

- *Brand name*: the transfer of a well-established brand name to the off-line world gives greater credibility to the Internet site, particularly when brand communication is consistent in both environments.
- *Research*: the opportunity of freely seeking information and data in Internet sites permits a better relationship of trust to be created between the company and its users.
- *Fulfillment*: even the smallest promise must be fulfilled online, for example, replies to e-mails within twenty-four hours, or real updating of online data compared to information received off-line and vice versa. These small accomplishments allow the development of the perception of reliability of the company, which can be extended to any transactions or giving out of personal data.
- *Presentation*: even the graphic presentation must be simple and allow smooth flowing surfing, as it gives a greater perception of the intrinsic and visible qualities of the Internet site. This communication must be consistent with the traditional company presentation and must not diverge from the other channels of communication adopted by the company.
- *Technology*: the presence of sophisticated databases and advanced technology improve the perception of quality of the company and the integration between the channels of communication.
- *Information*: online information, according to research, must have certain key features which are accuracy, completeness, the presence of neutral

reviews, continuous updating, and the possibility to personalize the content of the Internet sites, even using other multimedia tools, such as mobile phone, booths, satellites, and so on.

- *Accurate information on safety*: the presence of regulations that ensure correct functioning of the informative or commercial relationship, the presence of logos such as Visa, trade associations, and recognized institutions create a greater perception of safety for customers and users.

In conclusion, trust is an essential component for building online relationships, and must be planned and programmed carefully by the company through all online and off-line contacts with the customer.

Personalization

From the beginning of the 1990s, even the modern final customer has moved closer to the industrial customer, mainly due to the increase in his/her buying power toward enterprises. In fact, although the number of final consumers is greater compared to industrial consumers, and subsequently the individual market quotas are less, repeated buying is of great importance to the modern seller. Also, the same final customer has become more careful of his/her spending, is more informed, and appreciates the exchange of information with other consumers to a greater extent.

Consumption in the new millennium, therefore, moves from mass models to individual consumption models, more personalized to the preferences of each customer. The development of these models force the company to get to know its customers better, anticipating their preferences and needs. Only until a few years ago was this realized exclusively through long-term and medium-term relationships; today, this occurs automatically in a few minutes thanks to sophisticated software for online personalization.

Interaction, in fact, foresees a two-way communication, in which the customer not only replies to company communications but using the Internet and other multimedia systems, he/she can even influence the productive decisions using the stated activities of personalization (Rayport & Jaworsky, 2001).

Personalization online can be created in two ways:

1. directly by the user by selecting and arranging the site content, or compiling a questionnaire; or
2. automatically by the enterprise according to the previous behavior of the customer or other customers belonging to the same target. In this case, the

customer has a passive role in the formation of the product and service online.

In the first personalization process, in particular, all information given out directly and automatically by the customer is used by the business to create subjective solutions of the Internet site, the product, and connected services including payment, assistance, and the help with the use of the company offer. This new idea of developing online communication and relationships was conceived by Godin (1999) using the term *permission marketing*. This theory suggests that explicit permission given by the customer is the basis for creating personalized advertisement and promotions. With this authorization, the company can build a synergic relationship and at the same time it can increase targeting precision. Authorized advertising, for example, which means not only the authorization to receive company information but also any information that may be interesting to the user, has much higher returns in terms of commercial effectiveness compared to results from the simple activity of spamming.[7] Permission marketing to a large public can only be achieved if the company has advanced technology and powerful databases; without this, it would be impossible to achieve personalization on a vast scale due to the high off-line contact costs. Despite of Godin's imprecision in explaining how firms can earn different levels of trust from customers (Krishnamurthy, 2000), this theory gives another option to increase interaction between customers and businesses.

The second personalization approach, instead, can be achieved automatically with less cognitive effort on the part of the user. The pages are subjectivized, in fact, autonomously by enterprises, thanks to monitoring tools applied to the Internet, the most powerful of which is the traceability of user behavior (the so-called log files[8]). This last activity allows development of ad hoc Internet pages constructed according to behavioral preferences and type of surfing carried out by the users during their online sessions. In this way, businesses try to attract the attention of the user to promotions, product advertising, and to information concerning the interests shown by the same user. This automatic personalization, in fact, even though revealing itself, for example, with standard online advertising messages, concerns exclusively the interests or products previously bought or visited by surfers. Although they are unaware of it, surfers are hit with targeted and subjectivized advertising messages. This all occurs without the permission of the customer and is automatically controlled by the enterprise.

The use of both these activities of personalization, even though they have evident benefits to the users, must not be exaggerated. On the one hand, the first type of personalization can bring problems of surfing and use of company multimedia services, because the subjectivization of the online products and services requires direct activation by the customer and selection of the various different options, filling in of questionnaires or personal interviews may take a long time. The user, however, often does not want to spend too much time in front of the monitor answering questions on his/her personal preferences. The time required for these activities becomes, in this way, a burden for surfers, and a request for personalization that is too demanding may decrease the perceived value of the online commercial transaction. On the other hand, the second type of personalization does not require direct action by the buyer, but may be invasive. In fact, Web pages that are continuously tailored according to surfing or to previous purchases of the customer, or other similar customers, may make the user feel "under observation" and less free to surf and choose the many options that exist online. This kind of personalization, therefore, although at times is considered an added value for "lazier" users, is instead perceived as an infringement for those users who do not want to feel "observed" during their online purchasing.

For the reasons mentioned above, companies should avoid the danger of excessive personalization that may cause users to alienate their affections. As mentioned above, in fact, the cognitive effort required by the buyer to fill in a product personalization form, or the continuous automatic personalization of Internet site content, may lead the user to abandon the purchase.

Not all buyers, therefore, desire a personalized version of products. In reality some are seeking to select a standard product in the minimum time possible and with the least amount of commitment. In order to remedy this, Internet sites should always include a standard version of their products and services, together with the option of personalization. During the automatic personalization of online commercial supply, instead, many users would like to feel free to select and evaluate a large amount of products without being manipulated by the company. The enterprise should first verify the tendency to tailoring of the products using behavior analysis of its target customers and therefore verify the level of monitoring that the customer will be submitted to in order to buy the product.

For these reasons, these activities must be carefully measured according to the target. Another important aspect is the cost of personalization of online commercial supply. In fact, investments in monitoring technology, archive databases, and management of information on users may be extremely high. From a recent survey it was shown that it costs from $250,000 to over $1 million to personalize a site (Jagannathan, Srinivasan, & Kalman, 2002).

In spite of all the problems mentioned above, if these activities are balanced and carried out well, they offer the customer an excellent possibility for personalizing multimedia configuration tools, including composition of the product, communication structuring with the enterprise (e-mail, SMS, satellite, Web TV, and Internet site), delivery methods, logistics timing, and the different payment options. All this creates a better relationship between the company and customer and therefore a greater possibility of exchange of information and products between the two sides.

The Impact of Internet on Marketing Research

Marketing research is based on information concerning the various agents that influence the commercial performance of the enterprise. This information is the predominant feature of any transaction and information that travels over the Internet is particularly important. The driving force of Internet business, as illustrated by Kalakota and Whinston (1996), is the perception that the spread and ease of access of information is crucial for the effective functioning of any market. The Web, therefore, can be seen as an informative resource and a tool for gathering data, which is evolving rapidly. The main use of this temporary information is for managerial decisions (Holsapple, Joshi, & Singh, 2000). Structuring of the units of information within a specific organizational context, therefore, creates the fundamental knowledge for strategically developing each decisional process.

The ability to gather, manage, and use online information in commercial transactions, in particular, determines the competitive advantage. Information exchange, given the low costs of transactions, lead to the creation of information-rich environments that give rise to new methods of approach to markets by all people involved in a particular transaction.

There are many different types of online market research and these can be subdivided into

a) content research; and
b) online behavior and preferences monitoring.

Content research blends perfectly with the often-mentioned characteristics of the Internet, which allow improvement in the circulation of information and increase knowledge, essential for the development of managerial decisions. Thanks to the Internet, macroeconomic information can be gathered (e.g., market trends, consumption tendency, competition, etc.) from different consulting and research companies, trade associations, and public organizations, such as chambers of commerce and employer's associations.

Often data may concern single subjects or market segments in a well-defined sector. In this case, the greatest difficulty will be the retrieval of very diffused data, sometimes referring to only one customer (recurring often in industrial sectors). It is worth underlining that so-called infomediators, exist on the Internet who resell sensitive data of Internet users gathered through free online services (e.g., Internet connections).

This type of data is now easily accessible online through subscriptions to research services or simple paid file downloads, that is, the direct loading of data from an external database onto one's PC. The Internet, in this case, does not change the nature and value of the research content but makes information and reports required by the company more accessible and usable.

Thanks to Internet, research into the profile and behavior of Internet users may also concern individuals, and has the aim of planning one-to-one marketing (Miller, 1995a), and particularly to

- construct user profiles according to their surfing behavior;
- personalize the Internet site or differentiated Web advertising activities;
- monitor the effectiveness of communication schedules and online merchandising;
- suggest new product allocations in the virtual store, or even, eliminate the least visited products from the virtual shelves; and
- optimize the technical performance of the site or surfing.

These data can be gathered and analyzed directly by the enterprise or studied by outsourcing them to specialized research companies. The sources in this case are as follows:

- registration data
- log files (surfing data)
- online transactions in the case of an e-commerce site

Personal data are gathered from forms for registration to Internet sites or services, Internet addresses from received mail, and forums activated on the Internet site. These data, however, are not very significant, especially when the monitoring system is not very efficient as data could be falsified by the user or when a service does not exist or a high-value product is not available online (e.g., banking services). These data, as stated in the previous paragraph, are not significant to predict consumer behavior.

Gathering of surfing data, instead, concerns gathering the preferences of the user. Traditional qualitative research is greatly limited by the impossibility to verify that declared in questionnaires of customers interviewed during company monitoring. During interviews and focus groups, in fact, customers often declare preferences which are subsequently disproved by the real behavior of the customer at the point of sale. Research carried out directly at the point of sale, however, is prohibitive in economic terms. On the Internet, instead, data concerning online preferences of users are disseminated throughout the network in online forums, discussion groups, mailing lists, and by surfing behavior. This information indicates the preferences of the target user. Certain Internet sites exist, which gather, in a logic and organized way, the opinions of consumers diffused throughout various forums, newsgroups, and mailing lists. Furthermore the statistics per page (generally called a *hit*), and sellers who have divided products per sub-page can potentially determine the number of users who have surfed the site, where, in what way, and for how long. By studying the path of the Internet user, sellers may perceive what are the products that attract greater attention. In this way, they can easily gather surfing data and, if necessary, data on products that have not been selected by the buyer. Analysis of surfer behavior can also be gathered according to brand, or the order in which they were consulted.

The analysis of buying behavior concerns control of the buying activity of online products which was traditionally performed by the sales force in physical distribution points (Burke, 1996).[9] This caused great difficulty in interpretation of both the data gathered and of the problems relating to the relationships with retailers. These barriers preventing the gathering of information were usually overcome by direct monitoring activity at the point of sale. This, however, was extremely costly to realize, for example, with video cameras, audio recorders, and interviews. It is evident that this type of activity can only be sustained economically by multinationals. The Internet has the advantage of implying that it is simple to implement by monitoring log files. Some of the most used measuring systems are the conversion rates from simple Web users to site visitors, from site visitors to prospective customers, from prospective customers to buying customers, and from buying customers to loyal customers.

Despite the usefulness of the monitoring systems stated, the problems subsist however for those customers who do not use Internet as a commercial tool and use other channels such as telephone, fax, e-mail, and personal visits. In this case, online data gathering represents only a minimum part of the real and potential customers. In order to acquire sufficient knowledge of the profiles and behavior of one's customer, it is therefore desirable to integrate online data gathering with data from all the other front-office tools. In order to prevent this discrepancy, the business must develop and promote the integration of different marketing channels: traditional and new. The aim is to create a system of integrated communication. All online marketing activities already occur within conventional marketing channels and therefore must be considered inside any company integration strategy. In spite of this, complete integration of different channels is still "an intriguing idea rather than a practiced reality" (Davenport, Harris, & Kohli, 2001). This situation is due mainly to the problem of technical realization, costs, and implementation times.

The Impact of the Internet on Marketing Management and on the Marketing Mix

Introduction to Online Management and Marketing Mix

Marketing management is "the process of planning and realization of the conception of pricing, promotion, distribution of ideas, goods and services, to create exchanges that permit the aims of individuals and organizations to be achieved" (Kotler, 1984). The process of marketing management starts with the gathering, analysis, and study of market data (e.g., examination of the customer, potential demand, competition, distributing channels, etc.) that together lead to the identification of the opportunities and threats present in the market. These data, once processed by the company strategy management, becomes part of marketing campaign processing. Investments for these marketing campaigns are processed according to the resources available to the company to coincide with the company operational units. The marketing campaigns are then carried out and finally monitored to check their levels of efficiency and effectiveness.

As we have seen previously, the reference environment, customer behavior, analysis means and the capacity of managerial control, as well as company resources are modified on the Internet.

In this section, the classic and traditional elements of marketing management will be analyzed, that is, the marketing mix (product, price, promotion, and place [distribution]), explaining how they evolved in light of new technology.

Product

Marketing strategy linked to product aims to direct a particular product toward a particular market (Booz Allen & Hamilton, 1982). To this end, two marketing activities are necessary: communication and effectiveness (Kotler, 1984). The informative task of "product marketing" concerns information, mainly conveyed by the price, promotion, product label, and packaging. This information is used to position the product on the market, to inform, and/or to persuade current or potential customers to buy.

The effective task of product policy, instead, is to remove any barriers to transactions or exchanges so that the consumer perceives how the products/ services may satisfy his/her needs and preferences with the minimum amount of effort (Kotler, 1984).

Barriers are concentrated onto the product in terms of the following:

- accessibility
- availability
- properties and use
- correct perception and appeal
- differentiated use

Traditionally the effective task was to continually improve the transaction by offering the right product, at the right time and in the right place, together with the most suitable service for the potential customer.

The Internet can participate actively helping to bring down these barriers. In fact, as well as its contribution in an informative way, it is also able to bring down transaction barriers in an effective/operational level, particularly for those products that can easily be transferred online (digital products). For physical products, the Internet can reduce the bureaucratic process of consultation–order–dispatch–possession.

In marketing tradition, the products are subdivided into categories according to the effort and risk perceived by the consumer. Referring to the well-known classification of Copeland (1923), it is possible to identify four product categories: convenience, preference, shopping, and specialty products. The Web allows a comparison of well-defined characteristics of the product (Subramaniam, Shaw, & Gardner, 1999).

Table 2 shows in which matter convenience, preference, shopping, and specialty products can be compared and bought online.

From Table 2 we can deduce that

- the purchase of frequently used, low-risk goods (convenience and preference products) could be carried out online, avoiding long lines at counters and check outs.[10]
- some shopping products require sensorial involvement (smell, taste, and visual perception) for their selection. In this case the Internet is not very significant as a buying tool.
- specialty products can be easily sold over the Internet if the consumer has defined certain variables, among which are trust in the online distributor, product information, contract terms, and brand and model of the product.

Table 2. How convenience, preference, shopping, and specialty products can be compared online

	convenience	preference	shopping	specialty
price	√	√	√	not relevant
additional services	√	√	√	not relevant
technological characteristics	√	√	√	not relevant
sensorial characteristics	not relevant	not relevant	relevant but not possible online	relevant but not possible online
product brand	not relevant	√	√	relevant only if also the brand of the distributor is well known

From the topics covered up until now, we can deduce how much, on one hand, information research on products/services is a strong requirement of the consumer, and on the other hand, how the Internet and multimedia systems can contribute on more levels to satisfy this requirement. In order to understand the dynamics on this online contribution better, we must take into consideration another important author, Nelson (1974, 1981), who subdivided products into two macrocategories according to their characteristics: "search" products and "experience" products. The "search" products are characterized by the possibility of obtaining complete information on their key characteristics before purchase; for example, the automobile.

The "experience" products, instead are goods

- whose complete information of their key characteristics cannot be known without direct experience, especially if they are intrinsic characteristics the concern the key variables of the product;[11]
- whose research on information and key characteristics are too costly or difficult to achieve compared to direct experience. For example, technical information of certain products and the comparison of many suppliers.

The influence of the Internet on both categories is very strong and we can even ascertain that on the Internet certain "experience" products have been transformed into "search" products (Klein, 1998). The Internet, in fact, has made the buying process of "search" products easier, thanks to the possibility of being able to search more information, in a more personalized form and at reduced cost with respect to traditional search methods. For the "experience" products, those that can be easily transformed into bits via the Internet can easily be tested before buying. For example, the effectiveness of certain software programs and the quality of certain sounds using files known as shareware.

Internet has succeeded in transforming goods whose information gathering was too costly into simple "search" products, thanks to the possibility of seeking previously inaccessible information, and above all to be able to receive relevant data and information from direct sources.

Another decisive factor when buying "experience" products is word of mouth, which enables the consumer to make use of the testimony of direct testing without ever testing the product personally.[12] This aspect is very important especially when the perceived buying risk is very high or when the products have strong distinguishing elements to their characteristics.

Marketing is also often concerned with reducing the level of stress and perceived risk of consumers during their decision to buy, particularly for purchases with a high level of involvement, establishing communication with the customer and helping him/her to have access to all information on the product and relative services.[13]

In particular, the elements that lead to a reduction in perceived risk are as follows (Subramaniam, Shaw, & Gardner, 1999):

- Access to all services that are complementary to the buying process using a single interface
- Communication with other consumers to learn and know about the product and service
- Development of sensorial experiences using virtual reality without having access to physical products
- Ability to personalize the product or service to adapt individual need and preferences

Managers can take advantage of the opportunity of a single Internet interface to create a rich and realistic virtual environment for the consumer that allows him/her to experiment and evaluate the product, building loyalty and trust of the consumer with advise or opinions from the distributor, forming support groups online, such as virtual communities, that act as image editors of the product or service offered. Finally, group together suppliers of a particular service on a single interface to assist cross-selling.

Price

Price is the only element of the marketing mix that produces a return, while the other three factors (product, place, and promotion) essentially require investment (Kotler, 1984). In particular, marketing deals with this variable during determination of price, change in price of a product/service in time and space. In the last analysis, marketing activities relative to price verify how to answer or introduce a change of price in a competitive market.

The Internet has a strong impact even on price, both for the customer and for the company. For the consumer, in the first place, the greatest advantage of a virtual purchase concerns the reduction in the search costs of a product and other information. Sellers, on the contrary, can benefit from the great flexibility of the Internet tool which permits price updating in real time, allowing an alignment with the dynamics of the market. Next, we will analyze these advantages and the problems connected to them for each of the parties involved.

As we have seen several times in this chapter, the Internet allows a comparison between supply from different markets, reducing the so-called search costs for the consumer. This may be divided into the following:

- Costs of price search
- Costs of quality information
- Costs of comparing supply from different sellers

The reduction in these costs can, however, be interpreted by many manufacturers and sellers as a way of increasing the price sensitivity of the customers. Some enterprises, in fact, fear that these reductions in search costs will increase competition and reduce company margins, extending the competition beyond the country's borders. For this reason many virtual malls and portals have been abandoned by manufacturers and sellers, who have preferred to open single, private Internet sites (Alba et al., 1997).[14]

Although it is true that in many cases this phenomenon has already occurred, it must be considered that this occurs in a particular way when online distributors only give prominence to information concerning price. A well-structured e-commerce site must be able to give information, not only in terms of price but above all give information on quality. The information given out online must therefore be superior and incomparable with respect to that supplied by stores and traditional distributors (Hoffman, Novak, & Chatterjee, 1995).

If there is a real differentiation between online retailers in terms of products, information, choice, complementary products, and services, then the interactive channel will become much more efficient with respect to traditional channels of distribution. Bakos (1997) indicates two factors influencing the degree of importance of information on quality with respect to price search information. The first factor is the differentiation of the product and the personalization of supply, the second concerns the number of suppliers of the product. In fact, the more a product can be personalized, the more difficult a comparison between products in the same category can be carried out. This, for example, occurs with car insurance costs. Finally, the greater the number of suppliers, the more the search and comparison costs increase.

In order to better understand how online price perception occurs, Lynch and Ariely (2000) conducted an empirical survey testing the sensitivity to price of a sample of online users. They discovered that online price perception decreases or increases with a reduction in the costs of the three types of search mentioned initially. This analysis was conducted comparing products and prices in two electronic stores selling wine. They showed that price sensitivity varies according to a reduction in the costs of price search, quality search, and comparing prices. From this, the authors have shown that

- for differentiated products such as wine, a reduction in quality search costs causes a reduction in price sensitivity;
- however, price sensitivity increases when it is possible to compare standardized products found in several Internet sites but remains unchanged for products found in only one site; and
- the reduction in search costs causes an increase in the well-being of consumers. They seem to appreciate the buying experience more and their retention level is greater.

Finally, from the analyses of market shares (Lynch & Ariely, 2000) it emerged that the presence of transparent information and the possibility of comparison between products in different virtual stores pays above all in the presence of a good differentiation in the range of products of the company.[15]

If, on the one hand, the Internet changes the perception of price of users, on the other hand, it allows the enterprise to develop more flexible price strategies, mainly in terms of the following:

- *Timeliness*: as well as the cost advantages that companies have gained with savings in printing of catalogs and price lists, on the Internet they may vary in real time

- *Adaptation to market trends*: the price, furthermore, change according to the consumer's requirements, by his/her online behavior or by direct e-mail
- *Better price segmentation*: for example, according to the buying frequency, the type of products, and the price models chosen, the enterprise can vary the levels of the prices online

From this, we can deduce that a marketing variable such as price, that traditionally was considered complex and not easily malleable, has today become a marketing lever that can be developed and used creatively online.

Despite these benefits, however, as stated previously, the Internet has placed great pressure on prices for companies especially since the rise of search agents and virtual auctions. The necessity to create different mechanisms for price creation has therefore emerged. Dolan and Moon (1999), in particular, identified three different price mechanism types online, subdivided in turn into subcategories, and in particular

- strategies of fixing the price in advance;
- strategies of negotiated price; and
- strategies of price at auction.

The strategies of fixing the price in advance involve a sales price fixed arbitrarily by the seller according to market regulations. These prices may be updated periodically (e.g., catalogs) or updated continuously (e.g., "take or leave" formulas). With this strategy, due in particular to its standard nature, prices of similar products from other companies can be compared more readily, especially using the search agents that work to "hunt" the lowest price on the net, causing companies to engage in a price war. In order to stem these "attacks," the company must work to build trust and brand name, especially with novice users and consumers who want well-grounded payment assurances online and punctuality of delivery. Companies can also aim to create a buying experience online, namely, the offer of information and service above the market average. They can also adopt the so-called "lock-in," or stickiness strategy that consists of creating particular incentives for already-acquired customers, to make it more difficult for them to leave the site for other rival sites. Finally the strategy of fixed but dynamic prices allows the enterprise to adapt the price according to the customer's requirements and according to his/her preferences recorded in the log files.

The strategies of negotiated price, instead, are the classic methods of transaction still used today mainly in the industrial goods market. These price trends can begin at a specific starting point for negotiation (e.g., list of potential suppliers), or without a specific starting point for negotiation (e.g., personalized research). Even in this case, the Internet proves to be an extremely suitable interactive means, in particular for reducing negotiation times, usually very long and costly in terms of resources. The Internet is also very efficient at extending the bargaining to elements other than price, and using different software, the sales proposals can be personalized according to the features of the product or the services that are complementary to the sale. Sellers can also construct automatic negotiation systems with the customer to reduce costs and the risk of human error. Finally, one particular negotiated price strategy is the purchase aggregate, that is, the simultaneous purchase of the same product by many buyers unknown to one another, the demand for which is aggregated on the Internet site with the aim of achieving a discount on the bought quantity.

Last, there are the strategies of price at auction, which were traditionally used for very targeted sectors, such as the antiques or furniture sector. The Internet has allowed this model to be widened to more markets, so that the search for peculiar products or an excess in production have has allowed auctions to be used by potential online customers. In this way, search costs, particularly for rare items, decrease and suppliers have the possibility of reducing warehouse excesses. There are different types of auctions and the company may select the most suitable according to its product.

- *"Name your price"*:[16] the starting price is not specified by the seller, it is left to potential customers to suggest the ideal price. The enterprise will then verify the fairness of the price with respect to its internal conditions.
- *Reverse auction*: in this case, it is the customer that activates the auction and suppliers participate until they arrive at a price which is as near as possible to that requested by the customer.
- *Bargaining*: these are market places in which sellers and buyer meet and bargain in an unstructured way.

It can therefore be concluded that if, on the one hand, Internet eases the comparison of price between the different online offers for the user, putting many enterprises in difficulty, on the other hand, it gives the enterprise a wide choice of pricing strategy, more flexible and involving compared to more traditional strategies.

Advertising

The third component of the marketing mix here considered is the so-called communication, promotion, and advertising. Communication has already been fully dealt with in the paragraph above; in this section, the contents regarding promotion and advertising will be analyzed.

Among the elements that make up a marketing plan, communication—even in its advertising aspect—is the key factor for the commercial development of the Internet. The Internet has, in fact, all the characteristics of interactivity, integration of texts and moving images, entertainment, high dynamism and updating, and above all of flexibility toward consumers' needs. Moreover, the Internet enjoys a wide possibility of targeting communication through thematic sites, portals, search engines, and the interactivity itself with the consumer. And last, the Internet is the mass media with the lowest advertising contact cost.

Because of the above-mentioned unique characteristics of this virtual instrument, the definitions of marketing and advertising are not so clear; this difficulty often arises from the impossibility of drawing a line between the neutral communication for the construction of a marketing relationship and actual commercial advertising. Much more than in other media, on the Internet advertising merges with written contents or with technical and value information. It is easy, in fact, to find online editorials with direct links to the companies that offer the products in questions, or banners connected to the kind of news search online, the so-called advertorial.

In his study on Web advertising, Ducoffe (1996) shows that more than 75% of his sample survey considers shopping guides, online catalogues, graphic displays of products, and offers for free samples as commercial advertising, not as information.[17]

As far as online communication is concerned, in the fifth paragraph we dealt with the substantial difference between the "push" and "pull" nature of the traditional communication strategy as compared to the online communication. It has also been considered how the technological framework and culture developed on the Web do not allow intrusive policies of mass marketing. The choice of being involved or not in an advertising policy is left to the consumer. In this way, advertising is more effective, as it is aimed directly to people who are really interested and self-selected.

Examples of pull online advertising activities are as follows (Subramaniam, Shaw, & Gardner, 2000):

- *Banners*: they are advertising images present in Internet sites that are aimed at the traffic of users interested in the advertised company. The online user, at his/her discretion, can click on the banners and directly enter the company site or the page dedicated to the offer advertised.

- *Buttons*: they include only the name or the brand of the product. Such buttons can be used by companies to create brand awareness, as they are constantly present on the Web page.
- *Advertising on key words*: it is an advertising software situated in the search engines which autonomously connect to advertising banners linked to a text or to key words typed directly in the search engine.
- *Interstices (gap)*: ads that, like television commercials, can be audio or video. When the user clicks on a specific topic, a separate window opens with advertising connected to that topic.
- *Advertising on request*: it is a new instrument used by some Internet sites. The first in Italy was www.google.com which gives the possibility of viewing advertising banners only by specific request of the user. Another existing version is the possibility given to the user of eliminating advertising present on the Internet site he/she is visiting.

Intrusive advertising aims to reach and foster the needs—not yet evident—of the possible consumers toward the company's products. The aim of such strategies of online advertising is to study methods that can connect in some form the push culture of the traditional marketing with the pull culture of Internet. The list of "push" advertising techniques which follows, with the indication of some devices, should be considered mainly for the "pull" culture of the Internet instrument (Schlosser & Kanfer, 2000):

a) *E-mail marketing*: to avoid spamming and benefit from the e–mail marketing technique, messages should be sent only to users who have directly requested information to the company. The addresses of the bidders or users could be supplied by specialized or targeted infomediators.

b) *Discussion groups*: these thematic and virtual meeting points represent good opportunities to advertise company products and services. But before sending commercial messages to all discussion groups more or less relating to the company products, the specific scope of the virtual community should be analyzed, considering all netiquette rules, that is, written and not written regulations for the participation in discussion groups.

c) *Target*: the best target to address "push" advertising ventures are users who have already responded positively to other activities of direct marketing, such as home shopping or mail orders through catalogues. These users are more positively disposed toward Internet marketing ventures than traditional consumers, possibly because they are used to remote buying and searching information through texts, without the necessity of a physical approach to goods (Schlosser, Shavitt, & Kanfer, 1999).

d) *Customization*: companies should give up mass marketing messages in favor of more customized messages. A way to begin with the targeting of messages is to prepare messages suitable to the interests of newsgroups or to specific requests for information received by the company.

e) *Interaction*: creating a dynamic and interactive Internet site helps the company to be in tune with the online consumer, who will consider the interactive Internet site as a reference point for his/her shopping.

f) *Advertising integration*: it is important for the company to use all the available information channels to advertise its Internet site, but it is important that the advertising policy developed online is consistent with the one traditionally adopted by the company. For example, it is important to exactly indicate the specific Internet address of the products on special offer, rather than leave the Internet address of the home page which would cause the user to get lost while searching the product offered on the company Internet site.

Once the surfer has been persuaded to visit the Internet site, advertisers must also find the way to get him/her to visit it regularly. Promotional games, contents, serialized stories, updated news, and any other material regularly and frequently updated may help in keeping an Internet site always active. Hoffman and Novak (1994) state that the play aspect of the surfing instruments of the Internet sites help the netsurfers to concentrate more on the interactivity. High levels of playfulness in the man–machine interconnections are related to higher experimentation levels. Games, surfing or fluidity are the basic elements for a steady permanence of surfers on the sites, as well as the continuity of their visits.

As for the rating of the effectiveness of advertisements (Subramaniam, Shaw, & Gardner, 1999), as mentioned earlier, the new technologies allow the advertisers to better identify the individual behavior of the buyers, both when searching for and purchasing the product. The number of entries (access) to a home page, the repeated visits for each individual customer, the number of internal pages visited, and the amount of time spent on each page are all data that are easily gathered on the Internet. These statistics can be used to measure the contacts, the frequency of visits, and the interest level of an Internet site. Moreover, it will be easier to distinguish the effectiveness of an advertisement from the effectiveness of the product advertised.

Distribution

At the beginning the Internet seemed the instrument that could create a highly transparent and informative environment, where the producers could exchange goods and information directly with the final consumers, thanks to the low contact costs. But as the few years of experience online have demonstrated, "the complete de-brokerage is an unattainable myth" (Kalakota & Robinson, 2000). The company must decide where and how to present its product online: search engines, portals, medium-sized Internet sites, or even personal sites. These are the *new digital brokers* that have come up in the net economy and that, like the old agents in the business world, live on sales commissions.

Therefore, contrary to what was thought at the beginning of the Internet era, that the Internet was believed to be a commercial instrument capable of eliminating all intermediary figures between producers and final customers, today it is evident that the online brokerage is a highly developed and profitable business model. Therefore, Coase's law (1937) is once again reconfirmed and the three kinds of transaction costs have allowed the birth and the flourishing of online brokers:

- *Research costs*: they relate both to the survey costs of the products and to the costs for the search of suppliers.
- *Negotiation costs*: such an activity is less developed in B2C. If, hypothetically, even for the final consumers, a fixed price or a previous negotiation on behalf of the broker did not exist, they would have to spend time and resources negotiating the price and the delivery and payment terms every time.
- *Coordination costs*: the customer would have to carry out further research to find out whether there are complementary products that can replace or be added to the goods of his/her interest.

As mentioned more than once before, on the Internet it is possible to easily access the information one may need to make a decision and coordinate complex activities, virtually in real time and at a low cost. But all this has not eliminated the need to rely on business brokers to reduce the above-mentioned brokerage costs. Indeed, the Internet is a virtual place based on such a quantity of information that often confuses the users, who then have to spend time to evaluate the sources, coordinate the contents and bargain over the goods and services offered online. For this reason, on the Internet there is a proliferation of brokers, who under the condition of acquiring the trust of the users, are involved in the reduction of the research, negotiation, and coordination costs, be they real or perceived by the Internet users.

The list that follows has some of the most common brokers who can be found online, with a short description of the business models they use.

On the Internet two particularly interesting brokerage models can be found: brokers and merchants. Brokers are pure virtual brokers, who exclusively assume the responsibility for selecting the products, reaching specific segments of the market, and guaranteeing the complete execution of the exchange activities. Therefore, he/she does not take part in the business risk of the company, but deals only with the processes of matching and negotiation between demand and offer. Some examples of brokers are as follows:[18]

- *Market exchange sites*: the Internet site administrator supplies a virtual space in which the potential buyers and sellers freely meet, exchange information, and may begin negotiations.
- *Buyer aggregators*: they are brokers who deal with the collecting of requests for the same product/service from users, thus guaranteeing a saving based on the total quantity purchased from a supplier.
- *Virtual malls*: these are proper virtual shopping centers that bring together offers from different virtual shops and wholesalers.
- *Metabrokers*: they are virtual malls that, as well as offering virtual windows, offer common services, such us online payment, distribution, and advertising services.
- *Auction brokers*: these are Internet sites that organize virtual auctions on request, open to a more or less limited public.
- *Inverted auctions*: they are Internet sites that organize virtual auctions in which the participants are not the users but the suppliers themselves.
- *Classifiers*: these Internet sites classify and submit offers/requests from Internet users, such as the traditional free magazine *Secondamano* (where you can find offers of second-hand products).
- *Research agents*: they are search engines for the most economical prices in the net. The business model is based on the presence of a search engine that allows the classification of goods requested by customers according to their price.

The merchant models, unlike the brokers, take on the responsibility for what is sold and what is left unsold; they are, therefore, intermediary commercial subjects between producers/distributors and the final buyers of the goods or service. Their role becomes central for the final consumer, who often relies on this kind of broker even for the pre- or after-sales activities. These models of distributive brokerage in Internet can be divided into the following:

- *E-tailers*: they are the traditional wholesalers and sellers of goods and services, but for the virtual world, for example, www.esperya.it.
- *Price list model*: the sale of goods or services occurs on the basis of a price list per product which the user can view directly on the site or download onto his/her computer.

There are further categories of virtual merchants, amongst which the most developed are the clicks-and-bricks models, where the user has the possibility of paying for the goods and receiving it directly at his/her home, or collecting and paying for the goods from physical locations scattered over the territory. This solution requires a widespread network of shops on the territory for the sale of products.

These are only a few examples of brokers and direct interaction models that can be created online. This is just to demonstrate that, even in the distribution field, the Internet can modify some cornerstones of company business.

The Impact of the Internet on Marketing Performance

From the very first developments in marketing theories, the contribution of this discipline has been studied in terms of company cost effectiveness, efficiency, and effectiveness (Clark, 1999). Moreover, what is important is that the company goal is subjective to each individual firm, and that confrontation with the market often does not take into consideration long-term company objectives (Ambler & Kokkinaki, 1997).

To measure the performance of marketing activities on the Internet is even more difficult, due to this interdisciplinary instrument, the intangibility of some benefits brought about by the multimedia systems, and the lack of experience of the management in the measuring systems of the new generation. Therefore, to understand how and in what measure Internet affects company performance positively or negatively is really a different task. Even Ghosh (1998, p. 126) asserts that for the manager it is more and more difficult to carefully evaluate—in commercial terms—the returns on Internet investments. Many companies are in fact attracted by the Internet due to the possibility of opening their business toward a number of users—albeit potentially unlimited—from all over the world, whereas other companies shy away from this, as they fear the price wars that could be triggered off in an online business world. None of the two hypotheses, however, has been backed up by empirical research in the field to prove their validity. Many are theoretical models that have been developed to show how the Internet can potentially increase a company's performance, but none of these can support its theory with empirical studies which are statistically relevant.

Stephen G. Butler, of the consulting company KPMG, has listed the major advantages of the businesses that could be developed within the new economy: globalization, technology, speed, communication, and information (Butler, 2001). All these factors, however, need to be adapted to each single company strategy, and obviously a standardized measurement is not desirable, above all for the companies that operate in the virtual channel, where the business models and the methodologies of approaching customers constantly change. This notwithstanding, an idea of the possible measurements of successful applications of business strategies—even online—can be given by the Balanced Scorecard Model of Kaplan and Norton (1992). The authors suggest that the performance indexes are measured on the company's own Critical Factors of Success, which differ according to sector, product, and company of reference. Such indexes can also be extended to companies that operate online. They can be divided into four microareas: finance, customer satisfaction, internal procedures, and innovation/growth of staff.

On the other hand, as far as e-commerce is concerned, the performance measurement, although similar to the traditional one, has distinctive characteristics. Its performance, however, is based on financial and accounting indicators. The measurement of the Internet marketing activities, that for their nature—as shown in the previous paragraphs—present high evaluation criticalities relating to the powerful presence of quality elements present in the activities themselves.

Due to these complexities, the indexes on the intangible assets when using the Internet for sale activities—which are also considered in the literature as positive factors that, more than others, influence the online business performance—were not taken into consideration. This for two different reasons: pragmatically, the quality factors are difficult to quantify and few companies are in a position to measure their value, as happens, for example, for consumer perception, brand, and satisfaction. Moreover, the actual measurement of the Internet investment in terms of cost savings and proceeds increase is invalidated by other quality elements that are difficult to identify and calculate, amongst which the integration terms with the internal company procedures.

According to Avlonitis and Karayanni (2000), in fact, the business activities linked to online sales influence company performance in all areas in terms of

- product management;
- sales management; and
- sales performance.

Products management benefits from online activities, first, as it is possible to customize products and services, thanks to a greater monitoring and understanding of consumers' needs.

The better understanding of one's own customer expectations fosters, therefore, the interaction and exchanges between company and customer. Moreover, as demonstrated, market surveys and tests carried out online give results in real time, and the possibility of verifying the substantial buying behavior of online users confers these studies a greater effectiveness and efficiency for the commercial advice they can give. Last, the Internet allows product management to shorten the life cycle of products. These can be added or eliminated from online catalogues, or modified within a very short time, without having to spend resources for printing new catalogues or literature.

As far as sales management is concerned, the Internet can be a good instrument to identify the different characteristics of the users according to their ways of approaching an Internet site. This process can facilitate a different typology of segmentation that is no longer based on socio-demographic features, but on more significant aspects relating to the business in question. Such an innovative identification of the segments can lead to a more effective targeting of company products and services, according to real requirements and needs—expressed or not—by Internet users. Even sales can be facilitated through the Internet, thanks to several services that can be automatically offered online (e.g., customization, payment methods, information service, and FAQ), while the services offered with the help of the company staff can be supplied on request. The Internet site, in fact, can become an instrument for the retention of the customer, thanks to the updating services and to interactive communication.

Last, the Internet also has direct and indirect effects on sales performance, in particular, direct effects through sales via Internet. These allow high savings on costs, such as the absence of a proper sales outlet, the reduction of agents, and better information capability. The indirect effects are through interorganizational connections: the Internet, as stated several times, allows a greater circulation and sharing of information and data among the different resources of the Internet and external to the company. This allows a saving on paper cost, and savings on time and cognitive exchange. Moreover, indirectly the Internet is good for sales performance, thanks to cutting-edge sales systems, that is, new models of sales that—although with some difficulty—can improve and enhance the company image. Last, the Internet allows an improvement of sales performance, thanks to higher levels of investment opportunities. The information exchange, the monitoring of the customer and a wiser segmentation allow companies to identify more opportunities for the implementation and widening of their business.

It is not our intention to analyze the more or less indirect benefits an e-commerce project can bring to company performance. Hereafter some performance indexes are listed, without giving unnecessary details. The indexes identified have been divided into the following six categories (Amber & Kokkinati, 1999):

- *Financial*: sales volumes, turnover, profit contribution, return of sales (ROS) and prices
- *Competitive*: the share of voice, the relative price as compared to competitors, and the share of promotion toward the competitors
- *Consumer behavior*: the number of users compared to the number of buyers, the penetration ratio, the profit (losses) on the users, the percentage of dropout customers, and the rate of fidelity of the users
- *Consumer awareness and attitude*: the perception and awareness of the brand and of the company products can be inferred through discussion groups and online forums. The attitude, the perceived quality, and customer satisfaction can also be analyzed through requests for quotations, the purchasing intentions, and possible complaints sent directly to the company
- *Direct trade customer*: through the analyses of direct trade customer it is possible to measure the profitability for each individual customer in a precise and not approximate way as may happen in the traditional way
- *Innovativeness*: the number of new products/services, the earnings generated by each new product or service in percentage compared to the total sales can be investigated

These are only a few of the indexes that could be used to monitor and check how the Internet can concretely improve company performance.

Conclusion

It is the intention of this chapter to demonstrate how the Internet and new technologies—on a theoretical and practical level—have not changed the marketing nature and its aims. In particular, this is true of its main aim, that is, the facility and the improvement of the exchange company/customer. The company reality shows a change especially in the strategic and operative methods and models, integrated—even with some difficulties—with the more traditional communication and interaction channels. Strategically, companies are trying to establish closer and more lasting relations with the customers with the help of the new multichannel instruments; from an operative point of view, they are looking for an integration among the different channels and instruments at their disposal.

The logical process of this chapter is based on the customer considered as an active subject in the creation and fulfillment of the company offer. The involvement of the customer can occur only and exclusively if a relationship based on trust between the company and the customer can be established. In such cases, Internet and other interactive instruments can offer several interchange channels. Moreover, the new technologies can bring about further improvement in the activities of interaction and relation, if used as means of investigation of the preferences and behaviors of consumers. All this brings about an improvement of the commercial offer, that integrates with services and products customized on the basis of the characteristics and preferences more or less expressed by the users. Finally, in such a context, the performance indexes must also be modified because of the new technologies to shed light on the relational value of the new systems.

References

Alba, J., Lynch, J., Weitz, B., Janiszewski, C., Lutz, R., Sawyer, A. et al. (1995). Interactive home shopping: Incentives for customers, retailers and manufacturers to participate in electronic marketplaces. *Journal of Interactive Marketing, 61*, 38–53.

Ambler, T., & Kokkinati, F. (1999). *Marketing performance assessment: An exploratory investigation.* (Working paper, report no. 99-114). Marketing Science Institute.

Avlonitis, G. J., & Karayanni, D. A. (2000). The impact of Internet use on business-to-business marketing—Examples from American and European companies. *Industrial Marketing Management, 29*, 441–459.

Bakos, J. Y. (1997). Reducing buyer search costs: Implication for electronic marketplaces. *Management Science, 43*(12), 1676–1708.

Bell, R. M., & Pavitt, K. (1993). Technological accumulation and industrial growth: Contrasts between developed and developing countries. *Industrial and Corporate Change, 2*(2).

Berthon, P., Holbrook, M. B., & Hulbert, M. H. (2000). Beyond market orientation: A conceptualization of market evolution. *Journal of Interactive Marketing, 14*(3).

Blattberg, R. C., & Deighton, J. (1991). Interactive marketing: Exploiting the age of addressability. *Sloan Management Review, Autumn*, 5–14.

Booz Allen & Hamilton. (1982). *New product management for the 1980's*. New York: Booz Allen & Hamilton Inc.

Bradlow, E. T., & Schmittlein, D. C. (2000). The little engines that could: Modelling the performance of World Wide Web search engines. *Marketing Science, 19*(1), 43–62.

Burke, R. R. (1996). Virtual shopping: Breakthrough in marketing research. *Harvard Business Review, 74*, 120–131.

Burke, R. J. (1997). Do you see what I see? The future of virtual shopping. *Journal of the Academy of Marketing Science, 25*(4), 352–360.

Butler, S. G. (2001, Summer). A global education for a global economy. *Beta Gamma Sigma News,* pp. 1–2.

Carter, D. (1996). Perspectives—The future of interactive marketing. *Harvard Business Review*, November–December, 157.

Cheskin Research. (2000). Trust in the wired Americans—2000. Retrieved from *www.cheskin.com*

Clark, B. H. (1999). Marketing performance measures: History and interrelationships. *Journal of Marketing Management, 15*, 711–732.

Coase, R. H. (1937). The nature of the firm. *Economica*.

Compaine, B. M. (2001). *The digital divide: Facing a crisis or creating a myth?* Cambridge, MA: MIT Press.

Copeland, M. T. (1923). The relation of customers' buying habit to marketing methods. *Harvard Business Review,* April, 282–289.

Cronin, M. J. (1994). *Doing business on the Internet*. New York: Van Nostrand Reinhold.

Davenport, T. H., Harris, J. G., & Kohli, A. K. (2001). How do they know their customers so well? *Sloan Management Review*, Winter.

Deighton, J. (1996). Perspectives—The future of interactive marketing. *Harvard Business Review*, November–December, 151–152.

Dolan, R. J., & Moon, Y. (1999). Pricing and market making on the Internet. *Journal of Interactive Marketing, 14*(2).

Ducoffe, R. H. (1996). Advertising value and advertising on the web. *Journal of Advertising Research*, 21–35.

Ghosh, S. (1998). Making business sense of the Internet. *Harvard Business Review, March–April*, 126–135.

Godin, S. (1999). *Permission marketing: Turning strangers into friends, and friends into customers*. New York: Simon & Schuster.

Grönroos, C. (1994). "Quo vadis marketing? Toward a relationship marketing paradigm. *Journal of Marketing Management, 10*, 347–360.

Grönroos, C. (2000). The relationship marketing process: Interaction, communication, dialogue, value. Retrieved from *www.viu.unive.it/tedis/sdilab/ebusiness/papereb.htm*

Gupta, S., & Chintagunta, P. K. (1994). On using demographic variables to determine segment membership in logit mixture models. *Journal of Marketing Research, 31*, 128–136.

Haeckel, S. H. (1998). About the nature and future of interactive marketing. *Journal of Interactive Marketing, 12*(1), 63–71.

Hoffman, D. L., & Novak, T. P. (1996). Marketing in hypermedia computer-mediated environments: Conceptual foundations. *Journal of Marketing, 60*, 50–68.

Hoffman, D. L., Novak, T. P., & Chatterjee, P. (1995). Commercial scenarios for the Web: Opportunities and challenges. *Journal of Computer-Mediated Communication, 1*(3).

Hoffman, D. L., Novak, T. P., & Yung, Y. F. (2000). Measuring the customer experience in online environments: A structural modelling approach. *Marketing Science, 19*(1), 22–42.

Holbrook, M. B. (1999). *Consumer value: A framework for analysis and research*. Routledge.

Holsapple, C. W., Joshi, K. D., & Singh, M. (2000). Decision support applications in electronic commerce. In *Handbook on electronic commerce*. Berlin: Springer-Verlag.

Iacobucci, D. (1998). Interactive marketing and the meganet: Networks of networks. *Journal of Interactive Marketing, 12*(1), 5–16.

Jagannathan, S., Srinivasan, J., & Kalman, J. L. (2002). Internet commerci metrics and models—In the new era of accountably. Upper Saddle River, NJ: Prentice-Hall.

Johanisson, C. (1987). Organizing: The network metaphor. *International Studies of Management and Organization, 17*(1).

Kalakota, R., & Robinson, M. (2000). *e-Business 2.0—Roadmap for success*. Addison-Wesley.

Kalakota, R., & Whinston, A. B. (1997). *Electronic commerce: A manager's guide*. Reading, MA: Addison-Wesley.

Klein, L. R. (1998). Evaluating the potential of interactive media through a new lens: Search versus experience goods. *Journal of Business Research, 41*, 195–203.

Kotler, P. (1984). *Marketing management: Analysis, planning and control*. Englewood Cliffs, NJ: Prentice-Hall.

Kotler, P. (1999). *Kotler on marketing: How to create, win, and dominate markets*. New York: The Free Press.

Krishnamurthy, S. (2000). " ... New book in review—Permission marketing: Turning strangers into friends, and friends into customer. *Journal of Research in Marketing, 37*(4), 525–526

Leeflang, P. S. H., & Wittink, D. R. (2000). Building models for marketing decisions: Past present and future. *International Journal of Research in Marketing, 17*, 105–126.

Levin, M. (1996). Perspectives—The future of interactive marketing. *Harvard Business Review*, November–December, 154–155.

Lynch, J. G. Jr., & Ariely, D. (2000). Wine online: Search costs and competition on price, quality, and distribution. *Marketing Science, 19*(1).

Mandelli, A. (n.d.). Nuove regole per un nuovo marketing [New rules for new marketing]. Retrieved from *www.mymarketingnet.com/agora/editoriali/contributi/dettaglio.asp?i=4&id=75*

McCarthy, & Jerome, E. (1960). *Basic marketing: A managerial approach*. Homewood, IL: Irwin.

McKenna, R. (1997). *Real time*. Boston: Harvard Business School Press.

McKinsey & Company & Media Matrix, October 2000.

Nelson, R. R., & Winter, S. G. (1982). *An evolutionary theory of economic change*. Cambridge, MA: Belknap.

O'Connor, G. C., & O'Keefe, R. (2000). The Internet as a new marketplace: Implication for consumer behavior and marketing management. In *Handbook on electronic commerce*. Berlin: Springer-Verlag.

Parson, A., Zeisser, M., & Waitman, R. (1998). Organizing today for the digital marketing of tomorrow. *Journal of Interactive Marketing, 12*(1), 31–46.

Peppers, D., & Rogers, M. (1997). *Enterprise one to one*. New York: Currency Doubleday.

Peterson, R. A., Balasubramanian, S., & Bronnenberg, B. J. (1997). Exploring the implications of the Internet for consumer marketing. *Journal of the Academy of Marketing Science, 25*(4), 329–346.

Pew & American Life Project. (2000). New Internet users: What they do online, what they don't and implications for the net's future. Retrieved from *www.pewInternet.org/reports*

Porter, E. M. (1985). *Competitive advantage*. New York: The Free Press.

Powell, W. W. (1990). Neither market nor hierarchy: Network forms of organization. In B. Staw & L. Cummings (Eds.), *Research in organizational behaviour*. Greenwich, CT: JAI Press.

Quelch, J. A., & Klein, L. R. (1996). The Internet and international marketing. *Sloan Management Review, 37*, 60–75.

Quinn, C. (1999). How leading-edge companies are marketing, selling, and fulfilling over the Internet. *Journal of Interactive Marketing, 13*(4), 39–50.

Ravald, A., & Grönroos, C. (1996). The value concept and relationship marketing. *European Journal of Marketing, 30*(2), 19–30.

Rayport, J. F., & Jaworsky, B. J. (2001). *E-commerce*. Boston: Irwin/McGraw-Hill in association with the Monitor Group.

Rayport, J. F., & Sviokla, J. J. (1994). Managing in the marketspace. *Harvard Business Review*, November–December, 141–150.

Rosenberg, N. (1993). Why technology forecasts often fail. *The Futurist, 29*(4), 16–21.

Rullani, E. (1993). *Reti di marketing*. Milan: Etaslibri.

Schlosser, A., & Kanfer, A. (2000). Culture clash in Internet marketing: Implications for marketing practices. In *Handbook on electronic commerce*. Berlin: Springer-Verlag.

Schlosser, A., & Kanfer, A. (1999). Current advertising on the Internet: The benefits and usage of mixed-media advertising strategies. In D. Schumann & E. Thorson (Eds.), *Advertising and the Internet*. Hillsdale, NJ: Lawrence Erlbaum.

Schlosser, A., Kanfer, A., & Shavitt, S. (1999). Survey of attitudes toward Internet advertising. *Journal of Interactive Marketing, 13*(3), 1–21.

Simon, H. (1957). *Models of man*. New York: John Wiley & Sons.

Subramaniam, C., Shaw, M. J., & Gardner, D. M. (2000). Product marketing on the Internet. In *Handbook on electronic commerce*. Berlin: Springer–Verlag.

Ugolini, M. (1999). Tecnologie dell'Informazione e Fiducia: la nuova Sfida per l'Impresa. *Sinergie*, 50(99).

Venkataraman, N. (2001). Five steps to a dot-com strategy: How to find your footing on the Web. *Sloan Management Review*, Spring, 15–28.

Webster, F. Jr. (1996). Perspective—The future of interactive marketing. *Harvard Business Review*, November–December, 156–157.

Whitener, E. M., Brodt, S. E., Korsgaard, , & Werner, J. M. (1998). Managers as initiators of trust: An exchange relationship framework for understanding managerial trustworthy behavior. *Academy of Management Review, 23*(3), 513–530.

Wind, Y., & Mahajan, V. (2001). Convergence marketing. *Journal of Interactive Marketing, 15*(2), 64–79.

Endnotes

1 In this work, the term *Internet* does not refer exclusively to the World Wide Web, but it means *multimedia channel par excellence.* This concept includes remote connection tools, including e-mail, FTP, Web TV, wireless connection, and video conferencing. It refers to the World Wide Web in those cases that state that the activities of marketing are linked to the construction and management of Internet sites. *New technology*, instead, means the set of multimedia channels and "devices" that allow connection and exchange of information, including mobile phone, computer, lap tops, satellites, handhelds, databases, software, and connection and interaction controls.

2 Webster (1996): "IT modifies the knowledge, the focus on the customer, the market segmentation, targeting and positioning. All becomes flexible: information and activities interact in a more holistic way."

3 The 4Ps of the marketing mix are the variables that can be directly controlled by marketing in order to achieve the targets put before in the objective market (Kotler, 1988). This model proposed by McCarthy (1960) consists of the following elements: product, price, place, and promotion.

4 In this chapter the concept of "customer" refers particularly to business-to-consumer (B2C), even though much of the content that follows may suitable in a business-to-business (B2B) context.

5 In the distribution sector, for example, a difference is recognized, even in lexical terms, between the expressions "buying" and "shopping." The first suggests a transaction based on a rational need to possess the goods to meet primary needs: cleaning products, food for the family, school equipment for the children. On the contrary, "shopping" has a more emotional meaning

and includes the pleasure of looking at windows, trying on clothes, meeting friends, and involving complete sensorial activities.

6 Secondo Grönroos i processi chiave del Relationship Marketing sono: l'interazione, la comunicazione ed il valore

7 These are considered spamming activities:

- unauthorized sending of an e-mail proposing a Web site or product to purchase
- insertion, in a discussion forum or newsgroup, of a message not related to the discussion taking place which has a commercial or provocative purpose
- use of Windows internal messaging system to make a dialog box with an advertising message appear
- insertion of a distribution list without permission of user or impossibility to cancel a subscription

8 Log files are files that sit on the server hosting the Internet site to be analyzed. They register what happens in the site itself. Within the log files are contained all the information relevant for checking visits and itineraries the customers use in the site, including its advertising spaces. There are four types of log files:

- transfer log: records all files transferred from the server to the user
- error log: records errors that occur during transfer
- agent log: identifies the user agent (browser or search engine) from which the request left to the server
- refer log: records origin of visitors

9 Many enterprises, because of their economic activity, do not have any direct contact with the consumer (e.g., manufacturing companies, assemblers, industrial intermediaries, etc.). These companies, therefore, when monitoring the buying behavior of their products, must base their information on that declared by the distributors, or invest in equipment or resources to directly analyze the consumers (e.g., video cameras at sales points, focus groups, store testing, etc.). These data may be, on the one hand, contaminated by contractual relations with distributors, and on the other, may be very costly due to the considerable investments.

10 A typical example of frequent use, perceived low-risk buying is online buying of travel tickets.

11 Some key variables of the product can be monitored by the buyer only at the moment of use, for example, comfort, resistance, answer to unexpected events, technical assistance, guarantees, and so forth.

12 Typical examples are newsgroups and online forums.

13 These marketing activities connected to communication allow the perceived buying and consumption risk to be reduced. Before the Internet, the problem was that traditional media did not fully allow this process, while today the Internet gives the possibility of creating a direct contact between supplier/distributor and customer.

14 E-commerce portals are virtual spaces where different supplies of particular goods and services are concentrated. Many of these initiatives have failed, however, because the comparison between commercial supplies, in terms of price, was not well accepted by the supplying companies, which abandoned these spaces causing their near closure.

15 Differentiation of the production range is strongly perceived by potential buyers especially in the presence of personalization tools of the online supply.

16 The "name your price" formula was invented and used by PriceLine, an American airline ticket site.

17 The same research shows that more than the half of the sample consider an Internet site as an advertising form.

18 The features of the brokers listed hereafter have been taken from the Internet site http://ecommerce.ncsu.edu/business_models.html.

19 A search agent is a program that has the task of carrying out particular search information on the Internet. In this case, the task requested concerns the search of products classifying them in price levels. Furthermore, the application may also not be physically connected to the computer of who is activating the search, but may be hosted by a remote server (or even "distributed" among several remote servers), operating without using the resources of the PC of the user carrying out the search.

20 The term *word of mouth* means informal communication between people discussing products, services, and ideas. These people are not connected to the company offering the product or service mentioned and they communicate using a channel unconnected to enterprise itself.

Chapter IX

The Internet and Global Markets

José Manuel Ortega Egea, University of Almería, Spain

Manuel Recio Menéndez, University of Almería, Spain

Abstract

This chapter examines the impact of the Internet and related technologies on global marketing activities (global e-marketing), under consideration of the following aspects:

- *Special implications for multinational corporations (MNCs) and small and medium-sized companies (SMCs)*
- *Distinction between business-to-consumer (B2C) and business-to-business (B2B) markets*
- *Role of the Internet as a complementary or supplementary marketing channel*

In order to clarify the special characteristics and challenges involved in global e-marketing practices, the authors have carried out a review of related empirical and conceptual research. The following conclusions can be drawn with regard to the characteristics of reviewed studies:

1. *Due to the global nature of the Internet, relatively little research explicitly accounts for the differences between domestic and global e-marketing practices. Further research is needed on issues directly related to the Internet "global reach."*
2. *Relatively more studies analyze global Internet marketing from a theoretical point of view. Academics are recently recognizing the need to carry out empirical research, both in B2C and B2B online environments.*

Introduction

The Internet and its main related services—the Web, e-mail services, intranets, mobile technologies, instant messaging systems, and so forth—foster direct, fast, and flexible communication between producers, suppliers, and final customers across countries. One of the most differential characteristics between the Internet and other traditional media relates to the relatively easier "global reach" enabled on this new medium. The possibilities for instant cross-national data flows have led several authors to argue that the development of true global markets is possible (Javalgi & Ramsey, 2001; Rudraswamy & Vance, 2001).

The Internet global reach is likely to have relevant implications for both business-to-consumer (B2C) and business-to-business markets (B2B). Though the effects on B2C markets are likely to be very significant (Angelides, 1997), several authors point out that B2B transactions will benefit significantly more from the global information flows over the Internet. Internet-related technologies are also argued to have "equalizing effects" (Cavusgil, 2002; Hamill, 1997; Samiee, 1998a), as skills and information assets tend to be more critical factors than financial resources or firm size in order to achieve success in global e-markets. Nevertheless, companies will necessarily have to face important challenges and risks in this new global business environment. Most of the issues that companies usually deal with in off-line global markets will continue to be relevant on the Internet: complexities related to successful international negotiations, global marketing effectiveness, international distribution and logistics, and so forth. Global marketing practices are especially likely to be changed by the introduction of Internet technologies, due the differential characteristics of the Internet medium—speed, ubiquity, interactivity, and two-way communication.

This chapter examines the impact of the Internet and related technologies on global marketing activities (global e-marketing), under consideration of the following aspects:

- Special implications for multinational corporations (MNCs) and small and medium-sized companies (SMCs)
- Distinction between B2C and B2B markets
- Role of the Internet as a complementary or supplementary marketing channel

In order to clarify the special characteristics and challenges involved in global e-marketing practices, the authors have carried out a review of related empirical and conceptual research. The following conclusions can be drawn, with regard to the characteristics of reviewed studies:

1. Due to the global nature of the Internet, relatively little research explicitly accounts for the differences between domestic and global e-marketing practices (Samiee, 1998b). Further research is needed on issues directly related to the Internet global reach.
2. Relatively more studies analyze global Internet marketing from a theoretical point of view (Bennett, 1997; Hamill, 1997; Samiee, 1998a, 1998b). Academics are recently recognizing the need to carry out empirical research, both in B2C (Hamill & Gregory, 1997; Lituchy & Rail, 2000; Moen, 2002) and B2B online environments (Eid, 2002; Leek, Turnbull, & Naudé, 2003).

The Internet and Global Markets

Internet markets have special characteristics that will change significantly the way products and services are marketed and distributed through traditional domestic and international distribution channels.

Interactivity and Two-Way Communication

Interactivity and two-way communication between suppliers and customers are highly interrelated concepts, and have been identified as differential characteristics of the online channel. Two types of interactivity are possible on the Internet and the Web (Berthon, Pitt, Katsikeas, & Berton, 1999):

- Interactivity *with the medium* (e.g., interactively modifying the contents of a Web page), and
- Interactivity *through the medium* (e.g., customer-to-customer, company-to-customer, and company-to-company interactions through the Web, chats, e-mail, online forums, etc.). Online services such as chats or instant messaging services—e.g., MSN Messenger, Yahoo! Messenger, or AOL Instant Messaging—enable two-way communication on a global basis.

Global Market Reach

On the Internet, both consumers and businesses can benefit from the access and exchange of information across national and regional boundaries (Berthon et al, 1999). Diverse authors explicitly recognize the relevance of the Internet global market reach, arguing that the Internet will become an essential element of global marketing strategies (Hamill & Gregory, 1997; Lazer & Shaw, 2000; Lewis & Cockrill, 2002; Samiee, 1998b).

The Internet and the Web promise an easier and cheaper global market presence, "regardless of company size" (Bennett, 1997). Less time and financial resources are required to market goods and/or services to worldwide customers over the Internet, compared to other distribution channels. The Internet global reach has the potential to increase the variety of products available in different national markets, especially in emergent markets increasingly demanding the newest technology (Deshpandé, 2000). The Internet and the Web are also likely to increase the international competitiveness of companies from developing countries (Morris, Marais, & Weir, 1997).

Quelch and Klein (1996) argue that companies with an online presence become automatically multinationals. However, certain companies, especially SMCs, which have traditionally served only their domestic markets, may have extended their potential customer base on the Internet, but not deliberately. Such companies may not be aware of the Internet's suitability for building international relationships (Hornby, Goulding, & Poon, 2002; Melewar, Hunt, & Bridgewater, 2001; Samiee, 1998b; Wymbs, 2000).

Profiles of Global Internet Users

The Internet is commonly regarded as a global medium, but Internet use has evolved at significantly differing paces worldwide—the United States continue to be ahead. Thus, companies willing to use the Internet for global marketing communications should account for current regional differences in Internet adoption.

In this section, the authors examine the demographic profiles of Internet users and the existing national differences with regard to Internet adoption.

Demographic Characteristics of Global Internet Users

As a result of regional differences in Internet use, the demographic characteristics of global Internet users are currently not homogeneous. These demographic differences are likely to determine the market potential of certain products in different countries (Bain, 1999; Lin, 1999). In this regard, Guillén (2002) points out that "the sell of health-care products and services online can be limited in countries where few women use the Internet—e.g., in Latin America, as women make most of decisions on health-care." Nevertheless, as Internet adoption generalizes, the demographic characteristics of Internet users are likely to resemble those of the general population, and should be less helpful in predicting Internet usage behaviors such as online shopping (Bennett, 1997; Korgaonkar & Wolin, 1999).

Table 1. Internet users' demographic characteristics

Average age	37.6 years
Sex	33.6% women
Race	87.2% of participants identified themselves as white
Education	Highly educated, as 87.8% had some kind of college education, and 59.3% had obtained at least one degree
Average income	$57,300
Marital Status	47.6% of participants were married. European respondents showed a higher tendency to be single
Nationality	Most participants were U.S. Internet users (84.7%), followed by Europe (7.3%), Canada (3.8%), and Oceania (2.0%)
Location	Internet users in suburban areas (48.9%), 37.3% in urban areas, and 13.8% in rural areas U.S./Europe differences: U.S. Internet users more likely to live in suburban areas (52.4%) while Europeans live predominantly in urban areas (62.9%)

Source: Kehoe et al. (1999)

Table 1 shows the demographic characteristics of Internet users, according to the Tenth WWW User Survey conducted by the Graphic, Visualization and Usability Centre (GVU) in 1999 (Kehoe, Pitkow, Sutton, Aggarwal, & Rogers, 1999).

Adoption of Internet-Related Technologies: Growth Trends in Different Countries

The term "digital divide" (Ngini, Furnell, & Ghita, 2002) has been recently used to refer to national and regional differences in the Internet adoption levels of consumers and companies. These differences limit significantly the potential benefits to be obtained on the Internet by international companies and consumers.

International differences in the Internet diffusion processes are influenced by diverse factors (Rogers, 1983; Rudraswamy & Vance, 2001): (1) characteristics of the Internet medium, (2) communication channels, (3) time elapsed since the introduction of the Internet, (4) social and cultural characteristics of different social systems, and (5) differences in technological and economic development. Although regional differences are being progressively reduced, and connectivity levels in international markets are increasing rapidly, Internet adoption and the development of digital infrastructures are still higher in the United States. It must also be noted that Internet markets are developing in uneven patterns around the world, that is, lower Internet penetration in certain countries, lower availability of broadband Internet access (Crosby & Johnson, 2002).

Regional Trends in Internet Adoption

The following regional trends can be observed, with regard to the development of Internet markets (Javalgi & Ramsey, 2001; Jevons, 2000):

- *United States:* The United States is still leading with regard to the number of Internet users and online transactions.
- *Europe:* Europe is around 10–15 months behind the United States in terms of Internet use, but is the worldwide leader in the use of mobile devices. Turner (2001) points to the following reasons for the slower development of Internet markets in Europe: "wait and see" approach by most organizations; regulations; high prices of Internet access; lower penetration of PCs; and limited culture of distance shopping among Europeans. In this regard, the eEurope initiative aims at developing modern Internet infrastructures

and achieving an integrated European information society by 2010 (European Council, 2002).

- *China:* It is the fastest growing Internet market in Asia, and will account for a large share of the global Internet market.

According to market estimations by Forrester Research for 2004, the regional distribution of worldwide e-commerce will be as follows: the United States will

Table 2. Distribution of Internet users in different countries

Country	Population	Telephones	Cellular Phones	Internet Service Providers (ISPs)	Internet Users	Literacy (total)
	Thousand	thousand	thousand		thousand	%
Argentina	37812.817	7500.000	3000.000	33	3880.000	96.2
Australia	19546.792	10050.000	8600.000	603	10060.000	100.0
Belgium	10274.595	4769.000	974.494	61	2807.000	98.0
Brazil	176029.560	17039.000	4400.000	50	11940.000	83.3
Canada	31902.268	18500.000	4207.000	760	14440.000	97.0
Chile	15498.930	2603.000	944.225	7	1750.000	95.2
Czech Rep.	10256.760	3869.000	4346.000	300	1100.000	99.9
Denmark	5368.854	4785.000	1444.016	13	2930.000	100.0
Estonia	1415.681	501.691	711.000	38	540.000	100.0
Finland	5183.545	2861.000	2162.574	23	2270.000	100.0
Germany	83251.851	50900.000	55300.000	200	28640.000	99.0
Greece	10645.343	5431.000	937.700	27	1330.000	97.0
Hong Kong	7303.334	3839.000	3700.000	17	3930.000	92.2
Iceland	279.384	168.000	65.746	7	168.000	99.9
Italy	57715.625	25000.000	20500.000	93	19250.000	98.0
Japan	126974.628	60381.000	63880.000	73	47080.000	99.0
Kenya	31138.735	310.000	540.000	65	250.000	78.1
Liechtenstein	32.842	20.000	-	44	-	100.0
Lithuania	3601.138	1142.000	500.000	32	341.000	98.0
Luxembourg	448.569	314.700	215.741	8	100.000	100.0
Mexico	103400.165	12332.000	2020.000	51	3420.000	89.6
Netherlands	16067.754	9132.400	4081.891	52	8700.000	99.0
New Zealand	3908.037	1920.000	2200.000	36	1780.000	99.0
Norway	4525.116	2735.000	2080.408	13	2450.000	100.0
Poland	38625.478	8070.000	1780.000	19	3500.000	99.0
Portugal	10084.245	5300.000	3074.194	16	2000.000	87.4
Romania	22317.730	3777.000	645.500	38	800.000	97.0
Russia	144978.573	30000.000	2500.000	35	9200.000	98.0
Serbia & Montenegro	10656.929	2017.000	87.000	9	400.000	93.0
Slovakia	5422.366	1934.558	736.662	6	700.000	-
Slovenia	1932.917	722.000	1000.000	11	600.000	99.0
South Africa	43647.658	5000.000	7060.000	150	2400.000	85.0
Spain	40077.100	17336.000	8394.000	56	7380.000	97.0
Sweden	8876.744	6017.000	3835.000	29	5640.000	99.0
Switzerland	7301.994	4820.000	1967.000	44	3410.000	99.0
Taiwan	22548.009	12490.000	16000.000	8	11600.000	86.0
Thailand	62354.402	5600.000	3100.000	15	2300.000	93.8
Turkey	67308.928	19500.000	17100.000	50	4000.000	85.0
Ukraine	48396.470	9450.000	236.000	260	750.000	98.0
United Kingdom	59778.002	34878.000	13000.000	245	33000.000	99.0
United States	280562.489	194000.000	69209.000	7800	166000.000	97.0
Uruguay	3386.575	929.141	350.000	14	370.000	97.3
Uzbekistan	25563.441	1980.000	26.000	42	7.500	99.0
Venezuela	24287.670	2600.000	2000.000	16	950.000	91.1

Source: CIA World Factbook

account for 47% of worldwide e-commerce; Asia/Pacific countries, 24.3%; Europe, 22.6%; and Latin America, 1.2%.

Table 2 offers an overview of current Internet use across countries.

As shown in Table 2, though significant regional differences still exist, Internet access in non-U.S. markets is reaching acceptable levels. These Internet adoption trends will contribute to a generalized increase in international transactions, which will enable international consumers to benefit from access to a wider variety of products, services, and information. Companies should not underestimate the market potential of less developed countries, as the Internet may make these markets more accessible than through traditional media (Mahajan, Pratini De Moraes, & Wind, 2000).

Effects on Competition

Advantages based on size and economies of scale enjoyed by multinationals and large companies will lose part of their influence in Internet markets. Internet-related technologies have introduced significant changes into the competitive configuration of global markets:

- *Globalized, dynamic, and highly competitive business environment:* The Internet and the Web provide by nature global market reach, which will increase the number of companies competing in different national markets (Singh & Kundu, 2002). Companies that have traditionally served only their domestic markets will face increased competition, both from multinational companies and "foreign-born global companies." Samiee (1998b) points out that a Web presence will be a must for the survival of most companies, rather than a source competitive advantage in global markets.
- *Lower entry barriers to foreign markets for SMCs:* The relevance of advertising, financial resources, company size, previous market experience, or location as barriers for international market access will be much lower (Cavusgil, 2002; Hamill, 1997; Hamill & Gregory, 1997; Samiee, 1998a). The Internet is expected to have equalizing effects on current global markets, though larger firms will be better positioned due to their higher financial power.
- *Higher relevance of "virtual or soft assets":* Sources of competitive advantages on the Internet (Cavusgil, 2002; Singh & Kundu, 2002; Tetteh & Burn, 2001): information and technological skills, fast and global flows of

information, digital and network resources, technological integration of global operations, and relationships with consumers and businesses.

- *Technology will be key to competitive advantage more than size:* The recent success of companies offering file-sharing services, based on peer-to-peer technology (P2P), has shown the potential of technology to provide competitive advantage in Internet markets. While technological innovations will be more accessible to smaller companies online, multinationals have more resources for internal technological innovation (Quelch & Klein, 1996).
- *Lower costs and higher efficiency of global marketing communications* (Hornby et al., 2002; Javalgi & Ramsey, 2001).

Global SMCs

The activities of SMCs account for a significant share of most countries' economies. Therefore, increasing research is being carried out into the implications of the Internet and the Web for SMCs' marketing and business practices (Bennett, 1997; Hamill & Gregory, 1997; Hornby et al., 2002; Lewis & Cockrill, 2002; Moen, 2002).

The Internet offers special benefits to SMCs, as the establishment of a global business requires fewer efforts, both in terms of time and investments, than in traditional physical markets (Bennett, 1997; Hornby et al., 2002). Several authors have referred to the emergence of a new kind of company on the Internet, *born-global companies* (Deshpandé, 2000, 2002; Quelch & Klein, 1996), which enjoy access to global markets at early stages. On the Internet, activities such as international market access, global sourcing, global promotion, development of international relationships, or global coordination are more affordable to companies of different sizes (Hamill, 1997; Melewar et al., 2001; Samiee, 1998a).

Small producers of "niche products" can serve small and geographically dispersed customer groups over the Internet, which may significantly increase the profitability and sustainability of their businesses (Martin & Matlay, 2003; Moen, 2002).

Despite all of its potential benefits, certain companies, especially SMCs, may not properly recognize the strategic relevance of an online presence. Online companies may select between active versus passive approaches to Internet use in marketing: while certain companies actively seek to serve international customers over the Internet, others may regard potential foreign customers as an added "bonus," deriving from the Internet global characteristics (Lituchy & Rail, 2000; Hornby et al., 2002). Recent empirical research shows that few

SMCs can be classified as proactive Internet users (Hamill & Gregory, 1997; Lewis & Cockrill, 2002).

Most SMCs are not fully seizing the opportunities afforded by Internet technologies for global marketing communications. Important deficiencies can be found in SMCs' global e-marketing strategies, for example, Website's contents offered only in English. Perceived barriers to Internet uptake are also expected to be higher among smaller companies, including financial constraints, lack of previous experience in foreign markets, suitability of companies' offerings for international markets, time constraints, availability and requirements of skilled staff, IT expertise, and so forth. These complexities are likely to reduce the market reach of these companies, targeting only their domestic markets through the Internet (Lewis & Cockrill, 2002).

Differential Characteristics of B2B Markets

Most of previous international Internet marketing research has focused on B2C e-markets. Relatively little research has been conducted on the global implications of B2B Internet markets (Karayanni & Baltas, 2003; Klein & Quelch, 1997). Although most of the issues reviewed in this study are valid for both market types, it will be useful to offer a brief overview of B2B e-markets' differential characteristics.

Market analysts predict that the impact of Internet technologies will be more pronounced on B2B rather than B2C transactions (Klein & Quelch, 1997; Samiee, 1998b). Forrester Research (2001) estimates that by 2006, B2B online exchanges will account for around 53% of worldwide e-commerce. B2B e-commerce is currently growing at higher rates than B2C markets. According to estimations by the Gartner Group, there are currently around 500 B2B markets worldwide, and 10,000 new markets will appear in the next few years.

Network relationships are critical for success in B2B markets. Wymbs (2000) suggests that the value of B2B business grows consistent with Metcalfe's Law: "the value of the network is equivalent to the square of the number of nodes connected to it." The Internet global nature increases both the number of potential B2B relationships and a company's customer base, which may contribute to achieving a sustainable competitive advantage (Eid, 2002; Leek et al., 2003).

Samiee (1998b) argues that both structural and functional issues are expected to have greater impact in B2C business settings than in B2B transactions. Common barriers to growth in B2C e-commerce, such as credit card security or online shopping enjoyment, are not likely to be relevant in B2B contexts (Klein & Quelch, 1997). The main purposes of B2B e-shopping are in most cases related to cost efficiency. Nevertheless, in a study by Forrester Research (2000, cited in Guillén, 2002), it was found that 60% of B2B e-companies experienced difficulties arising from differences in business practices across countries. Therefore, B2B online enterprises should not underestimate the potential complexities (e.g., geographic, infrastructural, political, cultural, etc.) for success in the Internet global markets.

Internationalization of E-Commerce Corporations

Diverse products and services industries are undergoing significant internationalization processes (e.g., music, books, banking, or technological products). The Internet is expected to increase the internationalization of companies in diverse sectors. Several authors agree that, on the Internet, the critical decision to be made by managers will not be whether or not to go global. Much more important will be selecting the most suitable global strategy for the firm (Singh & Kundu, 2002). Market entry strategies should be selected according to the product/service characteristics: when pressures for local responsiveness are high (e.g., costly worldwide distribution is involved, or language and cultural differences are critical factors), foreign markets should be entered on a country-by-country basis; on the other hand, online companies should pursue a fast global presence if transactions are not involved, or "winner-takes-all" advantages are high. Fist-mover advantages are expected to be especially important for potential B2B market makers (Klein & Quelch, 1997).

Previous research suggests that new international marketing paradigms may be needed to account for the internationalization processes on the Internet (Bennett, 1997; Hamill, 1997; Kim, 2003). Due to improved information flows and lower costs of information collection and transmission on the Internet, the gradual, incremental approach to business internationalization (Jatusripitak, 1986) may no longer be relevant to describe e-firms' internationalization processes. In this regard, Kim (2003) showed that the internationalization of e-commerce corporations supports the gradual and sequential internationalization of firms, under consideration of a sociocultural index to account for the "psychic distance" between national markets. According to these results, Internet firms (1) tend to enter strategically important countries first, (2) may enter multiple markets in a shorter period of time, and (3) in some cases, firms may follow business networks rather than psychic distance or market potential as a basis for the internationalization decision.

Internationalization of Service Industries on the Internet

Service industries have been traditionally much less internationalized than physical product industries. Diverse factors have contributed to this situation, such as the special characteristics of services or protection by national governments (Wymbs, 2000). Nevertheless, several factors have contributed to an increasing internationalization of service industries (Berthon et al., 1999): (1) exponential growth of world trade in services, (2) increasing role played by services in international trade negotiations, (3) importance of international services as a determinant of a nation's economic development and societal welfare, and (4) governmental deregulation worldwide.

The Internet promises to accelerate significantly the internationalization processes of diverse service sectors. Kim (2003) points out that the internationalization of online service firms has been faster than for online providers of physical products. Logistics and problems involved in worldwide distribution of tangible products are not barriers to the global expansion of online service providers.

Internet-Based Technologies and Traditional Media for Cross-Border Communications

Although Internet uptake among businesses has not yet reached the penetration levels of more traditional communication channels (e.g., telephone or fax), the usefulness of online services is expected to increase substantially in the near future (Leek et al., 2003).

While certain communication methods will be gradually replaced by more efficient online methods, Internet communications are not likely to become a substitute for all older communication technologies. Rather, online and off-line communication systems are expected to coexist in the future. Diverse technologies are available to develop global Internet marketing strategies:

- The Web and related services, such as e-mail, online forums, newsletters, chat services, search engines, and so forth, are powerful vehicles for global marketing communications. E-mail is currently the world's most widely used online service among businesses and consumers (Hamill, 1997; Wei,

Ruys, van Hoof, & Combrink, 2001), and it is expected to become the most useful method for global business communication (Leek et al., 2003).

- Other technological applications are currently being used, such as electronic data interchange (EDI), enterprise resource planning (ERP), customer relationship management (CRM), work flow and groupware systems, intranets, extranets, and other data transfer systems (Cavusgil, 2002; Rao, 2001).
- Peer-to-peer (P2P) software applications offer great potential for global e-marketing communications. File-sharing software's underlying technology (e.g., Napster, Kazaa, and eMule), leaving aside legal concerns, can become a valuable source of competitive advantage in the future.

These diverse technological possibilities have a great potential to improve several business areas of global e-commerce companies, both in B2B and B2C business contexts. Possible global applications of the Internet include global supply chain management (SCM), e-procurement, e-fulfillment, knowledge portals for knowledge management, global knowledge repositories, horizontal communities, global talent pools, e-learning, and e-training (Cavusgil, 2002).

The relevance of the Internet as a global marketing channel will depend on the added value that it provides compared to traditional media. It should generate revenue and reduce costs (Quelch & Klein, 1996). These authors also suggest that the impact of the Internet will be more significant in countries with less developed traditional distribution channels.

Role of Mobile Technologies (M-Commerce)

M-commerce applications enable transactions and information distribution, regardless of the user's geographical location. The following market trends point to an increasing potential of these mobile technologies across countries:

- While in 2001 there were around 180 million PCs, there are currently around 400 million users of cellular phones worldwide. By 2004 the number of mobile phones will surpass that of fix telephone lines. By 2005 there will be more than 1,000 million users of mobile phones worldwide (Accenture, 2002).

- Globally, it is expected that 240 million people will use their mobile phones for data exchanges by the end of 2004. In 1999 there were only 26 million users of mobile appliances.
- The estimated growth in the global m-commerce market is around 75% annually, and is expected to reach $80,000 million by 2005.
- There are likely to be increasing interrelations between mobile markets and other online and off-line markets. For example, some European companies are offering mobile services through their Web sites (i.e., downloading logos and music, sending SMS messages from the Web site, receiving e-mails on the cellular phone, etc.).
- Regional trends:

  M-commerce markets, unlike e-commerce markets, are more developed in Europe and Japan than in the United States. Reasons include the following: (1) high penetration rates of cellular phones in Europe, (2) unique standard for mobile communications, and (3) appropriate pricing structures that promote a mobile culture.

  The eEurope initiative aims to strengthen Europe's leading position in mobile technologies (European Council, 2002).

  - Great growth potential for U.S. m-commerce markets in the near future.

Challenges to global m-commerce:

- Existence of diverse technological standards in different regions.
- Limitations related to speed and functionalities of mobile appliances.
  - Newer mobile standards, such as WAP, GPRS, and UMTS, are expected to overcome these limitations.

Internet Potential for Relationship Building (eCRM)

Several authors acknowledge the Web and the Internet's suitability for relationship building, especially with geographically distant customers and suppliers (Angelides, 1997; Leek et al., 2003; Melewar et al., 2001). Global e-marketing communications are likely to benefit from the implementation of e-CRM systems, both in B2C and B2B contexts.

Building online relationships can help e-marketers to deal with the complexities involved in global markets, for example, differences in national legislations, cultural differences, or the need for localization of marketing communications (Melewar et al., 2001). On the Internet, companies have the potential to establish new customer relationships, regardless of where they are located. E-CRM systems enable companies to customize product offerings, due to the identification of the customer's previous online behavior and preferences. The collection of customer data through e-CRM systems is likely to face restrictions from country-specific privacy regulations (Crosby & Johnson, 2002).

Internet technologies facilitate global and close collaborations, but e-companies must also face certain limitations, mainly associated with the lack of personal interaction, which is commonly believed to strengthen business bonds. The need for personal contact for online relationships should not be underestimated, and it is likely to be dependent on the products and services' specific characteristics.

On the Internet, it is relatively easy for customers to swap between different providers from different countries. Adequate implementation of e-CRM systems can help companies avoid customer switching behaviors, potentially deriving from unsatisfactory distribution or customer service (Crosby & Johnson, 2002; Deshpandé, 2000). E-CRM systems may increase customer loyalty in online global markets, which avoids price competition by making customers less price sensitive (Melewar et al., 2001).

Challenges and Risks

More challenges and risks are involved in global than in domestic markets. Diverse issues have been identified in previous research as barriers for the success of global e-marketing communications (Cavusgil, 2002; Eid & Trueman, 2002; Melewar et al., 2001; Palumbo & Herbig, 1998; Samiee, 1998a; Tractinsky & Jarvenpaa, 1995): (1) variations in technological and commercial infrastructures across countries (e.g., PC ownership); (2) system compatibility issues; (3) psychological distance between national markets; (4) different currencies; (5) organizational barriers (e.g., available resources for global operations); (6) diversity of local regulations (product standards, privacy and security laws, intellectual property, censorship, taxes, tariffs, etc.); (7) security concerns and consumer trust; (8) competitive factors in global markets; (9) customer support in foreign markets; (10) understanding foreign markets; (11) distribution issues; and so forth.

Previous research has shown that the perceived relevance of the above barriers is likely to differ significantly between companies with and without prior experience on the Web (Bennett, 1997). Issues related to the "need of foreign representation" and "lack of export skills" were perceived as relatively more important in smaller firms without Web experience. On the other hand, companies with previous Web experience included "easier export marketing" and "not needing foreign representation" as major advantages provided by the Internet.

Infrastructural Issues in Foreign Markets

Infrastructural constraints limit the potential success of global e-commerce and e-marketing communications. Global e-marketers should assess the availability and requirements of both technological and commercial infrastructures in the target markets.

Technological Infrastructures in Target Markets

It is critical for companies to evaluate the development of technological and telecommunication infrastructures in countries targeted through the Internet and the Web. The suitability of the Internet channel for marketing communications will be lower in those countries with less developed digital infrastructures.

In many developing countries, two factors will make it difficult for companies to fully benefit from the opportunities offered by the Internet for global marketing communications (Guillén, 2002; Morgan, 1996; Ngini et al., 2002; Palumbo & Herbig, 1998; Samiee, 1998a, 1998b):

- *Underdevelopment of information technology and telecommunications infrastructure:* In many countries, digital infrastructures tend to be far less developed than in developed Western countries.
- Differences with regard to the availability of broadband Internet access solutions should be taken into account at the design stages of Web sites with international focus (e.g., reducing Web pages' download times for markets with less developed digital infrastructures).

- *Unaffordable prices for Internet access:* High prices for Internet access limit significantly the adoption and development of Internet technologies in certain markets.

Firms' Technological Infrastructures

Together with the necessary technological development in different markets, it is equally important that managers make the right decisions on the development of their own technological infrastructures, for example, setting up their own Web servers or contracting with an ISP, necessary bandwidth, and so forth (Javalgi & Ramsey, 2001; Morgan, 1996). In order to seize opportunities offered by the Internet, significant investments in diverse computer equipment will be required. These investments can reduce the potential market reach of smaller companies.

Commercial and Support Infrastructures

With regard to the commercial and support infrastructures available in foreign countries, two main factors are likely to influence success:

- Availability of local offices and representation (Bennett, 1997; Samiee, 1998a). Setting up local offices can be a costly decision. Other solutions include contracting the services of local distributors.
- Sophistication of foreign markets' commercial infrastructure. The availability of high-quality support services facilitates the activities of global marketers in different countries, for example, local availability of banks and financial institutions, and providers of computer and Internet services (Javalgi & Ramsey, 2001).

Structural Issues

Previous research has focused on the potential effects of diverse structural issues on global e-marketing success. Among such relevant issues, the following can be identified: computer literacy, PC ownership, Internet access, location, local regulations, and culture.

PC Ownership

The international availability and adoption of computer equipment enabling Internet access—mainly personal computers and Internet servers—is required to support the development of e-commerce on a global scale (Javalgi & Ramsey, 2001; Samiee, 1998a). While personal computers are widely available in developed countries, the purchase of PCs is less affordable for consumers in less developed countries. National and regional differences are also significant in the ownership levels of other devices enabling Internet (laptops, "set-top boxes," cellular phones, PDAs, etc.). Diverse estimations suggest that such regional disparities are not narrowing, and higher penetration rates of PCs and high-quality Internet terminals are expected in developed Western countries, such as the United States. These market trends point to a geographically limited potential for Internet use as a communications and distribution channel. Ngini et al. (2002) argue that Asian countries are the only developing nations likely to approach the Internet access levels of more developed countries in the near future.

Staff and Consumers Skills

Diverse authors acknowledge that the effective use of Internet technologies for global e-commerce demands threshold levels of skills by both companies' staff and consumers. Several skills are required in order to fully benefit from the use of the Internet and the Web for global marketing communications (Hamill & Gregory, 1997; Javalgi & Ramsey, 2001; Klein & Quelch, 1997; Morgan, 1996; Wei et al., 2001):

- Educational and technological skills (e.g., familiarity with PCs and Internet technologies)
- Proper understanding of foreign markets (e.g., linguistic and specific skills to deal with foreign customers and partners)

Computer and Internet Literacy

Computer and Internet literacy-related factors refer to consumer perceptions on the usefulness of personal computers and the potential benefits offered by Internet technologies. Education and previous experience with these technologies determine to a great extent the perceptions that people from different nations hold on this issue and contribute largely to the adoption and use of Internet technologies. The persistence of regional inequalities, with regard to the technological expertise of the population, further limits the suitability of the Internet as an international distribution channel (Samiee, 1998a). Training programs should be continually promoted by both private and public institutions. In this regard, the eEurope initiative, promoted by the European Commission, aims to develop an "inclusive digital society" and increase the technological skills of Europeans (European Council, 2002).

The companies' staff is expected to play a key role in the implementation of effective global e-marketing strategies. Skilled managers and marketers will be needed to "recognize the Internet's marketing potential and build on it" (Martin & Matlay, 2003). On the other hand, the successful implementation of global e-marketing will depend greatly on staff skills. Hamill and Gregory (1997) argue that Internet technologies are easily available to most companies, but there is a steep learning curve involved in the effective use of these technologies.

SMCs with limited resources will have to make a careful assessment of the available and needed staff resources; staff training or new hirings may be needed (Bennett, 1997; Hamill, 1997; Tetteh & Burn, 2001). Another limitation for smaller companies relates to the availability of enough "staff time" for tasks such as Web site maintenance and updates, or responding to online customer inquiries and feedback.

Geographic Location

Several authors suggest that location and geographic restrictions are less relevant to commercial success on the Internet, due to the Internet potential for building an integrated worldwide network of people and organizations, regardless of where they are situated (Angelides, 1997; Bennett, 1997; Cavusgil, 2002; Lazer & Shaw, 2000; Palumbo & Herbig, 1998; Samiee, 1998a). Nevertheless, the Internet does not alleviate certain difficulties involved in foreign markets, such as perceived market risk or distribution and logistic complexities.

Government Regulations

Due to cross-border information flows on the Internet, governments will play a key role in the development of Internet markets. Traditionally, the degree of government intervention in consumer and business markets differs significantly between different nations (Javalgi & Ramsey, 2001; Tractinsky & Jarvenpaa, 1995). While the United States relies more on free markets, European and Asian countries rely more on higher political instances and business elites for the promotion of new digital technologies among their citizens.

Differences in Local Regulations

On the Internet, global marketers will have to deal with diverse national regulations, and bilateral and multilateral agreements (Tran & Atkinson, 2002; Zugelder, Flaherty, & Johnson, 2000). There is little international homogenization of regulations on consumer protection, copyright issues, taxation, and so forth. Different online marketing practices could conflict with national regulations. Therefore, increased localization may be needed in order to comply with the requirements of diverse regulatory environments (Rudraswamy & Vance, 2001).

Local governments can limit the advantages offered by the Internet through the following practices:

- *Limitations to global information flows:* some countries have already developed local regulations that restrict the access to foreign information sources.
- *Restrictions to imports and exports:* there is a risk that certain countries set up import controls to the goods and services available for purchase on the Internet (Bennett, 1997; Quelch & Klein, 1996).
- *Security aspects:* currently there is a diversity of country-specific regulations to protect data transfers on the Internet (e.g., countries such as France do not allow the transfer of encrypted data through the Internet). Regulations such as the Data Protection Act, Safe Harbor, and the Gramm-Leach-Bliley Act (GLBA) coexist in the protection of customer data (Samiee, 1998a; Tran & Atkinson, 2002).
- *Privacy regulations:* companies will have to deal with foreign regulations on consumer privacy (Crosby & Johnson, 2002; Rudraswamy & Vance, 2001; Samiee, 1998a; Zugelder et al., 2000).
- *Censorship:* companies operating in sectors related to pornography are likely to face censorship attempts in several nations (Palumbo & Herbig, 1998).
- *Intellectual property issues:* intellectual copyright regulations face diverse problems on the Internet, as several countries do not even recognize the validity of the Berne Convention on copyright law (Morgan, 1996; Zugelder et al., 2000). Recent intellectual property-related problems include free audio and video downloads, copying the design and contents from other Web pages, Web domain names, and so forth.
- *Tariffs, taxing, and pricing regulations* (Hughes & Glaister, 2001; Zugelder et al., 2000).

- Diversity of product regulations (Guillén, 2002).
- Complex jurisdictional problems raised by global e-commerce.

Samiee (1998b) points out that governments react generally slowly to conflicts between companies' online practices and national laws. In this regard, Hughes and Glaister (2001) suggest that current regulations should be gradually updated, according to the encountered problems and trends in global e-commerce.

Influence of Cultural Factors on the Effectiveness of Global E-Marketing Communications

A key decision in global marketing relates to the extent to which marketing communications should be standardized or localized across countries. There has been a long debate among marketing academics on this issue, with authors supporting the preference of standardized marketing communications (Levitt, 1983), while others suggest that standardized approaches fail to account for the differential characteristics of diverse social contexts (De Mooij, 2003).

The global flows of information on the Internet have been argued to contribute to an increasing globalization and homogenization of customers' preferences. These authors suggest that global communication is possible, regardless of economic, cultural, and commercial differences (Bennett, 1997). Other authors conversely argue that, along with opportunities, the Internet global markets involve significant complexities associated with the diversity of cultures (Becker, 2002; Samiee, 1998b).

Arguments Favoring Localized Marketing Strategies

According to the findings of recent research on the preference of standardized/localized marketing communications in international marketing, fully standardized marketing communications are very difficult to apply. Various authors criticize the ethnocentric approaches to international and global marketing of diverse companies, especially U.S. global companies, and suggest that localization is a much more suitable strategy to take into account cultural and regional differences between markets (Crosby & Johnson, 2002; Jevons, 2000).

Depending on the product and the sector, varying degrees of local responsiveness may be necessary (Guillén, 2002). In this regard, Crosby and Johnson (2002) argue that the effectiveness of globalized approaches may be limited to certain products, such as consumer electronics for which price and quality are the most relevant considerations.

Due to the easy global market access through the Internet, there is a risk that global marketers overlook the potential implications of regional and cultural differences for effectiveness of their global e-marketing communications (Quelch & Klein, 1996). These risks are likely to be higher for smaller "born global" companies, lacking the experience and knowledge that multinationals have about international markets. Diverse factors may contribute to the selection of standardized strategies on the Internet: (1) Internet "global nature," (2) easier implementation (Hornby et al., 2002), and (3) beliefs that cultures and societal practices are converging (Lee, 1998; Levitt, 1983).

The decision on the degree of localization is a crucial determinant of Web site marketing effectiveness. Issues such as the translation and cultural localization of Web sites' contents must be carefully considered, according to the individual market's characteristics. Developers of Web sites with international focus should account for the following factors:

- *"Psychic distance" between the home country and the target market:* The concept of psychic distance has been previously used to refer to cultural and social differences between national markets (Bennett, 1997). Standardized e-marketing communications will have more potential for success if psychic distance between the targeted markets is low.
- *Limitation of potential market reach on the Internet:* If a localized approach is selected for all markets, smaller companies with higher resource constraints are likely to focus on certain countries first (e.g., markets with less psychic distance and higher market potential).
- *Costs of Web site localization:* More financial and staff resources will surely be necessary for Web site development and maintenance if Web sites are localized. The management of local contents involves significantly higher complexities.

In global marketing through Web sites, a standardized approach would involve the use of a single Web site or domain name for all countries. A localized approach would require content translation and adaptation (e.g., local events or regional promotions). Kim (2003) points out that localization approaches may be especially important for Internet portals, as Internet users usually look for customized and locally relevant contents on such Web sites. Global online marketers should find a balance between global integration and localization (Becker, 2002; Guillén, 2002; Wrobel, 2002). While the advantages of globalized Web marketing are mainly related to cost effectiveness, local marketing increases the effectiveness of e-marketing communications due to higher local sensitivity.

Cultural Factors

Cultural barriers may limit the success of both multinationals and SMCs' global e-marketing communications. Cultural diversity is related to differences in the values, beliefs, and language of international customers. Cultural factors may influence the success of global e-marketing strategies in several ways:

- There is a lack of universal management and marketing practices, which are subject to cultural influences (Tractinsky & Jarvenpaa, 1995). For example, cultural differences are important limitations for the development of international relationships.
- Psychic distance between national markets has been used to explain the internationalization process of firms in traditional markets. Using a "socio-cultural distance index" to measure psychic distance, Kim (2003) was able to explain online companies' internationalization processes.
- Culture influences a country's "technological sophistication" (Hornby et al., 2002; Javalgi & Ramsey, 2001), for example, consumers' attitudes, familiarity and experience with Internet technologies.
- Preferences on the suitability of diverse distribution channels differ internationally (Guillén, 2002). For example, online shopping adoption can be limited in countries where consumers regard the Internet as a less suitable distribution channel.
- Culture is a valuable resource for the differentiation of local companies' offerings (Ger, 1999).
- Cultural influences on Web site design (e.g., different attitudes toward colors and images).
- The relative importance of privacy and security concerns is related to culture (Rudraswamy & Vance, 2001).
- Increased impersonalization on the Internet may not be well perceived in certain cultures (e.g., high-context cultures) (Samiee, 1998a).

- The staff of "born global" companies on the Internet, who lack previous experience dealing with cultural factors in global markets, may need "cross-cultural training" (Lituchy & Rail, 2000).

Cultural considerations are not only limited to B2C contexts. B2B markets, where cultural considerations might be regarded as less relevant due to more impersonal transactions, are also subject to the influence of "psychic and geographical distance" between the home and foreign markets (Melewar et al., 2001). For example, industrial purchasing decisions will generally involve different decision makers, who will generally need Web information in their local language (Samiee, 1998a).

Language

Effective Web site translation is one of the most challenging tasks if a localization approach is selected. The use of different languages also needs to be integrated into business practices. For example, customer service via e-mail, fax, and phone should also be available in the local language (Guillén, 2002).

On the Internet, English has been referred to as a "global language," with a significant higher number of single-language Web sites (Samiee, 1998a). Nevertheless, most Internet users do not properly understand English, for example, in Southern Europe and Asia (Becker, 2002; Gerritsen Korzilius, van Meurs, & Gijsbers, 2000), and Internet adoption among non-English speaking consumers is growing at very high rates. According to recent estimations, native English speakers will account for less than 30% of the total Internet population by 2005 (Guillén, 2002). On the Internet, like in traditional off-line markets, consumers prefer to purchase products and services in their native language. Even Scandinavian consumers, who generally have a very good knowledge of the English language, seem to prefer linguistically localized Web sites. Therefore, linguistic adaptation will be further required in the future.

Offering contents in local languages is not absent of problems and diverse complexities. Successfully offering locally relevant contents and language localization may require partnerships and local cooperation (Kim, 2003; Palumbo & Herbig, 1998).

Diverse solutions for linguistic adaptation have been identified:

- *Automatic translation solutions:* The accuracy of content translation may not be accurate.

- Offering multilanguage options
- Development of localized Web sites

Several companies, which started offering their Web contents only in English, are starting to develop multilanguage Web sites. Customers of Hotmail.com, the leading provider of Web-based e-mail services, have the chance to select between several languages. Other companies such as Yahoo! have developed fully localized Web sites in different countries.

Organizational Barriers

Organizational barriers arise from the difficulties and resources required to engage in global marketing. Potential barriers range from staff skills, for example, education, technological expertise, or previous experience in international markets, to product/market barriers, for example, the suitability of the firm's products and services for foreign markets, and market selection (Hamill, 1997).

The application of Internet technologies to commercial activities involves the integration and adaptation of the firm's technology, business processes, and staff, according to the characteristics of the online environment and the target markets.

Information Management

Another challenge for online companies may be the effective management of the sheer amount of diverse data available on the Internet (e.g., information on customers' preferences and online behavior or diverse reports and market analyses). Hamill and Gregory (1997) point out that an effective information management (information collection, organization, and interpretation) will be more relevant in SMCs due to more limited staff and time available.

Web Sites' Development and Maintenance Costs

Though the Internet reduces significantly the financial requirements for global marketing communications, the costs involved in effective Web site development and maintenance are not negligible. The costs of the following activities should be carefully managed:

- Development and maintenance of global Web sites. In several sectors, Web sites' contents need to be updated on a daily basis, increasing significantly the costs involved in Web site maintenance.
- Local content management and maintenance of multilingual Web sites: a strong financial commitment must be made to localize Web sites' contents.
- Necessary financial resources for the implementation of an "Internet infrastructure": computers, software, security systems, broadband Internet access, technological maintenance, and so forth.

According to estimations by Forrester Research, the costs of developing and managing a company's Web site range from $300,000 for promotional sites to $3.4 million for shopping sites (Samiee, 1998a, 1998b). The maintenance of effective Web sites is an ongoing process, and depending on the purposes and the degree of Web site localization, the total costs of global marketing on the Web may be too high for smaller companies with limited financial resources.

Operational and Procedural Problems

Further problems posed by the global implications of Internet markets relate to dealing with operational and procedural problems (Samiee, 1998a). These problems are largely transaction-specific and include such practical problems as dealing with documentation and paperwork, international logistics, and managing payments in different currencies.

Global Marketing on the Internet

In this section, the chapter will review the main implications of the Internet and the Web for global marketing. The authors strive to offer a thorough analysis of the potential effects of the Internet global information flows on marketing practices.

Global E-Market Segmentation

Market segmentation on the Internet will differ significantly from traditional consumer and business segmentation. The Internet provides a context where potential audiences are easier to target and reach on a global scale. The differential characteristics of the Internet channel for market segmentation have been referred to as "mass customization" (Lazer & Shaw, 2000): it incorporates the best of mass markets (e.g., global market reach), together with possibilities for individual customization.

Steenkamp and Hofstede (2002) propose a two-step approach for the identification of cross-national consumer segments with certain similarities (e.g., similar responses to marketing efforts). At the first stage, countries are grouped on general attributes such as socioeconomic and cultural characteristics, or geographic continuity. Second, on the basis of consumers' needs and preferences, cross-national segments are identified inside the previously identified market segments. This two-step approach to international segmentation enables the identification of more geographically continuous segments (lower costs of logistics) and the identification of homogeneous cross-national segments (possible standardization of marketing efforts for the different segments). This segmentation approach may be especially useful in the Internet global markets, as it solves largely problems related to the selection of cost-effective standardized marketing communications versus more effective localized marketing communications.

Identifying Global Customers' Preferences

Traditional market segmentation involves the use of criteria such as geographic and demographic attributes. Internet technological capabilities allow marketers to identify the individual customer's preferences and accordingly customize marketing communications. On the Internet, segments of one can be identified (Morris et al., 1997).

On the Web, it is easier for marketers to analyze and track consumers' shopping behavior than in off-line markets. Diverse online services help companies gain an overview of the needs and preferences of people from different cultures (Melewar et al., 2001). The Internet enables the longitudinal monitoring of changes in consumer segments like no other marketing medium in the past. Steenkamp and Hofstede (2002) argue that the structure of global consumer segments may change over time.

Samiee (1998b) argues that the identification of potential customers from different countries should not rely only on online market segmentation, as significant barriers to the use of the Internet are likely to remain in several countries.

Improved Opportunities for Global Market Research

Effective marketing research is essential for successful marketing in complex and globalized markets. The Internet improves market research in several ways, due to the easier collection of information (Hamill, 1997; Samiee, 1998a, 1998b). Diverse free-of-charge and low-cost sources of relevant information are available online for global marketing research and planning, for example, market selection and country screening processes (Ger, 1999; Lituchy & Rail, 2000). Available information includes market research reports, demographic information, regional development of Internet markets, local regulations, and so forth.

The Global E-Marketing Mix

The Internet global reach has introduced significant changes into the traditional components of the marketing mix. Next, the authors examine special characteristics of the "global e-marketing mix."

Global Online Promotion

The Internet is regarded as a very effective promotional channel, with a huge potential for global advertising (Angelides, 1997; Eid & Trueman, 2002; Kassaye, 1997; Quelch & Klein, 1996). E-mail and the Web are the most widely used methods for global advertising on the Internet.

The decision on the degree of standardization versus localization is critical for the effectiveness of global online advertising. Online marketers should not underestimate the need for advertising localization on the Internet, depending on the target market characteristics (e.g., developing multilingual Web sites). Samiee (1998b) points out that the Internet global nature may promote a standardized approach, which may reduce the effectiveness of online advertising in different countries. Recent research shows that there are no universal values that standardized advertising can appeal to (De Mooij, 2003).

An important aspect in online advertising relates to its integration into the company's integral advertising strategy. The promotion of the company's Web site should be an important part of the global advertising strategy (Berthon et al., 1999; Eid, 2002; Hamill, 1997; Morgan, 1996). Companies should promote their Web sites' addresses (URLs) through online and off-line media, in order to increase online visibility: placing the URL in off-line advertisements, registering the Web site with global and local search engines and Web directories, and including reciprocal links to other Web sites.

SMCs can especially benefit from the relatively lower costs of Web global promotion, compared to other traditional media. Nevertheless, smaller companies continue to be more constrained than larger companies on the Internet. Diverse low-cost methods for online advertising are available online (e.g., indexing in diverse search engines), but the fees charged for more sophisticated services are significantly higher (e.g., leasing keywords) (Samiee, 1998b).

Roles of Web Sites in the Company's Global E-Marketing Strategy

Diverse marketing functions can be transferred to a company's Web site: marketing and sales, customer support, public relations/corporate communications, purchasing, and internal communications (Morgan, 1996). A well-developed Web site involves several decisions of great strategic importance:

- In-house development versus contracting out
- Web development staff: depending on its functionalities, Web site development is likely to require the interaction of interface designers, content editors, technical staff, marketers, and managers.
- Web site design: an important aspect of Web site design involves reducing customer confusion (Berthon et al., 1999; Samiee, 1998b). Customer errors may result from the amount of data presented on the Web site, confusing information organization, or lack of content and linguistic localization.
- Update periodicity: depending on the information and product characteristics, Web sites' contents may need continuous updates (e.g., online newspapers).
- Selecting a mechanism for measuring e-marketing effectiveness: there should be continuous assessment of global customers' perceived value.

Markets to be Targeted through Web Sites

This is a decision of great strategic relevance, as Web sites are expected to make the most significant contribution to a company's global e-marketing strategy. All companies with a presence on the Web have the potential to serve foreign markets, but several issues determine a company's real market reach (Quelch & Klein, 1996):

- Business model: information or transaction model
- Product characteristics: information products are more easily distributed through online media than tangible goods
- Target market: domestic or global
- Degree of Web site localization

Global Branding on the Web

The Internet offers great opportunities for branding and image building, previously unavailable in off-line business environments. The information transparency and international reach, facilitated by Internet technologies, enable companies to build a worldwide identity much faster (Cavusgil, 2002).

The brand-building process differs on the Internet and other communications channels, especially in globalized markets. Both domestic and international consumers are usually at different stages in the relationship- and loyalty-building process with a specific company, product, or service. By means of Internet technologies, companies can achieve the goal of adapting marketing communications according to the specific customer's preferences (Chiagouris & Wansley, 2000).

Established Versus Emergent Brands

Previous research suggests that the most suitable strategies for managing global e-brands are likely to be different, depending on the companies' specific characteristics (Becker, 2002; Chiagouris & Wansley, 2000; Deshpandé, 2000; Palumbo & Herbig, 1998).

- *Emergent brands:* In order to compete with established brands and achieve market stability, these companies should focus on building trust and brand credibility (e.g., Yahoo.com), innovation (e.g., Paypal.com), and first-mover advantages (e.g., eBay). Lindstrom (2001) argues that first-mover advantages are decisive for successful online branding in diverse sectors. True virtual companies such as Amazon.com have been successful in promoting universal branding, as factors influencing the online shopping experience have been homogenized across countries, especially Web site design.
- *Established brands:* For "click-and-brick" companies, operating both in online and physical markets (e.g., Barnes & Noble), online and off-line

branding strategies should be adequately integrated in order to fully take advantage of the potential for brand building offered by diverse media.

Need for Branding on the Internet

Reputation and branding-related issues are expected to be as relevant on the Internet as in physical markets (Guillén, 2002). Image building is critical for international customers to be aware of a company's existence among the sheer amount of information available online. Furthermore, "trust" is one of the most decisive factors for online shopping adoption (Lin, 1999), so companies should not expect international Internet users to purchase "unfamiliar brands through unknown vendors in the foreseeable future" (Samiee, 1998b). Lindstrom (2001) points out that e-brand building will not take place until trust has been earned.

Registering the company's Web site in global and local search engines and directories is necessary in order to increase a company's visibility on the Web (Guillén, 2002; Hamill, 1997; Hornby et al., 2002). In this regard, recent research has shown that global search engines (e.g., Google.com) offer better global and local coverage than local ones (Smith, 2003). This may be due to differences in the technology underlying diverse online search services.

Branding through Web Sites

The management of a global brand and corporate logo on the Internet is an important challenge to be managed by e-companies. As in traditional markets, companies may decide to use a single brand or multiple brands. On the Internet, Web sites are the most powerful branding medium, and various approaches to Web site development are available, according to the desired degree of identification between (1) product or services brands, (2) global Web sites, and (3) corporate identity:[1]

- *Centralization of all product lines on a single Web site:* this approach involves the highest degree of identification between product brand and corporate identity. The control over global e-marketing efforts is likely to be highly centralized.
- *Multiple local Web sites for a single brand:* companies such as Yahoo.com have developed localized Web sites in diverse countries. While this strategy accounts for country-specific differences, there is a need for control over local marketing efforts in order to avoid potential conflicts between local e-marketing communications and the global brand (Eid,

2002). Consumers may become confused if a company and its subsidiaries have different Web sites, each communicating a different format, image, message, and content. Therefore, companies should use available technologies, formats, and contents to provide a consistent brand image in the Internet global markets (Kassaye, 1997).

- *Different Web sites for each brand:* Quelch and Klein (1996) suggest that this approach is suitable for brands from different markets and sectors. Companies must then decide whether to develop global Web sites for each brand, or to develop localized Web sites in different countries. The latter approach increases the complexity and coordination costs of global e-marketing efforts.
- *Development of local Web sites by independent sellers or intermediaries:* the company would not possess its own Web site in this case (Quelch & Klein, 1996).

Importance of Virtual Communities

Virtual communities are groups of geographically dispersed Internet users or consumers with shared interests or needs. These communities usually develop on Web sites, newsgroups, online forums, and so forth, where people exchange information about specific topics, but also on commercial Web sites, where consumers share opinions about the company' products and services.

The global dialogue between consumers and between consumers and companies in online communities provides great opportunities for global branding and building customer relationships (Chiagouris & Wansley, 2000). Companies such as Amazon.com have been very successful in developing profitable relationships with Internet users that exchange opinions and review the products offered on the Web site.

Country Differences

Brands, even in Internet markets, are in most cases regional, not truly global (Crosby & Johnson, 2002). Global marketers should take into account that international consumers may have different perceptions of their brands. Yahoo!, commonly regarded as a global brand, had to adapt significantly to the characteristics of the Japanese local market (Lindstrom, 2001).

Perceptions of global brands are likely to be influenced by diverse factors. Country-of-origin effects (e.g., manufacturer and production country of origin), which have been widely documented in off-line markets, cannot be ignored in the online business environment. On the Web, two main factors are expected to be relevant: product's country of origin, and Web site's country of origin. Guillén (2002) argues that the influence of a product's country of origin on the Internet should be higher for branded goods. Internet domains, as part of the companies' Web addresses, are also a branding issue that companies have to deal with (Jevons, 2000). While global Web domains (e.g., .com, .net, .org, or .edu) are commonly used for U.S. organizations and companies targeting the U.S. market, the use of country-specific Web domains (e.g., .de, .es, .co.uk, or .fr) is more common in non-U.S. countries. Local domains may be perceived by customers as a signal of local sensibility; on the other hand, global domains should be more suitable for building global brands.

White (1997) showed in an empirical investigation on U.S. consumers' perceptions of U.S. and international Web sites that international Web sites received consistently lower ratings in the following issues: (1) speed, (2) ease of navigation, (3) Web site information, (4) order options, and (5) overall site rating. Consumers seem to be more critical of international Web sites with regard to Web site design and quality. White (1997) argues that consumers will not make purchases on international Web sites if they do not perceive unique benefits in the products offered on those Web sites, compared to the products available through local Web sites.

Pricing Strategies

Effective pricing on the Internet represents a great challenge for companies operating on a global basis. The Web increases consumer power to acquire information and compare prices between domestic and international service providers (Deshpandé, 2000, 2002; Lazer & Shaw, 2000; Lituchy & Rail, 2000). This has led to certain predictions toward a generalized price reduction in online global markets, as direct competitors are just a "mouse-click" away.

Palumbo and Herbig (1998) suggest that traditional territory-based pricing is ineffective on the Internet. Diverse possibilities are available for online sellers to track online buyers' behavior (e.g., cookies, IP tracking, or data mining), which can significantly contribute to price discrimination attempts, based not only on traditionally used criteria, such as geographic location of customers and prospects, but on the individual consumer's behavior (Guillén, 2002). Price discrimination strategies involve certain risks that may arise if consumers become aware of price differences between countries. Internet technological appliances such as smart search agents will help consumers fight price discrimination through worldwide price and product comparisons. In this regard, several authors suggest that the Internet will increase price standardization across borders (Deshpandé, 2000, 2002; Eid & Trueman, 2002; Quelch & Klein 1996).

The easier price comparison might suggest that factors concerning customer loyalty, branding, and store atmospherics are no longer relevant on the Internet. On the contrary, recent research has shown that factors that reduce price sensitivity are important in online consumer markets. Even in B2B markets, factors other than price (e.g., lower transaction costs or access to more products and providers through the Internet) have been identified as key drivers of the adoption of online purchases (McKinsey, 2000). Different tactics can be used by online sellers to reduce consumers' willingness to switch to other Web sites and compare prices.

Although it is easier for consumers to swap between different online providers, consumers must invest significant time and effort in learning how to use different Web sites and online services (Eid & Trueman, 2002). Therefore, satisfactory online experiences should contribute to customer loyalty and limit customers' switching behaviors.

Challenges to global e-pricing:

- *Global standardization of promotions:* Locally sensitive pricing strategies, such as occasion-based promotions on events such as Halloween, Mother's Day, or Valentine's Day, can be difficult to standardize due to regional and national differences. While some celebrations are important only in certain countries, others are celebrated in several countries, although on different dates.
- *National differences in price sensitivity:* Differences in purchasing power and consumers' price sensitivity among countries may force companies to compete on a country-by-country basis (Guillén, 2002).
- *Customer dissatisfaction:* Due to improved information on the Web, consumers may become aware of regional price discrimination attempts. This is likely to increase customer dissatisfaction (Deshpandé, 2000, 2002; Quelch & Klein, 1996).
- *Competition:* Competitors' reactions to online pricing strategies are likely to be faster, since they can easily access competitors' price information, and accordingly modify their marketing programs (Samiee, 1998b).
- *Pricing regulations:* Pricing is subject to country-specific regulations. Dealing with pricing rules may involve significant efforts and management time, and may limit the chances for price discrimination between different markets and consumers.

- *Currencies:* Companies targeting foreign markets through the Internet will surely need to quote prices in local currencies (Guillén, 2002). Generally, customers realize if a product is cheap or expensive when the price is quoted in their local currency. When prices are shown in a foreign currency, a higher cognitive effort on the customer's side is required, and this may jeopardize one of online shopping's main advantages over other traditional channels: convenience. White (1997) argues that Internet sellers should not expect online shoppers to search for information on currency conversion rates. Customer identification through IP addresses could help companies quote prices in the customer's local currency. If the local currency is not the one that the customer prefers, the Web site should offer the possibility to quote prices in alternative currencies. Customers' preferences should be identified for future visits. Technologically easier solutions could be adding a link to a currency converter or providing approximate conversion rates for the different local currencies (White, 1997). Although the introduction of the euro softens price quoting problems for companies targeting the European market through the Internet, these barriers are expected to remain in the future and should be carefully addressed by online marketers.
- *Shipping charges:* Companies delivering products in international e-markets should clearly indicate the applicable shipping charges and local taxes in each of the served countries (Hornby et al., 2002; Samiee, 1998a; White, 1997).

Payment Systems

There are significant differences in the commonly used payment systems in different countries: some payment methods are preferred by consumers from certain countries, and some payment methods may not be even available or safe enough in several countries (Guillén, 2002). For example, more recently developed payment methods such as e-cash has only been introduced into certain local markets and few consumers already use these systems (Hornby et al., 2002).

Credit cards are the most widely used payment system on the Internet, but online sellers should not offer only this payment possibility in all countries, as there are diverse limitations to credit card use in certain countries. Credit cards are widely accepted in the United States, while this payment method faces diverse problems in other countries: in Germany, credit cards have traditionally not been used; certain Japanese credit cards are not accepted worldwide; in China, credit cards are restricted to people who can use foreign currencies (Palumbo & Herbig, 1998); and very few Asians and Latin Americans have a credit card (Guillén, 2002). Credit card use for online payments raises important security concerns among Internet users in different countries. Some Internet users are reluctant to provide their credit card information online for security reasons. Online shoppers from Western European countries tend to prefer alternative payment methods, such as cash on delivery (e.g., in Spain) and bank transfers (e.g., in Germany).

The decision on the acceptable payment methods is crucial for companies conducting transactions over the Internet. E-sellers should be flexible with regard to the accepted payment systems in different national markets.

Distribution

In both domestic and global markets, distribution is a critical determinant of customer satisfaction with online shopping services. Based on the production country and the served markets, companies will have to develop an appropriate distribution channel (Samiee, 1998b): for example, online sellers may decide to keep their own product inventory, or make arrangements with suppliers that ship the products directly to the customers.

Online Disintermediation

The online channel is expected to introduce significant changes into the traditional configuration of companies' global distribution infrastructures. The Internet is expected to change the functions performed by traditional intermediaries in local markets. Rather than displacing local intermediaries through direct relationships between sellers and buyers, current intermediaries will have to perform new functions.

A new kind of intermediary has also appeared on the Internet: infomediaries (Samiee, 1998b). The functions performed by these new intermediaries involve the specialized recollection, interpretation, and distribution of information to customers, both suppliers and consumers.

Certain authors suggest that companies accessing foreign markets through the Internet will not need to rely on local intermediaries, because customers from those markets can find information about a wider variety of products on the Internet than in local markets (Javalgi & Ramsey, 2001; Quelch & Klein, 1996). The Internet channel, though, does not solve logistic problems associated with the distribution of tangible products to international markets. Due to these restrictions, companies will need to carefully manage logistics and transport issues in foreign markets (Ryans, 1999).

Configuration of the International Distribution Channel

Both "click-and-brick" and "born-global" companies will have to make relevant decisions on the configuration of their international distribution channels:

1. Should they rely solely on the Internet for distribution in foreign markets?
2. Should they establish their own local distribution offices or contract the services of local distributors?

Samiee (1998b) argues that companies are not expected to close local sales offices in foreign countries and deal strictly through the Internet. Nevertheless, the successful experience of Dell™, relying only on the Web for global marketing and distribution, shows that such strategies are feasible. SMCs will particularly benefit from a global market reach on the Web, without investing in local distribution infrastructures in every national market.

Foreign representatives may be needed in other markets: either companies' own staff or contracted local distributors (Bennett, 1997). Most of global marketers are not likely to rely solely on their Web sites for global marketing; they should be regarded as an element of the company's integral global marketing strategy.

Local agents and local distribution infrastructures usually contribute to strengthen companies' relationships in foreign markets. Finding the right agent or distributor overseas is especially critical for SMCs' international market access over the Internet. Hamill (1997) points out that information about available local distributors is readily available on the Web.

Coordination Between Online and Off-Line Distribution Channels

Established "brick-and-mortar" companies should take into account the risks involved in the integration of the online channel into their previous distribution strategy. Bypassing local distributors may be a source of significant conflicts. Therefore, managers should manage carefully the interrelations between online and traditional distribution channels and current relationships with local distributors (Palumbo & Herbig, 1998).

Distribution Fulfillment

The fulfillment of international orders is one of the most important challenges faced by global e-sellers. Although U.S. online-selling companies receive a significant number of international orders, between 40%–50% of such orders go unfulfilled (Guillén, 2002). Therefore, many e-companies are not seizing the opportunities offered by the Internet to increase their customer base internationally. Most of the problems related to international order fulfillment are associated with the required logistics to distribute tangible goods in foreign markets. Conversely, the Internet is a very suitable medium for the distribution of information and "digitizable" products.

International customers not receiving or receiving late the products they have ordered and paid for online will surely not consider those companies for future purchases. The attitudes toward online purchasing could also be damaged, due to such unsatisfactory online shopping experiences. Global e-sellers should find logistical solutions, which ensure a smooth and cost-effective distribution to foreign customers. The Internet forces established multinationals and start-ups to adjust their current distribution infrastructures, as the Internet increases consumers' expectations on issues such as speed of delivery and after-sales services. A satisfactory navigational experience on the Web is not enough for customer satisfaction with online shopping services. Companies should deal very carefully with distribution problems, as consumers may switch easily from one provider to another.

Companies will have to decide whether it would be desirable to control global access to product information, as customers from countries where products are not distributed can be disappointed when they realize that they cannot purchase the products advertised on the Web site. The unavailability of worldwide delivery is likely to damage brand perceptions by foreign customers (Palumbo & Herbig, 1998).

Other factors have been identified to influence the decision to purchase from international online sellers (Eid & Trueman, 2002; Samiee, 1998b; White, 1997): (1) clear shipping information, including delivery times to different countries and packaging procedures, (2) information on quality guarantees and possibility of international returns or refunds, (3) availability of 24-hour worldwide customer service, and so forth.

Product

Global online marketers should assess and emphasize the unique advantages of their own products and services in local markets, compared to those available through traditional channels (Quelch & Klein, 1996; White, 1997).

On the Internet, international customers will benefit from a wider product variety. Some products, not distributed in certain local markets, will usually be available for purchase online. Consumers from such markets can access foreign

Web sites for purchases. A clear example is Amazon, the leading online bookseller, with customers scattered across countries. While Amazon has established local Web sites in countries such as the United Kingdom (Amazon.co.uk) and Germany (Amazon.de), it still sells to foreign customers through its original Web site (Amazon.com). Prices for international customers are higher than for domestic U.S. customers, mainly due to higher shipping costs. Nevertheless, total prices are competitive in most cases and the wider product assortment is highly appreciated by Amazon's customers.

Niche Products

Smaller companies with limited financial resources can gain easier access to international markets through the Internet. Quelch and Klein (1996) suggest that companies with specialized offerings, thanks to the Internet, will be able to gather the necessary number of customers.

Product Development and Product Design

Among the benefits provided by the Internet for product development, it leads to easier identification of customer needs, individual product customization, and global and faster product testing (Avlonitis & Karayanni, 2000; Eid & Trueman, 2002). The Internet helps in the design of products that match customers' preferences like no other communications channel, by incorporating the views and tastes of global customers into the product design and product development phases.

On the Internet, product design and product development can be improved by forming virtual teams, which integrate knowledge from different countries (Cavusgil, 2002). The use of Internet-based platforms can be very beneficial for product development processes involving specialization and modular product design, for example, modular software design, and decentralized research and development (R&D) functions in multinational companies (Rao, 2001). According to Wymbs (2000), companies such as Cisco Systems are using the Internet for the coordination of product design processes from geographically disperse research centers.

Services

Service offerings need to be managed differently than physical products online, due to the defining characteristics of services: intangibility, simultaneity, heterogeneity, and perishability. With regard to online distribution of services, Berthon et al. (1999) argue that the Web offers diverse possibilities for managing the special characteristics of services, mainly related to the ability of the Internet to enable both mass production and customization on a global scale.

Automation, Industrialization, and the Role of Personal Contact in Global E-Marketing

The Internet and the Web contribute to an increasing industrialization and automation of services (Berthon et al., 1999). There is a risk for e-companies that an increasing dehumanization and mechanization damages their interactions with customers and business partners. In this regard, Melewar et al. (2001) point out that the Internet must be supplemented by human interaction to sustain long-term relationships and build trust in foreign markets. This author also argues that delivering complex products to international markets may pose significant challenges to online marketers, arising form the high degree of personal interaction and customization required.

Internet technologies like e-mail and the Web should be seen as "supporting rather than replacing personal, face-to-face relationships" (Hamill, 1999). Interpersonal contact may be needed for negotiations with global customers and business partners, which are more likely to be influenced by factors like cultural influences.

Internet technologies allow companies to provide a wide variety of mass customized services without staff involvement. Nevertheless, online marketers should not regard the possibilities for standardization and mechanization as a panacea for replacing the need for personal interaction.

Conclusions

The Internet provides great opportunities for global market access to companies of different sizes. This new channel is expected to change global marketing like no other communications technology in the past. Lower access costs to foreign markets, as well as better knowledge of global consumers' preferences are two of the main improvements offered by Internet technologies, compared to traditional distribution channels. But online companies will necessarily have to face diverse complexities derived from the peculiarities of globalized environments, in order to develop an effective global e-marketing strategy.

In Internet global markets, companies will have to deal with complex market conditions related to the existence of national and regional differences in the target markets' economic, infrastructural, cultural, legal, and political characteristics. A higher environmental diversity and the lack of familiarity with the target markets are serious risks for the success of global marketing efforts through the Internet.

Diverse structural issues, such as current differences in Internet use and the development of digital infrastructures among countries and regions, should be taken into account by online marketers for the development of their online marketing strategies (Mahajan et al., 2000). Diverse aspects of global e-marketing communications should be adapted in accordance with the environmental characteristics of the local market: PC and Internet adoption rates, attitudes toward and acceptance of the Internet as a distribution channel (Javalgi & Ramsey, 2001). Other challenges to be carefully managed by online marketers relate to organizational issues, such as ensuring a smooth distribution, integrating the Internet into the companies' global marketing strategies, coordinating online and off-line distribution channels, or evaluating the need for local representation in the local market (Samiee, 1998b). The most suitable strategies to cope with structural and organizational problems will be highly dependent on both the characteristics of the target market and the offered products or services.

Governments will play a significant role in the development of global e-markets, promoting Internet adoption by both companies and consumers, and improving local information and technological and commercial infrastructures. Proactive public and private participation is critical to increase the potential of Internet markets in technologically less developed countries, reducing the effects of the "digital divide" phenomenon. This is one of the main purposes of the eEurope initiative for countries belonging to the European Union (Turner, 2001).

Internet technologies provide great improvements in global market segmentation and market selection, which is likely to increase the effectiveness of online companies' global e-marketing efforts. The Internet channel will also have a significant impact on the diverse elements of the companies' global marketing mix (global e-marketing mix). Internet technologies will introduce significant changes into the pricing, promotion, distribution, and product elements of the marketing mix. Most of the improvements provided by Internet technologies relate to higher possibilities for adaptation, according to the preferences of the individual customer.

It seems clear that the Internet should not be regarded as a panacea for global market access. According to diverse recent investigations, localization of marketing communications is expected to be further necessary on the Internet in order to account for local markets' differential characteristics. The improved possibilities for global market research offered by the Internet should help companies find a balance between standardization versus localization approaches, according to the target market's specific characteristics. Global e-marketers should prove their skills in finding a balance between the higher effectiveness of localization approaches and cost advantages provided by standardization strategies.

References

Angelides, M. C. (1997). Implementing the Internet for business: A global marketing opportunity. *International Journal of Information Management, 17*(6), 405–419.

Anonymous. (2002). The high cost of Web content management. *Information Management Journal, 36*(5), 8-8.

Bain, M. G. (1999). Business to consumer e-commerce: An investigation of factors related to consumer adoption of the Internet as a purchase channel. Centre for Marketing Working Paper, No. 99-806.

Becker, S. A. (2002). An exploratory study on Web usability and the internationalization of US e-businesses. *Journal of Electronic Commerce Research, 3*(4), 265–278.

Bennett, R. (1997). Export marketing and the Internet. *International Marketing Review, 14*(5), 324–344.

Berthon, P., Pitt, L., Katsikeas, C. S., & Berthon, P. J. (1999). Executive insights: Virtual services go international: International services in the marketplace. *Journal of International Marketing, 7*(3), 84–105.

Cavusgil, S. T. (2002). Extending the reach of e-business. *Marketing Management, 11*(2), 24–29.

Chiagouris, L., & Wansley, B. (2000). Branding on the Internet. *Marketing Management, 9*(2), 35–38.

Crosby, L. A., & Johnson, S. L. (2002). The globalization of relationship marketing. *Marketing Management, 11*(2), 10–11.

De Mooij, M. (2003). Convergence and divergence in consumer behavior: Implications for global advertising. *International Journal of Advertising, 22*(2), 183–202.

Deshpandé, R. (2000, June 20–21). Leveraging the Internet for global branding. *Proceedings of the Marketing Science Institute's Conference on "Global Branding,"* Milan, Italy.

Deshpandé, R. (2002). Performance companies. *International Journal of Medical Marketing, 2*(3), 225–231.

Eid, R. (2002). A cross-industry review of B2B critical success factors. *Internet Research: Electronic Networking Applications and Policy, 12*(2), 110–123.

Eid, R., & Trueman, M. (2002). The Internet: New international marketing issues. *Management Research News, 25*(12), 54–67.

European Council. (2002). eEurope 2005: An information society for all. An Action Plan to be presented in view of the Seville European Council. Retrieved October 10, 2003, from *http://europa.eu.int/information_society/eeurope/2002/news_library/documents/eeurope2005/eeurope2005_es.pdf*

Ger, G. (1999). Localizing in the global village: Local firms competing in global markets. *California Management Review, 41*(4), 64–83.

Gerritsen, M., Korzilius, H., van Meurs, F., & Gijsbers, I. (2000). English in Dutch commercials: Not understood and not appreciated. *Journal of Advertising Research, 40*(4), 17–31.

Guillén, M. F. (2002). What is the best global strategy for the Internet? *Business Horizons, 45*(3), 39–46.

Hamill, J. (1997). The Internet and international marketing. *International Marketing Review, 14*(5), 300–323.

Hamill, J., & Gregory, K. (1997). Internet marketing in the internationalization of UK SMEs. *Journal of Marketing Management, 13*, 9–28.

Hoffman, D. L., & Novak, T. P. (1996). Marketing in hypermedia computer-mediated environments: Conceptual foundations. *Journal of Marketing, 60*(3), 50–68.

Hornby, G., Goulding, P., & Poon, S. (2002). Perceptions of export barriers and cultural issues: The SME e-commerce experience. *Journal of Electronic Commerce Research, 3*(4), 213–226.

Hughes, J. F., & Glaister, K. (2001). Electronic commerce and international taxation: A square peg in a round hole? *European Management Journal, 19*(6), 651–658.

Jatusripitak, S. (1986). An integrated model of the export marketing decision. In *The export behaviour of firms*. UMI Research Press.

Javalgi, R., & Ramsey, R. (2001). Strategic issues of e-commerce as an alternative global distribution system. *International Marketing Review, 18*(4), 376–391.

Jevons, C. (2000). Misplaced marketing—International marketing: With marketing misplaced, it's often not international. *Journal of Consumer Marketing, 17*(1), 7–8.

Karayanni, D. A., & Baltas, G. A. (2003). Web site characteristics and business performance: Some evidence from international business-to-business organizations. *Marketing Intelligence & Planning, 21*(2), 105–114.

Kassaye, W. W. (1997). Global advertising and the World Wide Web. *Business Horizons, 40*(3), 33–42.

Kehoe, C., Pitkow, J., Sutton, K., Aggarwal, G., & Rogers, J. D. (1999). Results of GVU's tenth World Wide Web user survey. Retrieved from *www.gvu.gatech.edu/user_surveys/survey-1998-10/reports/*

Kim, E. (2003). The internationalization of US Internet portals: Does it fit the process model of internationalization? *Marketing Intelligence & Planning, 21*(1), 23–36.

Korgaonkar, P. K., & Wolin, L. D. (1999). A multivariate analysis of Web usage. *Journal of Advertising Research, 39*(2), 53–68.

Klein, L. R., & Quelch, J. A. (1997). Business-to-business market making on the Internet. *International Marketing Review, 14*(5), 345–361.

Lazer, W., & Shaw, E. H. (2000). Global marketing management: At the dawn of the new millennium. *Journal of International Marketing, 8*(1), 65–77.

Lee, E. C.-Y. (1998). Cultural recognition and the Internet. Proceedings of the ISOC Conference: INET'98. Retrieved April 3, 2002, from *www.isoc.org/inet98/proceedings/5e/5e_1.htm*

Leek, S., Turnbull, P. W., & Naudé, P. (2003). How is information technology affecting business relationships? Results from a UK survey. *Industrial Marketing Management, 32*(2), 119–126.

Levitt, T. (1983). The globalization of markets. *Harvard Business Review, 61*(3), 92–102.

Lewis, R., & Cockrill, A. (2002). Going global—remaining local: The impact of e-commerce on small retail firms in Wales. *International Journal of Information Management, 22*(3), 195–209.

Lin, C. A. (1999). Online-service adoption likelihood. *Journal of Advertising Research, 39*(2), 79–89.

Lindstrom, M. (2001). Corporate branding and the Web: A global/local challenge. *Brand Management, 8*(4 & 5), 365–368.

Lituchy, T. R., & Rail, A. (2000). Bed and breakfasts, small inns, and the Internet: The impact of technology on the globalization of small businesses. *Journal of International Marketing, 8*(2), 86–97.

Mahajan, V., Pratini De Moraes, M. V., & Wind, J. (2000). The invisible global market. *Marketing Management, 9*(4), 31–35.

Martin, L. M., & Matlay, H. (2003). Innovative use of the Internet in established small firms: The impact of knowledge management and organisational learning in accessing new opportunities. *Qualitative Market Research: An International Journal, 6*(1), 18–26.

McKinsey. (2000). Internet pricing—A creator of value not a destroyer. Retrieved May 5, 2001, from *http://www.mckinsey.com/practices/marketing/ourknowledge/pdf/Solutions_InternetPricing.pdf*

Melewar, T.C., Hunt, C., & Bridgewater, S. (2001). Business-to-business relationship marketing: An internet and international perspective. *The Marketing Review, 2*(2), 169–185.

Moen, O. (2002). The Internet and international marketing—An empirical analysis of small and medium sized Norwegian firms. *Quarterly Journal of Electronic Commerce, 3*(1), 31–41.

Morgan, R. F. (1996). An INTERNET marketing framework for the World Wide Web (WWW). *Journal of Marketing Management, 12*(8), 757–775.

Morris, M. H., Marais, P., & Weir, J. (1997). Is the Web World Wide? Marketing effects in an emerging market. *Journal of Strategic Marketing, 5*(4), 211–231.

Ngini, C. U., Furnell, S. M., & Ghita, B. V. (2002). Assessing the global accessibility of the Internet. *Internet Research: Electronic Networking Applications and Policy, 12*(4), 329–338.

Palumbo, F., & Herbig, P. (1998). International marketing tool: The Internet. *Industrial Management & Data Systems, 98*(6), 253–261.

Quelch, J. A., & Klein, L. R. (1996). International business and the Internet. *Sloan Management Review, 37*(3), 60–75.

Rao, P. M. (2001). The ICT revolution, internationalization of technological activity, and the emerging economies: Implications for global marketing. *International Business Review, 10*(5), 571–596.

Rudraswamy, V., & Vance, D. A. (2001). Transborder data flows: Adoption and diffusion of protective legislation in the global electronic commerce environment. *Logistics Information Management, 14*(1/2), 127–136.

Ryans, J. K. Jr. (1999). Global marketing in the new millennium. *Marketing Management, 8*(4), 44–47.

Samiee, S. (1998a). Exporting and the Internet: A conceptual perspective. *International Marketing Review, 15*(5), 413–426.

Samiee, S. (1998b). The Internet and international marketing: Is there a fit? *Journal of Interactive Marketing, 12*(4), 5–21.

Singh, N., & Kundu, S. (2002). Explaining the growth of e-commerce corporations (ECCs): An extension and application of the eclectic paradigm. *Journal of International Business Studies, 33*(4), 679–697.

Smith, A. G. (2003). Think local, search global? Comparing search engines for searching geographically specific information. *Online Information Review, 27*(2), 102–109.

Steenkamp, J.-B. E. M., & Hofstede, F. T. (2002). International market segmentation: Issues and perspectives. *International Journal of Research in Marketing, 19*(3), 185–213.

Tetteh, E., & Burn, J. (2001). Global strategies for SMe-business: Applying the SMALL framework. *Logistics Information Management, 14*(1/2), 171–180.

Tractinsky, N., & Jarvenpaa, S. L. (1995). Information systems design decisions in a global versus domestic context. *MIS Quarterly, 19*(4), 507–534.

Tran, E., & Atkinson, M. (2002). Security of personal data across national borders. *Information Management & Computer Security, 10*(5), 237–241.

Turner, C. (2001). Accelerating the development of the European information economy: The European Commission's eEurope initiative. *European Business Review, 13*(1), 60–66.

Wei, S., Ruys, H. F., van Hoof, H. B., & Combrink, T. E. (2001). Uses of the Internet in the global hotel industry. *Journal of Business Research, 54*(3), 235–241.

White, G. K. (1997). International online marketing of foods to US consumers. *International Marketing Review, 14*(5), 376–384.

Wrobel, U. (2002). "Not in front of your mother!": Online marketing for pharmaceutical products addressing taboo topics. *Qualitative Market Research: An International Journal, 5*(1), 19–27.

Wymbs, C. (2000). How e-commerce is transforming and internationalizing service industries. *Journal of Services Marketing, 14*(6), 463–478.

Zugelder, M. T., Flaherty, T. B., & Johnson, J. P. (2000). Legal issues associated with international Internet marketing. *International Marketing Review, 17*(3), 253–271.

Endnote

1 Classification adapted from Quelch and Klein (1996).

Chapter X

Stance Analysis: Social Cues and Attitudes in Online Interaction

Peyton Mason, Linguistic Insights, Inc., USA

Boyd Davis, University of North Carolina-Charlotte, USA

Deborah Bosley, University of North Carolina-Charlotte, USA

Abstract

In this chapter, we will first discuss what stance is and highlight how we identify and measure stance using multivariate techniques, using an ongoing example taken from an Online Financial Focus Group. We review differences in stance between online real-time focus groups and online chat, as well as between online and face-to-face focus groups; and finally, proffer examples of stance analysis in two very different online focus groups: older adults discussing financial services and teens discussing clothes. As marketers see that online focus groups offer valuable marketing information by understanding the significance of how *something is said as well as* what *is said, their confidence in the use of online focus-group data should increase.*

Background

Discourse is different in the online world. It takes place in an on-screen environment that is typically text based, devoid of the natural cues we typically interpret in face-to-face environments and which frame the participants' severely truncated, often terse and elliptical phrases. Synchronous (real-time) online interaction inhibits our usual reliance in face-to-face interaction on using body language or facial expressions to guess at meaning, or on listening to tone and intonation for clues to intention. The on-screen text of real-time interactions cannot replicate the back and forth, give and take of the normal face-to-face, two-party conversation that allows us to immediately modify our responses or clarify our intent.

Conventional wisdom holds that the limitations of online chats and focus groups are many: the interactants may or may not know each other (Campbell & Wickman, 2000); the size of the window available for text may affect the ways they send messages to each other (Cech & Condon, 2002); and turn-taking is affected because the line a person is typing is not always the line seen on the screen. In addition, the text-based universe of chat and online focus groups can have multiple conversants online at any one time, each of whom can be simultaneously sending small texts that "flash up on a participant's screen, or form part of the growing interactive text" (Yates, 1996, p. 77) being created in the online site for a particular chat room, chat channel, or focus group.

In this chapter, we will first discuss what *stance* is, and highlight how we identify and measure stance using multivariate techniques. Our examples and illustrations throughout will be keyed to an online focus groups about financial services. We will briefly characterize features differentiating online real-time focus groups and online chat, as well as between online and face-to-face focus groups; and finally, give extended examples of stance analysis applied to two very different online focus groups: older adults discussing financial services and teens discussing clothes.

Neuage (2003) comments that chat conversation has a double context. First, the reader sees the words in a line of text itself, which is often added a phrase at a time, in reference to words in preceding lines. Second, chatroom members can come and go during a conversation and reenter at any time, "bots" and "buddies"—programs that are automated to insert messages and even advertisements—show up on the screen at various intervals (Frey, 2002). Learning to read messages in online chat is one set of skills; learning to participate by reading, writing, and occasionally including emoticon faces demands another set. And all the while, the screen keeps scrolling.

Despite the debate over whether online real-time chats are trivial or incomprehensible and whether online real-time focus groups might be socially uninformative, a number of researchers have called attention to the social presence, gender and identity clues, and signals suggesting affect that are provided by interactivity in computer-mediated communications (Bellamy & Hanewicz, 1999; Davis & Brewer, 1997; Herring, 2002; Jacobson, 1997; Murphy & Collins, 1998). As Donath (1998) comments, in a discussion of online identity and deception, "Identity cues are sparse in the virtual world, but not non-existent" (p. 29). Taking our cue from corpus-based approaches to text analysis, we have developed a way to measure and interpret both the linguistic clues and the under-the-surface meaning of online focus groups with the multivariate techniques that collectively make up stance analysis.

What is Stance?

Stance is a person's affective or evaluative use of language based on an intellectual or emotional attitude taken toward something, about anything. This attitude stems from an evaluation or appraisal that a speaker makes, either consciously or unconsciously:

> *Whenever speakers (or writers) say anything, they encode their point of view toward it: whether they think it is a reasonable thing to say, or might be found to be obvious, questionable, tentative, provisional, controversial, contradictory, irrelevant, impolite, or whatever. (Stubbs, 1986, cited in Smith & Jucker, 2000, p. 207)*

Stance reflects different aspects of how speakers position themselves vis-à-vis other participants in a communicative interaction (Davies & Harre, 1990), or take a perspective on a particular topic being discussed in that interaction. The participants are not always conscious of such positioning since stance typically manifests itself as *emergent* and as *contingent*, evolving through various turns and sequences (Ford, Fox, & Thompson, 2002). The term *stance* is common parlance among researchers for work in language and communications on how people signal confidence or doubt, appraisal or judgment (Biber & Finegan, 1998; Martin, 2000; Precht, 2000, 2003).

How we say something is part of the "what" our recipient hears or reads as our meaning. Even though we are not consciously aware of the ways we use language, our words fall into patterns. Usage patterns can signal attitudes. For example, our patterns of where and how often we shade our phrases with auxiliary verbs like "might" or "gonna" actually signal how confident we are about what we are saying, or whether we intend to do something: look at the range of shadings in the following answers:

So, bottom line, you'd be willing to buy this?	I might	*Not yet ready to commit*
	Could be	*Still some doubts*
	Gonna think about it	*Almost ready to commit*
	You'd need more info	*Backing off a bit*
	I'd want to hear more	*Slowing things down*
	Like to hear more	*Positive and getting ready*

Usage patterns across the group as a whole, or for any individual section, can be identified, counted, correlated, clustered, factored, and scaled: that is what we do to the contents of a transcript in order to discover attitudes and emotions that lie beneath our spoken or written stance. Although much of current research looks at stance in relationship to the spoken word, we have applied the concept to written and online text through a methodology and intellectual framework that we call stance analysis.

Because the on-screen text for an online focus group looks like sentence fragments, and reads like an old-time telegram, it is all too easy to think that very little is being said—but that is not the case. Stance analysis of online text allows us to identify and monitor how people signal changes in their affect, intensity, and certainty toward a topic. When we analyze online focus groups, just as when we analyze face-to-face groups, we measure the ways participants shift their stance on issues, particularly by taking responsibility for their opinions, "owning" their feelings, and giving personal reasons for their opinions at different times during the course of a focus group discussion.

Measuring Stance: Overview of the Method

Stance analysis is an application combining techniques in content analysis and corpus analysis in order to measure how word usage patterns signal a speaker's emotional response or degree of certainty about a topic and a situation. Like content analysis, which compresses "many words of text into fewer content categories based on explicit rules of coding" (Stemler, 2001, n.p.), corpus analysis codifies and analyzes text. However, a corpus is considered to be a specific collection of machine-readable texts that is representative of the genre or variety its sample contains; its codification often reviews relationships and patterns among grammatical features or categories as well as words.

The techniques of corpus analysis have primarily been used to look closely at specific kinds of language use, such as appropriacy of style in business English, or at particular tasks, such as document queries or summarization. More recently, corpus techniques are beginning to be used for analyzing texts in areas of health or business (see, for example, the NIH-NCI Tobacco-Documents

Project at the University of Georgia, where corpus analysts are looking at possible deception in tobacco industry media statements [www.uga.edu/tobaccodocs/papers.html]). Corpus analysis is an empirical analysis, keyed to a machine-readable collection, or corpus. Ideally, a corpus is a collection of texts whose collection and arrangement is designed to be representative of a particular type, genre, or style of text. It is collected and stored in a machine-readable form which supports computational analysis (McEnery & Wilson, 2001).

In brief, we draw on the string, pattern, and word features of Code-A-Text©, which is a computer-assisted qualitative data analysis software (CAQDAS), to analyze stance across successive chunks of transcript and to get at the "story" of the whole focus group session. We have adjusted the software to identify and highlight those segments of text transcript that show frequency-cued shifts in patterns that characterize stance for a particular writer/speaker or section of the transcript. We compare these shifts with baseline data derived from our corpus of online interactions.

The computational approach we use, and our basic coding of variables, follows Douglas Biber's earlier multidimensional analyses of text (Biber, 1988). Biber, a corpus linguist, performs statistical operations such as factor and cluster analysis on standardized lengths of machine-readable texts to determine underlying associations across a speaker's or a group's language features. He conducts this research, finding language feature differences between newspaper articles, editorials, telephone and face-to-face conversations, academic prose, and so forth. His multidimensional approach is based on the assumption that statistical patterns reflect underlying "shared communicative functions" (Biber, Conrad, & Reppen, 1998, p. 149).

Corpus analysis differs from traditional content analysis in that it works with the co-occurrence of grammatical features as well as words, thus supporting the analysis of rhetorical moves across the span of a text. Rhetorical moves in a particular focus group might include shifts from an appeal to authority, to a timid demurral, or to a sudden backpedaling. The analysis of particular moves or themes within a focus group can highlight sections of a transcript of conversational interaction, as well as the changes throughout the whole session (Catterall & MacLaren, 1997).

We quantify both the frequency and the interconnections among the word patterns by which people indicate shifts in their stance. We derive scales created by multivariate statistical analysis of two dozen language categories, such as *adverbs-of-time* (e.g., "soon," "later") or *verbs-of-perception* (e.g., "see," "believe"), and use those scales to identify the key areas of a transcript. Those key areas locate where in the time span of the interaction the participants are:

- Comfortable or uncomfortable
- Tentative about their opinions or actions
- Qualifying what they say
- Ready to commit to an opinion or an action
- Edging away from commitment or opinion

Quantitative coding brings objectivity, reliability, and comprehensiveness to the qualitative task of unmasking and interpreting participants' convictions, opinions, and personal reactions toward ideas, concepts, services, or products.

Corpus of Task-Focused Conversation

Our corpus of Task-Focused Conversation, collected from 1999–2003, includes online chat groups, interviews and focus groups, and matching face-to-face (ftf) conversations, interviews, and focus groups. Each of these kinds of interaction has its own characteristics, constrained by both medium and by social situation. We collected the material in ways consonant with the ethics statements of several professional organizations, such as the Association of Internet Researchers (www.aoir.org/reports/ethics.pdf). For example, we obtained chat at rotating hours during the day and night over a 4-month period, from open public chats, self-listed on the Internet as available to anyone, and sponsored by major commercial portals (Yahoo!, MSN, and AOL).

Our Task-Focused Conversation corpus currently contains about 750,000 words, representing several social and geographic varieties of English across a number of topical areas. To ensure a broad base of language usage in different contexts, the full collection contains groups and chats on such subjects as travel, family, friendship, money and finance, music, religion, friendship, health, hobbies (including shopping), book talk, sports, and politics. In the online universe of chat groups, topics serve as "places" where language styles can differ in the same way the different sections of a high school—classroom, auditorium, lunchroom, gym—constrain the way teens choose their words, their tone of voice, even the choice of who speaks to whom. The subset of online focus groups currently has 93,000 words of predominantly North American English. This subset covers topics of finance, travel, fashion, and online retail, and includes both male and female participants from different regions and ages. Names, nicknames, user IDs, and aliases are deleted from the captured text before being entered into our corpus. The remainder of this chapter will examine the online focus group segment of our corpus. We first describe how we prepare the text for analysis.

Standardizing and Coding Units of Text

The text is first divided into 200-word units or segments to standardize for length. The use of standardized word units (segments) supports

- the capture of conversational narrative between participants;
- normalization for the comparison of unequal-length discussions;
- two screens of dialogue to provide context for any discussion; and
- the inclusion of infrequently used categories of words or word patterns.

200-Word Unit of Text From Online Financial Focus Group

When my husband is ready to retire, we will need to make some changes.
We discuss certain financial decision if it involves both of us.
When we focus on a large purchase we have at times changed something
Cut down on expenses.
my wife handles half of the responsibility
Unexpected expenses involving my children change my financial situation.
Buying more stocks - sometimes we disagree
Not often. Again, I might tend to charge items more, but investments are agreed upon by us.
sometimes the cost
we always disagree, but we seem to always work something out
not often
No, we generally agree with each other after a discussion.
My husband is more conservative and likes to wait until we have the money instead of charging.
I consult with my wife on major purchases, but investments are primarily my decision. We rarely disagree, but when we do, we invariably compromise.
My husband is more conservative with regard to investments than I am
could always use more $$$$$$$$$$$$
Fairly comfortable
we seem to have a good balence
Our financial situation seems to be fine
This past year has put a significant dent in our investments. Generally, I feel that we are a bit short of where we would like to be financially.

The next step is coding the 200-word units for those language features that are our variables. We use Code-A-Text© because it can search for an individual word as well as strings of words: that supports the identification of an array of language features to represent the syntax and semantic possibilities of usage in synchronous online discourse. Our set of 23 variables, which reflects the literature on stance and evaluation, represents the following classes of language features: adverbials marking place, time, condition, degree, manner, stance, coordination, and concession; adverbs of intensification, emphasis, and mitigation; personal, impersonal, and indefinite pronouns; modal auxiliary verbs expressing possibility, probability, futurity, and inclination; adjectives signaling elaboration; specialized verbs of perception and persuasion; negation; and discourse markers such as "Well."

Frequencies obtained for the tagged variables by segment are placed in a spreadsheet.

Spreadsheet Excerpt:

Variables 1–7 for Segments 1–5, Online Financial Focus Group (Note: adv – adverb)

Segment	Adjective	advADDITIVE	advCONDITIONAL	advDEGREE	advLINKING	advSTANCE	advTIME
1	14	0	2	5	0	1	0
2	13	1	0	3	2	1	0
3	22	3	2	0	2	3	0
4	5	0	0	2	2	2	2
5	2	0	1	1	0	1	0

The spreadsheet is the end product of the conversion of focus group text into quantitative units for further data analysis.

Data Analysis

Factor analysis helps identify the structured relationship of language features to one another, and allows the data to be reduced to its underlying patterns. Given a large set of language features, the factor analytic approach identifies underlying patterns of relationships to determine if the original set of features can be reduced to a smaller number. Factor analysis summarizes the language features in a multidimensional view. We assume that language features present multicollinearity, which is why we use a principal components factor analysis with an oblique Promax rotation, following Biber (1988) and Park, Dailey, and Lemus (2002). That is, specific parts of speech or word usages are covariant, as they come together in certain communicative acts and are identified as "dimensions." The following graphic displays dimension scores derived from the data analysis segments of the Online Financial Focus Group; successive graphics will show how the interpretation is developed.

Dimension Scores: Opening Segments of Online Financial Focus Group

Dimension scores by word segment

Dimension:

1 represents people's generalized recommendations of wishes or opinions.

2 identifies opinionated undifferentiated wishes or dissatisfactions of the participants.

3 identifies strong personal feelings.

4 indexes where in the discussion the speakers identify conditions for their personal opinions: here, they take a weaker stand and back off from stronger positions.

1 & 2 intersect to signal when participants take a strong stand to present strong generalizations, projected recommendations, and rationales for negative opinions. (This intersection is stronger than either dimension in isolation.)

Dimensions

Segment	1	2	3	4
1	-6.88	0.16	6.45	3.54
2	-0.69	-2.31	8.79	0.10
3	-8.13	-1.73	11.18	5.84
4	-10.93	-3.29	8.09	6.66
5	-7.83	8.74	6.72	8.75
6	-0.73	8.81	9.43	2.41
7	-1.28	4.92	14.22	4.01
8	2.03	9.77	11.21	4.86
9	-2.19	13.44	5.78	3.60
10	-0.58	5.82	10.99	6.23
11	-4.69	3.48	6.96	1.18
12	-3.62	6.75	10.78	-1.07
13	-5.72	7.00	5.53	3.11
14	3.49	16.77	10.57	1.03
15	6.93	18.27	11.57	1.01
16	-12.18	3.60	8.75	7.44
17	4.00	12.06	6.32	1.02
18	10.07	14.81	0.49	-0.87
19	-1.46	9.79	11.19	2.91
20	-2.86	11.08	12.66	6.73
21	4.74	17.26	8.14	2.74

Our original set of variables, features used by Biber and other corpus analysts to characterize specific kinds of texts, included 73 categories. However, not all of those variables have significance for isolating and identifying stance. Prior to conducting a factor analysis specifically on the focus group data, we eliminated variables based on several criteria: (1) very low frequency of usage variables that would not be significant to the factor analysis (less than 2% of the 93,500 word database), (2) word usage that was not related to the appraisal or evaluative component of stance, and (3) word usages known to be highly correlated and potentially duplicative, that is, nouns and definite/indefinite articles. Consequently, this left 49 variables to be factor analyzed.

A second factor analysis was then performed, using only those variables with factor score coefficients greater than .30 (a lower score is considered to play a theoretically minor role in defining language scales; see Biber, 1988). This procedure led to the elimination of 26 more variables, resulting in the final 23 language features noted below. They measure five dimensions of stance. Our decision to use the first five factors as the source of the scales is based on the results of the scree plot for each genre. Only those factors that exhibit a decline in eigenvalues to the point that scree plot exhibits a flattening of the plot are used as measures of stance (Park, Dailey, & Lemus, 2002).

The variables or language features fall into the following categories, discussed further in the *Longman Grammar of English* (Biber, Johansson, Leech, Conrad, & Finegan,1999); examples of words in categories are italicized:

- Adverbs:
  additive (*also, too*)
  linking (*anyway, however*)
  conditional (*if, unless*)
  time (*afterwards, soon*)
  degree (*exactly*)
  stance (*actually*)

  Adverbs/adverbial phrases used as:
  amplifiers (*completely*)
  emphatics (*really!*)
  downtoners (*barely, only*)
  hedges (*almost*)
  discourse particles (*well*)
- Adjectives (*bitter, cheap, rich*)
- Negatives (*not, –n't*)
- Pronouns: first, second, and third person; indefinite (*anybody*); impersonal (*it*)
- Verbs: public (observable: *walk*) and private (*anticipate, believe, feel*)
- Modal verbs: possibility (*can*), necessity (*should*)

The next illustration shows how different language features are grouped along dimensions identified by factor analysis scores:

Factor Score Dimensions of Online Focus Group Language Features (Note: adv – adverb, mod – model verb, pro – prounoun, v – verb, neg – negative element)

	1		2		3
EMPHATICS	0.744	advDEGREE	0.665	proFIRST	0.560
advSTANCE	0.687	AMPLIFIER	0.624	negANALYTIC	0.518
advADDITIVE	0.685	Adjective	0.521	advDEGREE	0.493
proTHIRD	0.483	proIMPERSONAL	0.482	AMPLIFIERS	0.481
advLINKING	0.346	discoursePARTICLE	0.376	advCONDITIONAL	0.343
vPRIVATE	0.304	advCONDITIONAL	-0.345	proINDEFINITE	-0.323
advTIME	-0.307	proFIRST	-0.446	proSECOND	-0.358
	4		5		
discoursePARTICLE	0.655	modNECESSITY	0.537		
advTIME	0.608	modPOSSIBLITY	0.481		
proIMPERSONAL	0.409	proSECOND	0.389		
negANALYTIC	0.340	advCONDITIONAL	0.347		
proINDEFINITE	0.321	DOWNTONER	-0.357		
		HEDGE	-0.406		

To capture the covariance of language features, the factor score dimensions are used as scales to measure stance. For example, the first scale for Online Focus Groups measures the amount of information participants give about *how* as well as *what* other people think, monitoring the intensity assigned, ranging from "probably" to "really" and "very." Reporting and predicting the thoughts and actions of others, in relation to questions about a product, brand, or service can also be a weak projection of potential personal interest, so we check how segments highlighted for scale 1 show relationships with scale 3, where participants report as 'I,' or scale 4, where participants project future choices onto a generic "you." Reporting as "I" indicates that the respondent is taking responsibility and/or moving toward ownership of his/her opinion; reporting as "you" indicates that the respondent is moving away from ownership by projecting responsibility outward and away from self. Scale 5 typically signals what "you" could or should do: it suggests some notion of obligation, if not full commitment.

To date, each genre of task-directed talk has its own set of scales, reflecting a slightly different covariance in each genre, a covariance we think to be affected by the choice of medium (face-to-face or online), the social situation (which includes the relationship of participants to the moderator or chief discussant as well as to each other), and to the constraints of the particular task (such as respond to survey, interact in an interview, respond online in multiparty discourse, etc.).

Stance in Online Compared to Face-to-Face Focus Groups

In an online focus group, as in any other type of focus group, participants are asked to react or to take a stand. Their stand is their "stance," which includes how they appraise a topic, a product, a brand, and even the experience of being part of the group. In short, they signal attitudes. Appraisal theory examines how people use language to signal attitude in interpersonal interaction. Martin (2000) explains the term as "the semantic resources used to negotiate emotions, judgments and valuations" (p. 145).

Analyzing how speakers make an appraisal (or take a stand), we can glimpse how they continually shift positions as a conversing self, designing remarks for different participants, and shifting among various roles—a narrating self, a character in the story, even a commentator (Gumperz, 1981). These shifts are intended to move toward or away from relationships with others as their stance shifts in response to self and others. Our notion of stance emphasizes the continuous, ongoing nature of appraisal or evaluation. In task-oriented, evaluative interaction, the speaker presents some aspect or feature of stance at multiple points in the discussion. As Koven (2002) notes, evaluation as such is not "clearly locatable, bounded entity"; instead it is "interactional, negotiated, and emerges cumulatively" (p. 171).

Schneider, Kerwin, Frechtling, and Vivari (2002) note that since online participants cannot interrupt each other, online focus groups "often have more participants and last longer" than face-to-face focus groups. In addition, they find marked differences in the amount of social presence in the two formats. They compared four ftf focus groups (participant n = 29) with four online focus groups (n = 59), and found that once the length of group time was adjusted for, neither group contributed more comments, either on- or off-topic; however, online participants were more likely to signal short comments of agreement and contributed fewer words per group.

While online, people can respond only to what they see on the screen, and in general, what they see is text. With only text to provide communication cues, participants in online real-time electronic "talk" must be able to realign in seconds to

- changes in topics
- shifts of power in addressee–addressor relationships
- entrances and exits of conversationalists
- changes in the tone of general or specific interactions

The participant must do all this with text that arrives on the screen as fragments: phrases instead of sentences, single words instead of phrases. Important words found in a moderator's question or probe are usually the core words of a topic, or what school grammars call "subject" or "main verb": they are usually not repeated. The presence or repetition of any single core or content-bearing word may have strong impact. At the very least, participants invest time and effort in keyboarding it.

People do not repeat others' questions or comments; they "point" to them. By "pointing" we mean that people do not necessarily respond with a complete sentence to someone else's statement or question. Instead they typically give an answer that, while sufficient to respond in a manner intended to convey meaning to the recipient, is still a fragment. Readers of the constantly scrolling text apparently learn new habits if they are to follow a conversation or dialogue and respond (Murphy & Collins, 1998; Herring, 2002; Frey, 2002).

Table 1. Stance by participant-keyed situation

Scale	Online multiparty Group	FTF multiparty Group	FTF one-on-one Interview
I	What 'they' think: Emphatic opi weak ownership	What 'I' think/don't like: Elaborate, usually negative opir	What 'anybody/you' (=weak 'I') might think: Projection of opinions
II	What 'they' do: Projection through report	What 'they' should do: Projection of weak commitment	What 'I' don't like: Negative opinions
III	What 'I' don't like: Negative op	Qualifying comments about opinion	Qualifying comments about opinion
IV	What everybody should do: Proj of weak commitment	What 'they' think: Emphatic, elaborated opinions	What 'they' might do: Weak prediction; weaker commitment
V	Waffling/hedging	Waffling/hedging	Waffling/hedging

An Illustration: Stance Across Different Types of Focus Groups

Conversation analysts remind us that the social situation surrounding conversationalists will have an impact on the ways they answer questions and give their opinions. Part of their response will be keyed to the relationship between the moderator and the participants. It is also keyed to whether the participants can hear or see each other. We find that features of stance, present in any dialogue or conversation, will vary in intensity and in the ways they combine with each other when the perceived social situation or context changes. Table 1 suggests the most frequent configurations of features of stance for three typical social situations. These scales, listed in the order of importance of factors in the factor analysis for each situation, shift slightly when we rerun them for focus groups, whether online or face-to-face, as shown in Example 2. In some instances, the first scale will also include a component for "social engagement" with the moderator, usually signaled by the use of personal names.

Locating Shifts of Stance in Focus Groups

To summarize, we divide a focus group transcript into 200-word unit segments so that we can trace topic and language shifts as they arise. Next, the software codes the segments for the 23 variables that are the minimum by which to characterize stance. Frequency counts for the variables are weighted by the factor scores we have established for each genre of task-directed talk in our collection: oral or keyboarded, face-to-face or online, one-to-one dialogue or multiparty, moderated or free form. It is these weightings that make up the scales. As noted earlier, each genre or type of interaction has its own set of scales. Each new transcript is assigned to a genre, coded, and its frequencies are run against the scales for that genre. The scale scores for each successive segment highlight changes in the affective or evaluative use of language throughout the course of the focus group.

Two Examples of Stance Analysis

Example 1. Adult financial concerns: The following example illustrates how our earliest scales for stance analysis (2000) were used to analyze financial services and retail marketing strategies of a very large bank. The figure below, taken from our report to the Large Bank, illustrates the scales for the different segments in an online focus group on financial services. When we tracked how participants changed their stance, from topic to topic, we were able to identify where and how they wanted immediate response from their bank, and the extent to which they wanted face-to-face contact with bankers as opposed to ATMs. Most telling, however, were the sections in which people revealed their recommendations and the degree to which they expected those recommendations to be heard. In this online focus group, participants spent a good bit of time developing a relationship with the moderator.

Scales for Initial Segments, Online Financial Group

Stance analysis scores for an online focus group

The group discussion is on people's financial situations and futures.

Segments	Social Engagement Dimension 1	Strength of Stance Dimension 2	Conditional Stance Dimension 3	Hedged Stance Dimension 4	Action Oriented Stance Dimension 5	Discussion Topics
1	1.11	13.26	0.81	0.14	0.39	Greetings and introductions
2	1.06	18.16	1.33	0.3	0.73	Introductions
3	-0.3	-9.32	1.7	0.74	1.37	Sharing financial responsibility
4	0.68	-6.89	1.45	0.47	0.92	Describe how you feel about your financia
5	0.39	7.68	1.12	1.28	1.08	In downturn do you think your investments
6	0.09	-2.58	0.41	2.26	1.43	What is a safe investment & prediction for
7	1.61	9.16	0.39	1.96	1.22	Will the economy ever come back to the w
8	1.94	-2.79	0.95	1.06	1.22	Use outside advice for certain decisions
9	0.82	-4.89	0.81	1.03	0.92	Cutting back expenses
10	0.96	-2.21	0.56	0.98	0.93	Cutting back expenses
11	1.93	14.58	0.64	1.38	1.35	What would change your financial situatior
12	1.56	-3	1.09	1	1	Win $32k, what would you do & discuss re
13	0.73	-3.37	1.3	0.97	0.9	What factors make retirement easy
14	1.19	-2.42	1.21	0.6	0.85	What's the best thing about retirement
15	1.23	-0.11	1.57	0.17	0.71	Discuss vacation and travel
16	1.18	-1.11	1.26	0.9	0.91	What's your vacation planning process
17	1.57	7.79	0.83	1.59	0.98	When/where next vacation & how will it chą
18	0.66	-2.37	0.88	1.27	0.99	Change in 5 yrs & best buy and dream va
19	0.57	-11	0.7	0.91	1.1	Dream vacations & wrap-up

Group

Identifies actual text

As the scale scores increase so does the strength of the feature.

Mason & Davis 7

The interactions among our scales tell us certain things about each of the consecutive sections of an online group. In effect, they identify sections that warrant a closer look, for different reasons. In this focus group, sections 5, 7, 11, and 17 stand out for positive reasons, and 9 and 10 stand out for negative reasons.

Section 5 asks participants to focus on how safe they think their financial situation to be. It includes the following questions from the moderator:

mod:	Many of you mention your investments and the economic downturn. Do you think that your investments will be enough to weather this storm? Why or why not?
mod:	Michael, good question. I was wondering if you felt secure with your investments.
mod:	I've heard some ideas about what to do in the face of the current economy. What, if anything, have you done about your current financial concerns?

The scales that highlighted section 5 presents groupings of features that were one or more standard deviations above or below the mean for their scale. The section shows participants voicing

- fairly strong opinion ***[Scale: 7.58]***
- strong information and strong action ***[Scale: 7.68],*** but
- little active personal engagement with an issue or stimulus ***[Scale: .39]***
- above-average conditions on or qualifications about the opinion ***[Scale: 1.12],*** and
- above-average face-saving or backpedaling ***[Scale: 1.28]***

This combination suggests caution on the part of the participants. When we look at the actual text, we see participants using predictive "will," private verbs like "hope," qualifying adverbs like "maybe" and "enough," and a slight drop in idea ownership through a less-than-usual number of first-person "I" pronouns. Participants are reporting concerns about the future in response to questions about financial security, and their concerns are strong, but they are not offering—or are reluctant to identify—personal solutions or experiences.

Section 7 completes the group of segments discussing current financial concerns for the future. Participants are actively sharing their personal opinions, giving specifics, and elaborating them. In the text itself, we see numerous "mays" and "mights" and "wills," with adjectives such as "better" and "worse" battling each other as optimists and pessimists square off—but very politely. Of special interest to the Very Large Bank: in this section, participants used the adjectives to identify the types of sources these participants look to for news and information.

Section 11 is the "hottest" section in terms of integrating a number of factors: strongest of all groups in information, in predicting action, and in generalizing what anybody and everybody might do/think. It is the second strongest in personal engagement, off the charts in opinion projection, and low in presenting qualifications restricting opinions and involvement.

Participants know what they think and are confident in their assertions. The moderator asks:

Mod: What's the first thing that you would do with your winnings? Why?

The "wish list" offered by the participants is important in its detail, as is their action list. Initially, these participants predict they would spend money on "home" (key nouns include patio, car, kitchen, children) and give many details about their desire to keep or invest at least half of any "win": members of this focus group have been burned in a market downturn. Leisure, travel, and vacation come "second."

Example 2: Female Teen Shoppers. Each focus group is different, of course, as we illustrate with our second example. This focus group of teens was convened the same year as that of the Very Large Bank, in December 2000. It offers an interesting validity check for our approach in that it helps differentiate an age cohort by language behavior. The scales identify some crucial sections for opinions and plans from this group, but not as many sections as we typically see. The teens in this group were extremely adept at keyboarding, and self-reported their habit of daily online chats with friends. They were accustomed to, and conversant in, the "fleeting speech" of the online chat universe, as characterized by Neuage (2003):

Online fleeting text affects discursive connectiveness. Spoken language is dynamic, fleeting, irreversible speech, but printed language breaks the strictures of time and leads to permanence. The two together in an online environment has elements of both—what has been said can be "revisited" as long as the chatroom is showing previous turn takings.

As we illustrate, they carried on a running series of quips, questions, and comments that included the moderator but were not always focused on the task

Table 2. Teen shoppers

Segment	Scale 1	Scale 2	Scale 3	Scale 4	Scale 5
	Other-Directed Information	Generalized Rationale	Personalized Negative Opinion	Waffling & Hedging	Projected Probabilities
3	18.69	-1.91	8.30	9.54	-1.56
4	21.78	-4.37	9.17	12.24	-0.16
5	**25.64**	**-6.38**	**8.68**	**11.50**	**-0.03**
6	15.55	-12.88	21.33	12.59	-2.31

of responding directly and exclusively to questions. Their language usage was often more like a chat group on a topic with some substance, such as books or religion, than like focus groups on banking and financial services made up of older adults.

Table 2 displays a selection from the full set of scales for the teen shoppers. Segment 5 of the online transcript using our expanded scales for online focus groups.

The scales identify segment 5 as offering strong, elaborated reports and opinions about actions or products but not signaling strong personal engagement with any particular one. It illustrates a rolling interaction where teens finish their conversations with each other, en route to answering questions. To understand it, we must find its start in the preceding segment, segment 4.

As a topic switch in segment 4, the moderator keys to recent news stories, asking

mod:	Can you think of any brands that were so popular that kids would get mugged just for wearing them?

A lively conversation ensues about one formerly popular brand now seen as fallen from favor. The moderator tries twice to introduce a new topic, and with her third question, tries tweaking the discussion about muggings, asking whether public service announcements might caution teens and slow the pace of muggings for jackets. On the screen, each line follows another; we have modified font and spacing slightly, to display efforts of the moderator to get the group back on *her* track.

mod: So public announcements and things along those line wouldn't do any good in your opinion?

C__: i dont like starter either
R__: i got disconnected, sorry
J__ i doubt it
L__: starter isn't hot here in VA
T__: nah... no one listens to those things
J__: who wears Starter anymore?
A__: no, i don't think they would
R__: *starter's era has passed*
J__: *i wore a starter jacket 6 years ago*
C__: not really...none listens

mod: It wouldn't have to just be Starter we're talking about
K__: ah
J__: when i was in the 5th grade
A__: i think public announcements and stuff would just make the items more desirable
mod: Okay, topic switch...

J__ i just can't see someone getting mugged for their clothes

mod: **When you go shopping, do you like to hang out with your friends—make it a social thing, or do you get in, get out, get it over….**

T__: like i said before, no one ever listens to those announcements. I honestly leave the room when they're on TV or something
C__: yeah people are just that way

After a sizable number of teen turns and two more efforts at switching the topic, the moderator is able to elicit information about teen retail preferences. Other segments with significant scores for strong positive opinions (segments 29 and 31) identify brand names in clothing and the names of stores that attracted teens because they were *unique* in concept, as well as in the brands stocked, which lead to their being seen as *trendy* and *trend setting.*

Such sidebar conversations or continued, overlapping threads seldom surface in segments whose participants predict, project, or hedge in significant ways. For example, negative opinions surfaced several times throughout the focus group, often accompanied by predictions of what others do or think. Segment 6 shows all the teens reacting immediately to the first in a set of three related questions about parental influences on teen clothing choices; in the next part of the segment they explain parents' desire for their respectability through coverage of body parts such as bellies.

mod2: Do you ever wear the brands or clothes that your mom wears?

L__: I'm very picky in clothes!
C__: if i didnt have time
J__: some of the time
T__: There are some things my mom and i disagree upon (my clubbing clothes) but we mainly have the same tastes
C__: yes
L__: NONONONONONONO
A__: no, my mom and I dress completely different

Implications for Marketing and Consumer Research

The methodology and results of stance analysis have implications for both marketing and consumer research in that each scrap or fragment of online interaction can be scrutinized with greater confidence. Previously, qualitative analyses of ftf focus and online groups have focused almost exclusively on the content of the participants' remarks. Using stance analysis, we now have a method to focus on meaning by *how* the participants express themselves. Although online focus group writing appears fragmented and occasionally random, it is not without meaning. A single word can have great significance to the "speaker" and the "listener." Participants express their concerns, want to be heard, expect to be responded to, all the while forming opinions about products, services, or whatever the topic at hand. We have "unpacked" the cues and clues to understanding the language interaction in environments far more interactive than traditional face-to-face focus groups. Stance analysis allows us to answer this question: "How do you know what people mean beneath the surface?" Our combination of qualitative and quantitative approaches gives an interpretive method that points to places in the text where statistical significance indicates what they mean, and how much they meant it, which suggests whether they are likely to act upon their opinion. The language they choose to use (whether consciously or unconsciously) implies much about their stance toward the product, service, or topic being discussed. In addition, stance analysis lets us understand how people express evaluation in Web-based interaction. It moves us closer to understanding how people suggest intention—critical to understanding feedback comments on Web sites, open-ended responses to online surveys, and other ways that people signal attitudes through language in online environments.

Yardena Rand, in "Revisiting Online Focus Groups," suggests that online focus groups offer much for market researchers: (1) increased information from respondents, (2) efficient, to-the-point conversations, (3) increased methods for data collection, (4) a reduction of inhibitions leading to greater intimacy among participants, and (5) increased sense of "partnership" between participants and moderators (www.quirks.com, last accessed September 30, 2003). We add that using stance analysis with online focus groups also offers a combined qualitative and quantitative methodology, a way to move below what is said to what is meant, and a new way to look at the affect wrapped up in the language of written text.

References

Bellamy, A., & Hanewicz, C. (1999). Social psychological scales of electronic communication. *Electronic Journal of Sociology, 2*(1). Retrieved September 30, 2003, from *www.sociology.org/content/vol004.001/bellamy.html*

Biber, D. (1985). Investigating macroscopic textual variation through multi-feature/multi-scaleal analyses. *Linguistics, 23*, 155–178.

Biber, D. (1986). On the investigation of spoken/written differences. *Studia Linguistica,* 40, 1–21.

Biber, D. (1988). *Variation across speech and writing*. Cambridge, UK: Cambridge University Press.

Biber, D., Conrad, S., & Reppen, R. (1998). *Corpus linguistics, investigating language structure and use.* Cambridge, UK: Cambridge University Press.

Biber, D., & Finegan, E. (1989). Styles of stance in English, lexical and grammatical marking of evidentiality and affect. *Text, 9*, 93–125.

Biber, D., Johansson, S., Leech, G., Conrad, S., & Finegan, E. (1999). *Longman grammar of spoken and written English.* London: Longman.

Campbell, C., & Wickman, S. (2000). Familiars in a strange land, a case study of friends chatting online. *M/C, A Journal of Media and Culture, 3* [Special CHAT issue]. Retrieved September 30, 2003, from *www.media-culture.org.au/past_vol_3.html*

Catterall, M., & MacLaran, P. (1997). Focus group data and qualitative analysis programs, coding the moving picture as well as the snapshots. *Sociological Research Online, 2*(1). Retrieved September 30, 2003, from *www.socresonline.org.uk/socresonline/2/1/6.html*

Cech, C., & Condon, S. (2002, July–August). Does attentional load affect discourse management in on-line communication? *Proceedings of the 4th*

International Conference on Advances in Infrastructure ... on the Internet, L'Aquila, Italy.

Davies, B., & Harre, R. (1990). Positioning, the discursive production of selves. *Journal for the Theory of Social Behaviour, 20*, 43–64.

Davis, B., & Brewer, J. (1997). *Electronic discourse, linguistic individuals in virtual space*. Albany: State University of New York Press.

Donath, J. (1998). Identity and deception in the virtual community. In M. Smith & P. Kollock, (Eds.), *Communities in cyberspace* (pp. 29–59). London: Routledge.

Ford, C. E., Fox, B. A., & Thompson, S. A. (Eds.). (2002). *The language of turn and sequence*. New York: Oxford University Press.

Frey, C. (2002, July 18). Web friend or faux? *Los Angeles Times*. Retrieved September 30, 2003, from *www.dstc.edu.au/ListArchive/eclectika/archive/2002/08/msg00068.html*

Gumperz, J. (1981). *Forms of talk*. Philadelphia: University of Pennsylvania Press.

Herring, S. C. (2002). Computer-mediated communication on the Internet. *Annual Review of Information Science and Technology, 36*, 109–168.

Koven, M. (2002). An analysis of speaker role inhabitance in narratives of personal experience. *Journal of Pragmatics, 34*, 167–217.

Martin, J. R. (2000). Beyond exchange, appraisal systems in English. In S. Hunston & G. Thompson (Eds.), *Evaluation in text*. Oxford: Oxford University Press.

McEnery, T., & Wilson, A. (2001). *Corpus linguistics* (2nd ed.). Edinburgh, UK: Edinburgh University Press.

Murphy, K. L., & Collins, M. P. (1998). Development of communication conventions in instructional electronic chats. *Journal of Distance Education, 12*, 177–200.

Neuage, T. (2003). *Conversational analysis of chatroom talk.* PhD thesis, University of South Australia. Retrieved September 30, 2003, from *http://se.unisa.edu.au/boo.htm*

Park, H. S., Dailey, R., & Lemus, D. (2002). The use of exploratory factor analysis and principal components analysis in communication research. *Human Communication Research, 23*, 562–577.

Precht, K. (2000). Patterns of stance in English. PhD dissertation, Northern Arizona University. Retrieved January 27, 2004, from *www.kprecht.net/cv.htm*

Precht, K. (2003). Stance moods in spoken English, attitude, emotion and evidentiality in British and American conversation. *Text,* 37, 239–257.

Rand, Y. (2003, January). Revisiting online focus groups. *Quirk's Marketing Research Review*. Retrieved September 30, 2003, from *www.quirks.com*

Schneider, S., Kerwin, J., Frechtling, J., & Vivari, B. (2002). Characteristics of the discussion in online and face-to-face focus groups. *Social Science Computer Review, 20*, 31–42.

Smith, S., & Jucker, A. (2000). Actually, and other markers of an apparent discrepancy between propositional attitudes of conversational partners. In G. Andersen & T. Fretheim (Eds.), *Pragmatic markers and propositional attitude* (pp. 207–237). Amsterdam: John Benjamins.

Stemler, S. (2001). An overview of content analysis. *Practical Assessment, Research & Evaluation,* 7(17). Retrieved March 10, 2004, from *http://PAREonline.net/getvn.asp?v=7&n=17*

Stubbs, M. (1986). A matter of prolonged field work, notes toward a modal grammar of English. *Applied Linguistics,* 7, 1–25.

Yates, S. (1996). English in cyberspace. In S. Goodman & D. Graddol (Eds.), *Redesigning English.* London: Routledge.

Chapter XI

Application of Internet-Based Marketing Instruments by Multichannel Retailers:

A Web Site Analysis in the U.S. and the UK

Maria Madlberger, Vienna University of Economics
and Business Administration, Austria

Abstract

Online and off-line retailers fulfill a wide range of functions that are beneficial to manufacturers as well as to individual consumers. In doing so, they apply a mix of marketing instruments for their store-based and Internet-based distribution channels. As the Internet offers many different innovative alternatives of marketing instruments, the question arises as to what extent online retailers apply Internet-based marketing strategies in order to attract online customers. The empirical study presented in this chapter aims at finding out to what extent powerful multichannel retailers utilize these different Internet-based marketing instruments. The study is conducted by Web site observation in order to represent the customer's point of view. A total of 60 online shops in the United States and in the United Kingdom are analyzed using 17 marketing-related observation criteria. The study reveals that the observed multichannel retailers still prefer "traditional" retail marketing instruments on their online shops and often do without innovative Internet-based marketing instruments such as personalization or content and information offering. Additionally, we identified fewer differences between the observed U.S. and UK retailers than expected. These findings should spur further research on the use of e-marketing by online retailers especially in an explanative manner.

Introduction

Internet-based marketing has experienced a very dynamic development since the emergence of electronic commerce. On the one hand, the Internet can influence traditional marketing instruments. On the other hand, it offers innovative alternatives for the marketing mix of online and off-line business-to-consumer (B2C) distribution channels. Internet-based marketing instruments strongly depend on the overall Internet business model a company pursues. The most common way of using the Internet for marketing purposes is its utilization as a distribution channel, as this is the case for electronic retailing in the B2C sector. If Internet-based retailers also conduct store-based distribution channels, referred to as multichannel retailing (Balabanis & Reynolds, 2001; Madlberger, 2004; Schoenbachler & Gordon, 2002; Webb, 2002) or bricks-and-clicks, valuable synergies in marketing can be realized (Krishnamurthy, 2003). Such a strategy is used by well-established store brands to leverage customers' confidence in building an online presence (Balabanis & Reynolds, 2001). Other synergies hold for physical distribution (Webb, 2002). This makes multichannel retailers often more successful than their virtual competitors (Bertele, Balocco, Gandini, & Rangone, 2002).

In the marketing literature, a variety of innovative Internet-based marketing instruments are described. In this context we define marketing instruments as a set of different action alternatives in order to address customers, such as product, price, distribution, and communication (Kotler & Armstrong, 2001). Together they constitute the marketing mix. Internet-based marketing instruments range from adaptation of classical marketing instruments to the Internet to innovative approaches that combine online with off-line marketing measures.

In contrast to that, only few publications can be found that present empirical data about companies' utilization of these instruments.

This chapter brings some insights in this area by empirically investigating the utilization of Internet-based marketing instruments by major multichannel retailers. For this purpose, the Web sites and online shops of 100 leading retailers in two countries, the United States and the United Kingdom, were analyzed with respect to different retail marketing instruments.

The discussion of online marketing instruments covers two aspects. On the one hand, marketing instruments influence an enterprise's success, measurable by performance figures as well as customer acceptance and behavior. In this context, existing marketing instruments can be understood as the independent variable of e-tailing performance. On the other hand, marketing instruments themselves are subject to influence as they are applied in reaction to different conditions an enterprise is operating in. From this point of view, online marketing instruments are the dependent variable that is influenced by independent environmental conditions.

The investigation at hand focuses on this second aspect and regards online marketing instruments as the dependent variable. As a consequence, we apply a research framework that can be used for a structured analysis of influencing factors of the online marketing mix and e-commerce business models. The main components of this framework are market conditions including customers and competitors, the online offered product and service range, the IT infrastructure of consumers and households, and the enterprise's IT background. For this investigation we apply a research model that investigates Internet-related customer attributes and IT infrastructure as possible influencing variables of online marketing activities on the basis of empirical data of both analyzed countries. In the following section we explain the theoretical background of this study which is based on findings upon retail marketing instruments. The next section outlines the analysis framework that structures the independent variables that influence the online marketing mix. In the fourth section, the methodology and design of the empirical investigation are presented and the reasons for country selection are explained. In section five we discuss the results of the empirical investigation. Finally, section six gives a critical discussion of the findings and contribution to research and shows an outlook to possible further research approaches.

Theoretical Background and Analysis Framework

Retailers fulfill a number of beneficial functions that affect many economic entities. By acting as an intermediary, they provide a benefit to customers as well as to manufacturers. For consumers, they ease product purchase; for suppliers, they support product distribution. Retail functions are categorized into space- and time-related bridging, the quantity function (adaptation of production-oriented product units to household-oriented units), the quality function (improvement of product quality by sorting, blending, etc.), and the assortment function that implies the offer of a product range consisting of different competing brands from different suppliers. Additionally, retailers contribute to opening up of markets for manufacturers, and they fulfill an advertising function as well as an advice and credit function (Berekoven, 1995). All these functions that cover only a part of retailer's scope of activities are supported by retail marketing instruments. Consequently, retail marketing instruments can be derived from retail functions.

As retail functions can be fulfilled both off-line in the form of immobile and mobile physical stores and online in the form of Internet shops, retail marketing instruments are applied online as well as off-line. Discussion of retail marketing instruments in literature very often differs considerably from the classical marketing mix that consists of product, price, place, and promotion (Kotler & Armstrong, 2001). In many publications, retail marketing instruments comprise assortment and presentation of merchandise, pricing, advertising, customer service, store location, and store layout (Berman & Evans, 2001; Dunne & Lusch, 1999; Levy & Weitz, 1992; Pearce, 1992). Interestingly, fewer authors, for example, Gilbert (1999) and Omar (1999), also add distribution to retail marketing instruments. The sum of the applied marketing instruments strongly influences the applied e-commerce business model (Hansen & Neumann, 2001).

An Analysis Framework

The design of business models depends on a set of variables that are characterized by the enterprise's environment. In order to integrate these independent variables into the empirical analysis discussed in the following section, a research framework developed by Hansen (1998) is applied. This framework consists of four basic elements that represent different influencing factors that cannot be changed in the short run and therefore act like environmental conditions. Originally, the framework was developed in order to identify factors that support or impede disintermediation and reintermediation in retailing. The systemized

Figure 1. Influencing variables on e-commerce business models (Hansen, 1998)

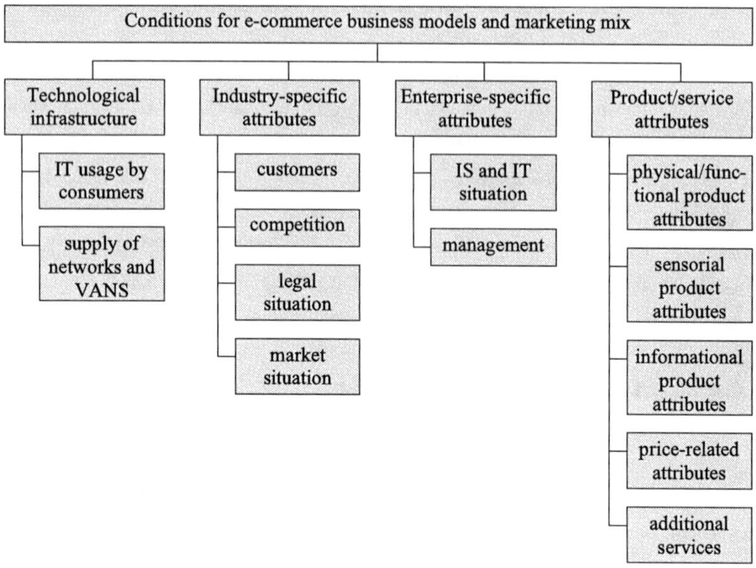

factors are, however, also applicable to explain adoption of e-commerce marketing instruments as they influence e-commerce business models as a whole. Figure 1 shows the four core elements of the general conditions and the respective subcategories.

As Figure 1 shows, there exists a variety of different factors that are subject to further categorization and operationalization. The analysis at hand focuses on Internet usage behavior, represented by Internet access, usage habits, and online shopping behavior, thus setting the other variables aside. Therefore this analysis mainly follows an explorative research approach regarding Internet usage behavior as a starting point.

Table 1 shows empirical data on different dimensions of Internet usage and shopping behavior in the United States and the United Kingdom. All data refer to the year 2002 unless other dates are quoted (European Internet Use, 2003; OECD, 2001, 2003; Population Explosion, 2003; World Resources Institute, 2003).

Table 1 reveals that the United States is more advanced than the United Kingdom in many respects of e-commerce diffusion although the relative number of Internet users is almost the same in both countries. This may be due to the differences in development of Internet diffusion. In the United States Internet

Table 1. Technological infrastructure and Internet usage behavior in the United States and the United Kingdom

technological infrastructure	US		UK	
population in million (Population Explosion 2003)	280.5		59.8	
Internet penetration (Population Explosion 2003)	59.1%		57.4%	
active Internet users as a percentage of all Internet users (Population Explosion 2003)	72.9%		51.5%	
development of Internet diffusion (World Resources Institutes 2003)	% of population	relative growth p.a.	% of population	relative growth p.a.
1992	1.6%	45.5%	.3%	50.0%
1993	2.1%	31.3%	.5%	66.7%
1994	4.6%	119.0%	1.0%	100.0%
1995	8.9%	93.5%	1.8%	80.0%
1996	10.7%	20.2%	4.0%	122.2%
1997	21.3%	99.1%	7.2%	80.0%
1998	30.1%	41.3%	13.4%	86.1%
1999	36.2%	20.3%	21.0%	56.7%
2000	44.1%	21.8%	30.3%	44.3%
2001	50.8%	15.2%	40.3%	33.0%
Length of time household connected (European Internet Use 2003)	US		UK	
< 6 months	16.0%		27.1%	
6 to 12 months	10.0%		18.3%	
> 12 months	74.0%		54.8%	
Internet usage behavior (OECD 2003)	US		UK	
Internet use by type of activity (US: year 2001, UK: year 2002)				
Sending/receiving e-mail	84.0%		76.0%	
Finding information about goods and services	67.2%		76.0%	
Purchasing/ordering goods or services	39.1%		38.0%	
Reading/downloading online newspapers/news magazines	62.0%[1)]		28.0%	
Playing/downloading games and music	42.0%[2)]		19.0%[3)]	

usage began to expand earlier than in Europe resulting in more moderate relative growth since the late 1990s. The United Kingdom shows a much more dynamic Internet diffusion process leading to a similar level of Internet penetration in 2002. These facts are mirrored in the length of time households have had Internet access. Almost three-quarters of American Internet users have been online for more than one year compared to slightly more than half of British Internet users. On the other hand, among American users 16% have had Internet access for less than half a year which is much less than the corresponding figure of 27.1% in the United Kingdom.

Table 1. (continued)

technological infrastructure	US	UK
Downloading free software	not available	19.0%[4)]
Using banking services	17.9%	28.0%
Job search	16.4%	20.0%
Interacting with public authorities	30.9%[5)]	17.0%
Using online services	34.9%	not available
online shopping behavior	US	UK
value of transactions (million $, year 2000) (OECD 2001)	25.845	1.040
penetration rate of retail sales (year 2000) (OECD 2001)	1.01%	.37%
number of buyers in 1.000 (year 2000) (OECD 2001)	19.666	970
number of buyers as a percentage of Internet users (year 2000) (OECD 2001)	27%	18%
Internet shoppers as a percentage of working age population (year 2000) (OECD 2001)	16%	5%

1) Reading/downloading newspapers also includes movies.
2) Playing games only instead of downloading games and music.
3) Downloading music only instead of games and music.
4) Downloading other software instead of free software.
5) Obtaining information from public authorities' Web sites only instead of interacting with public authorities.

When it comes to Internet usage behavior and preferred activities on the Internet, some main activities can be identified. In general, e-mail communication and information search about goods and services are the most important Internet activities in both countries (general surfing activities such as information search have not been recorded by the quoted survey). Direct comparisons between the United States and the United Kingdom are limited to those criteria that are related to the same basis. This is true for e-mail, information about goods and services, purchasing or ordering goods and services, banking services, and job search. In the context of these criteria, British Internet users apply banking services and product-related information search more intensively than their American counterpart.

Purchasing and/or ordering goods and services via the Internet are the activities of central interest for this study. According to this activity, there are almost no differences between the two countries in question showing a percentage of 39.1% and 38.0%, respectively. This number specifies how many Internet users at least have bought on the Internet in the past or occasionally buy on the Internet. But it tells nothing about frequency or expenses of Internet-based purchases. When it comes to e-commerce-generated turnover and regular buyers, more noticeable differences are identified. Whereas penetration rate of retail sales (i.e., the proportion of electronic retailing in overall retail sales) amounts to

1.01% in the United States, this number is much smaller in the United Kingdom, showing .37%. Also the number of buyers is considerably lower in the United Kingdom than in the United States. These discrepancies may be due to an apparently more intensive and frequent online shopping behavior in the United States.

Generally speaking, the United States is in a more advanced stage of e-commerce development in different respects. Moreover, in the United States there are more active Internet users being online regularly, also user experience and online shopping behavior indicate this difference.

Methodology of the Empirical Study

The empirical investigation focuses on the question of whether major multichannel retailers also offer broader marketing instruments and more consumer-oriented shopping conditions in the United States than in the United Kingdom. For this purpose we have chosen the methodology of content analysis for empirical research. Content analysis is an observational research method that allows systematic evaluation of the symbolic content of different forms of recorded communication (Kolbe & Burnett, 1991). This approach has been adopted by several researchers for the analysis of Web presence in different industries (Doherty, Ellis-Chadwick, & Hart, 1999; Ghose & Dou, 1998; Huizingh, 2000; Liu, Arnett, Capella, & Beatty, 1997; Perry & Bodkin, 2000).

The application of content analysis requires reliable measures, a system of observation categories, and adequacy of operational definitions in order to obtain valid and comparable results. In order to evaluate which retail marketing instruments are preferentially used by retailers in practice, the marketing mix components mentioned in the previous section are split up into observable items. We have done this on the basis of an in-depth analysis of retail and Internet marketing literature (Berman & Evans, 2001; Chaffey, Mayer, Johnston, & Ellis-Chadwick, 2002; Dunne & Lusch, 1999; Gilbert, 1999; Hanson, 2000; Levy & Weitz, 1992; Omar, 1999; Pearce, 1992; Sheth, 2001; Strauss & Frost, 2001; Zimmerman, 2000).

The result is a set of 17 observation criteria that are used for evaluating major retailers' utilization of the above-mentioned marketing instruments (see Table 2).

Many of these criteria are only meaningful in respect of online shops. For this reason the criteria are applied exclusively to those retailers' Web sites that conduct an online shop. The retailers' industries are also recorded.

Table 2. Observation criteria of the analysis of online shops

Criterion	observation instruction	answer categories	related to retail marketing instrument/Internet feature
Industry	industry the retailer is operating in		general information
online presence	website available	yes/no	filter criterion
online shop	online shop available	yes/no	filter criterion
online promotions	1. visible presentation of brands and product logos 2. general utilization of promotion measures 3. special solely Internet-based promotions	yes/no yes/no yes/no	advertising
content and commerce	4. information in the context of the product offer (e.g. nutrition, fashion) 5. general information not concerning the product offerings (e.g. news, leisure) 6. avatar that offers a range of products	yes/no yes/no yes/no	advice and information
convenience	7. facilities that ease shopping	- shopping cart with selected products - information about current total spending amount	advice and information
search engines	8. internal search facility	yes/no	advice and information
store location	9. availability of store locator (e.g. the nearest store)	yes/no	advice and information
scheduled delivery date	10. how long is time for delivery?	classification: - within 24 hours - 24 hours to three days - three days to one week - more than one week - no statement	distribution
order status information	11. online order status information provided?	yes/no	distribution
online payment	12. which payment methods are offered?	classification (multiple assignments are possible): - cash on delivery - credit card - invoice and bank transfer - electronic cash - others	credit function
feedback	13. online or e-mail feedback possible?	yes/no	advice and information
recruitment	14. online job offers with online application	yes/no	advice and information

As the focus of this investigation concerns multichannel retailing, the basic population is defined as store-based retailers in the selected countries, that is, the United States and the United Kingdom. We have selected these two countries for the following reason: e-commerce is situated in different development stages in different countries (BCG, 2000). As a consequence, conditions for electronic retailing are also different. Figure 2 compares Internet penetration in different industrialized countries (Nielsen NetRatings, 2001).

According to BCG (2000), European countries can be classified into different clusters: There is a group of large countries that count for a significant proportion of Europe's online sales. This is, however, not due to huge online sales but to absolute market size. Examples for this cluster are Germany and the United Kingdom. Another group consists of countries with a medium-scale retail market size that show a smaller share of e-tailing in retail sales. These countries play a

Figure 2. Internet penetration in selected industrialized countries (Nielsen Netratings, 2001)

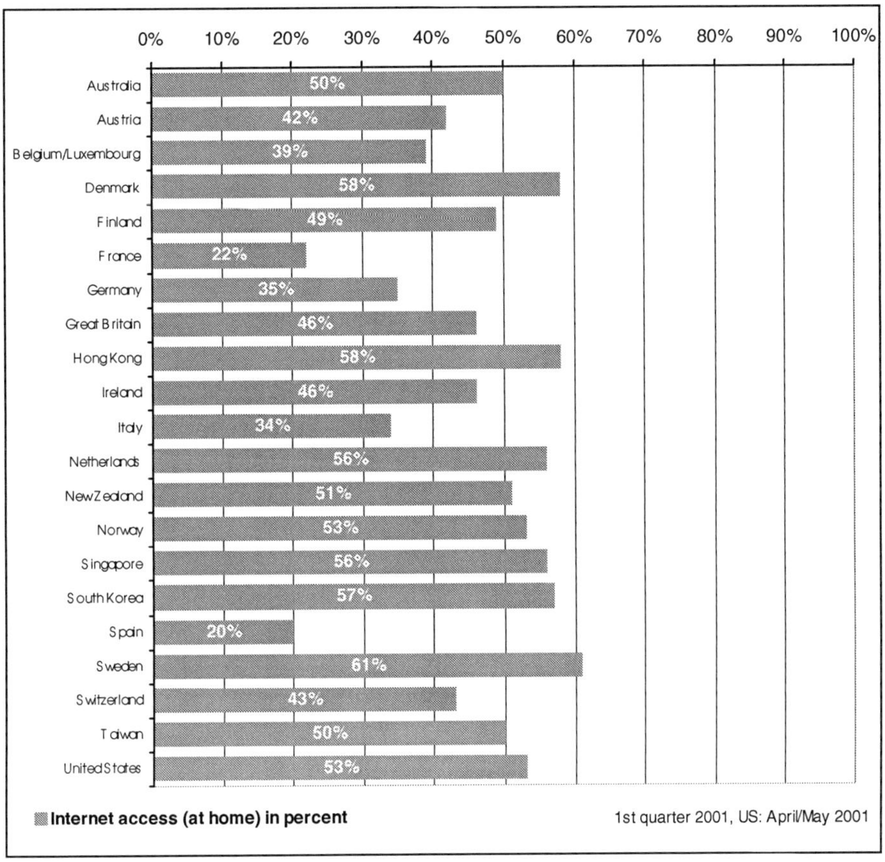

minor role in European e-tailing. Examples are France, Spain, and Italy. Finally, there are countries that are characterized by showing little e-tailing sales figures at present but are supposed to feature considerable growth in the near future. This development bases on indicators such as Internet access and Internet user behavior. Countries that belong to that cluster are many Scandinavian countries, Switzerland, and Austria (BCG, 2000). From a worldwide perspective, the United States is considered the leading nation in e-commerce and e-tailing in general and is therewith different from e-commerce diffusion in Europe (BCG, 2000).

In order to analyze online marketing activities in countries that are considered important in respect of e-commerce, we decided to focus our investigation on the United States and the United Kingdom although this sampling is not representative for a comparison between the United States and Europe.

Table 3. Design parameters of the Web site observation

Research method	Observation of Web sites
Basic population	Store-based retailers in the United States and Great Britain
Sampling	The respective 50 largest retailers in the United States (Stores, 2001) and Great Britain (Mintel, 2001), according to annual turnover
Sample size	50 store-based retailers in the US 50 store-based retailers in Great Britain
Observation period	December 2001 to January 2002
Used Internet browser	Netscape Navigator 4.76

The following step concerns the sample selection method. As this research focuses on multichannel retailing, the basic population are U.S.-American and British store-based retailers. Random sampling that supports representativeness is not applicable for Internet-based observation as there is no directory of all retailers' Web sites available. As an alternative, we decided to select the observation sample on the basis of enterprise size and market power, expressed by annual turnover. Following the assumption that large enterprises tend to adopt new technological developments earlier and act therefore as first movers (OECD, 2002), we chose the respective largest retailers according to annual turnover for the empirical study. As a result, the sample consists of comparable retailers. In doing so, small and medium-sized enterprises that are usually faced with different conditions (Kleindl, 2000; Daniel, Wilson, & Myers, 2002; Sadowski, Maitland, & van Dongen, 2002) are excluded from the observation. For the observation a sample of 100 retailers' Web sites in the United States and the United Kingdom have been chosen, each with a sample size of 50 (see Table 3).

Among the total of 100 observed retailers, 34 U.S.-American (68%) and 26 British retailers (52%) run an online shop. This corresponds to a valid sample size of 60 retailers that are further analyzed in the study. Additionally, no significant differences between the United States and the United Kingdom concerning the industries can be identified.

Study Results

In the following, the results according to all observation items are presented. For each criterion we have conducted a chi square test that evaluates whether differences between the U.S. and UK sample are statistically significant. We apply a significance level of (α) of 5%.

At first the assortment function is analyzed by observing the *size of the assortment*. Except two British retailers, all enterprises in the sample offer large assortments that exceed several hundred articles by far. As a consequence, all observed multichannel retailers use the Internet as a channel of distribution and not only for demonstration or promotion purposes. This implies that these retailers have to provide a satisfactory logistics and IS infrastructure that copes with order processing and fulfillment of comprehensive assortments.

Next, we observe category management-related criteria. *Classification* of online offered products into categories and *consumer-oriented article combinations* are examined. The results reveal that there is a large gap between those two criteria. Whereas all e-tailers except two classify the assortment into categories, only 28.3% of all observed e-tailers offer consumer-oriented article combinations that go beyond mere classification and therewith encourage cross-selling.

Focusing on the advertising function of e-tailing, we examine visible *presentation of brands and product logos* next. A total of 80% of the e-tailers put images and product logos on their online storefronts. In this context, a significant difference between the U.S.-American and the British sample can be identified. In the United States, this number amounts to 94.1%; in the United Kingdom, only to 61.5%. This results in an α of .002. The next two criteria are related to the Internet as a medium for *promotion* measures. According to Krishnamurthy (2003), there are two models of Internet-based promotions: in the direct model the e-tailer itself provides the customers with promotions, for example, coupons. The indirect model consists of promotions that are carried out through an intermediary that can exploit synergies across several participating e-tailers. In our analysis we focus on direct promotions only. Concerning application of *general promotions* that are published on the Web site but are related to store-based distribution channels, we find out that 73.1% of the observed e-tailers utilize this Internet-based marketing instrument. A different picture shows the next criterion that examines special *solely Internet-based promotions*. In this context, only 33.3% of the observed online shops include this feature. This leads to the conclusion that the observed e-tailers chiefly do not utilize Internet-based promotions as an incentive for customers to buy online. They rather apply the online shop as a support for their existing physical branch network. Both promotion-related criteria do not show noticeable differences between the U.S. and the UK sample.

Facilities that *support the customer during the shopping process* and therewith ease shopping are analyzed next. This criterion, like the following two, is derived from retailers' advice function. Facilities that ease shopping in the observed sample are exhibited in Table 4.

Table 4. Measures that facilitate shopping

Facilities that ease shopping	Total	US	UK
shopping cart with selected products	97.7%	100.0%	92.3%
information about current total amount	91.7%	94.1%	88.5%
list of previous purchases	28.3%	20.6%	38.5%
individual product proposals	20.0%	20.6%	19.2%

Table 4 reveals that there are considerable differences between facilities that are to some extent also applicable for store-based retailing and those facilities that aim at a higher level of individualization of offers. More than 90% of all retailers offer a shopping cart and information about the current total amount what both is transaction-related and does not include personal information or shopping histories. In contrast, 28.3% offer a list of previous purchases and 20% offer individual product proposals on their online shops. Consequently, many of the observed e-tailers do not put much emphasis on individualization and one-to-one marketing approaches.

The following item investigates whether product search is supported by an *internal search function* on the Web site. In this context we find that except for one retailer all observed enterprises in the United States offer this function whereas this is true for only 80.8% in the United Kingdom. This difference turned out to be significant according to the chi square test ($\alpha = .037$).

The third criterion that is related to the advice and information function is *store location* that serves as a link between online and off-line distribution channels. We examine to what extent the observed multichannel retailers utilize their Web sites in order to support customers in finding out locations of physical outlets. The results show that this function is widely used in the entire sample. Overall, 88.5% of the observed retailers provide this service, with the U.S. sample showing a higher number than the UK retailers although the difference is not significant.

As most goods that are bought and sold are nondigital, we observe key items that concern physical distribution in the next step. For this purpose we have chosen *scheduled delivery time* as one of the typical measures of logistics performance (Schulte, 1995). The results are graphically presented in Figure 3.

In most cases the observed online retailers offer a scheduled delivery time between four days and one week followed by delivery time between one and three days. A more differentiated picture is revealed when the two observed countries are compared to each other. Whereas almost 60% of the U.S.-American e-tailers promise to fulfill delivery between four and seven days and 20.6% deliver between one and three days, the dominant delivery time in the United Kingdom is between one and three days (46.2%) followed by delivery

Figure 3. Scheduled delivery time

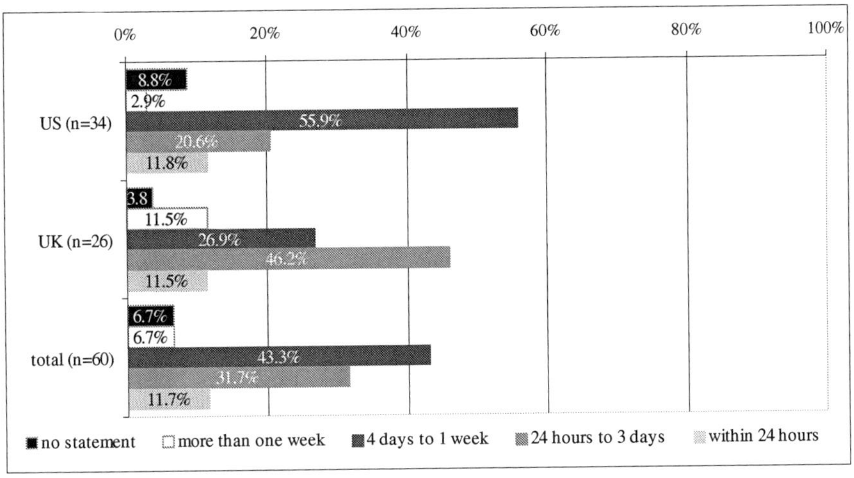

time between four and seven days (11.5%). There are no noticeable differences between the U.S. and the UK sample concerning delivery within 24 hours. This leads to the following interpretation: As there is no significant correlation between delivery time and delivery area (this attribute has been observed but is not discussed further here), we assume that the observed differences, although not significant, are mainly due to the different country sizes. Based on the fact that almost all observed retailers offer at least nationwide delivery areas it is comprehensible that U.S.-wide delivery takes more time than UK-wide delivery. There are, however, other possible reasons for these differences, for example, corporate strategies, product categories, logistics and transportation costs, and infrastructure or different delivery fee models that depend on delivery pace.

The second logistics-related item concerns the availability of *online order status information* that represents the ability and accordingly the willingness of an e-tailer to provide customers with up-to-date information on order processing and delivery status. In this respect a clear difference between the U.S.-American retailers and the UK retailers in the sample can be observed. Whereas the U.S. sample offers this service in more than half of the cases, this function can be identified in 11.5% of the UK sample. This difference also turns out to be highly significant ($\alpha = .001$). Obviously, the analyzed U.S. retailers put more emphasis on this information service than their UK counterparts do.

The next retail function of interest is the credit function, represented by offered *means of payment*. The results of the Web site observation are depicted in Figure 4.

Figure 4. Online payment methods

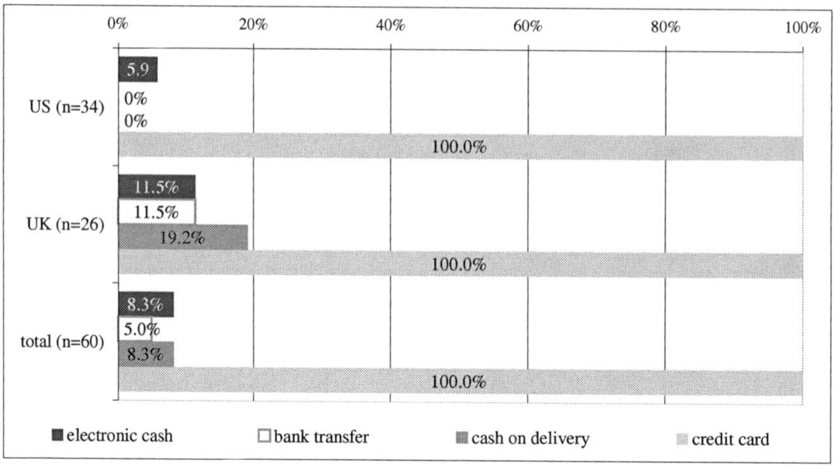

Among the observed retailers the offered payment methods show a clear preference. All analyzed online shops allow credit card payment that mirrors the intensive utilization of credit cards in general. Besides the fact that consumers are familiar with credit cards, this payment method shows the advantage that it allows online payment by electronic transfer of the credit card information. This enables a convenient way of payment for the customer but requires security measures as well as confidence from the customers. Most observed retailers offer only this method of payment. Cash on delivery is offered by almost 20% in the United Kingdom but by no U.S. retailer in the sample. Electronic cash is offered in 8.3% of all cases.

Further, the study investigates *Internet-based feedback* alternatives that allow the customer to contact the retailer. The related items are derived from the Internet's interactivity as it allows synchronous and asynchronous communication. In this context we find that most of the observed retailers (81.7%) allow for e-mail-based feedback with the UK sample showing a slightly higher level than the U.S. sample. When it comes to Web forms, considerably less retailers, namely 35%, could be identified. Also in this respect, the percentage is higher in the United Kingdom than in the United States. Finally, the Web sites are also analyzed in respect of their utilization for *recruitment,* meaning that a user can apply online for a vacant position. The results reveal that this function is widely used: 70% of the observed e-tailers offer online job application.

Conclusion and Contribution to the Community

The presented empirical investigation gives an overview of utilization of Internet-based marketing instruments by online multichannel retailers. The study reveals that many of the observed online shops apply Internet-based marketing instruments similar to their traditional off-line marketing instruments. The results show which instruments are preferred by retailers and whether differences between the two observed countries and industries can be identified. The main findings indicate that in many respects the online marketing mix is similar in both countries in many respects. Significant differences are only identified in the context of online brand and logo presentation, internal search function, and delivery status information. Therewith the analyzed U.S. retailers seem to offer more navigation and order-related information.

The investigation also shows that most multichannel retailers in the study apply online marketing instruments that are similar to the off-line marketing mix. Obviously, the online shops are intended to support the store-based distribution channels in the first instance. Personalization or interactive elements are found only in few cases, independent from the retailer's origin. Consequently, many of the Internet's attributes that can be utilized for commercial purposes are still not applied broadly.

From a methodological point of view some considerations about the research method that utilizes the Internet directly as a source of information should be done. One of the major strengths of this method is its customer-oriented point of view. Similar to the mystery shopping approach in store-based retailing (Finn & Kayandé, 1999) the analysis of Web sites allows to gain insights into competitors' Internet marketing strategies what would otherwise not be possible (e.g., by means of inquiries). For this reason this method is especially interesting for practitioners who want to get a picture of their rivals' marketing efforts. Another advantage that is also relevant for enterprises is the possibility of gathering data very quickly and cheaply independent from spatial distances. But this approach also has its limitations. Web site analyses only allow descriptive empirical work but are not able to give insights into motivations and success of different applied marketing instruments. Therefore this research method is suitable for exploratory investigations that are accompanied or supplemented by deeper surveys focusing on different special aspects. In combination with analyses of customer satisfaction or financial results, valuable insights into the appropriateness of different Internet-based marketing instruments can be obtained.

The study at hand documents the state-of-the-art of multichannel retailing among leading U.S. and UK retailers. From a long-term perspective, this investigation design is applicable for monitoring purposes in order to show the dynamic development of online marketing instruments. It can also be extended to purely online retailers as well as to other countries.

The present study has to be understood as an exploratory contribution to e-commerce research that should be continued by analysis of causal relationships. Investigating the applied marketing instruments as the dependent variable of the basic conditions described in section three requires inquiries among the analyzed retailers. Focusing on performance and success of the applied marketing strategies requires interviewing retailers as well a final consumers. In any case, our study shows that there are still many unanswered questions in the e-commerce research discipline.

References

Balabanis, G., & Reynolds, N. L. (2001). Consumer attitudes towards multi-channel retailers' Web sites: The role of involvement, brand attitude, Internet knowledge and visit duration. *Journal of Business Strategies, 2,* 106–131.

Berekoven, L. (1995). *Erfolgreiches Einzelhandelsmarketing. Grundlagen und Entscheidungshilfen.* Munich: C. H. Beck.

Berman, B., & Evans, J. R. (2001). *Retail management: A strategic approach.* Upper Saddle River, NJ: Prentice-Hall.

Bertele, U., Balocco, R., Gandini, I., & Rangone, A. (2002). B2C e-commerce: The Italian market. *International Journal of Business Performance Management, 2–4,* 182–201.

Boston Consulting Group (BCG). (2000). The race for online riches—E-retailing in Europe. Retrieved May 28, 2003, from *www.bcg.com/publications/ files/ E_Retailing_Europe_report_Feb00.pdf*

Chaffey, D., Mayer, R., Johnston, K., & Ellis-Chadwick, F. (2002). *Internet marketing: Strategy, implementation and practice.* Financial Times Management.

Daniel, E., Wilson, H., & Myers, A. (2002). Adoption of e-commerce by SMEs in the UK. *International Small Business Journal, 20*, 253–268.

Doherty, N., Ellis-Chadwick, F., & Hart, C. (1999). Cyber retailing in the UK: The potential of the Internet as a retail channel. *International Journal of Retailing & Distribution Management, 27*, 22–36.

Dunne, P., & Lusch, R. F. (1999). *Retailing* (3rd ed.). Fort Worth, TX: Dryden.

European Internet Use. (2003). European Internet use still behind the US. Retrieved August 8, 2003, from *http://cyberatlas.Internet.com/big_picture/geographics/article/0,1323,5911_ 351591,00.html#table1*

Finn, A., & Kayandé, U. (1999). Unmasking a phantom: A psychometric assessment of mystery shopping. *Journal of Retailing, 2*, 195–217.

Ghose, S., & Dou, W. (1998). Interactive functions and their impacts on the appeal of Internet presence sites. *Journal of Advertising Research, 38*, 29–43.

Gilbert, D. (1999). *Retail marketing management.* Financial Times, Prentice-Hall.

Hansen, H. R. (1998). Ausschaltung des Institutionellen Handels Durch Informations - und Kommunikationssysteme. In D. Ahlert, J. Becker, R. Olbrich, & R. Schuette (Eds.), *Informationssysteme fuer das Handelsmanagement* (pp. 123–166). Berlin: Springer.

Hansen, H. R., & Neumann, G. (2001). *Wirtschaftsinformatik 1.* Stuttgart: Lucius & Lucius.

Hanson, W. (2000). *Principles of Internet marketing.* Cincinnati, OH: South Western College Publishing.

Huizingh, E. K. R. E. (2000). The content and design of Web sites: An empirical study. *Information & Management, 37*, 123–134.

Kleindl, B. (2000). Competitive dynamics and new business models for SMEs in the virtual marketplace. *Journal of Developmental Entrepreneurship, 5*, 73–85.

Kolbe, R. H., & Burnett, M. S. (1991). Content-analysis research: An examination of applications with directives for improving research reliability and objectivity. *Journal of Consumer Research, 18*, 243–250.

Kotler, P., & Armstrong, G. (2001). *Principles of marketing.* Upper Saddle River, NJ: Prentice-Hall.

Krishnamurthy, S. (2003). *E-commerce management. Text and cases.* Mason, OH: Thomson, South-Western.

Levy, M., & Weitz, B. A. (1992). *Retailing management.* Homewood-Boston: Irwin.

Liu, C., Arnett, K. P., Capella, L. M., & Beatty, R. C. (1997). Web sites of the Fortune 500 Companies: Facing customers through homepages. *Information & Management, 31*, 335–345.

Madlberger, M. (2004). *Electronic retailing. Marketinginstrumente und Marktforschung im Internet.* Wiesbaden: Deutscher Universitaetsverlag.

Mintel International Group. (2001). *Top 50 UK retailers. Retail Intelligence's UK Retail Rankings 2001.*

Nielsen NetRatings. (2001). Nielsen/NetRatings finds global Internet users spend up to twice as much time online at work as home users. Retrieved January 9, 2002, from *http://eratings.com/news/20011126.htm*

Omar, O. (1999). *Retail marketing*. London: Financial Times Management.

Organisation for Economic Co-operation and Development (OECD). (2001). Business-to-consumer e-commerce statistics. Retrieved August 11, 2003, from *www.dtifueyo.cl/docs/estudios_recursos/b2cstadisticsoecd01despues.pdf*

Organisation for Economic Co-operation and Development (OECD). (2002). Measuring the information economy, information and communication statistics. Retrieved August 11, 2003, from *www.oecd.org/dataoecd/16/14/1835738.pdf*

Organisation for Economic Co-operation and Development (OECD). (2003). OECD science, technology and industry scoreboard 2003. Retrieved November 20, 2003, from *www1.oecd.org/publications/e-book/92-2003-04-1-7294/*

Pearce, M. R. (1992). *Retail marketing management*. Scarborough, ON: Nelson Canada.

Perry, M., & Bodkin, C. (2000). Content analysis of Fortune 1000 company Web sites. *Corporate Communications: An International Journal, 5*, 87–96.

Population Explosion. (2003). Population explosion. Retrieved August 11, 2003, from *http://cyberatlas.Internet.com/big_picture/geographics/article/0,1323,5911_151151,00.html*

Sadowski, B. M., Maitland, C., & van Dongen, J. (2002). Strategic use of the Internet by small- and medium-sized companies: An exploratory study. *Information Economics and Policy, 14*, 75–93.

Schoenbachler, D. D., & Gordon, G. L. (2002). Multi-channel shopping: Understanding what drives channel choice. *Journal of Consumer Marketing, 1*, 42–53.

Schulte, C. (1995). *Logistik* (2nd ed.). Munich: Vahlen.

Sheth, J. N. (2001). *Internet marketing*. Fort Worth, TX: Harcourt College Publications.

Strauss, J., & Frost, R. (2001). *E-marketing*. Upper Saddle River, NJ: Prentice-Hall.

Stores. (2001). Top 100 retailers. Retrieved October 11, 2001, from *www.stores.org/ 2001top100_1.html*

Webb, K. L. (2002). Managing channels of distribution in the age of electronic commerce. *Industrial Marketing Management, 2,* 95–102.

World Resources Institute. (2003). Variable: Access to information: Internet users, number. Retrieved July 24, 2003, from *http://earthtrends.wri.org/text/POP/ variables/551.htm#2*

Zimmerman, J. (2000). *Marketing on the Internet* (4th ed.). Gulf Breeze, FL: Maximum Press.

Chapter XII

The E-Mode of Brand Positioning: The Need for an Online Positioning Interface

S. Ramesh Kumar, Indian Institute of Management, Bangalore, India

Abstract

Brand positioning is a crucial strategy to any brand's strategy. Given the rapid development of technology and its impact on online strategies, changing lifestyles of consumers, and the consumer interaction required as a part of contemporary brand strategy, there may be need for brands to synergize their positioning strategies with online positioning strategies. This would enable brands to adapt to an environment that is increasingly becoming digital. This chapter, after taking into consideration the published literature on brand positioning, attempts to formulate online positioning strategies using different aspects of brand positioning, price, customer interactivity, and consumer community orientation. Implications for marketing managers are provided.

Introduction

Brand positioning has been the cornerstone of marketing strategy in recent times in fast-moving consumer product categories, durable categories, and services. It would be difficult to think of a strategy for any brand without a well-thought-out strategy for entering the consumer's psyche (Ries & Trout, 1987).

Thus, Nike's success could be attributed to the positioning that it is worn by the world's best athletes as reflected by the Michael Jordan campaign (Trout & Rivkin, 1999). While the challenges concerned with positioning strategies still remain with marketers, the environment has been changing with the influence of Web-based marketing. In the year which closed in September 1999, there was an increase of 221.5% of goods that were traded over the Internet. Consumer goods registered an increase of 665% over the same period (Wind & Mahajan, 2001).

The consumer is becoming more evolved in terms of information control. The consumer is no longer likely to receive information without the interactive component being present when he/she becomes involved in consumer decision making. Hence, the traditional positioning strategies may not succeed as segments are becoming smaller and less homogenous (Solomon, 2003). A number of established brands have also started using the Internet and the Web to adapt to the changing environment. Some of the global brands making this transition include Levi's, Dockers, and Barbie (Ries & Ries, 2000).

Even in a developing country such as India where less than 5% of the total retail sales come from organized supermarkets/malls and the penetration of the Internet is miniscule, supermarkets such as Subiksha and FabMall (www.fabmall.com) have started *online* marketing of groceries and consumer goods. FabMall started as an online store in Bangalore with books and music and over time has added several categories such as groceries, jewelry, and gifts. It has since added physical retail stores around the city of Bangalore. Today, its model attempts to synergize the advantages of retail outlets and online dimensions. The physical retailing model of the company has grown from revenues of 4 million rupees to 15 million rupees per month from April 2003 to November 2003 (Kumar & Mahadevan, 2003).

The trend of having multiple channels to reach the consumers could result in building a good brand besides the profitability aspects. Subiksha is a discount grocery store at Chennai (previously known as Madras) which deals with low-priced groceries. The store has a network of stores around the city and has started online operations by which customers could order groceries. The unique aspect of this store is that the residential neighborhoods are located close to the network of stores and hence the delivery charges, which are normally significant, are saved.

This integration of physical and online presence is commonly observed in global brands. Charles Schwab transacts 80% of its business over the Internet but increased its off-line presence as both channels would be required to service its customers (Lindstorm, Peppers, & Rogers, 2001). Tesco, the U.K.-based retail chain with 600 stores, 60,000 product lines, and 10 million customers who are members of a loyalty program has illustrated how the combination of online and off-line retailing could develop a successful retail brand. Amazon.com with a customer base of 8.4 million and 66% of sales being contributed by repeat purchasers is a brand that has an association of customizing products (books, music, etc.) to the needs of consumers by suggesting a number of options which they may not have otherwise considered (Rust, Zeithamal, & Lemon, 2000).

Given the rapid challenges in the marketing environment and consumer lifestyles and the growing influence of technology with regard to consumer retailing and marketing communications (e.g., advergaming and SMS messages), there is a distinct need to explore new conceptual frameworks for the concept of positioning. There are two stages that would lead to the development of such frameworks which could assist practitioners in a marketing environment. The first stage is concerned with analyzing existing dimensions of brand positioning with a view to examine how they could be used for a brand that will have both online and off-line retail channels. The next stage is to develop a framework for categories of consumer products from the insights gained from the first stage.

Different Dimensions of Brand Positioning

The challenge for marketers in India is not just to create an online experience: there is a need to "move" the consumer from the traditional ways of buying to the digital ways of buying after understanding certain shopping aspects which are unique to the Indian context. While some of these aspects may involve providing a kiosk in a traditional store for customers to browse through several dimensions of brand comparison, the most critical factor is the manner in which such prospective buying experiences are communicated. Given the Indian diversity with regard to demographics and psychographics, positioning challenges need to be market specific and product specific. The second challenge is to ensure that positioning propositions of brands are fulfilled and this involves infrastructure demanded by positioning strategies in a manner that would bring in price differentiation.

There are various dimensions that could be used for positioning a brand. Brand equity is a set of assets and liabilities linked to a brand, its name, or symbol. Brand loyalty, brand name awareness, perceived quality, brand associations, and other brand assets such as patents and trademarks are some of the components of brand equity (Aaker, 1991). Brand positioning involves developing, nurturing, and sustaining brand associations and brand imagery in such a way that it offers a long-term competitive edge through the consistency of such associations, which could be called sustainable competitive proposition (SCP) (Kumar, 2003). Hence, most components of brand equity could be used to develop positioning strategies.

Loyalty as a Positioning Dimension

Amazon.com uses loyalty as a strong positioning strategy. It provides a customer not just value in terms of the price of the merchandise. Rather, its unique value comes from specific strategies such as recommendation of book and music titles after capturing the customer's preferences on its database. It found that customers who bought books also bought CDs and expanded its product-line base to satisfy the base of loyal customers. It could be noted that the interactive nature of online marketing was effectively made use of by Amazon.com and this enabled the company to sustain a dialogue with its customers.

Peapod, an online grocery shopping store in the United States has sustained the loyalty of its customers based on its "virtual supermarket" strategy. Customers could access a list of categories, brands in the categories, (continue) brands by package size, by unit price, or in some cases even by nutritional value. Customers can have standardized and special shopping lists which could be used by them any time. The customer retention rate for Peopod is 80%. The retail outlet also uses the Internet to develop "learning relationships" by which it could adapt itself to the needs of consumers (Gilmore & Pine, 2000).

In both the Amazon.com and Peapod cases, the organization uses customization and interaction with customers to gain loyalty and the outlets are positioned on "value-based customization." In contrast, in a typical brick-and-mortar outlet the loyalty is built up in a different manner. Tesco has collected massive data on its customers and divided them into 5,000 needs segments. It sends coupon assortments to various customers depending on their needs and the redemption rate of these coupons is 90% (Kotler, 2003). From 1980 to 1993, the number of sales promotion coupons distributed tripled from 100 billion to 300 billion in the United States and the number of coupons redeemed has only grown over only by about a third since 1981 (Hallberg, 1995).

Shoppers Stop in India, which has a considerable degree of loyalty, also attempts to research the needs of consumers to formulate its loyalty programs. Large off-line retail outlets could develop loyalty-related positioning by analyzing the purchase data of consumers belonging to different segments. As the number of consumers in these off-line retail formats are likely to be large in numbers, "value-based loyalty" arises from the purchase patterns. FabMall uses recency of purchase, frequency of purchase, and monetary value (RFM) to formulate its loyalty programs. RFM could be useful both in off-line and online retailing environment. It is possible for a multiple channel retailer (with both online and off-line channels) to follow strategies that would enhance loyalty. In a country such as India where shopping for both fast-moving consumer goods and durable categories such as television, music systems, and kitchen appliances could be a ritual of entertainment, it is possible for a retailer to provide information on the Web and attract retail traffic base on the information being given on the Web for a specific segment (Kumar, 2002).

By this approach, while the information provided enables a consumer to be appraised of the offerings of the company, the "touch and feel" factor—a major prerequisite in the Indian shopping context—is also retained. This would be possible only for a specific segment of a market (niche) as the penetration of computers is low in India. The positioning of the brand is based on information support as well as the retail service when the customer visits the retail outlet. There has been a proliferation of brands in most categories and the traditional positioning methods may not result in customer retention. In a low-involvement category such as soap, consumers will have a tendency to try many brands even if they express a dominant loyalty to one brand. In other low-involvement categories such as antiseptic lotion or floor cleaning solution, penetration levels have to be enhanced especially in developing markets. In both these kinds of categories, there is a need to combine off-line and online positioning strategies and hence mass-based advertising approach, which has been followed for decades, may not produce sustainable outcome in terms of brand loyalty.

In the case of soaps, Indian brands continue to position themselves on fragrance, skin care, and prevention of bad odor while expanding on herbal offerings. One Indian herbal soap brand, Ayush, claims in its advertisements that it would kill 99% of seven types of bacteria. Pears, a well-known glycerin soap, has launched the germ-shield variant. Another brand, Lifebuoy, with variants is positioned as a family soap on the health platform and the brand has been in the Indian context for more than four decades. Lyril, which was positioned on product freshness with its lime ingredient and "waterfall" freshness, has not been doing well in recent times because of highly competitive positioning strategies. All four brands mentioned are from the same company, and except for the herbal brand, the other brands have a distinctive identity of their own and they have been nurtured for several decades by the company.

Given such a competitive situation, positioning has to go beyond the traditional imagery created by advertisements and the blitz of mass media. It may be worthwhile to follow the principle of combining the product benefit with the life benefit (Buchhold & Wondemann, 2000) while the positioning strategy is being formulated by brands in the competitive context. Incidentally, Lifebuoy was also positioned for several decades as a soap with a germ-killing action to the rural target segment characterized by a lower income and a different type of lifestyle. In fact, using a Lifebuoy a few decades back in the rural areas meant that the consumer has graduated to a branded offering from several low-end regional substitutes. Pears is a high-priced soap that has a small niche market and it has been positioned on long-term skin care. At the outset there is a need to provide differentiation in terms of how the product benefit of brands is relevant to the respective segment and even to segment the market combining life benefit with the product benefit would be useful. The product benefit of a herbal brand such as Ayush (killing of bacteria) may be relevant for a target segment that is exposed to dust and pollution in the environment in a developing country such as India. Children and several thousands of middle-class consumers of soaps traveling by crowded buses can be the target segment. The life benefit for this target segment is to stay fresh in the context to which they are exposed. Lifebuoy, which is currently positioned to the urban target segment as a "family soap" on the health platform (rather than on its original germ-killing proposition) could have the same demographic segment but address the same life benefit of staying fresh with regard to consumers who are exposed less of the dusty environment—probably self-employed business people who do not travel to work—as the target segment for Ayush.

The Internet enters into the mix as an information channel. It could provide information on the various brands, the various life benefits, the context (user situation) in which the core benefit of the brand could offer the maximum benefit and the ingredients used by each brand which is appropriate to the context (user situation). From this approach, it is apparent that there is a very clear differentiation not only in terms of benefits offered by the brands but also in terms of usage situation, which is a very strong criterion to segment consumers. Consumers would be able to appreciate how they are made to select the offering closest to their needs (not just in terms of fragrance or odor prevention which is very generic). This would make them buy the brand more frequently as there is a strong rationale to buy the specific brand (than just trying a few brands as more a variety seeking behavior). The problem of low penetration of the Internet in India (and hence the information) could be addressed at the important retail outlet and consumers could be educated by the company at these outlets with digital kiosks.

Shiseido, a Japanese cosmetic brand, has outlets where consumers could simulate several color combinations to suit their skin/desired aesthetic appeal and if they wish, they could leave their details in the database (Johansson & Nonka,1996). For the category of soaps, for instance, consumers could take a look at the kinds of ingredients and their benefits based on life benefit for an appropriate segment. With the database the company could obtain feedback on the effectiveness of the claims of the brand used by the consumers. This method of contemporary positioning even for a low-involvement product category could enable a brand to build up a relationship with the consumer base than just satisfying the positioning function of differentiating the offering from the competitors. Customer lifetime value has to consider the duration of loyalty and the profitability of customers during the duration of loyalty (Reinartz, Thomas, & Kumar, 2003). In a specific category the duration of loyalty is critical and the contemporary positioning suggested is likely to result in a longer duration of loyalty. Besides the company that has several brands across a price spectrum, the duration of loyalty could also enable the consumer to graduate to updated offerings. One of the reasons for customer migration is because the consumer does not find the company offering a broad spectrum of offerings which the consumer could adapt to based on his/her changing lifestyle (Coyles & Gokey, 2002).

Positioning Framework–I

My framework (Figure 1) uses two dimensions—price and interactivity with consumers—to provide guidelines for marketers to position their products on the dimension on loyalty:

The framework has four dimensions from which a brand can choose to employ its online and off-line positioning strategies depending on the selection of target segment for the brand. This framework would also be useful to develop specific "loyalty associations" through appropriate reward systems as applicable for the respective segment. Needs to be integrated with the framework more systematically. For example, low price–low interactivity (LEAD consumers as a target segment) would clearly understand that they would not be in a position to get rewards on loyalty as they are a part of the bargaining segment which is only

Figure 1. Price-customer interactivity linkages

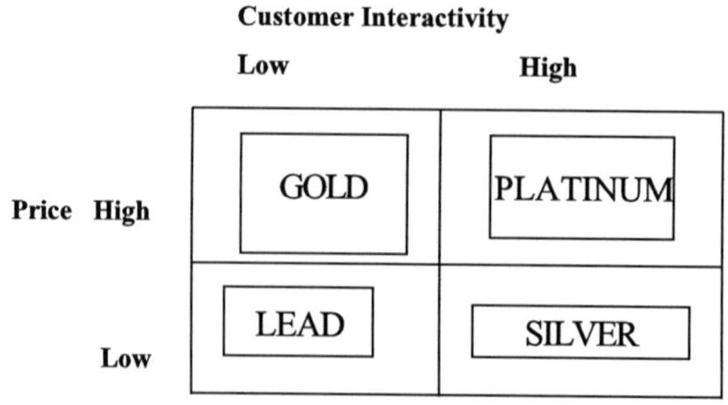

price conscious. The understanding comes from the positioning signal provided by the company's reward system for retaining customers.(continue) break down into smaller paragraphs. Such type of positioning is not possible through traditional ways.

For a brand that wants to consider high price–high customer interactivity (PLATINUM consumers as a target segment), the company should customize its product (even a tea brand could do this) to the consumer based on the finer needs of the consumer and the Internet-based interactivity could be used for changes in customization whenever it is required by the customer when it is bought frequently. For example, a brand of glycerin soap may customize such an offering based on the constant feedback received on usage, changing climatic conditions, and the customer's skin-specific reaction to the brand. The high-end customer getting involved in this interaction with the brand also perceives a value for the price he/she is paying and is aware that the price-conscious consumer is clearly differentiated by the brand. The Internet could throw up several customization options and give the customer specific guidelines on product usage after ascertaining feedback on brand performance with the inclusion of a dermatologist. A new variant of the soap could be initially introduced exclusively through a loyal base of consumers belonging to this segment, and this adds exclusivity to the value positioning.

High price–low customer interactivity (GOLD segment of consumers) could find application in hedonic products such as coffee, tea, and perfumes. While the interactivity may not be much on product performance, it may be associated with trends or recipes and the interaction may be low but customer information on new offerings may be required. This type of interaction would be helpful to build a relationship with customers by emphasizing the superiority of the offering, taking into consideration the category and competition together. An interesting example could be provided from the ready-made apparel industry which has a number of brands generally positioned on lifestyle aspects. The brand Van Heusen has brought in a fabric which reduces the temperature of the wearer. Another brand, Louis Phillippe, has introduced a shirt which is called "Permpress" (it offers a fabric that remains permanently pressed because of a specific technology). Even diapers, which have a very low penetration in the Indian market, could be a category that involves high price–low customer interactivity. These categories could reach out to the consumer on the net with information on the state of the artwork in the category and how such critical applications are treated with technology to deliver the relevant benefits to consumers. This approach would also add credibility to the brand. Product development efforts could also be highlighted and if the brand is able to get a testimonial from the scientific community on the credibility of claims, they could be discussed on the Web. Providing consumption-related services could be another dimension that may be appropriate to this segment. For example, a new user of baby foods may be interested in clarifying a few doubts about the usage and the Web is a very effective venue for providing a service of this kind.

Low price–high customer interactivity (SILVER segment of consumers) may not be a very feasible option for the company as costs of maintaining a system of this kind may offset the profits. However, there are a few aspects that could be considered for this segment. While individual consumer-specific information may not be a distinctive possibility, there could be a Web page that addresses the common concerns of consumers regarding the product. The brand offering this service would have to be priced slightly higher than the one in low price–low customer interactivity. If a company offers several shampoo brands, the mid-priced brand could have some customer interactivity if not high interactivity. On the Web site, the brand could answer a few questions on hair care, and the buyer of the brand could be given a password with which he/she could get three specific questions of her choice answered. SILVER target segment of consumers offer the possibility of a future potential in terms of interactivity as well as prices and hence could be moved to other segments. The four aspects of loyalty positioning could be useful in a variety of product/market situations and each aspect conveys a distinct positioning that is likely to enhance customer loyalty in the appropriate segment.

Positioning Framework–II

There are two dimensions of positioning strategies, namely perceived quality and associations that have been successful in the marketing history in both developed and developing markets. It would be useful for marketers to consider them while attempting the positioning synergy suggested in this article. These dimensions are portrayed in the backdrop of specific situations/contexts which reflect the realities of Indian markets. The contextual aspects are given in such a way that the positioning strategies suggested with these vital dimensions would be one of the primary components of a brand's strategy.

1. Perceived Quality as a Positioning Dimension

Perceived quality has three aspects—objective quality based on the performance of the brand on the intended direction, manufacturing quality in terms of how defect free the brand is, and product-based quality, which is associated with features, parts/ingredients, and services offered by the brand (Aaker, 1991). Perceived quality is the psychological because it involves consumers' perception of how the brand addresses their needs. The expectations of the target segment is crucial in assessing perceived quality. There may be two kinds of televisions:

one an upscale plasma version and the other an entry-level model. Both of these versions are targeted toward different segments. The higher-end consumer would expect specific features, the state-of-the-art features, which would also add some symbolic appeal to the television (which is normally kept in the visitors' hall in the typical Indian household) and effective after-sale service when there is a need for it. The expectations of the lower-end customer would be very different and hence perceived quality would be different for these two segments.

Perceived quality is used by the consumer in his/her decision making. A customer who is convinced of the perceived quality of a car would select the brand from among several alternatives. This aspect is especially applicable for a premium-priced brand. There are several car brands competing in the higher-end of the market. While off-line strategies would be associated with conventional advertising support, online promotion could be done through the Internet highlighting certain aspects that could not be done in an advertisement. For example, the engineering excellence in terms of safety or comfort could be conveyed through a special effect film shown to the prospective customer after assessing his/her needs. The preferences of several individuals could vary and several dimensions associated with the brand could be shown in accordance with the preferences of each individual prospective consumer. Perceived quality of an offering could also be enhanced by the services offered. OnStar is a service offered by General Motors and several million consumers have availed this service. The service ranges from remotely opening the door of a car (when the consumer loses the key) to tracking the car when it is stolen (Prahalad & Ramaswamy Venkat, 2004). The very positioning of such a service triggers a superior quality of service beyond the mundane after-sale service offered by car makers. Retail outlets of such brands could demonstrate such instances through simulations when consumers visit the outlets to learn more about the brand. The Internet could also be used in carrying the experience of consumers who have used the features of a brand (as testimonials) prospective consumers are thus encouraged to have a dialog with consumers who have experienced the brand. Such word-of-mouth references on reliability (which could be spread quickly from a variety of consumers on the web/e-mail) could enhance the perceived quality of the brand as reliability is one of the factors affecting product quality. Other aspects of product quality such as serviceability, finish (look and feel of the product), features, and durability (Garvin, 1984) could also be dealt with on the Web. Besides customers, experts from specific fields of engineering could offer an impartial assessment of the brand and its competitors. If the brand offers a product that is superior to that of the competitors, this approach of using experts to compare brands would be more effective than a company-sponsored comparison based on advertisements in which several competing brands are compared on a number of factors. The brand could also showcase the internal systems in the organization which assure quality on several aspects of the brand. There are also extrinsic cues that could influence perceived quality of the brand (Schiffman & Kanuk, 2002). The brand and its advertising are extrinsic cues that could influence perceived quality. A brand such as Sony can mention on its Web site the various high-tech experiments it had carried out to enhance its entertainment products. Consumers may not understand the technology involved but are likely to perceive the products of the brand as high in quality. The digital media in combination with such information creates a quality perception among consumers because elements of advertising enter the consumers' awareness as technology portrayed through digital media is used as a metaphor for quality of the product (Zaltman, 2003).

2. Associations as Positioning Dimensions

A number of dimensions of brand associations could be nurtured for positioning purposes. Prominent among them are product attributes, customer benefits, lifestyle associations, celebrity associations, and user imagery. Product attribute association is concerned with the association of a specific characteristic of the brand with its positioning. For example, Volvo is associated with safety and Mercedes is associated with its engineering excellence. In the digital context digitizability would be the extent to which the existing functional attribute could be converted into information-based functionality (Wind & Mahajan, 2001). This offers interesting possibilities for e-positioning of brands. National Semiconductor offers a simulation program on its Web site which would enable engineers to plug in their own parameters to experiment with their designs. Over 500,000 engineers keep coming back to Cisco's Web site (Seybold & Marshak, 2000).

In consumer product categories such aspects of positioning (digitizable positioning) is possible as well. Tide, the brand of detergent, has a Web site in which consumers can find information on removal of various kinds of stains. Amazon.com offers consumers several kinds of information that would enable them to consider several alternatives revolving around their preferences. E-positioning of brands extend the conventional positioning to offer whole customer experience which spans the entire decision-making stages of consumer's selection process from prepurchase to postpurchase (Bloch, 1995). The lifestyle positioning associated with a number of consumer categories, too, could effectively use e-positioning to be in line with the changing environment.

Consumer community is a concept that is evolving rapidly with the online marketing context cyberspace offers several innovative types of positioning. Forrester Research estimates that in the year 2000, 400,000 communities existed on the Internet (Solomon, 2002). Gartner opines that by 2005, 50% of all Fortune 1000 companies will launch virtual communities linked to their Web site (Zetlin & Pfleging, 2001). Sony's www.station.com has millions of users who participate in computer gaming online. Toyota has a digital racing game called Tundra, and as gaming's popularity has been increasing, marketers are merging advertisements that are interactive and they are placed with online games and this kind of technique is known as advergaming (Solomon, 2003). Ninety-four percent of British youth have mobile phones (Dana, 2001), and Nestlé held an innovative contest for its brand Kit Kat which involved mobile phones. Off-line lifestyle positioning, high-tech gadgets as status symbols, and cyberspace meeting spaces with an evolving youth population offer several online positioning strategies which could be sued in synchronization with lifestyle brand associations. The concept of consumer mind-set (Gollwitzer, 1986) distinctively divides the consumer mind-set into two categories—goal-oriented mind-set and experiential mind-set. The goal-oriented mind-set may be focused on feature-based information, whereas the experiential mind-set may be directed toward hedonic or sensual pleasure and this aspect could be used in online positioning of brands with contests and games being a trigger to make the hedonic mind-set more involved for sensual pleasure. Over time a brand could build a community of users who would be able to display brand passion as in the case of Harley-Davidson. Celebrity associations have been increasingly used in the recent times both globally and in India. Pepsi, Coke, Nerolac Paints, Cadbury's, Perk (chocolates), and Dabur's over-the-counter medication in consumables, and Palio and Santro in passenger cars, Victor two-wheelers (motorcycles), Samsung (washing machines), and Sahara (airlines) are some of the categories in which celebrities have been used in the Indian context.

Santro was a car introduced by Hyundai a few years ago and the brand has crossed 100,000 cars in terms of sales in 2003–2004 in a total passenger car market of one million. Santro was literally an unknown brand and also had a "tall boy" design unknown to Indian consumers. The brand initially used a topical male celebrity to create awareness about the brand and later after the brand picked up in terms of sales, it introduced a topical female celebrity and positioned the brand as "sunshine" brand with the imagery of the advertisement indicating a clear lifestyle positioning. The buyers of the brand are urban young adults who are upwardly mobile in terms of aspirations, income, and status. The celebrity positioning was strengthened (by the inclusion of the second celebrity) after the product was accepted for its functional features such as design and performance and comfort. It is surprising even such a celebrity-oriented advertising, very rarely brands use online positioning to "connect" with these target segment especially in durable categories. An online consumer chat session with the celebrities starring in the brand's advertisement (e.g., in Santro's) on the functional features of the car and the celebrities' experience with the car brand would have added fun and charismatic credibility to the campaign. Fanta, the orange-flavored soft drink from Coca-Cola, uses celebrities in its television commercials, and the script and the visual revolve around humor. An online session with consumers with the humor theme and the brand would have added excitement to the brand, and in the soft drink category, excitement is a useful positioning. In durable categories, an expert could also be roped in with the celebrity to provide a commentary on brand benefits and an online program could be made available on the brand's Web site for consumers to access any time.

A chat among the registered consumers as a rub-off strategy could also open up the possibilities of a community of brand users being formed. User imagery is another positioning dimension that is very useful in a competitive environment full of communication clutter. User imagery is very useful because the viewers of the advertisement using the imagery would be able to readily figure out the typical user depicted by the brand, and this is very important especially because there are several brands vying for the attention of the consumer. Fast track is a brand of watch targeting youngsters in urban markets and the advertising imagery shows the watch alongside a can of soft drink/beer (as perceived by the consumer with the can's image in India) indicating that it is clearly positioned toward youth who belong to the "cola/beer" culture and the imagery speaks volumes about the lifestyle association of the brand. Johnson & Johnson clearly carries the images of children when its products are advertised. Imagery for an edible oil brand would be different because the product is more under the focus of the consumer than the typical user imagery. Online positioning could carry complementary imagery (complementing the print/television advertisement imagery) to create an "experience." A chocolate drink aimed at youth could carry several innovative imagery visuals linking the typical drinker of the brand and the pleasure of the drinker in having consumed the brand. Experiential marketing, which involves several sense organs (Schmitt, 1999), could be used by a brand with its graphics on the Web. A high-end shaving razor, which claims several technological points toward providing consumer benefits, could create a product imagery on the Web (supplementing the user imagery in off-line advertising), which could vividly portray the finer aspects of the razor with the linked up benefits. Online advertising imagery as an extrinsic cue concerned with the brand could provide a significant enhancement of the intention to try the product in the case of consumables and could offer an enhanced image for durable categories. Such imagery could also provide information on product usage whether it is a recipe for a new fast food or for the first-time user of a fully automatic washing machine. A consumer may buy a vacuum cleaner but may not know how to use it and company-based off-line assistance is "timebound" and an online format would be available to the consumer any time he/she wants it. Timestyles of consumers differ depending on their personality (Cotte, Ratneshwar, & Glen Mick, 2003), hence online communication would take into consideration several types of consumer personality. Given the variety of associations and the contexts in which they could be put to use, the following frame work (Figure 2) with two dimensions, namely attribute orientation and online customer community orientation, would enable marketers to choose a strategy best suited to their product/market situation.

Positioning Framework–III

Given the fact that almost half the population in the Indian subcontinent is below the age of 25, the youth segment is an attractive one for several fast-moving consumer good categories. Changing lifestyles and the diffusion of digital products and the emergence of neo-youth segments such as software professionals offer tremendous scope for synergizing off-line and online positioning strategies with a focus on "community orientation." Consider a 2x2 matrix formed by Functional attributes (high, low) and Consumer Community (high, low). This provides us with an interesting way to explore positioning brands.

A brand could have a high attribute orientation and a high community orientation. Brands that have been launched on lifestyle to build themselves over the years, but which are required to enhance their attributes due to intense competition, could follow this approach. Close Up is a brand of toothpaste that was launched in the mid-1970s in India with the lifestyle appeal of "Close up smile" which featured a boy and girl with romantic overtones. Over the years, the brand has followed the same positioning slant and has been targeting the youth. With competitive brands following the same approach and brands from several other categories following similar positioning the brand seems to have lost its positioning luster. The brand could be revitalized by an online contest that emphasizes the functional attributes of the product.

A brand having a low attribute orientation could have a high community orientation. Brands faced with low levels of product differentiation could develop a community of brand users in a sustained manner. Mountain Dew's positioning which involves a group of youth is in tune with the online community orientation.

Low online community orientation with high attribute orientation could be applied to brands in any category that is highly innovative and sustains a product line which addresses changing customer needs. While community orientation could help any brand to build itself, in a country such as India where mass markets rule volumes, a durable category brand like Haier (the Chinese brand which has entered India) may want to address the mid-market and develop a strong product attribute association with thousands of consumers who may not have personal access to computers.

Low attribute orientation and low online consumer community orientation would be suitable to a number of no-frill brands at the lower end of the market which compete with unorganized offerings (offerings that are marketed at the local market and ones that may or may not be marketed in a systematic manner or the offerings that may not have completed the legalities required for marketing them) required for marketing the offerings in the category in a market such as India (electrical appliances ,watches, and footwear in the Indian market are examples of such product categories).

Other Topical Dimensions/Issues in Positioning

Points of difference associations (PODs) are strong, favorable, and unique brand associations for a brand and they may involve performance attributes or imagery that are unique to the brand (Keller, 2003). The various combinations of off-line and online positioning strategies could establish an appropriate POD for a brand in a given competitive context. The other aspect advocated by Keller was the points of parity association (POPs) which deals with category parity associations and competitive parity associations. Category parity associations refer to the extent to which a brand matches what consumers expect in a specific category.

Competitive parity associations refer to the extent to which a brand's associations match with that of its competitive brand's association with regard to its strengths. For example, if a new brand of car is launched in the market, competitive POP refers, for instance, to the state-of-the-art features of the brand which match with that of an existing competitive brand. The advantage of combining off-line positioning and online positioning is that in off-line positioning involving television or print advertisements (e.g., performance attributes of a detergent brand) could be highlighted and POP could be established. Online positioning of the brand (like that of Tide's) could establish the POD with suggestions on how the detergent brand could be used for various types of clothes or on how stains could be removed. Positioning could also involve linking attributes and benefits of the brand with the values that may be relevant to the target segment to which the brand is positioned. This concept is known as laddering (Reynolds & Gutman, 1988).

Marketing Implications: Creating a Synergy Between Off-Line and Online Positioning

Brands could be categorized as functional brands, symbolic brands, and hedonic brands from the viewpoint of brand positioning and this categorization is aimed at managing brand meaning over a brand's life cycle (Park, Jaworski, &

MacInnis, 1996). This is a very useful concept for brand positioning as it builds up a brand with a clear focus even when the brand attempts to enter a related diversification. When a brand has a strong functional appeal in terms of attributes and benefits, and if the company is able to sustain a product line with several offerings of the brand (over a period of time), having a focus on functional attributes or benefits, it could choose online and off-line positioning which has a focus on such dimensions.

Hero Honda is a two-wheeler bike company which entered the Indian context during the mid-1980s and for almost two decades it has focused on functional attributes/benefits with regard to all its offerings, namely Hero Honda CD100, Hero Honda SS, Hero Honda Splendor, and Hero Honda Passion. The last two offerings have had a symbolic positioning in terms but even such symbolism has been highlighted with additional features of the bike. While the brand has a clear focus on attributes, symbolism has been added based on innovative features. Hero Honda could have an online positioning that illustrates the processes within the factory on quality control, the rigor with which material is sourced from suppliers, and quality control with regard to suppliers to emphasize the efforts the company is making with regard to the attributes that consumers receive. The brand could also convey the developmental efforts being taken by the company to enhance customer-friendly features. This kind of secondary online positioning could build up credibility for the brand as consumers would also spread this information through word of mouth.

Conclusions

In sum, I argued that even in a developing market with low Internet penetration levels, the Web could be used as a channel to position a product effectively. Web sites could be designed to distribute product information that would enhance the differentiation of the brand in the marketplace.

References

Aaker, D. A. (1991). *Managing brand equity—Capitalizing on the value of a brand name.* New York: The Free Press.

Aaker, D. A., & Sthaler, J. (2000). *Brand leadership.* New York: The Free Press.

Bloch, P. (1995). Seeking the ideal forces: Product design and consumer response. *Journal of Marketing, 59*, 16–29.

Buchhold, A., & Wordemann Wolfram. (2000). What makes winning brands different? 21–26.

Cotte, J., Ratneswar, R., & Glen Mick David. (2003). The times of their lives: Phenomenological and metaphorical characteristics of consumer timestyles. *Journal of Consumer Research*, 2–4.

Coyles, S., & Gokey C Timothy. (2002). Customer retention is not enough. *The McKinsey Quarterly, 2*, 1–6.

Dana, M. (2001). M commerce will outperform e commerce. *RCR Wireless News*, 20(2), 4.

Gilmore, H. J., & Joseph II, P. B. (2000). Markets of one, creating customer—Unique value through customer. *HBS*, 62–65.

Gollwitzer, M. P. (1996). The volitional benefits of planning. In M. P. Gollwitzer & J. A. Bargh (Eds.), *The psychology of actions, living cognition and motivation or behavior* (pp. 287–312). New York: Guilford Press.

Hallberg, G. (1995). *All consumers are not created equal.* John Wiley & Sons.

Johansson, K. J., & Ikujiro, N. (1996). Relentless, the Japanese way of marketing. *Harper Business*, 143–148.

Keller, L. K. (2003). *Strategic brand management, building, measuring and managing brand equity.* New Delhi: Prentice Hall.

Keller, L. K., Sternthal, B., & Tybout, A. (2002). Three questions you need to ask about your brand. *Business Review*, 3–8.

Kotler, P. (2003). *Marketing management* (11th ed.). Pearson Education.

Kumar, K., & Mahadevan, B. (2003). Evolution of business models in B2C e-commerce: The case of Fabmall. *Management Review, 15*(4), 23–30.

Kumar, S. R. (2002). *Conceptual issues in consumer behaviour—Indian context* (pp. 82–89). Pearson Education.

Kumar, S. R. (2002). *Managing Indian brands.* (pp. 299–300). Vikas.

Linstrom, M., Peppers, D., & Rogers, M. (2001). *Clicks, bricks and brands.* Kogan.

Park, C.W., Jaworski, J., Bernard & MacInnis J. Deborah. (1996). Strategic brand concept—Image management. *Journal of Marketing*, 135–145.

Prahalad, & C K Ramaswamy Venkat. (2004). Future of competition—Co-creating unique value with customers. *HBS*, 83–85.

Reinatz, W., Thomas, J., & Kumar, V. (2003). *Linking acquisition and retention to maximize profitability.* (Working paper). University of Connecticut.

Reynolds, J. T., & Gutman, J. (1988). Laddering theory: Method, analysis and interpretation. *Journal of Advertising Research*, 11–23.

Ries, A., & Ries, L. (2000). *Immutable laws of Internet branding*. New York: Harper Collins.

Ries, A., & Trout, J. (1987). *Brand positioning: The battle in the mind* (pp. 1–5). Tata McGraw Hill.

Rust, R. J., Zeithmal, V. A., & Lemon, N. K. (2000). *Driving customer equity, how customer lifetime value is reshaping corporate strategy* (pp. 223–241). New York: The Free Press.

Schiffman, G. L., & Kanuk, L. L. (2002). Consumer behavior. Pearson Education, pp.141–153.

Schmitt, H. B. (1999). *Entrepreneurial marketing* (p.71). New York: The Free Press.

Seybold, P., & Marshak, T. R. (2000). Customers.com. *Times Business*, 99–102.

Solomon, M. (2003). Conquering the consumer mindspace. *Amcom, 10*, 151–153.

Trout, J., & Rivkin, S. (1999). *The power of simplicity* (p. 55). Tata McGraw Hill.

Wind, Y., & Mahajan, V. (2001). *Digital marketing* (pp. 210–320). Hoboken, NJ: John Wiley & Sons.

Zaltman, G. (2003). How consumers think: Insights into the mind of the market. *HBS*, pp. 80–90.

Zetlin, M., & Pfleging (2001, October). Creators of online community. *Computer World, 29*, 34.

Chapter XIII

Locked In By Services: Willingness to Pay More and Switching Behavior in a Digital Environment

Manlio Del Giudice, University of Milano-Bicocca, Italy

Michel Polski, Grenoble Ecole de Management, France

Abstract

We discuss a dynamic model of cognitive and behavioral e-loyalty developed through the analysis of barriers (perceived switching costs) which can be raised against customer's switching behavior. Using results from an empirical study, our chapter will be focused particularly on the determinants of the switching behavior online and on the opportunity to change Web site usability in a powerful lock-in strategy. Finally, as a result, we will discuss one of the main consequences of loyal behavior, in presence of positive perceived switching costs: the customer willingness to pay more.

Introduction

E-commerce is growing rapidly and has penetrated almost all industries. Given its enormous potential, the number of electronic stores has increased at an unprecedented rate during the last 5 years. Theory seems to support the prediction that online shopping will keep rising in the future, as online search engines and various intelligent agents can dramatically reduce search costs associated with purchase decisions (Alba et al., 2000; Bakos, 1997; Lee & Clark, 2001). However, online shopping lacks "look-and-feel" (Figueiredo, 2000; Rosen & Howard, 2000) and hence evaluation of product attributes or firms online can be still difficult (Bhatnagar, Misra, & Rao, 2000).

The limited empirical research done on online customer trust and loyalty has concentrated mostly on how customer perceptions of the online company affect their trust. However, while in off-line commerce it is the salesperson who often influences the buyer's trust in the seller (Doney & Cannon, 1997) thus inducing loyal behaviors, in the Internet context it is the Web site that should do that (Del Giudice & Del Giudice, 2003; Lohse & Spiller, 1998). Therefore, one would expect that the customer experience with the Web site would also have a strong effect on customer trust in the company. Following this approach, as in the marketing literature trust is positively related to the experience of the customer with the salesperson, in online commerce, instead, the salesperson is almost replaced by the company's Web site:[1] as a result, the customers' experience and perceptions of the quality service provided by the Web site's tools can influence their assumptions about the nature of the company and its trustworthiness (Friedman et al., 2000; Tan & Thoen, 2000–2001). Moreover, customers who do not trust an online vendor will be less inclined to do business with the vendor (Gefen, 2000; Jarvenpaa & Tractinsky, 1999) or to return for additional purchases (Reichheld & Schefter, 2000). Since quality service is something customers generally expect vendors to provide (Parasuraman et al., 1985; Zeithaml et al., 1996), high-quality service through Web site should arguably build customer trust and loyalty, as a recent study of customers of online vendors indicates (Reichheld & Schefter, 2000).

Following those premises, the aim of this chapter is mainly to highlight the absolute need for Internet-based firms to develop and manage, through the Web site, strategic tools able to increase customer loyalty in digital markets, thus reducing customer churn. Our work mainly starts from the emerging change occurring in customer loyalty management strategies through Internet customer service and on the strong difference between the customer behavior online, respect to the off-line one. Although trade and popular literature indicate much marketing concern about online retail customer satisfaction, little research has considered the customer's affective reaction to services provided by a Web site and their impact on customer behavior, one of the main goals of our work. Generally, the lack of satisfaction with a Web site would lead to customer intention not to purchase from that site (thus inducing switching behaviors). Accordingly, our work will attempt to discover the elements of online shopping experiences that influence the shopper's satisfaction with the online shopping experience, leading the shopper to purchase again from that site or alternatively to switch to another site. Starting from the evidence of an empirical survey, we aim to discuss a dynamic model of cognitive and behavioral e-loyalty developed through the analysis of barriers (switching costs) which can be raised against customer's switching behavior.[2] A Web site, by providing a supplier's material products in addition to a wide range of services, therefore, becomes a self-governing instrument of customer service. That would spur suppliers to search in customer service tools provided by a Web site a source of possible locking-in, through which cultivating customer's loyalty not so much as a result of a path dependence on preceding choices, but rather through customer's deep satisfaction stemming from the quantity and typology of services provided through the Web site. Our chapter will be focused particularly on the determinants of the switching behavior online and on the opportunity to change Web site usability in a powerful lock-in strategy; finally, as a result, we will discuss one of the main consequences of loyal behavior, in presence of positive perceived switching costs: the customer willing to pay more.[3]

Background

Although service quality through Web site usability has been very carefully studied in an online environment (Nielsen, 2002), there are few empirical studies examining the theory that service quality increases customer loyalty through increased trust in the online environment. At the same time, in the literature, there is little empirical research on cognitive lock-in based on superior service quality provided by the tools and key elements of a Web site (Del Giudice & Del Giudice, 2003; Johnson et al., 2003; Zauberman, 2002).[4] In the literature switching costs were classically grouped into three categories (Guiltinan, 1989; Klemperer, 1987, 1995):

1. continuity costs
2. learning costs
3. sunk costs

Continuity costs are typically linked to lost performance costs.[5] Continued patronage of a vendor often leads to the accrual of benefits and perquisites that are lost if the relationship is ended (Maute & Forrester, 1993; Turnball & Wilson, 1989). They appear as strictly linked to the highly personalised nature of services deriving from a strong and long-term relationship with the supplier's service personnel (Guiltinan, 1989). Continuity costs can be also represented by uncertainty costs, associated with the failure of continuing an existing relationship: in this case, they seem to be linked to the psychological uncertainty of risk perception surrounding the performance of an unknown or untested supplier (Guiltinan, 1989; Schmalensee, 1982). *Learning costs* refer to the time and effort spent by the customer to understand and learn selling patterns of a new supplier in case of switching (Jones et al., 2002).[6] Finally, *sunk costs*[7] are the economically irrelevant but psychologically important investments in a business relationship (Guiltinan, 1998).

Particularly, they refer to customer perception of the unrecoverable time, money, and efforts previously invested in establishing and keeping a business relationship alive (Jones et al., 2002).

Papers regarding switching barriers coming from marketing or economics mention switching costs as an important switching barrier. Switching costs refer to various types of costly obstacles of changing supplier. High switching costs tend to lock customers to suppliers.[8] Moreover, customers remain loyal to a supplier either because they *want to* or they *have to* (Hirschman, 1970; Johnson, 1982; Levinger, 1979; Ping, 1993). Following this approach if customers will experience a feeling of "wanting to be loyal," probably they are perceiving *positive switching costs*.[9] Whereas if they will face a feeling or "being trapped" or "having to be loyal" (meaning that customers have to stay with suppliers irrespective of the satisfaction created in the relationship), probably they are experiencing *negative switching costs*.[10] Such "negative" barriers may do more harm than good in the long run. Positive barriers, which might include interpersonal bonds, which provide intrinsic benefits may be less likely to create feelings of entrapment and, therefore, less likely to result in sabotage-type behaviors.

The main goal of our model is just to explain the impact of positive barriers, stemming from the Web site, that are likely to lock in the customer in a satisfying relationship. In this vision, there are some similarities with romantic relationships: Rusbult, Johnson, and Morrow (1986), for example, in their study of romantic relationships see commitment or investments as factors that increase the probability of a continuation of the relationship. Rusbult's theory of investment regarding interpersonal and romantic relationships consists of two main variables: satisfaction with the relationship (defined as the positivity of affect or attraction to ones relationship) and commitment (the tendency to maintain a relationship and feel psychologically attached to it). The investment model asserts that satisfaction is a function of the rewards from the relationship (in a business context the utility created by the suppliers products and services), and the costs of the relationship (possibly in a business context what one has to pay for the products and services). Commitment to the relationship, which we in this study refer to as attitudinal loyalty, is a function of satisfaction, attractiveness of alternatives, and investment in the relationship.

The Switching Cost Model Conceptual Framework

Why Switching Costs Should be More Strategic in a Digital Environment

Many different strategies can be implemented to achieve switching costs, and many different strengths or degrees of switching costs can be obtained. The strategies and strengths available depend in large part on the context in which the firm competes. We find that several key changes brought on by the advances in technology and the growth in the use of the Internet make switching costs a more strategic force in today's competitive environment. The first change is the growth in the use of the Internet and other computer and communications technologies. This growth has enabled the developed countries of the world to change from economies based on the processing of resources and raw materials to economies based on the processing of information, knowledge, and ideas (Arthur, 1996; Gual & Ricart, 2001; Shapiro & Varian, 1999; Tapscott, 1997; Yoffie 1999).

This shift is important because as more and more economic activity is based on technology and information, and as firms and customers increasingly interconnect over the Internet's open standards, the world is increasingly becoming one large network. While switching costs are an important force in all business environments, they are significantly more pronounced in network environments (Economides, 1998) because of a network's structure: it is composed of links that connect nodes, many different components make up the links and nodes, these components are complements to one another, and to be complementary the components must be compatible (Economides, 1996). In other words, the network works as a unified system. This system is built around a standard with which the components are made compatible. Because of this system structure and the need for participants in the network to have complementarity between components, network industries contain network externalities and positive feedback, also called increasing returns (Arthur, 1989; Katz & Shapiro, 1985; Shapiro & Varian, 1999). The combination of these forces makes network industries high switching cost industries. Network externalities, also known as network effects or positive consumption externalities, exist when a user values a good or service more as the total number of users for that good or service increases. A common example is the fax machine—as more people own faxes, faxes become more valuable to each individual user. Positive feedback is a force that "makes the strong get stronger and the weak get weaker" (Shapiro & Varian, 1999, n.p.).

"Classical" or "Digital" Switching Costs

As we know from the literature, since investment locks the customer to the supplier, we classify high investments in the relationship and attractiveness of other alternatives by the customer as positive switching barriers. In fact, if the chosen supplier is better than the other available alternatives, the customer stays with, or is locked to, the supplier, because the supplier is perceived to be better than other potential suppliers. That is, there is a positive motivation to stay with the supplier. Positive interpersonal relationships are also viewed as positive switching barriers. They could be said to be a part of the product offered, especially if it is a service. It can be expected that customers stay with suppliers because of such positive relationships. We classify loyal customer discounts and customer habit (Fornell, 1992) as positive switching barriers, since they are positive aspects of the product or service bundle offered. They resemble the artificial switching barriers mentioned by Klemperer (1987) and Nilssen (1992).[11]

In order to introduce our conceptual model and its underlying hypotheses, we will try to shift from a classical market to a digital one. In a digital market, customised Web interfaces, key accounts, defined cookies, filtering tools are to be considered powerful weapons to retain the customer on the Web site. We know that one would expect that the customer experience with the Web site would also have a strong effect on customer trust in the company. Moreover, as in classic marketing literature, trust is positively related to the experience of the customer with the salesperson, in online commerce, instead, the shopping experience is "lived," in the major part, with the company's Web site: as a result, the customers' experience and perceptions of the quality service provided by the Web site's tools can influence their assumptions about the nature of the company and its trustworthiness (Friedman et al., 2000; Tan & Thoen, 2000–2001). Following this approach, the Web sites' tools likely to let the customer deal the purchase and place the order by means of just "one click" (thus gaining time for his/her business and saving money) may be a possible source of positive switching costs. In this way, an efficient lock-in strategy should be thought of to retain the customer in a business relationship with the supplier's firm which might lever up his/her cognitive and behavioral costs. On the Internet it is possible to reach such a goal by revising and updating classic switching costs (continuity costs, learning costs, sunk costs). In the next section we will describe how to shift from a classical view of switching costs to a digital environment.

Empirical Results

The Model's Hypotheses

In a precedent study (Del Giudice & Del Giudice, 2003) we hypothesized six dimensions of possible source of switching costs on the Internet, quite similar to the classic switching costs known from off-line markets:[12]

cookie costs[13] (*digital continuity costs*);
interface tools costs[14] (*digital continuity costs*);
Web searching costs[15] (*digital learning costs*);
interface learning costs[16] (*digital learning costs*);
profile setup costs[17] (*digital learning costs*);
sunk costs.[18]

Table 1. Switching costs pattern definition in a digital environment (Del Giudice & Del Giudice, 2003)

CATEGORIES	E-SWITCHING COSTS	E-SWITCHING COSTS PATTERN DEFINITION
e-Continuity costs		
	Cookie costs	Customer's perception of the benefits involved in Customer's purchase pattern (cookie) being lost on switching
	Interface tools costs	Customer's perception of the likelihood of lower performance when switching (e.g., all the filtering tools that help the Web crawler to recognise in the Website a powerful business tool)
e-Learning costs		
	Web searching costs	Perception of the time and effort of gathering and evaluating information prior to switching
	Interface learning costs	Perception of the time and effort of learning a new Web site interface and routine subsequent to switching
	Profile setup costs	Perception of the time, effort, and expenses required to set up a new profile with an e-business
Sunk costs		
	Psychological costs	Perception of investments and costs already incurred in establishing and maintaining a business relationship

In Table 1, results of the *e-switching costs* analysis have been summed up. Thus we hypothesize the following:

H1: Each switching cost dimension relates positively with repurchase intentions (and thus negatively with customer churn rate).

H2: Cookie costs, interface tools costs, and interface learning costs relate more strongly with perceived Web site service quality (through better Web site usability, better Web design, etc.) than the other switching cost dimensions.

Starting from the premise that a loyal customer, being locked by his/her deep satisfaction stemming from his/her current supplier's Web site, can be willing to pay more in order to keep alive his/her business relationship, we then hypothesize the following:

H3: Each switching cost dimension relates positively with customer willingness to pay more.

Research Methodology

The main goal of this section is to test the hypothesized six dimensions of switching costs. Our empirical analysis followed two steps: in the first step, standard scale development procedures were followed in the development of the multidimensional switching costs scale. In the second step, we provide a more rigorous assessment of the dimensionality of the switching cost scale and we test the hypotheses.

Data Collection and Sampling Procedure

In-depth interviews with managers from a sample of 15 firms from the IT (B2B) sector (three e-suppliers and 12 of their e-customers [that had experienced shopping online with all of the three e-suppliers]) were conducted to define the scale items. Those interviews, our precedent study, and a review of the relevant literature allowed us to generate an initial set of nine acceptable items per switching cost dimension. A panel of five marketing faculty reviewed the items for clarity and face validity. Moreover, the original items were refined and pared to six items per dimension. Item-total correlation, Cronbach's alpha, and exploratory factor analysis were examined for each switching cost dimension (deleting the items based on low factor loadings, negative contribution to alpha, and/or low item-total correlation). After the exploratory factor analysis, we developed the confirmatory model and tested the propositions by administrating (through e-mail) the questionnaire to a sample of 180 e-customers (who had experienced shopping online from at least two of the original three e-suppliers). The following paragraphs show the result of our analyses.

Exploratory Factor Analysis

Item-total correlation, Cronbach's alpha, and exploratory factor analysis were examined for each switching cost dimension.[19] We calculated Cronbach's alphas for the scale items to ensure that they exhibited satisfactory levels of internal consistency (see Appendix, Table A). We refined the scales by deleting items that did not load meaningfully on the underlying construct and those that did not highly correlate with other items measuring the same construct. We deleted the items showing low factor loadings, negative contribution to alpha, and/or low item-total correlation. Finally we got just six factors reflecting the six proposed switching cost dimensions (eigenvalue >1). Cronbach's alpha gave positive results on all the six dimensions (see Appendix, Table A), supporting the proposed switching cost dimensions. Particularly,

Cookie costs (Alpha = .92)
Interface tools costs (Alpha = .83)
Web searching costs (Alpha = .86)
Interface learning costs (Alpha = .85)
Profile setup costs (Alpha = .95)
Sunk costs (Alpha = .83)

Table A in the Appendix presents the meaningful items (factor loadings less than .40 are not shown) and includes Cronbach's alphas for the hypothesized switching cost dimensions.

Analyses and Results: The Test

The Methodology

The hypotheses were tested using multiple multivariate analysis methodologies (we used SPSS 11.0 and LISREL 8.54). The switching cost items retained from the first part of the analysis were used in order to test the hypotheses. In order to pursue this goal, repurchase intentions, perceived Web site quality, and willingness to pay more were also measured. Particularly, repurchase intentions and perceived Web site quality were assessed on a 7-point Likert scale (from "unlikely" to "likely," from "impossible" to "very possible," from "no chance" to "certain scales" [Oliver & Swan, 1989]). Willingness to pay more (defined as the willingness on the part of the customer to continue purchasing from the e-supplier despite an increase in price) was measured on a 5-point semantic differential scale (with anchors "not at all likely" and "very likely"), by adapting relevant scale items from Zeithaml, Berry, and Parasuraman (1996). Moreover, after the factory analysis, we were ready to administer (through e-mail) the questionnaire to a sample of 180 e-customers (who had experienced shopping online from at least two of the original three e-suppliers). The answering rate was quite high (about 86%).

Confirmatory Model and Tests of Hypotheses

The exploratory factor analysis conducted provided strong support for the proposed switching costs dimensions. The second part of our analysis, instead, provided a more rigorous assessment of the dimensionality of switching cost scale and allowed to test the hypotheses. We conducted a confirmatory factor analysis for the overall sample (with LISREL 8.54). Fit statistics indicated acceptable fit (Tucker Lewis Index = 0.93; Comparative Fit Index = 0.92; Bollen, 1989). Results also support the internal consistency of each switching cost dimension since composite reliabilities (a LISREL-generated measure similar to Cronbach's alpha) were generally high (see Appendix, Table B). Moreover, estimates of variance extracted for each dimension were greater than 0.60, indicating high shared variance between indicators of each dimension (Fornell & Larcker, 1981). Propositions regarding switching cost correlates were tested using the phi estimates from the confirmatory model and chi-square difference tests of alternative models. H1 indicates that each switching cost dimension relates positively with repurchase intentions (and thus negatively with customer churn rate): it was supported since all phi estimates between switching costs and repurchase intentions were significant (phi's range from 0.21 to 0.57; see

Appendix, Table B). H2 indicates that cookie costs, interface tools costs, and interface learning costs relate more strongly with perceived Web site service quality (through Web site usability, Web design, etc.) than the other switching cost dimensions: it was supported by the higher association among cookie costs, interface tools costs, and interface learning costs (phi = 0.59, phi = 0.63, and phi=0.52, respectively) and perceived service quality, than that between the other switching cost dimensions and perceived service quality (phi's range from 0.19 to 0.32) (it was confirmed also by chi-square difference tests, all chi-square diff > 26,59, df = 1, Ps <.01).

Finally, H3 indicates that each switching cost dimension relates positively with customer willingness to pay more was supported since all phi estimates between switching costs and willingness to pay more were significant (phi's range from 0.45 to 0.69) (it was confirmed also by chi-square difference tests, all chi-square diff > 19,82, df = 1, Ps <.01).

In sum, all three hypotheses were supported.

Implications for Managers and Practitioners

Research that contributes to the understanding of customer experiences with online shopping has important implications for researchers as well as business managers and information systems managers (Adam et al., 1999). Although marketers are beginning to understand the innovative strategies that will attract visitors to Web sites (Hoffman et al., 1995; Morr, 1997), little is known about the factors that make Web use a compelling customer experience or about the key customer satisfaction outcomes of this compelling experience.

Nowadays, the high cost of attracting new customers on the Internet and the relative difficulty in retaining them make customer loyalty an essential asset for many online vendors. Attracting new customers costs online vendors at least 20% to 40% more than it costs vendors serving an equivalent traditional market (Reichheld & Schefter, 2000). To recoup these costs and show a profit, online vendors, even more so than their counterparts in the traditional marketplace, must increase customer loyalty, which means convincing customers to return for many additional purchases at their site. Customer loyalty, in general, increases profit and growth in many ways (Chow & Red, 1997; Heskett et al., 1994) to the extent that increasing the percentage of loyal customers by as little as 5% can increase profitability by as much as 30%–85%, depending upon the industry involved (Reichheld & Sasser, 1990), a ratio estimated to be even higher on the Web (Reichheld & Schefter, 2000). The reason for this is that loyal customers are typically willing to pay a higher price and are more understanding when something goes wrong (Chow & Reed, 1997; Del Giudice & Polski, 2003; Fukuyama, 1995; Reichheld & Sasser, 1990; Reichheld & Schefter, 2000;

Zeithaml et al., 1996). Indeed, the success of some well-known Web sites can be attributed in part to their ability to maintain a high degree of customer loyalty. Part of the success of Amazon.com, for example, is attributed to its high degree of customer loyalty, with 66% of purchases made by returning customers (The Economist, 2000).

Moreover, first of all managers must make sure that customers correctly perceive and accept the switching costs on at least one of the three dimensions of loyalty: cognitive, emotional, and/or behavioral. The cognitive dimension assumes the customers are voluntarily and consciously loyal because they are aware of sufficient and relevant information about exit and entry costs in favour of the firm. Structural and operational costs (implying for instance financial and technical risks) enter often into this consideration. The emotional dimension, entailing psychological and symbolical risks, is linked to brand equity and attachment of the brand by the consumer. Disappointment, regrets, complaining, and collector items are often materialization of a high psychological cost after the disappearance of a preferred brand for example. The behavioural dimension of loyalty regroups costs related to a change of buying or consuming habits: in learning, in time and space, in behaviour with others. This is why it implies social and environmental risks. Satisfaction inquiries, benchmarking with competition, and in-depth interviews can help to detect how the nature of switching costs are perceived, so that an appropriate communication campaign will put the emphasis on the right dimension of loyalty. A mismatch between the nature of imposed costs and loyalty can ruin the perceived value and brand equity. Table 2 shows, for instance, that if customers pay attention to social risks and are concerned about the symbolic dimension of value, it will be useless to advertise on minimizing operational costs and needless to try to make them loyal by operational means such as time saving.

Second, there must be a balance between exit and entry costs. If the exit costs are high, current customers are bound to be loyal, but if entry costs are high as well, winning market shares from competition or capturing again lost customers will not be an easy task. Moreover, "closing markets" can induce marketing myopia, few innovations, and less creativity. Similarly, this will be a way to

Table 2. The threshold nature of loyalty

Nature of loyalty and costs =>	Cognitive	Emotional	Behavioural : Operational/Structural
Nature of risks and value			
Physical			X
Financial	X		X
Practical (time, comfort)	X		X
Psychological (emotions)		X	
Social (symbols)		X	

Table 3. The relationship between entry/exit costs

	LOW ENTRY COSTS	HIGH ENTRY COSTS
LOW EXIT COSTS	Multiloyalty, volatility	Worse competitive situation
HIGH EXIT COSTS	Best competitive situation	Closed and shared markets

ensure "win-back" customers (former customers coming back from competition after having switched once), these customers are bound to be even more loyal than others and are often precious for firms because their decision was reinforced by a back-and-forth switch (long- term vision of businesses ⇔ long-term loyalty and trusts; short-term industries ⇔ one-shot approach) (Table 3).

Third, the intrinsic risk of a channel plays a major role as concerns the choice of environment. The scope of our study is limited to the digital environment: the pure players of the Internet. The Internet is still perceived as risky by a majority of people. Thus, the switching behaviour can occur inside the digital environment across brands (options 2 and 4, for example), or across environments inside brands (between options 1 and 2, for example), or across brands and environments (options 1 and 4, for example).[20]

By the way, the model proposed can be easily adapted to corporate managers' requirements. It is aimed at giving pragmatic support to managers wishing to maximize their customer's retention and loyalty by means of a streamlined management of customer service tools and through site customer stickiness. The empirical demonstration of the theoretical approach, tested in the IT market, has allowed us to propose a model easily applicable to digital enterprises by setting up a customer service environment so favourable to the customer to spur the rise of true switching costs. Following this approach, supplier switching which is

Table 4. Hypotheses on switching behavior

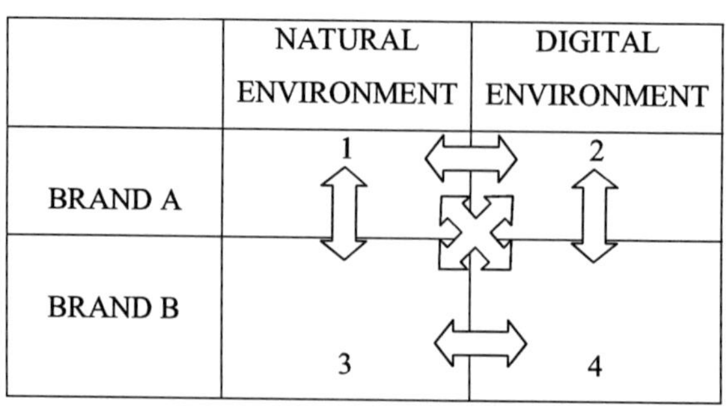

managers' main enemy in a digital era can be fought by devising a lock-in strategy based on customer's satisfaction rather than expecting a doubtful sort of customer loyalty emerging from the product features. Table C in the Appendix will help managers link customer service opportunities provided by an interactive Web site to the implementation of a lock-in strategy aiming at the strengthening of consumers' cognitive loyalty. In a few words it tries to give an answer to the following questions: How to implement this model? How to develop customer service and lock-in at the same time? How to raise e-switching costs from customer's satisfaction?

Conclusions and Suggestions for Further Research

The Internet has the potential to reverse the relationship of power between the supplier and the client. As the Internet increased customers' autonomy, customers have been considered only as sources of outlets for the firm's production. The only inputs from customers were profile data and opinions reflected in market studies. Consumerism is the first reason. As the Internet fostered customers' autonomy, customers are more informed, active, and critical. They can exchange information independently through chats, e-forums, thematic portals, or personal Web sites to compare products and share opinions. Thus, consumers can disparage a product even stronger than the stiffest competitor.

Second, customers can get their needs satisfied by virtual sources at lower cost. The book and entertainment industry had to adapt its strategy not to turn a threat into a growth opportunity. The "customer-as-competitor" should be turned into a "customer-as-partner." The link satisfaction and loyalty is necessary, but still not sufficient: genuine loyalty often goes through brand preference. The majority of the first studies about the Internet focussed on methods to create awareness and traffic. A second generation of concern was about how to transform traffic into purchases and building satisfaction through a quality and timely supply chain. Now the most topical concern deals with building relationship through the Internet by maintaining the level of satisfaction and increasing the willingness to pay (or buy) more. The problem of Internet loyalty seems to be tightly related to this concern. It lies often in the industrialisation of personalisation.

Call centres and customer relationship management systems are often misused, creating an asymmetry of information in this client–supplier relationship, which can be even worse than no relationship at all. As a matter of fact, firms can know almost everything of their customers, but the relationship is one way. For instance, in case of a disagreement and a complaint, call-centres are often subcontracted and unable to deal with individual demands, because the personnel is externalised, part time, and low skilled, sometimes in a foreign country, with just a phoning script to fill in, providing no personalized answers, nor any follow-up. This way, call-centres are not perceived by consumers as new link, but as a supplementary wall between them and the supplier, ruining the efforts of lock-in strategies setup in the Web. By expanding and refining the conceptualisation of switching costs and developing a switching cost framework, we believe that this chapter contributed to addressing the challenges occurring in digital marketing respect to classic one.

Our conceptualisation of switching costs should contribute by clarifying, unifying, and expanding upon this key strategic element. First, we have shown that while switching costs have long been considered an essential element for achieving competitive advantage, differences exist as to how it is portrayed in the literature. By clarifying the different approaches to switching costs we then are able to unify them in order to develop a more comprehensive and understandable conceptualisation of the phenomenon. The development of our switching cost framework provides several important contributions as well. First of all, it highlights the important role of switching costs in the firm's strategy and performance, a role emphasized consistently throughout the strategy, marketing, and economics literature that we reviewed. The framework explicitly links switching costs to the firm's strategic positions at the strategy level. It also explicitly links switching costs to firm performance at two different levels. At the strategy level, switching costs are linked to the performance the firm can potentially achieve, while at the operational level, switching costs are linked to the performance the firm actually achieves based on its ability to effectively manage the switching cost cycle. The second important contribution of the framework is the guidance it gives in understanding and dealing with the changing strategic role of switching costs as a result of the increasingly networked digital environment. Although there is debate over the direction in which switching costs may be changing, researchers consistently agree that change is occurring. Thus, while switching cost and lock-in economics have always been present, their form or appearance tends to change in the networked environment. By guiding a detailed analysis of switching costs, the framework helps firms to manage them in order to retain customers. It also helps firms to recognize when switching costs and lock-in are capable of creating "monopolies" (though perhaps only temporary monopolies) and locking-in markets due to the existence of networks, network externalities, and positive feedback. Finally, the framework's emphasis on *integration* ensures that firms go beyond a deep, broad, and long-term analysis of switching costs to include a dynamic analysis of the interrelationships between the different levels. Thus, while each of the existing tools we have discussed in the chapter makes a positive contribution to understanding and managing switching costs, each is limited on its own precisely because of a lack of such integration. Each of them effectively addresses the issues it was designed to address, but none of them was designed to provide a complete framework for managing switching costs, thus a new framework was needed. Finally we believe this new framework provides a powerful and, in our view, necessary strategic lens that can enable new insights and emphases when combined with other strategy tools or perspectives. Thus, when analysing the industry, competitors, or key resources and capabilities using existing approaches, the switching cost lens complements these approaches by prompting managers to recognise and manage switching costs' role in achieving competitive advantage. In addition to applying the switching cost lens to their own business, we suggest that firms apply the lens to their value net. The conceptualisation and development of the framework should reinforce the efforts made by other researchers to direct managers' attention to the importance of proactively managing switching costs. In addition, by linking the switching costs due to firm-specific retention strategies to the implementation costs, managers can better gauge the effectiveness of retention investments. While we believe this work contributes to the understanding of this strategic element, more research clearly needs to be done.

For one, due to the lack of empirical work and theoretical development on switching costs, there is a need to do more of both. One approach is to conduct multiple case studies to explore the role of switching costs empirically and to compare findings from different settings. This would be a logical progression with which we could evaluate the theoretical ideas put forth in this chapter. In addition, we see an opportunity for more cross-fertilization among the fields of research discussed in this paper, especially between strategy and marketing. Recent research (e.g., Mittal & Kamakura, 2001) has shown that customer characteristics moderate the relationship between customer satisfaction and retention. Hence, future studies might examine the impact that individual customer or situational characteristics have on the relationship between switching barriers and propensity to continue with an online supplier. Each of these fields provides valuable insight on switching costs and combining efforts should further enhance our understanding.

References

Bakos, Y. (2001). The emerging landscape for retail e-commerce. *Journal of Economic Perspectives*, January.

Beggs, A., & Klemperer, P. (1992). Multi-period competition with switching costs. *Econometrica, 60*(3), 651–666.

Boulding, W., Kalra, A., Staelin, R., & Zeithaml, V. A. (1993). A dynamic process model of service quality: From expectations to behavioral intentions. *Journal of Marketing Research, 30,* 7–27.

Bresnahan, T. (2001, November). The economics of the Microsoft case. Paper presented at the *MIT Industrial Organization Workshop*, Cambridge, MA.

Brynjolfsson, E., & Smith, M. (2000). *The great equalizer? Consumer choice behavior at Internet shopbots.* (Working paper). Cambridge, MA: MIT-Sloan.

Churchill, G. A. Jr. (1979). A paradigm for developing better measures of marketing constructs. *Journal of Marketing Research, 16,* 64–73.

Cingil, I., Dogac, A., & Azgin, A. (2000). A broader approach to personalization. *Communications of the ACM, 43*(8), 136–141.

Crosby, L. A., & Nancy, J. S. (1987). Effects of relationship marketing on satisfaction, retention, and prices in the insurance industry. *Journal of Marketing Research, 24,* 404–411.

Del Giudice, M., & Del Giudice, F. (2003). Locking-in the customer: How to manage switching costs to stimulate e-loyalty and reduce churn rate. In S. K. Sharma & J. Gupta (Eds.), *Managing e-business of the 21st century.* Heidelberg: Heidelberg Press.

Elzinga, K. G., & Mills, D. E. (1998). Switching costs in the wholesale distribution of cigarettes. *Southern Economic Journal, 65*(2), 282–293.

Farrell, J., & Shapiro, C. (1998). Dynamic competition with switching costs. *Rand Journal of Economics, 19*(1), 123–137.

Friedman, T. L. (1999, February 26). Amazon.you. *New York Times*, p. A21.

Gans, N., & Zhou, Y. (2000). *Customer loyalty and supplier strategies for quality competition: I and II.* (Working paper). Philadelphia: The Wharton School, University of Pennsylvania.

Gerbing, D. W., & Anderson, J. C. (1988). An updated paradigm for scale development incorporating unidimensionality and its assessment. *Journal of Marketing Research, 25*, 186–192.

Guadagni, P. M., & Little, J. (1983). A logit model of brand choice calibrated on scanner data. *Marketing Science,* (2), 203–238.

Henderson, P. W., & Cote, J. A. (1998). Guidelines for selecting and modifying logos. *Journal of Marketing, 62*, 14–30.

Hirschman, A. O. (1970). *Exit, voice, and loyalty: Responses to decline in firms, organizations, and states*. Cambridge, MA: Harvard University Press.

Johnson, E. J., Moe, W., Peter, S. F., Bellman, S., & Lohse, J. (2000). *On the depth and dynamics of online search behavior*. (Working paper). Philadelphia: The Wharton School, University of Pennsylvania.

Johnson, M. P. (1982). Social and cognitive features of the dissolution of commitment to relationships. In S. Duck (Ed.), *Personal relationships: Dissolving personal relationships* (pp. 51–74). London: Academic Press.

Jones, T. O., & Sasser, W. E. Jr. (1995). Why satisfied customers defect. *Harvard Business Review, November–December*, 88–99.

Katz, M. L., & Shapiro, C. (1985). Network externalities, competition, and compatibility. *The American Economic Review, 75*(3), 424–440.

Kim, M., Kliger, D., & Vale, B. (2001). *Estimating switching costs and oligopolistic behavior*. (Working paper). Philadelphia: The University of Haifa and the Wharton School, University of Pennsylvania.

Klemperer, P. (1987a). The competitiveness of markets with switching costs. *RAND Journal of Economics, 18*(1), 138–150.

Klemperer, P. (1987b). Markets with consumer switching costs. *Quarterly Journal of Economics, 102*, 375–394.

Klemperer, P. (1995). Competition when consumers have switching costs: An overview with applications to industrial organization, macroeconomics, and international trade. *Review of Economic Studies, 62*, 515–539.

Levinger, G. (1979). Marital cohesiveness at the brink: The fate of applications for divorce. In T. L. Huston (Ed.), *Divorce and separation: Context, causes, and consequences* (pp. 99–120). New York: Academic Press.

Lidsky, D. (1999, October). Getting better all the time: Electronic commerce sites. *PC Magazine*, p. 98.

McFadden, D. (1974a). Conditional logit analysis of qualitative choice behavior. In P. Zarembka (Ed.), *Frontiers in econometrics*. New York: Academic Press.

McFadden, D. (1974b). The measurement of urban travel demand. *Journal of Public Economics,* (3), 303–328.

Mobasher, B., Cooley, R., & Srivastava, J. (2000). Automatic personalization based on Web usage mining. *Communications of the ACM, 43*(8), 142–151.

Moe, W., & Fader, P. S. (2000). *Capturing evolving visit behavior in clickstream data*. (Working paper). Philadelphia: The Wharton School, University of Pennsylvania.

Novak, T. P, Hoffman, D. L., & Yung, Y. F. (2000). Measuring the customer experience in online environments: A structural modeling approach. *Marketing Science*.

Nunnally, J. C., & Bernstein, I. H. (1994). *Psychometric theory* (3rd ed.). New York: McGraw-Hill.

Pearson, M. (1998). Attractors: Building mountains in the flat landscape of the World Wide Web. *Director, 51*(12), 81.

Ping, R. (1993). The effects of satisfaction and structural constraints on retailer exiting, voice, loyalty, opportunism, and neglect. *Journal of Retailing, 69*(3), 320–352.

Polski, M. (1999a). *Le commerce des articles de sport sur Internet étude comparative entre les sites marchands de Décathlon et de Go-Sport.* Paper presented at Le Management du sport et l'Europe les acteurs, entre concurrence et coopération, Troisième Congrès de la Société Française de Management du Sport, University of Lille, Lille, France.

Polski, M. (1999b). *Structure Temporelle des Industries le cas de la distribution.* Unpublished PhD thesis, University of Strasbourg, Strasbourg, France.

Reichheld, F. F., & Schefter, P. (2000). E-loyalty: Your secret weapon on the Web. *Harvard Business Review, 78*(4), 105–113.

Shankar, V., Smith, A. K., & Rangaswamy, A. (2000). *Customer satisfaction and loyalty in online and offline environments*. (Working paper). University Park: Pennsylvania State University.

Shapiro, C., & Varian, H. R. (1998). *Information rules*. Boston: Harvard Business School Press.

Smith, M. D., Bailey, J., & Brynjolfsson, E. (1999). Understanding digital markets: Review and assessment. In E. Brynjolfsson & B. Kahin (Eds.), *Understanding the digital economy*. Cambridge MA: MIT Press.

Stalk, G., & Hout, T. M. (1990). *Competing against time: How time-based competition is reshaping global markets*. New York: The Free Press.

Varian, H. (1999). *Market structure in the network age*. (Working paper). Berkeley, CA: University of California.

Endnotes

1 This is not true for all Web sites, of course. For example some Web sites now use real-time chat to do this. If the customer is having trouble, he/she can click on a chat button and talk to someone for support.

2 A loyalty strategy stemming from a lock-in approach is completely different in online markets as compared to off-line ones (Del Giudice & Del Giudice, 2003). In classical economy the lock-in strategy has been approached as a strategy aiming at "locking in" the customer by making him/her dependent from his/her purchasing routines, rather than rendering him spontaneously loyal on the assumption that switching a product or a supplier the switching cost would be too high. In this approach the locking-in strategy has been closely related to the technical features of the product and only incidentally to customer support services. In a digital economy, instead, the greater space given to customer services on the Web site may turn out to be a sharper tool for cultivating customer loyalty than the tangible features of the product itself.

3 An online retailer can choose to increase the range of tools and services provided by its Web site in order to make easier the shop expedition and to stimulate the lock-in. This strategy may eventually reduce customer price sensitivity by distracting customers from focusing their purchase decisions on price alone (for example, Amazon.com does not have the lowest price [Smith, Bailey, & Brynjolfsson, 1999], but customers still regularly buy from it, which may be due in part to its exhaustive list of carried titles or to the tools and services provided by its Web site). This approach may attract those customers who value and are willing to pay premium prices for services (Grover & Ramanlal, 1999; Lynch & Ariely, 2000) and hence reduce price sensitivity for the segment of customers the retailer intends to attract and keep.

4 Quality service is something that customers typically want and value, providing high-quality service should arguably increase their willingness to come back and do more business with the vendor (Hesket et al., 1994; Reichheld & Sasser, 1990; Reichheld & Schefter, 2000; Watson et al., 1998).

5 They include the extent and likelihood of lost performance benefits and perquisites secured via continued patronage of a given provider (Jones et al., 2002). Examples include frequent flier miles, volume discounts, and special treatment based on previous usage.

6 They include the time and effort expended on information acquisition, exchange, and evaluation (Jones et al., 2002).

7 Sunk costs involve the economically irrelevant but psychologically important investments in the exchange relationship (Jones et al., 2002).

8 The assumption that barriers may enhance the probability of remaining in a social relationship was studied by Lund (1985). She posits that barriers are more important for the upholding of a relationship than positive pull (love of the partner and rewards from the relationship). She defines barriers as

investment in the relationship (measured by items like trying to encourage and support your partner, contributing financially to the relationship), and commitment (measured by items such as how likely one is to pursue another relationship, how likely the partner is perceived to be willing to continue the relationship, and how obligated one feels to continue the relationship). She found that the barrier variables were better predictors of whether a romantic relationship would continue than the positive pull variables.

9 For example Web site's elements allowing a customer "one-click shopping" can be seen as a source of positive perceived switching costs (Del Giudice & Polski, 2003).

10 Such constrained freedom of choice could, according to reactance theory, create lower satisfaction than a more unconstrained situation (Ringold, 1988). Positive switching costs are typically linked to *cognitive lock-in* policies, whereas negative ones have been linked in the literature to *behavioral lock-in* strategies (Del Giudice & Del Giudice, 2003; Del Giudice & Polski, 2003). From the economics literature we would like to add the degree of monopoly on the market, and supplier power, which, when high, may lock the customer to the supplier. Moreover, investment in the supplier by the customer (generally how much time, money, and effort are invested in the relationship) is also considered a negative switching barrier, since it tends to lock the customer to the supplier, especially if the customer has made physical investments in equipment.

11 Fornell also mentions financial, social, and psychological risk. We would put these under the heading of positive switching barriers. These risks should occur in a comparison of what you get from the current supplier and the probability that you will get the same utility from other suppliers. Thus, if one perceives high risks in a change of supplier, this is here classified as a positive switching barrier.

12 Our research has been inspired by Jones et al. (2002). That work was particularly focused on the underlying dimensions of services switching cost. Following their suggestions at the end of the paper, we conducted a similar analysis but focusing on a different industry (IT), on a different channel (Internet), and at a different level of the supply chain (B2B).

13 The cookie costs refer to the perception of the benefits involved in customer's purchase pattern (cookie) which will be lost on switching. The cookie is a file on a hard disk that records the identification number of the customer as well as other information useful to the Web server. If the server of the supplier does not find the customer's cookies on the customer entering the site, it will ship him/her another cookie not recognising him/her. Differently, if it recognises the customer's cookies, then he/she will have

much more information about him/her.[14] The cookies can have some disadvantages (such as multiple browser incompatibility, false identification of the customers, easy removal from hardware). For this reason many e-businesses use online registration and store all the information in a database.

14 Interface tools costs are strictly linked to cookie costs. They refer to the likelihood of lower site performance when switching: in one word, all the filtering tools that should help a Web surfer recognise the Web site are powerful business tools. The fast availability of information and the death of distances combine to minimise the browsing time of the consumer and to render its repurchase decision easier and more convenient. There are various tools that can improve customer satisfaction on the Web and are at the same time likely to raise switching costs. An example is provided by visual guides, answerbots, digital automatons, and videochat. The choice to repurchase is, however, often spurred by powerful filtering tools making the search for the product or service easier.

15 Web searching costs refer to the perception of the time and efforts necessary to gather and evaluate information prior to switching.

16 Interface learning costs which are typically postswitching behavioral and cognitive costs. They refer to the perception of the time and efforts necessary to learn a new Web site interface and a new surfing routine subsequent to switching.

17 They are costs connected to setting up a new profile (profile setup costs) with an e-business. They correspond to the classic market switching costs of filling in forms when changing banks, getting new X-rays when changing dentists, paying membership fees when changing gyms, and explaining a desired hairstyle when changing barbers (Jones et al., 2002). Profile setup costs, even if similar to, are different from cookie costs: in fact, they are related to the starting of a new business relationship, when the customer having switched a supplier is involved in *explaining*, to the new supplier, who he/she is and what he/she needs or wants (i.e., he/she has to transfer the *knowledge of old routines* to the new relationship); whereas cookie costs concern the perceptions of the benefits lost by switching and the efforts *to "build" them again* in new purchase routines (with the new supplier).

18 Sunk costs are the economically irrelevant but psychologically important investments in a business relationship (Guiltinan, 1998). Particularly, they refer to customer perception of the unrecoverable time, money, and efforts previously invested in establishing and keeping a business relationship alive (Jones et al., 2002).

[19] The exploratory factor analysis was performed on all six dimensions of the scale together by using SPSS 11.0. All the scale items were measured on a 5-point Likert scale (from "strongly disagree" to "strongly agree").

[20] In a pioneering study, Polski (2000) showed young sport athletes were reluctant to buy sporting goods online because of the risk of making a mistake because of a lack of information about goods and the annoyance of returning not suitable items by parcel. The Internet was the obstacle, but not the brand image of the retailer, because even trusted brick-and-mortar merchants were mistrusted online. The considered options were 1 and 3 only for retailers. The unexpected result was the following: respondents asked for an "option 5" in the open question, specifying they would rather trust a sporting manufacturer selling products directly at a lower price or exclusive limited series unavailable in stores. In order not to compete inside their traditional distribution channel, Nike used this strategy. Reversely, more and more pure players extend their marketing and communication strategy in the natural environment through traditional media or with alliances and partnerships with brick-and-mortar companies. In the coming years, the digital and natural environments will be part of strategies of almost all companies. Thus, studying the Internet specificities of loyalty is not enough to have a global outlook about possible interactions in case of choices of multiple brands across multiple channels.

Appendix

Table A. Exploratory factor analysis

Exploratory Factor Analysis						
Scale/items	F1	F2	F3	F4	F5	F6
Cookie costs (? ʒ						
(1) This IT online supplier provides me particular privileges I would not receive elsewhere.	0.92					
(2) By continuing to use the same IT online supplier, I receive certain benefits that I would not receive if I switched to a new one.	0.91					
(3) There are certain benefits I would not retain if I were to switch IT online supplier.	0.94					
(4) I would lose preferential treatment if I changed IT online supplier.	0.89					
(5) If I changed my current IT online supplier, it would take a great deal of time and effort to "reproduce" the benefits and privileges of my old purchase routines.	0.87					
(6) If I changed my current IT online supplier, it would take a lot of time to explain the benefits I used to have to the new one.	0.89					
Interface tools costs (=0.83)						
(1) I am not sure what the level of online customer service would be if I switched to a new IT online supplier.		0.75				
(2) If I were to change IT online supplier, the interface tools I might find on a new one's Web site could be worse than the one I have at my current supplier's Web site.		0.81				
(3) The online customer service from another IT supplier could be worse than the customer service I am now experiencing.		0.87				
(4) If I changed my current IT online supplier, I might experience a worse shopping way at a new one's Web site.		0.85				
(5) My current IT online supplier's Web site provides me interface tools I would not find elsewhere on the Internet.						
Web searching costs (=0.86)						
(1) If I changed an IT online supplier, it would take a lot of time to locate a new one			0.84			
(2) If I changed an IT online supplier, I would not have to search very much to find a new one			0.91			
(3) It takes a great deal of time and effort to locate a new IT supplier on the Internet.*			0.89			
(4) If I stopped using my current IT online supplier, I would have to crawl on the Internet for a new one to use.			0.88			
Interface learning costs (=0.85)						
(1) If I were to switch IT online supplier, I would have to learn how things work at a new one's Web site.				0.79		
(2) I would be unfamiliar with the Web site of a new IT online supplier.				0.89		
(3) If I changed IT online supplier, I would have to learn how the "system works" at a new one.				0.92		
(4) Changing IT online supplier would mean I would have learned about the Web site of a new one.				0.86		
Profile setup costs (=0.95)						
(1) If I changed IT online supplier, it would take a great deal of time to set up a new profile.					0.95	
(2) If I changed IT online supplier, it would not take a lot of time to set up a new profile.*					0.92	
(3) If I changed my current IT supplier on the Internet it would take a lot of time to explain who I am and what I need to the new one.					0.87	
(4) If I changed IT online supplier, I would have to explain many things to my new supplier.					0.92	
(5) There is much time and effort involved when you start using a new IT online supplier.					0.89	
Sunk costs (=0.83)						
(1) A lot of energy, time, and effort have gone into building and maintaining the relationship with my current IT online supplier.						0.72
(2) Overall, I have invested a lot in the relationship with my current IT online supplier.						0.83

Table B. Confirmatory factor analysis

Phi estimates

Construct	1	2	3	4	5	6	7	8	9
Cookie costs (1)	1.00								
Interface tools costs (2)	0.42	1.00							
Web searching costs (3)	0.41	0.44	1.00						
Interface learning costs (4)	0.49	0.56	0.53	1.00					
Profile setup costs (5)	0.55	0.63	0.79	0.84	1.00				
Sunk costs (6)	0.47	0.21	0.34	0.33	0.38	1.00			
Repurchase intentions (7)	0.57	0.32	0.25	0.44	0.39	0.21	1.00		
Perceived Web site quality (8)	0.59	0.63	0.19	0.52	0.27	0.29	0.32	1.00	
Willingness to pay more (9)	0.69	0.67	0.49	0.59	0.55	0.45	0.61	0.67	1.00
Mean	4.52	4.87	4.25	4.12	4.57	4.69	6.82	6.89	4.93
Standard deviation	1.34	1.62	1.83	1.25	1.49	1.94	1.36	1.85	1.27
Composite reliability	0.92	0.82	0.89	0.91	0.84	0.85	0.97	0.92	0.85
Variance extracted	0.65	0.62	0.68	0.59	0.70	0.68	0.95	0.89	0.82

Table C. Implications for managers (Del Giudice & Del Giudice, 2003)

CATEGORIES	E-SWITCHING COSTS	SUGGESTIONS TO MANAGERS
Continuity costs		
	Cookie costs	Employing tools (e.g., cookies, log files, restricted access pages) speeding up customer's shop expedition (considering customer's status and his/her purchase conditions)
	Interface tools costs	Devising tools easing up shop expedition on the Internet (as concerns selection of the products to purchase) and making purchase more satisfactory
Learning costs		
	Web searching costs	Increasing "Web presence perception" by promoting the company Web site through promotional banners, promotion in search engines, online co-branding, listing in what's new Web pages?, and so forth
	Interface learning costs	Facilitating interface surfing, Web site visiting, focusing on Web site consistency, simplicity, and contextualisation
	Profile setup costs	Designing essential profiling forms, allowing collaborative filtering and outlining a comprehensive customer's profile
Sunk costs		
	Psychological costs	Planning lock in strategies carefully so that, in case of switching, the customer feels uneasy about giving up benefits rising from regularly purchasing through his/her usual supplier's Web site

Chapter XIV

Comparative Analysis of International Approaches to the Protection of Online Privacy

Peter O'Connor, Essec Business School, France

Abstract

The Web provides unprecedented opportunities for Web site operators to implicitly and explicitly gather highly detailed personal data about site visitors, resulting in a real and pressing threat to privacy. Approaches to protecting such personal data differ greatly throughout the world. To generalize greatly, most countries follow one of two diametrically opposed philosophies—the self-regulation approach epitomized by the United States, or the comprehensive omnibus legislative approach mandated by the European Union. In practice, of course, the situation is not so black and white as most countries utilize elements of both approaches. This chapter explains the background and importance of protecting the privacy of personal data, contrasts the two major philosophical approaches to protection mentioned above, performs a comparative analysis of the current situation throughout the world, and highlights how the legislative approach is being adopted as the de facto standard throughout the world. The use of trust marks as an alternative to the self-regulation or legislative approach is also discussed, while the effectiveness of each of these efforts is also examined.

Introduction

One of the major advantages of using the Web as an e-commerce medium is its ability to tailor sales and marketing messages to the individual online consumer. To facilitate this process, many Web sites encourage users to register, define preferences, and then subsequently add value by providing content specifically tailored to these interests (Metz, 2001). Some sites go further by tracking user actions—how often they visit, what pages they view, what products they buy—and using this "click-stream" data to refine profiles based on actual behavior rather than stated preferences (Weber, 2000). According to Internet & American Life (2000), nearly 75% of users find it useful when Web sites remember basic information about them and use it to provide better service.

However, from the consumer perspective, such personalized service comes at a price—"the death of privacy" (Weber, 2000). As Andy Grove (1998), chairman of Intel, points out,

> *At the heart of the Internet culture is a force that wants to find out everything about you. And once it has found out everything about you and two hundred million others, that's a very valuable asset, and people will be tempted to trade and do commerce with that asset. (p. 2)*

Completing a retail transaction on the Web requires that certain personal data (for example, name, address, and billing information) be divulged. Problems arise when these data are used for purposes subsequent to the transaction for which they were collected—a process known as the secondary use of data (Hoffman et al., 1999). Such secondary uses can be internal, such as placing the consumer on the company's mailing list and subsequently marketing additional products or services to them, or external, such as the sale, lease, or other transfer of data to third parties. In the physical world, secondary use is generally limited to inferring broad characteristics about groups of consumers (such as geography or demographics) and drawing generalizations across such groups. However, with secondary data captured online, marketers can more easily take advantage of individual specific data, linking transactions to an identifiable person and subsequently individually customizing sales and marketing messages, often without his/her permission or even his/her awareness (Hoffman et al., 1999). As a result, as consumers increasingly use the Web for commercial purposes, they are becoming more concerned about who will have access to personal data once a transaction is completed and what use will subsequently be made of such data (Lourosa-Ricardo, 2001). A recent Forrester Research survey found that worries over privacy inhibit nearly 100 million people from shopping online (Gilbert, 2001). Similarly, Ryker et al. (2002) quote a PricewaterhouseCoopers study indicating that 92% of consumers who regularly use the Web are worried about online privacy, with 61% concerned enough to refuse to shop online.

A variety of different approaches to protecting online privacy have developed. Some Web sites try to reassure potential customers by publishing privacy policies—statements outlining what the site owners propose to do (or more importantly, not do) with personal data. Others have gone further and had their privacy policies "certified" by a third party in an effort to add credibility and build trust (Gilbert, 2001). Various industry bodies (e.g., Online Privacy Alliance, the Electronic Privacy Information Center) and third-party trust mark providers (e.g., TRUSTe, Better Business Bureau) have proposed sets of voluntary standards designed to reassure consumers as to a company's behavior with personal data (Grabner-Kraeuter, 2002). Governments have also acted to address the issue, although as will be discussed, philosophies as to how best to address the problem differ greatly. This chapter examines the background to protecting privacy in a wired world, compares the different approaches being used to address the issue, discusses the requirements of each approach (be it legislative, voluntary, or certification based), and highlights how despite differences in philosophy, alternative approaches are ultimately having the same result—a higher level of protection for personal data.

Background

Today's technology provides unprecedented opportunities for Web sites to monitor the actions of their visitors and to use such data to personalize the content presented in subsequent interactions. For the consumer, this reduces clutter, resulting in content more closely matched to their personal needs, wants, and interests (Krishnamurthy, 2001), while for sellers it facilitates a one-to-one marketing approach, allowing them to target their most valuable prospects, reducing dependence on wasteful mass marketing by tailoring their offering to individual needs, thus improving customer satisfaction and retention, all at a relatively low cost. Although such personalization brings benefits to both parties, its use comes at a price—a significant threat to personal privacy.

Because of its very nature, the Web presents opportunities to gather and disseminate detailed personal, demographic, and behavioral consumer data on a scale unprecedented in the past (Opplinger, 2000). The ability to observe and record browsing habits can reveal individual viewing behavior, shopping habits, and spending patterns as well as other data that people have traditionally considered to be personal and private. In the paper-and-ink world, the sheer effort of collecting, archiving, and analyzing such data protected privacy to a certain extent (Blanchette & Johnson, 2002). However, the use of technology-based systems not only changes the quantity, granularity, and quality of what can be collected, but it also allows it to be analyzed and cross-correlated in increasingly sophisticated ways. Efficient and cost-effective data-mining techniques and data-warehousing technology allow marketers to analyze the growing data pool, combine seemingly disparate morsels of information into fully integrated profiles, and ultimately understand their customers better (Rust, Kannan, & Peng, 2002). "It is this ability to connect, with electronic ease, dozens to literally thousands of isolated bits and pieces of information about an individual human being that is dramatically changing the rules and raising the stakes of privacy protection in modern society" (Jennings & Fena, 2000, p. 1). Technology has fundamentally altered the relationship between customers and merchants, potentially tipping the balance in favor of the latter's interests versus those of the former (Kelly, 2000).

In particular, the power of the Web to obtain, organize, and facilitate distribution of personal information is extraordinary (Valentine, 2000). Each and every site visit generates click-stream data, which can identify where the user came from and departs to, what was looked at and for how long, even the user's e-mail address—all collected automatically, invisibly, and often without the user's knowledge or permission (Kelly, 2000). Consolidating this data with what is voluntarily provided, such as names, credit card numbers, addresses, and demographic information, makes the resulting database a valuable marketing resource (Carroll, 2002). Furthermore, such monitoring tools, because they are automated, have greatly diminished the economic constraints on surveillance, meaning that more individuals and larger populations can be monitored for practically no additional cost (Ryker et al., 2002). Thus, the Internet is facilitating closer and more in-depth monitoring of personal data.

Proponents argue that marketers have been gathering such data manually for many years, that the Internet is simply an expansion of such efforts and that collecting these data allows companies to provide consumers with information and incentives that they are likely to use—an approach many customers like

(Grover et al., 1998). Indeed, consumers often willingly provide Web sites with highly detailed personal data for such purposes—for example, when supplying information to facilitate the aforementioned customization. Problems arise, however, when these data are used for "secondary" purposes (Hoffman et al., 1999). As information privacy is defined as "people's ability to control the terms under which their personal information is acquired and used" (Westin, 1967, p. 13), when data voluntarily entered into a Web site for one purpose are subsequently used for other purposes—either internally for marketing or externally as a result of selling/sharing data with third parties—without the knowledge or consent of the consumer, privacy clearly is compromised.

A variety of different studies have shown that consumers are concerned about lack of privacy on the Web. There is a growing belief among consumers that they have lost control over how their personal information is being used (Rust et al., 2002). In addition to the studies cited earlier, the Electronic Privacy Information Center (EPIC, 2000) found that 81% of consumers are worried about privacy invasion online. In his 2001 analysis, Krishnamurthy (2001) notes that privacy concerns negatively affect consumer interest and participation in permission marketing programs. Similarly, an October 2000 Harris Interactive survey found that more online Americans are concerned about loss of personal privacy than health care, crime, or taxes (Head & Yuam, 2001). A recent *PC World* survey identified fears over misuse of personal data as being the biggest challenge facing online retailers today (Kandra & Brandt, 2003), and nearly 90% of respondents to an EPIC survey felt that privacy was the most pressing concern affecting shopping online, rating it more important than prices and return policies (EPIC Alert, 2000).

This high level of distrust also has other effects. For example, studies have shown that consumers often react to these privacy fears by restricting the information they make available about themselves by declining to provide the data requested by a Web site (Nunes & Kambil, 2001), or even by providing false information (Georgia Tech Research Corporation, 1997). Nearly one in five online consumer maintains a secondary e-mail address to avoid giving a Web site real information (Phelps et al., 2001) and many surfers simply use the low-tech strategy of going elsewhere when required to provide personal information to proceed (EPIC Alert, 2000). Thus privacy fears may not only be limiting the growth of electronic commerce, but may also be affecting the validity and completeness of marketing databases, leading to inaccurate targeting, wasted effort, and frustrated consumers.

However, research has also shown that consumers do realize that surrendering personal data can be beneficial. Many realize that providing suppliers with detailed, accurate information is in their own self-interest as it will result in higher quality, more relevant messages and less clutter, and thus are open to providing such information in certain circumstances (Godin, 1999). For example, a Jupiter

Research survey found that 65% of respondents would be more inclined to provide personal information online if they had a guarantee that it would not subsequently be misused (Hinde, 1998), while other studies have shown that consumers would more readily cooperate if they had the right to force companies to delete personal information at a later date (Gilbert, 2001). In short, the issue comes down to one of trust. This is achieved when companies inform users in advance about how their personal data will be treated, and subsequently behave in a manner consistent with these disclosures (Culnan & Armstrong, 1999). Many analysts see this battle for trust as one of the prime barriers to the continued growth of e-commerce, and forecast that its impact is likely to increase as less technically sophisticated consumers come online and are less able to sort out valid threats from media hype and misinformation (Grabner-Kraeuter, 2002).

Approaches to Online Privacy Protection

Theoretical frameworks for understanding the concept of privacy are presented elsewhere (see for example Head & Yuan, 2001). In practical terms, such frameworks are generally implemented in the form of *fair information practices*—global principles that attempt to balance the privacy interests of individuals with the legitimate need of businesses to derive value from customer data (Culnan, 2000). Originally developed by the Organisation for Economic Co-operation and Development (OECD) in consultation with government organizations, academics, and privacy advocates, the guidelines focus on five core principles: *notice/awareness* implies that companies must disclose information practices before collecting data from consumers, must advise as to what information will be collected and how it will be used; *choice/consent* means that consumers must be given options as to whether and how the information is used for purposes beyond those for which it was originally provided; *access/participation* implies that consumers should be able to view and contest the accuracy and completeness of data, or delete that data if they so choose; *security/integrity* implies that companies must take reasonable steps to ensure that personal data are secure during transition and storage, and are protected from unauthorized use; *enforcement/redress* implies that facilities must be provided to resolve complaints about policy transgressions (for a comprehensive discussion of these guidelines, see Culnan, 2000). These voluntary guidelines are generally implemented to varying degrees by companies through their privacy policy—a statement that describes the personal information collected and how that information is used (Metz, 2001).

Although most people are in agreement as to the principle and importance of privacy protection (Bennett, 1992, p. 95) and to the validity of the fair information principles, philosophies vary greatly as to how best to implement these guidelines. Diametrically opposed viewpoints can be observed in Europe and the United States, where legislative protection and self-regulation, respectively, are (theoretically at least) the guiding principles. These approaches are contrasted below, and actual practice in the rest of the world is then discussed.

The European Approach: Legislative Protection for Personal Data

Within the European Union, privacy is considered to be a fundamental civil right that is too important to be left to chance (Zwick & Dholakia, 2001). Indeed, some European countries have had data protection legislation for nearly three decades (Hinde, 1999). For example, the first laws protecting personal information from unwarranted access were enacted in Sweden and Germany in the early 1970s (Mayer-Schonberger, 1998).

More recently, the European Community has introduced comprehensive and mandatory omnibus legislation regulating the processing of each and every piece of personal data. The European Union Directive on the Protection of Personal Data (1995) places severe restrictions on how personal data can be used (Mayer-Schonberger, 1998). In particular, it requires that personal data must be "processed fairly and lawfully" and "only collected for a specified, explicit and legitimate purpose"; that further processing incompatible with the original purpose is not permitted; that data must be kept "accurate and up to date"; that processing can only take place if the person to whom the personal data refers "has unambiguously given his consent"; and the data subject must also be given access to his/her personal data upon request and within a specific time frame, as well as the name of the processor, the purpose for which the data are being collected and details of all recipients of the data (European Community, 1995).

There are also prohibitions on the processing of data relating to racial origin, physical or mental health, religious belief, political opinion, trade union membership, criminal offences or sexual activity, unless with the explicit permission of the individual (Hinde, 1999). The Directive also compels organizations to take appropriate security measures to prevent unauthorized or accidental access to, alteration, disclosure, loss, or destruction of data, and gives individuals the right to have inaccurate data corrected or erased, as well as the right to prohibit the use of their personal information for marketing purposes. What are considered personal data are defined very broadly as "any information relating to an individual or identifiable natural person" (European Community, 1995).

Considered as a whole, these requirements both encompass and expand the fair information practice guidelines by placing severe restrictions both on what personal data can be collected and how it can be processed. And while one could claim that these requirements do not apply to data processed on computers outside European Union countries, the Directive preempts such an argument by stipulating that personal data collected within the European Union can only be exported if the recipient country has similar levels of data protection (Lee Larson, Larson, & Greenlee, 2003). In giving the requirements of the Directive global reach, this clause has proved particularly problematic with regard to the United States, where, as will be discussed below, privacy protection is based around a right to privacy rather than any specific piece of data protection legislation (Camp, 1999).

The American Approach: Self-Regulation

In contrast to the European approach, in the United States the protection of personal data is based on a constitutional right to privacy, rather than on any specific data protection legislation. While the latter offers blanket guidelines for all data with an identifiable subject, the U.S. approach views each subject area as separate and requires each one to be addressed independently (Camp, 1999). Thus, a patchwork of federal and state laws has developed which regulate privacy in certain circumstances (such as credit records, driver's license information, family and educational privacy, telephone records, and video rental records) (Turinas & Showalter, 2002). However, these have been developed in an ad hoc piecemeal fashion usually in response to public outcry over topical events (Cain, 2002).

In general, the overriding philosophy in the United States has been to resist the introduction of comprehensive legislative protection in anticipation that the market will self-regulate through adherence to voluntary codes. This approach was enshrined in the Clinton administration's *Framework for Global Electronic Commerce* (Blanchette & Johnson, 2002). "The Administration considers data protection critically important. We believe that private efforts of industry working in cooperation with consumer groups are preferable to government regulation..." (Clinton & Gore, 1997). As a result, within the United States there is no comprehensive set of laws or regulations (at either the federal or state level) that address the collection, storage, use, or sale of personal information by the private sector (Finkel & McCrady, 2000).

The self-regulation approach entails the setting of standards by an industry group and the voluntary adherence to such standards by those within the sector (Zwick & Dholakia, 2001). For example, U.S. companies are encouraged (but not legally obliged) to comply with guidelines such as those drafted by the Federal Trade

Commission (FTC), the U.S. government's primary consumer protection organization, which are in turn based on the OECD fair information principles discussed earlier, and to post appropriate privacy policies on their Web sites (Metz, 2001). Enforcement is based on contract law where if a company does not comply with the promises and guarantees made in its privacy policy, it can be sued by either the consumer directly or by a consumer group or government agency acting on his/her behalf. The FTC has been particularly active in taking legal action against companies whose practices are at variance with their published privacy policies for engaging in deceptive trade practices (Culnan, 2000).

Strong arguments can be made for letting market forces take care of data protection. As discussed above, research has shown that people are sometimes willing to disclose personal information in exchange for some economic or social benefit subject to their own "privacy calculus"—a personal assessment of whether their information will subsequently be used fairly and whether they will suffer negative consequences in the future (Milne & Gordon, 1993). As a result, it is argued that ethical norms will emerge naturally as the market evolves, with consumers only doing business with sites they trust (Culnan & Bies, 1999). Proponents argue that consumers will migrate toward sites that provide strong privacy protection and will avoid sites that have breached privacy, thus eventually forcing all companies to provide greater protection, or at least the kind of protection that consumers want, in order to stay in business (Rust et al., 2002).

Unfortunately research has shown that this is not happening in practice and that the self-regulation approach has to a large extent failed (FTC Report, 2000). Since Web sites are not legally required to display a privacy policy, many choose not to, making it impossible to prosecute them for deceptive business practices. Even where privacy policies are displayed, the majority are limited in that they fail to address many key issues. In a study of major U.S. consumer Web sites, over 90% failed to comply with one or more of the suggested guidelines, indicating that stronger measures may be necessary to ensure adequate levels of protection (Ryker et al., 2002).

Last, since there are no commonly agreed-upon standards or legal requirements to have one in the first place, privacy policies can be abandoned or changed at will, without notification to the customer (Cain, 2002). As evidence mounts of more and more companies abusing their power to collect consumer information, the belief is growing that the desire to make profits inherently contradicts consumers' privacy interest (Zwick & Dholakia, 2001). As a result, industry watchdogs claim that comprehensive privacy legislation should be introduced to protect the privacy of consumers online (Hinde, 1999). Even the FTC, reacting to a glaring case of privacy policy violation by Geocities in May 2000, moderated its heretofore unfettered support for self-regulation and recommended that Congress enact legislation to protect the public's private data on the Internet.

The requirements of the European Directive on the Protection of Personal Data discussed earlier have also increased the pressure on the U.S. government to introduce legislation (Blanchette & Johnson, 2002). In particular, the stipulation that personal data can only be exported from the European Union if the recipient country has similar levels of legislative protection (unless individuals expressly consent to the transfer) leads theoretically to a situation where data cannot be transferred from European-based companies to divisions or parent companies in the United States (Hinde, 1998). To overcome this, in summer of 2000 the U.S. Department of Commerce and the European Commission formulated the Safe Harbor Agreement. While not emulating the European Union rules, the agreement establishes a "mechanism which, though an exchange of documents, enables the EU to certify that participating US companies meet the EU requirements for privacy protection" (Lee Larson et al., 2003, p. 38).

In short, the agreement states that consumers must be notified about the purposes for which the company collects and uses data and must be given the opportunity to choose whether and how the data are used by or disclosed to third parties. Third parties that receive personal information must provide the same level of protection as that provided by the collecting company. In addition, companies must protect data from loss, misuse, unauthorized access, disclosure, alteration, or destruction; must ensure that data are reliable for their intended use, are accurate, complete, and current; and must give individuals the right to view, correct, amend, or delete personal data. Last, firms need to provide mechanisms for ensuring compliance with these privacy principles and the company's privacy policy. U.S. organizations that decide to participate in the Safe Harbor Agreement must both comply with its requirements and publicly declare that they do so by registering with the U.S. Department of Commerce (Zwick & Dholakia, 2001). As of October 2003, over 250 organizations had completed this registration process.

Approaches to Privacy Protection in Other Regions

The two conflicting approaches discussed above—the self-regulation philosophy embraced by the United States and the legislative approach used by the European Union—have to a large extent become the norms throughout the world. Table 1 summarizes the findings of the 2003 report on Privacy & Human Rights, produced by EPIC and Privacy International in respect of non-European countries.

As can be seen from Table 1, approaches to privacy protection differ greatly throughout the world. In many countries there is a constitutional right to privacy that also provides basic safeguards with regard to the protection of personal data. Other countries also specifically guarantee the privacy of such data with a separate clause in their constitution. However, in the majority of cases this constitutional protection has been supplemented by comprehensive data protection legislation. In particular, analysis of the data shows how many countries have recently adopted comprehensive data protection legislation in order to comply with the requirements of the aforementioned European Union Directive on the Protection of Personal Data. While for certain countries (Poland, Latvia, Lithuania, Romania, Slovenia, and the Slovak Republic) the introduction of such legislation was a prerequisite for consideration for entry into the European Union,

Table 1. Findings of the 2003 report on Privacy & Human Rights

Country	Explicit Constitutional Right to Privacy	Explicit Constitutional Right to Data Protection	Base Legislation Governing Data Protection	Compliance with requirements of European Union Directive on Protection of Personal Data
Argentina	Article 43	No	Law for Protection of Personal Data 2000	Yes
Australia	No	No	Privacy Act 1988 as amended by the Privacy Amendment (Private Sector) Act 2000	Pending
Brazil	Article 5	Article 5	Consumer Protection Law 1990	No
Bulgaria	Article 32	No	Personal Data Protection Act 2001	Yes
Canada	No	No	Personal Information Protection and Electronic Documents Act (PIPEDA) 2001	Yes
Chile	Article 19	No	Law for the Protection of Private Life 1999	No
China	Article 38	No	None	No
Colombia	Article 15	No	None (various bills pending)	No
Czech Republic	No	No	On Personal Data Protection 2000	Yes
Estonia	Article 43	Article 44(3)	Personal Data Protection Act 1996, Databases Act 1997 as amended 2002	Yes
Hong Kong	Article 29	No	Personal Data (Privacy) Ordinance 1996	Pending
Hungary	Article 59	No	Protection of Personal Data and Disclosure of Data of Public Interest 1992	Yes
India	No	No	No (various bills pending)	No
Israel	Section 7	No	Protection of Privacy Law 5741-1981 as amended 1996	No
Japan	Articles 21 and 35	No	Personal Data Protection Act 2003	No
Jordan	Articles 10 and 18	No	None (announced intension to comply with EU Directive)	No
Latvia	Article 96	No	Law on Personal Data Protection 2000	Yes
Lithuania	Article 22	No	Law on Legal Protection of Personal Data 1996, 1998, 2000, 2002	Yes

Table 1. (cont.)

Country	Explicit Constitutional Right to Privacy	Explicit Constitutional Right to Data Protection	Base Legislation Governing Data Protection	Compliance with requirements of European Union Directive on Protection of Personal Data
Malaysia	No	No	None (various bills pending)	No
Malta	Article 38	No	Data Protection Act 2001	Yes
Mexico	Article 16	No	Mexican E-Commerce Act	No
New Zealand	Article 21	No	Privacy Act 1993	(Pending)
Peru	Article 2	Article 2	None (various bills pending)	No
Philippines	Articles 1, 2, and 3	No	None (various bills pending)	No
Poland	Article 47	Article 51	Protection of Personal Data Act 1997	Yes
Romania	Articles 26 and 27	No	Processing of Personal Data and the Protection of Privacy in the Telecommunications Sector 2001	Yes
Russian Federation	Article 23	Article 24	None (various bills pending)	No
Singapore	No	No	None	No
Slovak Republic	Article 16	Article 19	Protection of Personal Data 2001	Pending
Slovenia	Article 36	No	Personal Data Protection Act 1999, 2001	Yes
South Africa	Article 14	Article 32	None	No
South Korea	Articles 16, 17, and 18	No	None	No
Switzerland	Article 13	Article 13	Federal Act of Data Protection 1992	Yes
Taiwan	Articles 12, 13, and 14	No	Computer-Processed Personal Data Protection Law 1995	No
Thailand	Article 34	Article 58	None (various bills pending)	No
Turkey	Articles 20 and 22	No	None	No
Ukraine	Article 31	Article 32	None (various bills pending)	No

in other regions (e.g., Cananda, New Zealand, Malaysia, and India) legislation has recently been introduced or is currently being debated specifically so that the legislative framework provides sufficient safeguards to allow personal data to be transferred from the European Union (Long & Quek, 2002).

A small minority of countries offer little privacy protection. Protection is particularly limited in Arab countries, where the concept is viewed as one of family rather than one of individuality (EPIC, 2003). Certain countries, for example, Japan and South Korea, have made a deliberate decision to resist the introduction of comprehensive data protection legislation, preferring instead to follow the U.S. example of self-regulation of the private sector. Last, in some regions (e.g., Russia, South Africa), recent political changes have resulted in a situation where although the desire has been expressed to provide European Union-style protection for personal data, more pressing economic and political changes have taken precedence and data protection legislation is still in early draft stages and is unlikely to be enacted in the near future.

An Alternative Approach: The Use of Trust Marks

Somewhere in between the two approaches discussed above lies another possibility—the certification that a company's behavior with personal data is ethical by an independent third party. Known as "trust marks" or "privacy seals," these programs encourage companies to follow privacy principles by providing specific guidelines for privacy protection to ensure that certain minimal standards are met, compelling companies to undergo a compliance review to establish conformity of their practices to the requirements of the scheme, requiring approved companies to submit to periodic re-verification and to commit to a dispute resolution mechanism. Companies that comply with these requirements are awarded a branded "seal" for display on their Web site (Endeshaw, 2001).

Such trust marks have been shown to be quite effective at reassuring the customer as to the ethical behavior of the sites on which they are included (Grabner-Kraeuter, 2002). For example, a study by Miyazaki and Krishnamurthy (2002) provides evidence that displaying such a seal of approval of this type positively influences consumers' perceptions toward a Web site's privacy policy and may encourage them to surrender their personal information. There are several third-party certification programs currently available. The two most popular are TRUSTe and BBBOnLine, with nearly 2,000 and over 700 certified sites, respectively, at the time of writing. Other alternatives include having a company's information management practices audited by companies such as PricewaterhouseCoopers with its PWC Privacy program, or the WebTrust program administered by the American Institute of Certified Public Accountants (AICPA) and the Canadian Institute of Chartered Accountants (CICA) (Ragothaman, Davies, & DeVee, 2000).

Each of these schemes award privacy seals to companies that post comprehensive privacy policies and are willing to comply with oversight and consumer resolution procedures. Although the requirements of each scheme vary, in general they conform to the fair information principles discussed earlier. For example, TRUSTe requires licensees to disclose what personal information is being collected; how the information will be used; the choices available to users regarding collection, use, and distribution of their information; the security procedures being used to protect their data from loss, misuse, or alteration; and how users can update or correct inaccuracies (Miyazaki & Krishnamurthy, 2002). For a useful analysis and comparison of the detailed requirements of each scheme, see Jamal, Maier, and Sunder (2002).

However, the use of trust marks as a way of supplementing self-regulation and as an alternative to legislative protection faces a variety of challenges. First, not all Web sites belong to such programs (the FTC study cited earlier found that only

8% of sites were participants in such programs) and thus they provide only limited protection for consumer privacy (Kelly, 2000). Second, there is confusion about privacy seals and what they mean. Lee Larson, Larson, and Greenlee (2003) point out that while the Better Business Bureau's Online Reliability Program might sound like a privacy seal, it is in fact designed to help consumers find reputable businesses online and has little to do with privacy protection. However, most worrying is the lack of punishment when companies violate the terms of their seals. Trust marks as a concept can only succeed if they remain credible in the mind of the consumer. To achieve this, certifying organizations must be strict about upholding their standards. Unfortunately this does not appear to have been the case. In recent years, there have been a number of cases of high-profile companies (including Microsoft, RealAudio, Yahoo!, Chase Manhattan Bank, and Geocities) that have displayed privacy seals on their Web sites, subsequently engaged in practices that directly contradicted the terms of their stated privacy policies, and yet were not disciplined by the certifying body. Several analysts have noted that the trust mark providers do not seem inclined to discipline their members and sponsors (Endeshaw, 2001). If such practices continue, consumers are likely to lose confidence in privacy seals and the value of the entire concept will be questionable in the future.

Conclusions

The right to privacy has become a central issue in electronic commerce. Camp (1999) summarizes the situation well: "What is the state of Web privacy? It is neither ideal nor improving" (p. 250). Consumers have become more concerned about how their personal data are being used, and there is growing evidence that these concerns are limiting the growth of electronic commerce.

This chapter has outlined the three major approaches being used to address this issue—self-regulation, legislative protection, and third-party certification through trust marks or privacy seals. Although the concept of allowing markets to self-regulate is an attractive one, in practice the desire to make profits seems to be overriding many company's guarantees as to their use of personal data. The evidence shows that such an egalitarian concept simply does not work in practice. Although some studies (e.g., Jamal et al., 2002) have shown that the level of protection being given to personal information in the United States is gradually improving without legislation or regulations, it is clear that such progress has to a large extend resulted from the threat of sanctions. Similarly, supplementing self-regulation with the certification of good privacy practices by third-party organizations is also facing challenges, mainly because of a lack of adoption and enforcement.

Furthermore, it is clear that the more restrictive comprehensive legislative approach is, the one that is gaining acceptance as the global norm. Already, the combination of the European Union countries, the portfolio of countries wishing to join the European Union, and the large number of other countries that trade extensively with European countries have adopted this approach, making it in effect a de facto standard for the protection of data privacy throughout the world. Even the United States' nearest neighbors, Canada and Mexico, have rejected the concept of self-regulation in this case and introduced highly specific legislation designed to guarantee the rights of consumers as regards the personal use of their data (Taylor, 2003). It can only be a matter of time before the United States follows suit. Already dozens of bills concerning the protection of privacy have been introduced at both the federal and state levels (Lee Lawson, 2003). At the time of writing, the Online Privacy Protection Act of 2003 (H.R. 69) is being considered by the U.S. Congress. Despite objections from industry groups that its provisions will make them uncompetitive, it is likely that this bill or a similar piece of legislation will pass in the near future, bringing the United States into line with the rest of the world in terms of the protection of consumers' personal information.

A major question remains as to whether the legislative approach will result in better privacy protection in the long run. While legislation does help to ensure a certain minimum level of protection for everyone (assuming, of course, that such standards are adequately enforced), it may also result in poorer standards than might have existed in its absence. Proponents of self-regulation argue that customers will, in the long run, gravitate toward companies that provide adequate levels of privacy protection, or at least the types and levels of guarantees that are important to them. Legislative standards are unlikely to be as focused or flexible as those set by the market, but the fact that they exist may result in consumers becoming complacent about the issue and companies conforming with the minimum baseline but going no further. In addition to stressing the need to conform with their legislative demands, governments must stress that such guidelines are the necessary and encourage companies to provide higher levels of protection.

References

Bennett, C. (1992). *Regulating privacy: Data protection and public policy in Europe and the United States*. Ithaca, NY: Cornell University Press.

Blanchette, J.-F., & Johnson, D. G. (2002). Data retention and the panoptic society: The social benefits of forgetfulness. *The Information Society, 18*, 33–45.

Cain, R. (2002). Global privacy concerns and regulation—Is the United States a world apart? *International Review of Law Computers and Technology, 16*(1), 23–34.

Camp, L. J. (1999). Web security and privacy: An American perspective. *The Information Society, 15*, 249–256.

Carroll, B. (2002). Price of privacy: Selling consumer databases in bankruptcy. *Journal of Interactive Marketing, 16*(3), 47–58.

Clinton, W., & Gore, A. (1997). Framework for global electronic commerce. Retrieved from *www.ecommerce.gov*

Culnan, M. (2000). Protecting privacy online: Is self-regulation working? *Journal of Public Policy and Marketing, 19*(1), 20–26.

Culnan, M., & Armstrong, P. K. (1999). Information privacy concerns, procedural fairness and impersonal trust: An empirical investigation. *Organization Science, 10*, 104–115.

Culnan, M., & Bies, R. (1999). Managing privacy concerns strategically: The implications of fair information practices for marketing in the twenty-first century. In C. J. Bennett & R. Grant (Eds.), *Visions of privacy* (pp. 149–167). Toronto: University of Toronto Press.

Electronic Privacy Information Center (EPIC). (2002). Privacy & human rights: An international survey of privacy laws and developments. Washington, DC: Author.

Electronic Privacy Information Center (EPIC) Alert. (2000, July 16). *Privacy*. Washington, DC: Author.

Endeshaw, A. (2001). The legal significance of trademarks. *Information & Communications Technology Law, 10*(2), 203–230.

European Community. (1995). Directive 95/46/EC of the European Parliament and the Council on the protection of individuals with regard to the processing of personal data and on the free movement of such data. *Official Journal of the European Community, 23*, L 281.

Finkel, R., & McCrady, T. (2000). Facing the Web's phantom menace: Understanding online privacy fears and how e-business can respond. *Journal of Internet Law, 3*, 9–12.

Georgia Tech Research Corporation. (1997). Seventh WWW user survey. Retrieved from *www.cc.gatech.edu/gvu/user_surveys*

Gilbert, J. (2001, August). Privacy? Who needs privacy? *Business 2.0*, p. 20.

Godin, S. (1999). *Permission marketing: Turning strangers into friends, and friends into customers*. New York: Simon & Schuster.

Grabner-Kraeuter, S. (2002). The role of consumers' trust in online shopping. *Journal of Business Ethics, 39*, 43–50.

Grove, A. (1998). *Only the paranoid survive*. New York: HarperCollins Business.

Grover, V., Hall L. et al. (1998). The Web of privacy: Business in the information age. *Business Horizons, July–August*, 5–11.

Head, M. & Yuan, Y. (2001). Privacy protection in electronic commerce—A theoretical framework. *Human Systems Management, 20*, 149–160.

Hinde, S. (1998). Privacy and security—The drivers for growth of e-commerce. *Computers and Security, 17*, 475–478.

Hoffman, D., Novak, P. et al. (1999). Information privacy in the marketspace: Implications for commercial uses of anonymity. *The Information Society, 15*, 129–139.

Internet & American Life. (2000). New Internet users: What they do online, what they don't and implications for the Net's future. Retrieved from *www.pewinternet.org/reports/toc.asp?Report=22*

Jamal, K., Maier, M., & Sunder, S. (2003). Privacy in e-commerce: Development of reporting standards, disclosure and assurance services in an unregulated market. *Journal of Accounting Research, 41*(2), 285–309.

Jennings, C. & Fena, L. (2001). *The hundredth window: Protecting your privacy and security in the age of the Internet.* New York: The Free Press.

Kandra, A., & Brandt, A. (2003). The great American privacy makeover. *PC World, November*, 145–160.

Kelly, E. (2000). Ethical apects of managing customer privacy in electronic commerce. *Human Systems Management, 19*, 237–244.

Krishnamurthy, S. (2001). A comprehensive analysis of permission marketing. *Journal of Computer-Mediated Communication, 6*(2). Retrieved from *www.ascusc.org/jcmc/vol6/issue2/krishnamurthy.html*

Lee Larson, J., Larson, R., & Greenlee, J. (2003). Privacy protection on the Internet. *Strategic Finance,* June, 49–53.

Long, W., & Quek, M. (2002). Personal data privacy protection in an age of globalization: The US–EU safe harbour compromise. *Journal of European Public Policy, 9*(3), 325–344.

Lourosa-Ricardo, C. (2001,). New technologies aim to give Internet users more privacy. *Wall Street Journal Europe*, p. 22.

Mayer-Schonberger, V. (1998). The Internet and privacy legislation: Cookies for a treat? *Computer Law & Security Report, 14*(3), 166–174.

Metz, C. (2001, November 13). What they know. *PC Magazine*, pp. 104–118.

Milne, G. R., & Gordon, M. E. (1993). Direct mail privacy efficiency: Trade-offs within an implied social contract framework. *Journal of Public Policy and Marketing, 12*, 206–215.

Miyazaki, A., & Krishnamurthy, S. (2002). Internet seals of approval: Effects on online privacy policies and consumer perceptions. *Journal of Consumer Affairs, 36*(1), 28–49.

Nunes, P., & Kambil, A. (2001). Personalization? No thanks. *Harvard Business Review, April,* 32–34.

Opplinger, R. (2000). Privacy protection and anonymity services for the World Wide Web (WWW). *Future Generation Computer Systems, 16*, 379–391.

Phelps, J. E., D'Souza, G. et al. (2001). Antecedents and consequences of consumer privacy concerns: An empirical investigation. *Journal of Interactive Marketing, 15*(4), 2–17.

Ragothaman, S., Davies, T., & DeVee, D. (2000). Legal aspects of electronic commerce and their implications for the accounting profession. *Human Systems Management, 19*, 245–254.

Rust, R., Kannan, P., & Peng, N. (2002). The customer economics of Internet privacy. *Journal of the Academy of Marketing Science, 30*(4), 455–464.

Ryker, R., LaFleur, E. et al. (2002). Online privacy policies: An assessment of the Fortune E-50. *Journal of Computer Information Systems,* Summer, 15–20.

Taylor, S. (2003). Protecting privacy in Canada's private sector. *The Information Management Journal,* July/August, 33–39.

Turinas, A., & Showalter, B. (2002). Privacy in the electronic age. *Managing Intellectual Property, 124*, 72–78.

Valentine, D. (2000). Privacy on the Internet: The evolving legal landscape. *Santa Clara Computer and High Tech Law Journal,* (16), 407–408.

Weber, T. (2000,). On the Internet, everybody wants to be a nobody. *Wall Street Journal Europe,* p. 26.

Westin, A. F. (1967). *Privacy and freedom*. New York: Atheneum.

Zwick, D., & Dholakia, N. (2001). Contrasting European and American approaches to privacy in electronic markets: Property right vs civil right. *Electronic Markets, 11*(2), 116–120.

About the Authors

Sandeep Krishnamurthy is an associate professor of e-commerce and marketing in the business administration program at the University of Washington, Bothell. He obtained his PhD from the University of Arizona in marketing and economics. His research interests are in the area of e-marketing, e-commerce, and open source software. Most recently, he published a 450-page MBA textbook, *E-Commerce Management: Text and Cases*. His scholarly work on e-commerce and open source software has appeared in journals such as *Business Horizons, Journal of Consumer Affairs, Journal of Computer-Mediated Communication, Quarterly Journal of E-Commerce, Marketing Management, First Monday, Journal of Marketing Research,* and *Journal of Service Marketing*. Krishnamurthy also works in the areas of generic advertising and nonprofit marketing. His work in generic advertising has appeared in journals such as *Organizational Behavior and Human Decision Processes (OBHDP)* and *Marketing Letters*. His work in non-profit marketing has appeared in the *International Journal of Non-Profit Voluntary Sector Marketing*. He currently serves as associate book review editor for the *Journal of Marketing Research* and is a co-editor for a special issue of the *International Marketing Review*. He regularly reviews papers for a variety of journals including *Marketing Science* and the *Journal of Advertising*. His writings in the business press have appeared on *Clickz.com, Digitrends.net,* and *Marketingprofs.com.* His comments have been featured in press articles in outlets such as *Marketing Computers, Direct Magazine, Wired.com, Medialifemagazine.com, Oracle's Profit Magazine,* and *Washington Post.* He has developed and taught several innovative courses related to e-commerce to both MBA and undergraduate students. Most recently, he developed and taught a course titled "Search and the World Wide Web." He was responsible for founding the management information systems (MIS) concentration in the business program. He invites you to visit his Web site at *http://faculty.washington.edu/sandeep* and his blog at *http://sandeepworld.blogspot.com*.

* * * * *

Daniela Andreini is a professor of marketing and e-commerce at the University of Bergamo, Italy. She received her PhD from the University La Sapienza of Rome. Her current research and teaching activities concern the measurement of e-commerce and Internet marketing performance. She also teaches personal selling, sales management, service marketing, and principles of marketing to undergraduate and graduate students at the University of Bergamo.

Subir Bandyopadhyay is an associate professor of marketing at the School of Business and Economics, Indiana University Northwest in Gary, Indiana (USA). Dr. Bandyopadhyay can be contacted at: Subir Bandyopadhyay, Professor of Marketing, School of Business and Economics, Indiana University Northwest, 3400 Broadway, Gary, IN, USA.

Ann Blandford is a reader in interaction design at University College London Interaction Centre, and is also a visiting professor at Middlesex University (UK). She teaches and conducts research on human–computer interaction, with a particular focus on delivering theory into practical design situations. Her work covers various kinds of interactive systems, from specialist safety-critical systems to large, widely accessible systems such as digital libraries.

Deborah Bosley is the director of the university writing programs at the University of North Carolina - Charlotte, USA.

Gerald Braun teaches in the Department of Management Information Systems at the Williams College of Business at Xavier University in Cincinnati, Ohio (USA).

Boyd Davis is associated with the Department of English at the University of North Carolina - Charlotte (USA).

Liisa H. Dawson is a research fellow in the Faculty of Maths and Computing of The Open University, UK. Dawson is working on a project titled "Exploring Exceptions in User-Centred Requirements and User Interface Designs." Having completed an MSc in computing at the University of Northumbria, she was offered a three-year research studentship at Napier University, Edinburgh. Her PhD dissertation, *Articulating Activities: Getting to the Root of the Problem,* explores the practical application of activity theory to user-centred design (UCD). Her particular research goals have been to explore the benefits that activity theory can offer to UCD. The central aim of this has been to make activity theory accessible to the practitioner and to provide a more rigorous process of systems development. She has applied activity theoretic principles to the analysis and requirements building stages of a number of projects during her involvement with activity theory. However, since working with the Open University, she has been closely involved with the exploration of the customer's perspective of e-commerce experiences. The research that she has carried out on this multidisciplinary project, along side Dr. Minocha, has led to a wider understanding of the characteristics and behavior of e-commerce customers, which in turn can be employed in the development of e-commerce environments.

Manlio Del Giudice teaches at the University of Milan - Bicocca's Institute for Corporate Management, Italy.

José Manuel Ortega Egea is a PhD candidate and lecturer of marketing at the University of Almería, Spain. His main research interests are related to Internet technologies and services: global and cultural implications for e-marketing, e-health services, and studies on the acceptance and use of diverse Internet services. His scholarly work has appeared in sources such as the *Handbook for Market Segmentation* (2004), national and international conference proceedings, and he is currently working toward publication in international journals. He is also in the process of completing his thesis about the acceptance and use of e-health services.

Ram Krishna is a systems engineer with Tata Consultancy Services, India.

S. Ramesh Kumar is the head of the Marketing Department at the Indian Institute of Management, Bangalore, India.

Maria Madlberger is an assistant professor in the Department of Business Administration and Information Systems at the Vienna University of Economics and Business Administration, Austria. She received her PhD from the Department of Retailing and Marketing also at this university. Her PhD thesis analyzes Internet-based marketing and market research methods. Maria's research activities follow an interdisciplinary approach as she concentrates on the links between information systems and marketing, especially in the field of e-commerce. Her research interests are Internet application for supply chain management (SCM), influence of e-commerce on channels of distribution, bricks & clicks (multichannel retailing) versus dot-coms, electronic data interchange, efficient consumer response (ECR), disintermediation versus re-intermediation, home delivery and last mile logistics, and Internet-based market research. Maria has conducted several research projects in the field of e-commerce that have been published in *Electronic Markets* and the *International Journal of Physical Distribution and Logistics Management* as well as other marketing and e-commerce-related journals. Her new book, *Electronic Retailing,* has recently been published. Before Maria joined the department, she gained practical experiences as a specialized journalist at an Austrian trade journal for the grocery and FMCG sector.

Peyton Mason is associated with Linguistic Insights, Inc. (USA).

Manuel Recio Menéndez is a professor of marketing at the University of Almería, Spain. He obtained his PhD from the Universidad Complutense de Madrid, Spain, in business and economics. His specialization area is related to international marketing. He has published widely in Spanish and international books, journals, and conference proceedings about diverse marketing topics: tourism, health services research, Internet services, and global marketing.

Nicola Millard is lead customer experience consultant with British Telecommunications PLC, specializing in two "-ologies": technology and psychology. Millard works extensively with clients to ensure that they put the relationship into customer management. She looks at how the human factor can become central to the development and success of a customer experience. Millard joined BT in 1990 after graduating with a BA (Honors) in applied psychology and computing from Bournemouth University and is currently working toward a PhD in human–computer interaction at Lancaster University. As a consultant, she has worked extensively within BT's customer contact organization as well as clients in the finance, government, and telecommunications sectors on a wide range of customer experience projects. She is in demand as a "CRM evangelist" at international conferences, teaches CRM people and culture modules on the BT Master's Program and at the Institute of Direct Marketing, and is one of the virtual experts on the Insight Exec Web site.

Shailey Minocha is senior lecturer in human–computer interaction (HCI) in the Faculty of Maths and Computing at The Open University (OU) (UK), where she leads a research program in the area of customer relationship management and service quality of e-commerce environments. Her other research interests include the design and evaluation of e-learning environments for usability and learnability, the internationalization of products and systems, and the evaluation of interactive systems by eye-tracking analysis. She also teaches and provides consultancy and training in the usability interactive systems. She has a PhD in digital signal processing and did her post-doctoral work in adaptive user interfaces at the Technical University, Braunschweig, Germany. Details of her research projects and teaching activities are available at *http://mcs.open.ac.uk/sm577*.

Melissa Moore is an associate professor of marketing at Mississippi State University (USA), having received her PhD from the University of Connecticut. Dr. Moore's research interests concentrate on understanding the development and maintenance of customer–firm relationships. Her research has been published or is accepted for publication in the *Journal of Business Research, Transportation Journal, Journal of Consumer Psychology, Marketing Management Journal, American Journal of Agricultural Economics, European Review of Agricultural Economics, Food Quality and Preference, AgBioForum,* and *Economics Letters*. In addition, she has presented her work at both domestic and international conference venues.

Robert S. Moore (PhD, University of Connecticut) is an associate professor of marketing at Mississippi State University (USA). He has presented at numerous conferences and published his research in various outlets including the *Journal of Advertising, Transportation Journal, Journal of Public Policy and Marketing, Journal of Services Marketing, Journal of End User Computing, Advances in Consumer Research, Marketing Management Journal, Journal for the Advancement of Marketing Education, Albany Law Journal of Science and Technology,* and *Seton Hall Legislative Review*. His research interests center upon consumer behavior in e-commerce settings.

Peter O'Connor, PhD, has recently worked as an associate professor at the Institut de Management Hotelier International (IMHI), France, an MBA program specializing in international hospitality management jointly administered by the Cornell School of Hotel Administration and ESSEC Business School. He received his doctorate in hospitality e-commerce from Queen Margaret University College, Edinburgh, holds a master's degree in MIS from Trinity College, Dublin, and a Bachelor of Science in hotel and catering management from the

Dublin Institute of Technology. Dr. O'Connor's primary research, teaching, and consulting interests focus on the use of technology in the hospitality and tourism sectors. He has developed expertise in the use of electronic channels of distribution in tourism, and on how information technology can be used to enhance both the management and operational effectiveness of hospitality organizations. Based on his work, he has authored two leading textbooks on technology in the hospitality business—*Using Computers in Hospitality* (Cassell, 2000—now in its second edition) and *Electronic Information Distribution in Hospitality and Tourism Industries* (CABI, 1999)—as well as numerous articles in both the trade and academic press. In addition, he serves on the editorial board of the *International Journal of Hospitality Management, Information Technology & Tourism, International Journal of Hospitality and Tourism Technology,* and *The Cornell Hotel Administration Quarterly.* In 2002 he was awarded the prestigious Best Research Paper award at the ENTER Technology in Tourism conference by the International Federation for Information Technology in Tourism.

Michel Polski teaches at the Graduate School of Business, Groupe ESC–Department of Marketing, France.

Thomas W. Porter is an assistant professor of marketing at the Cameron School of Business at the University of North Carolina Wilmington (USA).

Mark P. Sena teaches in the Department of Management Information Systems at the Williams College of Business at Xavier University in Cincinnati, Ohio (USA).

Rosemary Serjak is a graduate student in the Faculty of Administration at the University of Ottawa (Canada).

Sanjeev Swami is an assistant professor with the Department of Industrial and Management Engineering, Indian Institute of Technology, Kanpur.

Merrill Warkentin (PhD, University of Nebraska) is a professor of MIS at Mississippi State University (USA). He has published more than 125 research manuscripts, primarily in e-commerce, computer security management, and virtual teams, in books, proceedings, and journals such as *MIS Quarterly, Decision Sciences, Decision Support Systems, Communications of the AIS, Information Systems Journal, Journal of End User Computing, Journal of*

Global Information Management, and others. Professor Warkentin is the co-author or editor of four books, and is currently an associate editor for the *Information Resources Management Journal*, *Journal of Information Systems Security*, and *eGovernment Quarterly*. Dr. Warkentin has also served as a consultant to numerous organizations and as National Distinguished Lecturer for the Association for Computing Machinery (ACM). Previously, Dr. Warkentin held the Reisman Research Professorship at Northeastern University in Boston, where he was also the director of MIS and e-commerce programs. He can be reached at *mwarkentin@acm.org* and *www.MISProfessor.com.*

Index

E

F

G

H

I

J

K

L

M

V

W